Mooring the Global Archive

Martin Dusinberre follows the *Yamashiro-maru* steamship across Asian and Pacific waters in an innovative history of Japan's engagement with the outside world in the late nineteenth century. His compelling in-depth analysis reconstructs the lives of some of the thousands of male and female migrants who left Japan for work in Hawai'i, Southeast Asia and Australia. These stories bring together transpacific historiographies of settler colonialism, labour history and resource extraction in new ways. Drawing on an unconventional and deeply material archive, from gravestones to government files, paintings to song, and from digitized records to the very earth itself, Dusinberre addresses key questions of method and authorial positionality in the writing of global history. This engaging investigation into archival practice asks, what is the global archive, where is it cited, and who are 'we' as we cite it? This title is also available as Open Access on Cambridge Core.

Martin Dusinberre is Professor of Global History at the University of Zurich.

Cambridge Oceanic Histories

Edited by

David Armitage
Renisa Mawani
Sujit Sivasundaram

Across the world, historians have taken an oceanic turn. New maritime histories offer fresh approaches to the study of global regions, and to long-distance and long-term connections. Cambridge Oceanic Histories includes studies across whole oceans (the Pacific, the Indian, the Atlantic) and particular seas (among them, the Mediterranean, the Caribbean, the North Sea, the Black Sea). The series is global in geography, ecumenical in historical method, and wide in temporal coverage, intended as a key repository for the most innovative transnational and world histories over the longue durée. It brings maritime history into productive conversation with other strands of historical research, including environmental history, legal history, intellectual history, labour history, cultural history, economic history and the history of science and technology. The editors invite studies that analyse the human and natural history of the world's oceans and seas from anywhere on the globe and from any and all historical periods.

A full list of titles in the series can be found at: www.cambridge.org/cambridgeoceanichistories

Mooring the Global Archive
A Japanese Ship and Its Migrant Histories

Martin Dusinberre
University of Zurich

CAMBRIDGE
UNIVERSITY PRESS

CAMBRIDGE
UNIVERSITY PRESS

Shaftesbury Road, Cambridge CB2 8EA, United Kingdom

One Liberty Plaza, 20th Floor, New York, NY 10006, USA

477 Williamstown Road, Port Melbourne, VIC 3207, Australia

314–321, 3rd Floor, Plot 3, Splendor Forum, Jasola District Centre, New Delhi – 110025, India

103 Penang Road, #05-06/07, Visioncrest Commercial, Singapore 238467

Cambridge University Press is part of Cambridge University Press & Assessment, a department of the University of Cambridge.

We share the University's mission to contribute to society through the pursuit of education, learning and research at the highest international levels of excellence.

www.cambridge.org
Information on this title: www.cambridge.org/9781009346511

DOI: 10.1017/9781009346535

© Martin Dusinberre 2023

This work is in copyright. It is subject to statutory exceptions and to the provisions of relevant licensing agreements; with the exception of the Creative Commons version the link for which is provided below, no reproduction of any part of this work may take place without the written permission of Cambridge University Press.

An online version of this work is published at doi.org/10.1017/9781009346535 under a Creative Commons Open Access license CC-BY-NC 4.0 which permits re-use, distribution and reproduction in any medium for non-commercial purposes providing appropriate credit to the original work is given and any changes made are indicated. To view a copy of this license visit https://creativecommons.org/licenses/by-nc/4.0

All versions of this work may contain content reproduced under license from third parties.

Permission to reproduce this third-party content must be obtained from these third-parties directly.

When citing this work, please include a reference to the DOI 10.1017/9781009346535

First published 2023

A catalogue record for this publication is available from the British Library.

A Cataloging-in-Publication data record for this book is available from the Library of Congress.

ISBN 978-1-009-34651-1 Hardback
ISBN 978-1-009-34652-8 Paperback

Cambridge University Press & Assessment has no responsibility for the persistence or accuracy of URLs for external or third-party internet websites referred to in this publication and does not guarantee that any content on such websites is, or will remain, accurate or appropriate.

To Asuka, Noah and Leah

Contents

List of Figures	*page* ix
List of Maps	xi
Acknowledgements	xii
Note on the Text	xvii
Preface	xix

1. **Archival Traps** — 1
   - The Ship — 2
   - Trap 1: History as Moments of Birth — 6
   - Trap 2: The Global as Googleable — 14
   - Trap 3: Fixation on the Written Word — 23
   - Kodama's Gravestone: A Mooring Berth — 31

2. **Between the Archives** — 39
   - A Painting — 39
   - Ship as Plantation Boot Camp — 46
   - The Nation Cheek by Jowl — 57
   - (Re)framing — 70

3. **Outside the Archive** — 80
   - A Transcript — 80
   - Outside (1): Hawai'i State Archives — 85
   - Labouring Bodies in Circulation — 91
   - Outside (2): Kaminoseki Municipal Archives — 103
   - 'Invaded by the Industrious' — 109
   - Interpreting — 118

4. **Archival Country, Counterclaims** — 122
   - A Map — 122
   - Claim 1: Lines Away from the Sinosphere — 129
   - Claim 2: Points of Contact — 136
   - Claim 3: Uniform Colours — 144
   - Archival Directionality — 153
   - Delineating — 161

5. **The Archive and I** 172
   - A Statement 172
   - I Was Born at Nishiyama 181
   - Seeing My Sister at Singapore 182
   - On the Representations of a Man Named Konishi 188
   - Transferred without Landing 198
   - Otaka the Keeper of the Lodging House 202
   - I Boldly Decided to Go 205
   - A Brothel at No 2 Yokohama Thursday Island 207
   - Her Finger Mark 216
   - Voicing 220

6. **The Burned Archive** 224
   - A Diary 224
   - Port: 'At Wukumoto We Visited…' 232
   - Passage: 'The Great Mineral Agent of Civilization' 235
   - Port: No Further than Sixty Steps Down 239
   - Passage: From Mine to Market 243
   - Port: Alternative Geographies of Japan's 'Opening' 250
   - Passage: Stevedores and Bronze Buddhas 256
   - Mining 261

Epilogue 267

Bibliography 271
Index 300

Figures

1.1	Graveyard of the First Hawaiian Church, Kapaʻa	page 1
1.2	The launch of the *Yamashiro-maru*, Newcastle upon Tyne, 12 January 1884	7
1.3	'Midship Section of Spardecked Steamer' (*Yamashiro-maru* and *Omi-maru*)	12
1.4	'Depiction of a Foreign Ship' (Ikokusen-zu 異国船図)	25
1.5	'The Rivals', *Japan Punch*, January 1885	27
2.1	Joseph Dwight Strong, 'Japanese Laborers on the Sugar Plantation in Spreckelsville, Maui', 1885	41
2.2	Japanese immigrants landing. Honolulu, c. 1893	56
2.3	Ex-*City of Tokio* migrants in Honolulu, February 1885	60
2.4	Photographic models for Strong	66
3.1	Utagawa Kunisada, 'Rules of Dietary Life' (Inshoku yōjō kagami 飲食養生鑑), c. 1850	94
3.2	Hāna plantation, Maui, c. 1885	110
4.1	'AUSTRALIANS, HOLD YOUR OWN!' *The Worker: Monthly Journal of the Associated Workers of Queensland* (Brisbane), 7 November 1896	141
4.2	'Japanese and trucks loaded with cane', Hambledon Mill, near Cairns, c. 1890	154
4.3	Djambawa Marawili, 'Baraltja', 1998	165
5.1	'Correspondence re alleged abduction of a Japanese woman', 1897	178
5.2	Nagasaki Harbour from Tateyama, after 1896	182
5.3	View of Thursday Island, 1899 (detail)	209
6.1	The *Yamashiro-maru* (1884–1910)	227

6.2 Detail from Kizaki Moritaka, 'Illustrations of Products from Hizen Province' ('Hizen-shū sanbutsu zukō' 肥前州産物図考), 1784 — 244
6.3 Yamamoto Sakubei, 'Mining Coal in a Lying Position' (Nebori 寝掘り), December 1964 — 247
6.4 'Loading Women', date and photographer unknown — 258

Maps

Map 1 'N. Y. K. Line', c. 1923   *page* 125
Map 2 Nagakubo Sekisui, 'Complete Illustration of the Globe, All the Countries, and the Mountains and Oceans of the Earth' (Chikyū bankoku sankai yochi zenzusetsu 地球萬國山海輿地全圖説), c. 1790   132
Map 3 'Chart of the Mother-Ship *Yamashiro-maru*'s Routes' (Bokan Yamashiro-maru kōseki ryakuzu 母艦山城丸航跡略図), 1894–5   134
Map 4 Karatsu and Sasebo Coal Fields (1913), detail, with Karatsu to the north and Fukumo (Ōmachi) in the south   240

Acknowledgements

I dedicate *Mooring the Global Archive* to my wife Asuka and our two children. Asuka listened to my madcap idea for a second book one tepid summer evening long before I was finished with the first, but her unwavering belief in the subsequent fifteen years, her suggestions of trips and traps and her laughter at chickens crossing the road, have kept me on some kind of course – even as our worlds were transformed by the arrivals of Noah and Leah. With deepest thanks to you three.

That summer of 2008, the late Ann Waswo's fortitude helped me get my doctoral thesis over the line, as did her priceless arrangement of the Nissan Institute flat in St Antony's College (for which Asuka and I additionally thank Roger Goodman and Jane Baker). Also in Oxford, Arthur Stockwin encouraged my early branching into Japanese–Australian relations. For welcoming me to my first job at Newcastle University in August 2008, and for providing a wonderful blend of collegial endeavour and self-deprecation, I thank former colleagues in history and in East Asian studies: in particular, Tim Kirk, Barbara Cochrane, Naomi Standen, Diana Paton, Felix Schulz, Scott Ashley, Andrea Germer and Laura Moretti. That Ben Houston and I effectively only overlapped in Newcastle for eighteen months is one of life's regrets; that he and Michelle will now rib me for expressing it thus, while also underlining my unfortunate double adverb, reassures me that our friendship has lasted. I thank many other colleagues for acts of friendship in those years. As I started to study the region's global entanglements, Joan Allen, David Saunders, Henrietta Heald and Marie Conte-Helm offered expert guidance. Ian Buxton shared an invaluable database of British-built NYK ships. My initial archival trip to Hawai'i, in 2011, was generously funded by a Newcastle University HaSS Faculty Research Grant.

Harald Fuess was the first to introduce me to Heidelberg University's incomparable Cluster of Excellence 'Asia and Europe in a Global Context' by generously inviting me to work on the book as a visiting scholar for the academic year 2011–12. At a conference we organized in 2012, I benefited especially from the expertise of Joshua Fogel, Jan Rüger and Robert Hellyer. The friendship and incredible intellectual curiosity of colleagues in Heidelberg set this book on an entirely new direction. I thank – and occasionally still cuss, for the difficulty of their questions – Joachim Kurtz, David Mervart (now Autonomous University of Madrid), Anna Andreeva (Ghent University), Martin Hofmann, Pablo Blitstein (EHESS), Monica Juneja, Enno Giele, Frank Grüner (Bielefeld University) and Steve Ivings (Kyoto University); my thanks also to Luke Franks, Fabian Drixler, Eric Hayot, Christian Henriot, Charlotte Kroll, Björn-Ole Kamm, Dominic Steavu and Hans Martin Krämer for Cluster conversations. Madeleine Herren has continued to be an interlocutor in the years since she and then I left Heidelberg. Regular Sunday brunches hosted by Joachim and Haipeng, David and Harumi, and Enno and Guo Jue, gave greater succour to sleep-deprived parents than the hosts will ever know, and the mountains of food had the added benefit that Asuka and I only had one – then two – mouths to feed for the rest of the weekend. Our thanks also to Shupin Lang, Nicole Tsuda, and Andrew and Kate Faulkner, and to the Yamamoto and Habe families.

My stay at Heidelberg was extended to 2014 thanks to a research fellowship from the Alexander von Humboldt Foundation, whose generous funding also supported several archival trips to Japan, Hawai'i and Australia. Heidelberg students Charlotte Schäfer, Katharina Rode and Rudolph Ng provided invaluable research assistance during this time, as did Joe Barnes in Tokyo. At the Cluster, Roland Wenzlhuemer (now LMU Munich) got me fired up thinking about ship passages back in 2011 and has offered moral and scholarly support ever since. Additional research travel funding for the book came from the Swiss National Science Foundation thanks to a DACH grant which I led with Roland, 2017–20; as part of this project, I also developed a text-based computer game, livesintransit.org, based on material from parts of the book. My grateful thanks to the 'Lives in Transit' technical team at Zurich and beyond: Ramun Riklin, Pim Witlox, Daniel McDonald and the Vitamin2 team, plus many other project-support colleagues and testers at UZH, especially Tobias Hodel (now University of Bern).

The questions, encouragement, close readings and critiques from colleagues and students at the University of Zurich since 2015 gave me the space to change direction yet again. Gesine Krüger, Monika Dommann and Simon Teuscher gave me an intellectual home in our weekly Geschichtskontor writing workshop, whose regulars over the years I also thank: in particular, Jan-Friedrich Missfelder (now University of Basel), Christa Wirth (University of Agder), Juliane Schiel (University of Vienna) and Matthieu Leimgruber. Team-teaching with Svenja Goltermann sharpened my thinking about thematic approaches to the history of the modern world; more recently, Roberto Zaugg and Debjani Bhattacharyya have been wonderful interlocutors in thinking about global history methodologies. Beyond the Department of History, Raji Steineck and David Chiavacci were the first colleagues to introduce me to Zurich, while Hans Bjarne Thomsen's selflessness and optimism – and his introduction to then Johann Jacobs Museum director Roger M. Buergel – led to the exhibition 'Ein Bild für den Kaiser' (2018), which itself profoundly shaped Chapter 2. Graham Corkhill and Vic Clarke very kindly agreed to loan the *Yamashiro-maru* model to the museum, 2015–18. My thanks also to Ana Sobral, Wolfgang Behr and Marianne Hundt for their friendship at UZH, and especially to Anne Kolb, Barbara Welter, Marietta Meier and latterly Barbara Holler for good cheer and professional collegiality during the book's final stages. For departmental IT support, booming laughter and reminders of Newcastle, I simply have to call Francesco Falone, whose wonderful team, including Ben Fritsche, are second to none. Across the Karl Schmid Strasse in ETHZ, Harald Fischer-Tiné has offered regular conversations about new developments in global history, and I thank members of his team – especially, in the early days, Robert Kramm (now LMU Munich), Bernhard Schär (University of Lausanne), and Patricia Purtschert (University of Bern) – for their warm welcome at our joint research colloquium. But my greatest debt at Zurich has been to my own team over the years, in ways only they will appreciate: Nadja Schorno, David Möller, Gonzalo San Emeterio Cabañes, Lina Zbinden, Tamara Ann Tinner, Birgit Tremml Werner, Helena Jaskov, David Aragai, Rojbaş Feiner, Selina Tuchschmid, Antonia Schulte-Brinkmann, Jonas Rüegg and especially Moe Omiya for help in the last push. My grateful thanks to you all, not only for your outstanding assistance but also for making our work fun and rewarding. UZH students and former students have been integral to my thinking and writing, especially those seminar groups to whom I've assigned drafts as part of their course reading: my thanks in particular to Fynn Holm (now University of Tübingen), Ulrich Brandenburg, Christina Wild, Maryam Joseph, Yannick Arnold and Dario Willi, and also to Mayumi Arai.

Beyond Zurich, Jordan Sand has cajoled me and brought his own historical sensitivity to the manuscript in ways far beyond the call of friendship, especially during the first Covid-19 lockdown. Mariko Iijima has been a friend and research collaborator supreme, her steadfastness and hospitality extending also to my family. Through Mariko's generosity, I got to know colleagues in Japan and North America who have also supported me through the years: in particular, Araragi Shinzō, Eiichiro Azuma, David Ambaras, Tsubota-Nakanishi Miki, Mori Akiko,

Acknowledgements

Yaguchi Yujin and Furukawa Toshiaki, plus many of Mariko's own postgraduate students. Nakamura Naofumi has posed provocative questions over dinner on each of my visits to Tokyo. I am also grateful to Kimura Kenji, Kokaze Hidemasu, John Breen, Takenaka Toru, Okubo Takeharu, Sven Saaler, Bill Wray, Harry Liebersohn, Jürgen Osterhammel and Andrew Gordon for conversations during the project's early stages, and to Osamu Saito for encouraging me to continue researching Japanese migration history at a crucial juncture in 2012. Conversations with Noelani Arista in Hawai'i, Switzerland and Britain helped focus the book's arguments in essential ways, and I am indebted to her students Ami Mulligan and Sarah Kuaiwa. The late Saneo Okada helped me greatly in Hawai'i in 2011 and 2013, as did Marylou Bradley of the Kaua'i Historical Society, by email, and most recently Vicky Shen. In Australia, Keiko Tamura, Simon Avenell and Nathan Woolley generously gave their time and advice. In Britain, Christopher Gerteis and Barak Kushner have been unwavering in their support, especially when Chris and I overlapped during an eventful summer in Heidelberg; Zoë Fritz gave advice on hernias (Chapter 5). Sujit Sivasundaram's friendship and own model of scholarship have been vitalizing, and I look forward to our future collaborations.

I could not have wished for a more wonderful reading group since 2014 than Naoko Shimazu, Lucy Riall and Pieter Judson, and the friends and colleagues, at Yale–NUS College and the European University Institute respectively, into whose circles they have drawn me.

I am particularly grateful to colleagues who invited me to present earlier versions of material that ended up in the following chapters (here acknowledged with their university affiliations at the time of invitation). Chapter 1: Gesa Mackenthun (Rostock University) – and thanks also to Bernd Zittlau; Robert Bickers (University of Bristol); Jun Uchida (Stanford University); thanks also to colleagues from the Zentrum Geschichte des Wissens, Zurich, and to Myriam Spörri. Chapter 2: Naomi Standen (University of Birmingham); Wolfram Manzenreiter (University of Vienna); Aleksandra Kobiljski (INALCO); Cyrian Pitteloud (University of Geneva); Noelani Arista (University of Hawai'i–Mānoa); Mariko Iijima (Sophia University, Tokyo); Cristiana Bastos and Nic Miller (University of Lisbon); and thanks also to Frances Steel, Tamson Pietsch, Johanna de Schmidt, and Dagmar Bellmann. Chapter 3: Andreas Eckert (re:work, Humboldt University); Roger Goodman (Nissan Institute, University of Oxford); Pol Dalmau (Pompeu Fabra University, Barcelona); and Cyrus Schayegh (Graduate Institute, Geneva). My thanks also to Brigitta Bernet, Juliane Schiel and Jakob Tanner, to Bill Mihalopoulos, and to Beth Dusinberre for generous comments and encouragement. Chapter 4: James Raven (University of Essex); Gopalan Balachandran and Gareth Austin (Graduate Institute, Geneva); Paul Kreitman and Carol Gluck (Columbia University); Asano Toyomi and Umemori Naoyuki (Waseda University), plus also Sayaka Chatani. My thanks to David Ambaras for commenting on an earlier draft of Chapter 5, as also Roland Wenzlhuemer. Chapter 6: Ian Jared Miller and David Howell (Harvard University), plus also Nadin Hée, Stefan Huebner and Bill Tsutsui; Helen Macnaughton (SOAS, University of London); my thanks also to Penny Francks, Julia Adeney Thomas and Ryan Tucker Jones, all of whom encouraged me to keep going with coal. Despite these many helping hands, and with apologies to anyone I may have overlooked, all errors are mine.

Two anonymous readers for Cambridge University Press gave me wonderfully detailed and constructive feedback in 2021–2. Lucy Rhymer encouraged me from early on and managed the whole editorial process expertly; I am grateful to her CUP colleagues Stephanie Taylor, Sari Wastell, Emily Plater and Rosa Martin for managing production, and to Cheryl Hutty for impeccable copyediting. I thank all the immensely helpful staff at the institutions listed under 'Archives, Museums and Libraries', many of whom went the extra mile to help me; and I gratefully acknowledge all permission to reproduce images (for details, see individual captions). A Swiss National Science Foundation grant (10BP12_214505/1) generously supported the Open Access costs in publication. Parts of Chapter 2 were published in a much earlier form in the *Journal of Global History* (2016) and *Historische Anthropologie* (2019). The 'Labouring Bodies' section of Chapter 3 is a shortened revision of an article published in *Historische Anthropologie* in 2016. Chapter 5 is a complete reworking of material I first wrote about in the *History Workshop Journal* (2017).

My parents, Bill and Juliet Dusinberre, and my brother Ed brought their own scholarly inquisitiveness to this project from the beginning, along with regular missives and acts of encouragement. My late grandparents, Merrick and Charlotte, and John and Thea, have been much in mind as I have written, as has my late mother-in-law, Reiko Kawaguchi. My dear dad did not quite live to hold a final copy of the book, but he is surely held in its pages.

Zurich, April 2023

Note on the Text

Aboriginal and Torres Straits Islander peoples should be aware that this book contains references to the names and work of deceased First Nation persons.

Japanese names are written in Japanese order (surname, given name), unless I am citing from a primary source, or unless the person in question is an author who has published in English.

When referring to ships, tonnage indicates a measurement of volume; elsewhere, where tonnage refers to weight (e.g. of coal), I have mostly not offered a metric conversion – partly due to the different definitions of a nineteenth century ton being used in the sources.

All translations are mine except where otherwise stated. In some instances I have included not just transliterated Japanese terms but also Chinese characters in the main text, where I judge they may be of interest to readers of Chinese.

Preface

I am just about old enough for my first trip abroad to have been by ship. In the summer of 1985, we went to the Netherlands: my mum and dad, my American grandma and I, to see my older brother in concert and, as it transpired, to do a bit of family history. These were the days before budget flights belched Brits into Europe's sunny climes, so we drove as far as Harwich and there boarded the ferry to the Hook of Holland. I was eight years old and remember little of the holiday except us visiting the small town whence a certain Mr Doesburg emigrated to New Amsterdam in the mid-1600s. And I remember that on the way home, the ferry's engines broke down mid-crossing. We sat for hours in the English Channel, waiting for the engineers to ship in from Rotterdam while watching the world on the horizon. Whatever my parents said about the situation – and I fancy they said plenty – I thought it was *brilliant*.

One hundred years earlier and on the other side of the globe, a slightly older boy experienced a similar thrill. Having left his childhood home in rural Hyogo prefecture, he arrived at the bustling port of Kobe, where he boarded a steamer bound for a new life in Tokyo. He would remember the quayside moment, in August 1887, as he wrote his autobiography in the late-1950s:

I think it was from around where the American Pier now is. Lighters were setting off from the wharves, and in the distance a ship was approaching. It was the 2,300-ton *Yamashiro-maru*, which subsequently served in the Sino-Japanese war. With a mixture of excitement and pride – 'it's a 2,000-plus-ton ship!' – I went onboard. But even then, I just couldn't sleep. Perhaps it was the vessel's smell, the rarity of everything. So despite it being forbidden, I sneaked in to look at the Westerners in the first class saloon. Everything was a complete surprise. This was the first time I saw the world.

Domestic migration was no rare thing in nineteenth-century Japan, be it for off-season labour away from the farm or for the pursuit of wealth and independence in the great metropolis of Edo (renamed Tokyo

a Japanese ship and its migrant histories, I shall cite documents from multiple archives; but I also attempt to site those archives, materially to moor them in particular geographical and political contexts.[7] This will at times involve both questioning the extent to which 'actual archives' are comprised of written documents,[8] and also challenging the assumption that the exponential digitization of sources has had the effect of 'unmooring our previously emplaced archive'.[9] Throughout, I examine the tensions between 'the global' and 'the archive' as I encountered them in my investigations. In this sense, *Mooring the Global Archive* is a personal confession of historical practices in the first decades of the twenty-first century. I can only speak for my own circumstances in what follows, but I hope that the various archival traps I fell into and clambered out of resonate with other scholars, too. Though I agree with Bloch's sentiment, I shall avoid a language of 'successes and reverses' per se, partly because the so-called reverse is often the moment of most surprising insight. You can be sailing along, then something happens to disrupt the journey – and suddenly there is the improbable excitement of being all at sea.

---

[7] On 'sites of citation', see Kris Manjapra, 'Transnational Approaches to Global History: A View from the Study of German–Indian Entanglement', *German History* 32, 2 (2014): 274–93, here p. 288, in turn inspired by the methodology of Ronit Ricci, *Islam Translated: Literature, Conversion, and the Arabic Cosmopolis of South and Southeast Asia* (Chicago: University of Chicago Press, 2011).

[8] The phrase is repeated in Markus Friedrich, *The Birth of the Archive: A History of Knowledge*, trans. John Noël Dillon (Ann Arbor: University of Michigan Press, 2018 [2013]), pp. 11–12.

[9] Michael Goebel, 'Ghostly Helpmate: Digitization and Global History', *Geschichte und Gesellschaft* 47 (2021): 35–57, here p. 39.

1 Archival Traps

Figure 1.1 Graveyard of the First Hawaiian Church, Kapaʻa. Author's Photo, 2011.

KEIJIRO, KODAMA
ARRIVED
HAWAII, NEI
JUNE 18, 1885
DIED
KAPAA, KAUAI
MEIJI XXIX
JULY 9, 1896

The Ship

Early on the morning of 17 June 1885, a steamship by the name *Yamashiro-maru* arrived in the Hawaiian port of Honolulu. A government-appointed physician boarded to carry out an all too perfunctory check of the passengers' health – there were nearly 1,000 Japanese labourers in the steerage accommodation – before giving permission for the vessel to dock.

This book follows a single ship to explore such moments of landfall in the Asia-Pacific world.[1] The iron-hulled *Yamashiro-maru* may have been an unremarkable vessel in the global scheme of things, but it steamed the seas in a remarkable age. A century or so before 1885, for example, this particular arrival would have been unimaginable. Japan, according to its most famous European chronicler of the eighteenth century, was all but closed to the outside world.[2] Ships were still powered by wind, their hulls constructed from wood. Japanese sea-faring vessels were neither capable of intentionally crossing the Pacific Ocean nor legally permitted to do so; overseas migration was also prohibited. And halfway across that vast expanse of water which Edo intellectuals labelled not the Pacific but the 'great eastern sea', islanders on the Hawaiian archipelago were only just beginning – after the year 1778 in European calendars – to explore the possibilities raised by their encounters with people from beyond the realm of their ocean-faring memories.[3] In the first decades of the twenty-first century, by contrast, the world is unimaginable *without* the transformations epitomized by the *Yamashiro-maru*'s Hawaiian arrival: that is, long-distance transport infrastructures; labour migrations and transnational families; fossil fuel consumption on an unsustainable scale; and tropes of a Pacific 'paradise' exploited by resource extraction. The

---

[1] On 'following' in global history, see John-Paul A. Ghobrial, 'Introduction: Seeing the World like a Microhistorian', *Past & Present* 242, Supplement 14 (2019): 1–22, especially p. 19.
[2] Engelbert Kaempfer, *Kaempfer's Japan: Tokugawa Culture Observed*, trans. and ed. Beatrice M. Bodart-Bailey (Honolulu: University of Hawai'i Press, 1999); Kaempfer's account was first published in 1727 in English. The fact that a Nagasaki scholar translated the term 'closed country' from Dutch into Japanese in 1801 suggested a more complex reality of knowledge, if not people, permeating tight borders: David Mervart, 'The Republic of Letters Comes to Nagasaki: Record of a Translator's Struggle', *Transcultural Studies* 2 (2015): 8–37.
[3] Marcia Yonemoto, 'Maps and Metaphors of Japan's "Small Eastern Sea" in Tokugawa Japan (1603–1868)', *Geographical Review* 89, 2 (1999): 169–87; David A. Chang, *The World and All the Things upon It: Native Hawaiian Geographies of Exploration* (Minneapolis: University of Minnesota Press, 2016). See also Chapter 4 for a discussion of early modern Japanese representations of the Pacific.

story of a Japanese steamship thus speaks to the world today as much as to its nineteenth-century context.

At least, such a sweeping overview of Asian and Pacific engagements was the book I originally thought I would write. Inspired by C. A. Bayly's *The Birth of the Modern World, 1780–1914*, and Jürgen Osterhammel's *The Transformation of the World*, I planned a 'global history' in terms of broad brushstrokes and apposite vignettes: in my case, of Japanese contributions to the period Bayly characterized as modernity's 'great acceleration' in the decades either side of 1900.[4] Japan fascinated non-Japanese people in these years, whether in the speed of society's perceived 'Westernization' after the 1868 Meiji revolution, or in the carefully curated image of national 'civilization' – wooden temple reconstructions, gorgeous silk kimonos – presented at world fairs in Europe and North America, or in the supposed anti-colonial vision its victory in the Russo-Japanese War (1904–5) constituted in the imaginations of colonized peoples in North Africa and South Asia.[5] My focus on a single steamship, especially on its migrant passengers, was initially intended to complicate these stereotypes by examining the socioeconomic costs of societal transformation during the Meiji period (1868–1912), alternative expressions of Japaneseness on Hawaiian plantations or Singapore streets, and the complex imbrication of overseas migrants with Japanese settler colonialism. And in the pages which follow I indeed address these issues, alongside the wider dynamics of labour, race, and environmental disruptions at the turn of the twentieth century. But the way I do so derives from my realization that the book I wanted to write was *not* a global history in the mode of all-encompassing vistas of modernity and globalization.

One problem was where to begin – a problem which quickly shifted from aesthetics to the epistemologies of archival position.[6] In an earlier age, whose logic still pervaded my historical training in the heart of the British establishment, the geographies of intellectual choice seemed simpler. If you wanted to write about local history, you began with local archives; if you were researching an aspect of the modern nation-state,

---

[4] C. A. Bayly, *The Birth of the Modern World, 1780–1914: Global Connections and Comparisons* (Oxford: Blackwell, 2004), p. 456; and Jürgen Osterhammel, *The Transformation of the World: A Global History of the Nineteenth Century*, trans. Patrick Camiller (Princeton, NJ: Princeton University Press, 2014 [2009]). Bayly's term lacks the environmental overtones later proposed by J. R. McNeill and Peter Engelke in *The Great Acceleration: An Environmental History of the Anthropocene since 1945* (Cambridge, MA: Harvard University Press, 2016).

[5] On the latter, see Pankaj Mishra, *From the Ruins of Empire: The Revolt Against the West and the Remaking of Asia* (London: Penguin, 2013).

[6] For one example of aesthetic angst about beginnings, see John Demos, *The Unredeemed Captive: A Family Story from Early America* (London: Paperman, 1996), pp. 3–10.

you would at some point end up in national archives. A recent book on 'the birth of the archive' reinforces this basic binary: the author first acknowledges institutions ranging 'from small *city archives* with the charm of improvisation to great *national archives* with sophisticated operations'.[7] But the problem of where or how to conduct *global* history research was not addressed in an older literature on historians' enamoured relationship with the archives;[8] and, as I shall argue, Ann Laura Stoler's crucial insight that colonial archives produce colonial ontologies, or 'categories of things that are thought to exist', has been inadequately pursued in a global history literature.[9] Bafflingly, the canonical works on global history methodologies have overlooked archival considerations, as have interventions on the 'prospect' or 'futures' of the field. Pamela Kyle Crossley went so far as to claim, in her *What Is Global History?* (2008), that 'the essential work of discovering facts and assembling primary history is not the work of those doing global history', while Sebastian Conrad's wide-ranging book of the same title (2016) eschewed global history archives as an explicit object of analysis.[10]

---

[7] Friedrich, *Birth of the Archive*, p. v (emphasis added).
[8] Arlette Farge, *Le Goût de l'archive* (Paris: Editions du Seuil, 1989): the English translation loses this sense of 'taste of' and 'taste for': Farge, *The Allure of the Archives*, trans. Thomas Scott-Railton (New Haven, CT: Yale University Press, 2013). See also Harriet Bradley, 'The Seductions of the Archive: Voices Lost and Found', *History of the Human Sciences* 12, 2 (1999): 107–22, here p. 110. For ways in which archives were used in early modern and nineteenth-century Europe, see, respectively, Friedrich, *Birth of the Archive*, and Bonnie G. Smith, 'Gender and the Practices of Scientific History: The Seminar and Archival Research in the Nineteenth Century', *American Historical Review*, 100, 4 (1995): 1150–76.
[9] Ann Laura Stoler, *Along the Archival Grain: Epistemic Anxieties and Colonial Common Sense* (Princeton, NJ: Princeton University Press, 2009), p. 4. I address other contributions to the archival literature later in the book.
[10] Pamela Kyle Crossley, *What Is Global History?* (Cambridge: Polity Press, 2008), p. 3; Sebastian Conrad, *What Is Global History?* (Princeton, NJ: Princeton University Press, 2016). The archives are only discussed in passing, and in strictly functional terms – e.g. the need for greater digitization – in Richard Drayton and David Motadel, 'Discussion: The Futures of Global History', *Journal of Global History* 13, 1 (2018): 1–21. In an explication of why global historians are attracted to notions of network, three leading historians contrast the 'modest' archival footprint of moving artisans, dealers and traders with the 'overbearing archives' generated by states and empires – but they and their fellow essayists offer no methodological discussions on how to mitigate the latter in favour of the former: James Belich, John Darwin, and Chris Wickham, 'Introduction: The Prospect of Global History', in James Belich, John Darwin, Margret Frenz and Chris Wickham, eds., *The Prospect of Global History* (Oxford: Oxford University Press, 2016), pp. 1–22, here p. 16. Methodological archival discussions are also absent in two Japanese-language introductions to global history, namely Mizushima Tsukasa 水島司, *Gurōbaru hisutorī nyūmon* グローバル・ヒストリー入門 [An introduction to global history] (Tokyo: Yamakawa shuppansha, 2010); and Haneda Masashi 羽田正, *Atarashii sekaishi e: Chikyū shimin no tame no kōsō* 新しい世界史へ：地球市民のための構想 [Towards a new world history: Making citizens of the earth] (Tokyo: Iwanami

The Ship

But if we accept that the past is a position, as Michel-Rolph Trouillot argued in his groundbreaking study of power and silence in Haitian history-making, then the physical site of the archive must be a key epistemological consideration in where a ship-centred history should begin, and what form its global dimensions might take.[11] Through histories of passage and landfall, *Mooring the Global Archive* attempts to answer a set of questions concerning the sites of 'global' archives, how they are constituted, and by whom. The standard answer to these questions, if they are asked at all, invokes some variation of the phrase 'multi-sited archival research', as if number and geographical breadth alone conjured up the global. But I shall argue that the production of global history emerges not only in archival breadth or archival silences – important though these are – but in the brackish spaces between archival sites, or between physical and digitized archives; in ontologies co-produced as a consequence of complementary agendas shared by record keepers across great oceanic distances; and also in the historian's imagination – or occasional failure thereof – as they try to bring different source collections into dialogue with each other. Broadly defined in ways I later discuss, 'the archive' disrupts 'the global' and the global reshapes the archive.

Through the heuristic device of the ship, I came to think of this mutual destabilization in terms of 'archival traps'.[12] I lay out three such traps below, all of which I unerringly jumped into as I drafted book beginnings and shapely structures. The first was my hope that the *Yamashiro-maru* could be narrated as a quasi-biographical history, in which a ship's 'life' could be told through moments of birth, death and achievements in-between. The second was my assumption that the global was googleable, such that the profusion of accessible, newly digitized sources might serve as my empirical base. And the third trap lay in the temptation to overlook the material contexts in which the languages of my sources were deeply

---

shoten, 2014). By the same token, the literature on archives in Japanese tends to overlook the turn towards global history: see, for example, Hosaka Hirooki 保坂裕興, 'Ākaibuzu to rekishigaku' アーカイブズと歴史学 [Archives and the discipline of history], in Ōtsu Tōru 大津透, Sakurai Eiji 桜井英治, Fujii Jōji 藤井譲治 et al., eds., *Iwanami kōza: Nihon rekishi* 岩波講座：日本歴史, Vol. 21 (Tokyo: Iwanami shoten, 2015), pp. 181–207.

[11] Michel-Rolph Trouillot, *Silencing the Past: Power and the Production of History* (Boston: Beacon Press, 2015 [1995]), p. 15. My thoughts on position and location are also influenced by Donna Haraway, 'Situated Knowledges: The Science Question in Feminism and the Privilege of Partial Perspective', *Feminist Studies* 14, 3 (1988): 575–99.

[12] In my focus on the relationship between archival work and global history narratives, I use 'traps' differently to Arlette Farge, *Allure of the Archives*, pp. 69–78.

embedded. Like all good traps, their cover was convincing: they led to several sources upon which I draw in future chapters, and they offered insights into how certain actors experienced change in the late nineteenth-century world. But they also led me to problematic narrative places in terms of my aspiration to write global history.

So here are three archival departures whose allure was all too real but whose intellectual logic I eventually came to jettison. Here is an explanation for why a gravestone inscription with the wrong date serves as this chapter's epigraph. And here, along the way, are some background sketches of the late nineteenth-century worlds of Britain, Japan and Hawai'i, between which the *Yamashiro-maru* steamed.

Trap 1: History as Moments of Birth

The most obvious place to begin was the ship's launch in Newcastle upon Tyne: the moment of its official birth. Indeed, one of only three surviving photographs of the *Yamashiro-maru* (to my knowledge) document this christening ceremony, in January 1884. On a temporary wooden platform at the base of the vessel's vast bow, around two dozen dignitaries pose for the moment of celluloid exposure (see Figure 1.2). The woman at the centre, Lady Margaret Armstrong (1807–93), wears a white fur cape; everyone else's overcoat is of a more sombre hue. The six Japanese men in the group sport top hats.[13]

Though a rare enough gathering to be worthy of a photograph, Japanese statesmen and businessmen had in fact been coming to the north-east of England for more than two decades by the time of the *Yamashiro-maru*'s launch. Back in 1862, the Tokugawa shogunate, weakened by the domestic unrest and foreign encroachment that would culminate in the 1868 Meiji revolution, had sent overseas embassies to Europe and Qing China, to build on the work of a similar mission to the United States in 1860.[14] To mark the ambassadors' arrival in 'our own neighbourhood' as part of their European tour, the *Newcastle Daily Journal* offered a summary of the region's historical achievements – in the modest prose typical of Victorian Britain:

---

[13] The Japanese attendees and various other dignitaries are listed in 'The Local Shipbuilding Trade', *Newcastle Daily Journal*, 14 January 1884 (accessed in Newcastle City Library). Mori Arinori is incorrectly named as 'Joushi Mari', along with his wife, 'Madame Mari', who officially named the ship.

[14] The classic account of the US-bound mission is Masao Miyoshi, *As We Saw Them: The First Japanese Embassy to the United States (1860)* (Berkeley: University of California Press, 1979); for more recent scholarship, see Natalia Doan, 'The 1860 Japanese Embassy and the Antebellum African American Press', *Historical Journal* 62, 4 (2019): 997–1020.

Figure 1.2 The launch of the *Yamashiro-maru*, Newcastle upon Tyne, 12 January 1884. Courtesy of Newcastle City Library, Local Studies Collections.

Here in the cradle of the locomotive and the railway system; in the home of the High-Level Bridge; in *the birthplace* of the hydraulic engine and the Armstrong gun; and in the great centre of the coal trade, where works for the manufacture of lead, iron, and glass rise up on every hand – where, with one exception, the largest ships in the world have been built, and where alone in England the beauties of Continental Street architecture are worthily rivalled, the illustrious [Japanese] party whom we entertain today will find the real secret of *England's greatness* among nations.[15]

Meanwhile, on the same day as the *Journal* published these breathless claims, the shogunate's embassy to China departed Nagasaki. Upon arrival in Shanghai, many in the group were appalled by what they perceived to be the decline of the Qing empire and the leeching of Asian resources at the hands of the 'barbarian' foreigners. But one

---

[15] *Newcastle Daily Journal*, 27 May 1862. Cited in Marie Conte-Helm, *Japan and the North East of England: From 1862 to the Present Day* (London: Athlone Press, 1989), p. 6 (emphasis added).

representing as it did one articulation of the 'level of enlightenment' which he had long hoped Japan would attain. And perhaps the *Yamashiro-maru* was in the back of his mind when he gave his final newspaper interview before departing London a few weeks later. 'People imagine here that Japanese progress during the last ten or fifteen years is a new thing to us,' he explained. In fact, nothing could be further from the truth: for centuries until the Tokugawa shogunate, Japan had taken 'that which is best from all worthy nations with which we [came] into contact'. Japanese strength was epitomized by this 'importation of ideas and institutions from foreign and alien civilizations'. And now, having overthrown the Tokugawa, and bolstered by the knowledge that the imperial dynasty had (allegedly) remained unbroken for 2,500 years, 'it is natural that we should feel a pride in our country – a pride that makes us smile with amusement at the idea that our importation of steam engines, telegraphs, or Parliaments can in any way affect our Japanese heart'.[22]

Such a profile of the most important Japanese dignitary attending the *Yamashiro-maru*'s launch served as one possible template for framing the history of the ship itself. It thus constitutes the first archival trap, namely my initial instinct to anthropomorphize the ship – to assume that the *Yamashiro-maru* was an object whose history could be narrated in the form of a biography, just as historians have written histories of modern Japan through the figure of Mori Arinori.[23] But the problem was that the genre of biography implied a moment of birth and thus, as deployed figuratively in histories of the modern world (or, indeed, the archive), a linear temporality departing from origin points.[24] Such narrative linearity in turn reinforces a universalizing, Enlightenment mode of imagining the modern world, in which 'progress' moved in one direction and as yet unenlightened people, whether they be in Europe's backwaters or

---

[22] 'The Japanese Ambassador on Public Affairs: An Interview on His Departure from England', *Pall Mall Gazette*, 26 February 1884 (accessed online through the *British Library Newspapers, Part I* database, 1 October 2011). For extended discussion of this interview, see Alastair Swale, *The Political Thought of Mori Arinori: A Study in Meiji Conservatism* (Richmond: Japan Library, 2000), pp. 82–112.

[23] On object biographies, see I. Kopytoff, 'The cultural biography of things: commoditization as process', in Arjun Appadurai, ed., *The Social Life of Things: Commodities in Cultural Perspective* (Cambridge: Cambridge University Press, 1986), pp. 64–91; also Chris Godsen and Yvonne Marshall, 'The Cultural Biography of Objects', *World Archaeology* 31, 2 (1999): 169–78. For biographies of Mori in English, Hall, *Mori Arinori*, and Swale, *Political Thought of Mori Arinori*.

[24] Dipesh Chakrabarty, *Provincializing Europe: Postcolonial Thought and Historical Difference*, 2nd edn (Princeton, NJ: Princeton University Press, 2008 [2000]), ch. 5, especially his concluding comments on p. 148; Friedrich, *Birth of the Archive*.

beyond the European metropole, were destined to follow a predetermined course in the pursuit of *catch-up*.

In practical terms, my imagination of the *Yamashiro-maru*'s January 1884 launch as such a moment of birth posed the danger of leading me towards a centrifugal narrative, whereby the ship equated to civilization bursting forth from a site of British 'greatness' and then proceeding – as the *Yamashiro-maru* did that July – towards a new home in Japan. In this mindset, my tendency was to shape even technical documents into a Mori-inspired mould of unidirectional history, in which the nascent ship both conformed to and reinforced standard narratives of modern world transformations. One afternoon in the autumn of 2009, for example, I visited the Tyne and Wear Archives, just down the hill from my office in Newcastle University's Armstrong Building. There I called up a design drawing for the midship section of the *Yamashiro-maru* (constructed in the Armstrong–Mitchell company's Low Walker yard 467) and its sister ship, the *Omi-maru* (yard 468).[25] On paper thick to the touch, a beguiling set of acronyms, numerals, annotations and calculations spoke to the physical heft of a vessel which – as we shall see – contemporaries hailed as 'handsome', 'lofty' and 'splendid' (see Figure 1.3). The '3″ [three-inch] teak deck' conjured up the tapped sound of polished leather shoes strolling from stern to bow during an afternoon promenade, the flesh of first-class hands resting on iron railings. In the *Yamashiro-maru*'s entry in the *Lloyd's Register (1884–5)*, the line *C.I.Cy.42″&78″ – 54″* similarly evoked a copper-sheathed, two-cylinder engine, both cylinders 54 inches in length but the narrower one – 42 inches wide – being where steam was compressed at high pressure.

Or, more to the point, such numbers *would* have translated into a basic materiality, had I known their meaning. As it was, I had to go online to fathom the drawing's *300′ PP* ('300 feet between perpendiculars', the *Yamashiro-maru*'s length) or *37′-0″ BMLD* (its breadth).[26] The engine had to be explained to me several years later by a retired shipbuilder in the German city of Rostock, with the help of a dictionary, a bottle of wine, and – on his part – infinite reserves of patience.

But even without grasping these technical details, I sensed what the numerals represented. Scaled up at half-an-inch to the foot, the result

---

[25] The Armstrong–Mitchell company dated from 1882, when Sir William (1810–1900) combined forces with renowned shipbuilder Charles Mitchell (1820–94), who boasted clients from around the world: see, for example, David Saunders, 'Charles Mitchell, Tyneside and Russia's First Ironclads', *Northern History* 48, 1 (2011): 75–95.

[26] To get really technical: the length 'between perpendiculars' referred to the ship's length at the waterline (a little over 91 metres). The length of the decks, including the *Yamashiro-maru*'s overhanging stern, would have been a few feet longer.

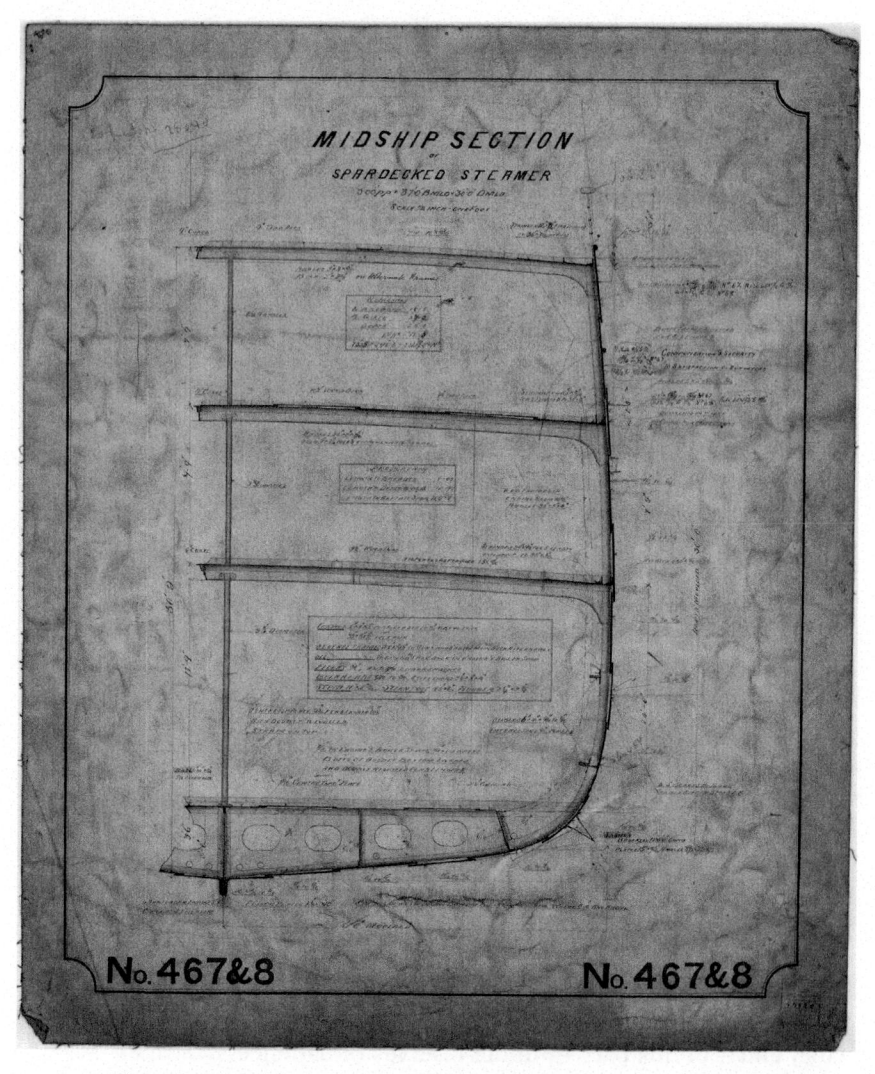

Figure 1.3 'Midship Section of Spardecked Steamer' (*Yamashiro-maru* and *Omi-maru*). Courtesy of Tyne and Wear Archives and Museums.

would be not merely a ship but a way of measuring the world: where those in the know, no matter whether they came from Kagoshima or Kronstadt (or Rostock), would recognize the technology as meeting international standards; where the publication of those standards – the post-launch *Yamashiro-maru* was awarded the highest possible 'A1'

Trap 1: History as Moments of Birth   13

Lloyds rating for hull and equipment – constituted global 'indicators of a ship's modernity'.[27] Thus, the design drawing's technical information served as a synecdoche for the increased standardization of nineteenth-century global time and space – itself symbolized by the October 1884 treaty to establish an international time regime.[28] Like the temporal marker of Greenwich Mean Time, the surviving traces of the *Yamashiro-maru* in the Newcastle archives would anchor my history to an hour zero: a base point from which to narrate, through the ship's subsequent journeys, what Bayly called the world's 'great acceleration' towards a modern age.

True, Mori Arinori himself apparently subscribed to the idea of base points when he spoke of Japanese 'progress' (*shinpo* 進歩) in comparison to a British civilizational standard, and of 'importation' as a means by which Japan might catch up with the West.[29] For many years, moreover, historians borrowed this rhetoric of the actors and ascribed it an analytical value. Thus, in an influential essay entitled, 'The Spread of Western Science', George Basalla argued that the steamboats introduced to the River Ganges in the 1830s were 'far more than a rapid and effective means of transportation'. In words which Mori could have uttered, Basalla continued, '[Steamboats] were *vectors of Western civilization* carrying Western science, medicine, and technical skills into the interior of India'.[30] But this imagination of the world, which my own vectors of assemblage in the Newcastle archives seemed likely to reinforce, served only to privilege certain metropolitan narratives.[31] To consider the ship's birth as one moment in the spread of civilization from Britain to Japan would be to entrench a modernist historiography of what Dipesh Chakrabarty has pithily called, 'first in the West, and then elsewhere'.[32] It would be to reinforce a diffusionist view of progress that the nineteenth-century discipline of history, at least as practised in Europe, itself validated – thereby undermining my aspiration to write any kind of global history.[33]

---

[27] This phrase was part of a narrator's voice-over in the Internationales Maritimes Museum Hamburg, which I visited in September 2013.
[28] Vanessa Ogle, *The Global Transformation of Time, 1870–1950* (Cambridge, MA: Harvard University Press, 2015).
[29] Mark Ravina calls the actorly rhetoric of Japanese catch-up in the 1870s 'nonsense': Ravina, *To Stand with the Nations of the World: Japan's Meiji Restoration in World History* (New York: Oxford University Press, 2017), p. 1.
[30] George Basalla, 'The Spread of Western Science', *Science*, 156, 3775 (5 May 1967): 611–22, here p. 620 (emphasis added).
[31] Cf. Stoler, 'vectors of official assemblages': *Along the Archival Grain*, p. 10.
[32] Chakrabarty, *Provincializing Europe*, p. 6.
[33] On 'progress' as central to the practice of history at the turn of the nineteenth century, see Reinhart Koselleck, 'The Temporalisation of Concepts', *Finnish Yearbook of Political Thought* 1, 1 (1997): 16–24. See also Priya Satia, *Time's Monster: How History Makes History* (Cambridge, MA: Belknap Press, 2020).

Obviously, this is somewhat of an exaggeration. There was nothing in the Tyne and Wear Archives that would *determine* a West-first reading of the *Yamashiro-maru*'s history, nobody insisting that I reconstruct Mori Arinori's career or cite his words. But the absence of other voices and genres of written sources (a problem that was becoming clearer by the day); the materiality of the magnificent red-bricked Armstrong Building from which I wrote; Armstrong's statue and the natural history museum and the other spaces bequeathed by this global engineering 'magician' in Newcastle and around the region;[34] the survival of the Armstrong–Mitchell company records; and even the drawing's thick paper in my hands: these seemed likely to launch me on a linear history pursuing tropes of greatness, progress and Japanese catch-up.[35]

There were other tropes hidden in this story, not least Mori's reference to the 'Japanese heart'. If I could find a way of fleshing out this claim, either through Mori himself or even better through the words of any of the thousands of Japanese migrants who had travelled on board the *Yamashiro-maru*, then this potentially offered an alternative vocabulary to 'civilization' for understanding Japan's late nineteenth-century engagements with the world, and thus a less standardized way of framing the ship's global history as a story of modernity. There were also alternative temporal scales suggested by the lived landscape of north-east England, in particular the histories of coal formation and extraction. These possible alternatives offered a way of imagining the ship, and, indeed, the modern world, not in terms of moments of birth but in terms of a *process* which encompassed parallel timelines.[36] Turning that imagination into a narrative that might work on the page was a different order of challenge, however. Back in 2009, my own design drawing of the *Yamashiro-maru* was merely a rough sketch, its calculations far from complete.

Trap 2: The Global as Googleable

Luckily, the internet was to hand – a different kind of archival trap. As I began imagining alternative points of departure, historians were

---

[34] Henrietta Heald, *William Armstrong: Magician of the North* (Newcastle upon Tyne: Northumbria Press, 2010).

[35] They seemed likely also to skew me towards a history of novelty, in that a newer ship was more newsworthy than an older one. In practical terms, this means that the source base for the *Yamashiro-maru* favours the 1880s and 1890s – that is, the ship's youth and middle age. On such problems, see David Edgerton, *The Shock of the Old: Technology and Global History since 1900* (Oxford: Oxford University Press, 2007).

[36] I draw here on Greg Dening's observation that the *Bounty* was a process: *Mr Bligh's Bad Language: Passion, Power and Theatre on the Bounty* (Cambridge: Cambridge University Press, 1992), p. 5.

debating new destinations, intellectual journeys made possible by the fact that 'networked access to online sources and to one another has completely changed the transaction and information costs that historians face'.[37] During my doctoral studies, my research had involved oral interviews and paper archives – the latter most haphazardly preserved in rural Japan. The transaction and information costs were high (as were my carbon costs), involving a flight to Tokyo at the very least. If digitized sources had aided my work at all, they had done so in a supplementary way, an extra gust of wind to my analogue sails. But now, in the long winter evenings of northern England, even something as methodologically unsophisticated as the single-box search engine promised an entirely new source of research power. I could sit at my screen, type some imaginative combination of *yamashiro* and *steamship* and *1880s* – and one night be presented with the search result, *Full text of "Reminiscences of an Ancient Mariner"*.[38] Tempted by this none-too-subtle allusion to Coleridge, I read on, turning yellowed pages with the tap of a touchpad, revelling in accessibility and drowning in detail.

Reminiscences had been published in Yokohama in 1918 by one of the city's English-language newspaper presses. Its author, John J. Mahlmann, had by that time been living in Japan for nearly fifty years – the 'New Japan', as he at one point described it. 'The Japanese people have undergone many changes,' he wrote, 'in some ways for the better, and in others not. They are endeavouring to raise themselves to the level of the most advanced nations, and I am of the opinion that if given enough time, their endeavour will be crowned with success.'[39] Here, more than four decades after Mori Arinori's 'First Essay on Enlightenment', was the undying trope of civilizational catch-up, replete with the language of nationally distinct 'levels'. And *Reminiscences* made clear that Mahlmann had played his own role in this Japanese 'success' story, most notably as harbour master at Kobe, 1888–98, and then as Meiji government adviser until his retirement in 1902. He had been decorated for his efforts with the Third Order of the Rising Sun.[40] But

---

[37] Observation by William J. Turkel, in Daniel J. Cohen, Michael Frisch, Patrick Gallagher, Steven Mintz, Kirsten Sword, Amy Murrell Taylor, William G. Thomas III and William J. Turkel, 'Interchange: The Promise of Digital History', *Journal of American History* 95, 2 (2008): 452–91, here p. 458.

[38] The technical term (I would later learn) is 'Boolean search', after a mid nineteenth-century English mathematician: another vestige of Europe-first standardization impacting the contemporary world.

[39] John James Mahlmann, *Reminiscences of an Ancient Mariner* (Yokohama: Japan Gazette Printing and Publishing, 1918), pp. 125, 132. Available through the Internet Archive (https://archive.org) (last accessed 26 March 2021).

[40] Mahlmann, *Reminiscences*, p. 236.

if Mahlmann had made the New Japan, then *Reminiscences* demonstrated that Japan had equally made the New Mahlmann. By 1918, he was a paragon of respectability, a man so far removed from the dubious associations of his youth that his memories merited publication – that in his dotage (this the greatest claim of all to respectability, arguably) he could afford to sojourn in Switzerland.[41]

Such a respectable future would have been unimaginable in 1864, the year *Reminiscences* begins. Mahlmann fails to make his anticipated £50,000 fortune in Hokitika during New Zealand's West Coast Gold Rush.[42] After working his way back to Australia (whence the reader is led to believe he comes), he finds various employments, including as chief mate on a commodity-trading ship sailing between Sydney and the Gilbert Islands.[43] In 1868 he joins a barque overloaded with coal, bound from Newcastle (New South Wales) to Shanghai. The vessel is wrecked in the Marshall Islands, but Mahlmann is eventually picked up by the notorious US trader Benjamin Pease (1834–70), for whom he will work on the Caroline Island of Pohnpei. And thus to one of Mahlmann's aims in penning his autobiography: he wants to 'clear away any misunderstanding among my acquaintances respecting the extent of my connection' with Pease and with William 'Bully' Hayes [1829(?)–77], also American, who were heavily involved in 'blackbirding' – that is, the abduction of tens of thousands of Pacific Islanders to work on colonial plantations in Queensland in particular.[44] Eventually, in mid 1871, Mahlmann makes his way to Shanghai but there discovers that Pease's company, for which he'd been promised employment, has collapsed.

---

[41] *Reminiscences* closes with several addenda, the last of which is a letter written from Geneva, in November 1911, during the two years Mahlmann spent there to be near his daughter's school at the Villa Brillantmont (Lausanne). Mahlmann's marriage to a Japanese woman from Wakayama prefecture goes unmentioned in *Reminiscences*, but is recorded on his gravestone in Kobe: Kōyama Toshio 鴻山俊雄, 'Gaijin bochi ni nemuru hitobito' 外人墓地に眠る人々(中) [Those who sleep in the foreigners' cemetery], *Nikka geppō 16* (1968), p. 5.

[42] Hokitika's Gold Rush is brilliantly evoked in Eleanor Catton's novel, *The Luminaries* (London: Granta Books, 2013).

[43] Also unmentioned in *Reminiscences*: Mahlmann was born in 1838 in Borstel, near Hamburg – according to his Certificate of Competency as Second Mate (accessed through www.ancestry.com) – and probably came to Australia for the first time in 1864. His sensitivity to his German roots may have been due to *Reminiscences* being published during the First World War.

[44] Mahlmann, *Reminiscences*, p. i. On blackbirding and on Hayes in particular, see Gerald Horne, *The White Pacific: US Imperialism and Black Slavery in the South Seas after the Civil War* (Honolulu: University of Hawai'i Press, 2007), pp. 33–62. On Pohnpei, see David L. Hanlon, *Upon a Stone Altar: A History of the Island of Pohnpei to 1890* (Honolulu: University of Hawai'i Press, 1988), who calls Mahlmann 'honest but incompetent' (p. 132).

Instead finding work on a steamer belonging to the Yokohama-based Walsh, Hall & Co, he arrives in Japan on 1 November 1871.

Though no Coleridge, Mahlmann offers the reader an intriguing insight into the changing economic dynamics of the Pacific world in the mid nineteenth century. We grasp the migratory pull of gold rushes; the increasing presence of US interests in the region, even as China remained a key market for Pacific commodities; the British imperial infrastructures which supported the shipping of coal to the strategic port of Shanghai; the continuation of a Pacific slave trade deep into the nineteenth century; and the emergence of Japan into East Asian trading networks during the 1860s and 1870s.[45] But there is nothing in these stories to suggest that Mahlmann was Third Order of the Rising Sun material, either in 1871 or in the years that followed – which boast the chapter titles 'Coasting and Loafing in Japan', and 'Here, There and Everywhere'. Late in 1884, however, Mahlmann's fortunes took an upward turn. Due both to his years of service in the Japanese merchant marine, and to his acquaintance with Robert W. Irwin (1844–1925) of the new KUK shipping company, he was offered command of the KUK's 'best steamer at the highest rate then going'.[46] This was the *Yamashiro-maru*.

During Mahlmann's three years in the ship's command, the *Yamashiro-maru* mainly ran the Kobe–Yokohama line, the key passenger and freight artery of Meiji Japan. Mahlmann was thus on the bridge when the young Yanagita Kunio travelled to Tokyo in 1887.[47] But in addition to these regular duties, in May 1885 the *Yamashiro-maru* was also 'chartered to take 1,000 Japanese emigrants to Honolulu, to be distributed from there among the different sugar plantations on the islands'.[48] The chapter Mahlmann writes on Hawai'i constitutes the most detailed episode in *Reminiscences*. In it, he describes a seventeen-day quarantine period that all first-class passengers and crew were forced to spend on the ship after the belated discovery, upon arrival in Honolulu, of smallpox among the migrant labourers. But the main story, accompanied in the text by imprints of King Kalākaua (1836–91, r. 1874–91) and Queen Kapi'olani (1834–99), concerns a working tour that the *Yamashiro-maru* took of the Hawaiian Islands, joined also by the royal couple. There is 'Hawaiian dancing' on the ship's decks, a 'charming'

---

[45] Robert Hellyer, 'The West, the East, and the Insular Middle: Trading Systems, Demand, and Labour in the Integration of the Pacific, 1750–1875', *Journal of Global History* 8, 3 (2013): 391–413. See also Matt Matsuda, *Pacific Worlds: A History of Seas, Peoples, and Cultures* (Cambridge: Cambridge University Press, 2012). For imperial coal infrastructures, see my Chapter 6.
[46] Mahlmann, *Reminiscences*, p. 182. [47] See the Preface.
[48] Mahlmann, *Reminiscences*, pp. 183–4.

dawn view of Mauna Loa and Mauna Kea (Mahlmann reaches for the cliché, 'Paradise of the Pacific'), and a respectful nod to the new monument honouring where Captain Cook 'was foully murdered by a native in 1779'. Upon the *Yamashiro-maru*'s return to Honolulu, there is more royal dancing late into the night. At an impromptu breakfast ceremony, Mahlmann is appointed Companion of the Royal Order of the Crown of Hawai'i in the presence of the king, government ministers, the aforementioned Mr Irwin and the Royal Hawaiian Band.[49] The author plays to the crowd in these pages, reinforcing an anti-Native Hawaiian stereotype of King Kalākaua which would later coalesce around the phrase, 'merrie monarch'.[50] But mainly the chapter is about Mahlmann himself: his newfound status as an acquaintance of monarchs and ministers; his royal honour in Hawai'i foreshadowing his imperial honour in Japan; his becoming, through the *Yamashiro-maru* ('the first Japanese merchant steamer that ever visited the islands'), a conduit of the New Japan.[51] Indeed, his command directly leads, at the turn of 1888 and in his fiftieth year, to his prestigious appointment as Kobe harbour master. Thus, Mahlmann's service as the *Yamashiro-maru*'s captain serves as a narrative bridge between his chequered life aft and his reputable life fore.[52]

As I say, a lot of detail. But reading *Reminiscences* in 2009, I became convinced that the ship as a narrative device, shaping however briefly the lives of historical actors and their subsequent memories, could be a model for my book as a whole. If I could interpret Mahlmann's biography in this way, then approximately 1,000 other opportunities for a similar approach presented themselves to me in the form of the Japanese migrants transported to Hawai'i in 1885, such that the ship would summon subaltern lives.[53] All I needed was to google a little more – although perhaps with a tad more search-term sophistication.

And so to the second archival trap. My online reading of Mahlmann's *Reminiscences* was one manifestation of what Lara Putnam has called the

---

[49] Mahlmann, *Reminiscences*, pp. 189–99. On Mahlmann's royal honour, see also *PCA*, 21 July 1885. Accessed online through https://chroniclingamerica.loc.gov.
[50] On the undermining of King Kalākaua's political authority through allegations of 'frippery and nonsense', see Jonathan Kay Kamakawiwo'ole Osorio, *Dismembering Lāhui: A History of the Hawaiian Nation to 1887* (Honolulu: University of Hawai'i Press, 2002), pp. 224–9, citation from p. 225.
[51] Mahlmann, *Reminiscences*, p. 194.
[52] Mahlmann describes his Japanese career as 'chequered' in *Reminiscences*, p. 101. In this reading of social advancement and narrative strategy, I am influenced by Scott Ashley, 'How Navigators Think: The Death of Captain Cook Revisited', *Past & Present* 194, 1 (2007): 107–37.
[53] Clare Anderson, *Subaltern Lives: Biographies of Colonialism in the Indian Ocean World, 1790–1920* (Cambridge: Cambridge University Press, 2012).

'digitized turn'.[54] Indeed, my research for *Mooring the Global Archive* in the 2010s coincided with an intensification of source digitization in the Global North especially.[55] English-language newspapers in Hawaiʻi that could only be manually searched on microfilm readers in 2011 were by 2014 miraculously available on the Library of Congress's 'Chronicling America' online directory. In the period 2012 to 2014, as I trawled through bound paper files in the Diplomatic Archives of the Japanese Ministry of Foreign Affairs, documents were being unbound and photographed at an adjacent table. The archivists' whispered consultations and the camera's electronic click formed a background soundtrack to my research. Over the months, staff updated their work in a colour-coded spreadsheet on the archive's website.

If the updates evoked a journey's progress similar to that measured by a shipboard log (a source genre which was proving frustratingly difficult to find in the *Yamashiro-maru*'s case), then comprehensive digitization was our promised destination – depending on what was meant by 'comprehensive'. Mahlmann had appeared in my Google search results because someone called Alyson-Wieczorek, working for the non-profit Internet Archive, had uploaded *Reminiscences* to archive.org on 10 May 2007.[56] As of June 2022, Alyson-Wieczorek has an upload history of 68,455 texts, 97 per cent of which were published in English. For the Internet Archive as a whole, 74 per cent of the 34.9 million digitized texts are published in English, with the three next most popular languages – French, German and Dutch – comprising another 6 per cent.[57] There was a similar imbalance in Chronicling America: after 2014, you could browse those Hawaiʻi-based newspapers founded before the overthrow of the Hawaiian monarchy in January 1893 – Chronicling America had nine – and come away with the erroneous impression that English was

---

[54] Lara Putnam, 'The Transnational and the Text-Searchable: Digitized Sources and the Shadows They Cast', *American Historical Review* 121, 2 (2016): 377–402, here p. 379.

[55] Archival digitization is itself old enough to merit a history: for an overview, see Adam Crymble, *Technology and the Historian: Transformations in the Digital Age* (Champaign: University of Illinois Press, 2021), pp. 46–78.

[56] On the founding of the Internet Archive in 1996, see Ian Milligan, *History in the Age of Abundance? How the Web Is Transforming Historical Research* (Montreal: McGill–Queen's University Press, 2019), pp. 74–5. On metadata analysis being the 'hermeneutic prerequisite of online source criticism', see Andreas Fickers, 'Towards a New Digital Historicism? Doing History in the Age of Abundance', *VIEW Journal of European Television History and Culture* 1, 1 (2012): 19–26.

[57] https://archive.org/details/@alyson-wieczorek. The equivalent text figure for the Internet Archive as a whole was 34,851,578, of which 25,842,575 were in (printed) English: https://archive.org/details/texts?tab=collection (both last accessed on 23 June 2022). On the wider problem of the 'marked Anglophone bias in digitized history', see Goebel, 'Ghostly Helpmate', especially pp. 51–5, citation from p. 51.

the only language of the islands.[58] Hawaiian-language newspapers do in fact exist in large numbers, and have been digitized by local institutions rather than by the Library of Congress; but as of mid 2022, neither Hawaiian nor any other Indigenous North American or Pacific Island language appears as a search filter option on Chronicling America.[59] In other words, I could read Mahlmann online because the vast majority of printed publications digitized by the Internet Archive and other similar services are English-language sources.

The trap's narrative consequence was that Mahlmann would all too easily become the textual embodiment of the *Yamashiro-maru* in Hawai'i, the ship's story *his* story. By contrast, it turned out that to study the *Yamashiro-maru*'s nearly 1,000 emigrants to Hawai'i in June 1885 still necessitated the transactional costs of multiple flights to Japan and their concomitant carbon footprint, because the very files I had been reading to reconstruct their migrations in the Japanese Diplomatic Archives came from exactly those source series which were not and will not be digitized (see Chapter 5). This discrepancy highlights what Putnam has identified as 'the systematic underrepresentation of whole strata of people in our now-massive digitized source base'.[60]

The chapters which follow offer a set of archival strategies for narratively countering this digitized source underrepresentation. But my narrative also occasionally pauses to reflect on why historians should practise greater methodological transparency in a digitized age. For example, my blithe assumption that the global was googleable overlooked the problem of traceable archival pathways. In an analogue world, archival collections are ordered according to certain organizational principles. To map these principles, and to understand how they affect results generated by a particular archival request, is partly to identify what Ann Laura Stoler calls the 'archival grain' – and thus to trace, as if fingering a piece of

---

[58] As of June 2022, Chronicling America included twenty-three digitized newspapers from Hawai'i, the date of their first issue ranging from 6 June 1840 to 1 July 1912: https://chroniclingamerica.loc.gov/newspapers/?state=Hawaii&ethnicity=&language= (last accessed 23 June 2022).

[59] For Hawaiian-language newspapers, see www.papakilodatabase.com (last accessed 23 June 2022); see also Paukea Nogelmeier, *Mai Pa'a I Ka Leo: Historical Voice in Hawaiian Primary Materials: Looking Forward and Listening Back* (Honolulu: Bishop Museum Press, 2010), pp. 58–104. The language imbalance I have described has many causes, one of which may be that newspaper digitization tends 'to be strongest in subjects and time periods that garner grant funding': Andrew J. Torget and Jon Christensen, 'Building New Windows into Digitized Newspapers', *Journal of Digital Humanities* 1, 3 (2012): http://journalofdigitalhumanities.org (last accessed 4 April 2021).

[60] Putnam, 'Transnational and the Text-Searchable', p. 391.

Trap 2: The Global as Googleable   21

timber, one's lines of archival enquiry.[61] If newly digitized archives and their browsing infrastructure maintain the original organizational principles of their physical counterparts – as was eventually the case with the Japanese diplomatic archives – then all to the better. But with invisible commercial algorithms driving general internet searches, some of the archival grain has become impossible to trace.[62] A decade on from 2009, and thanks to the Wayback Machine (itself developed by the aforementioned Internet Archive), I could reconstruct a decent approximation of the websites I had visited at the beginning of my research.[63] But I could never revisit the paths that had led from my browser one winter evening in Newcastle upon Tyne to Mahlmann's *Reminiscences*, nor explain how a similar search ten years later might throw up subtly different results. One principle of scientific reconstruction, manifested in the discipline of history in explanatory footnotes or endnotes, has thus been broken. The fact that the text-searchable is at some level irretrievable thus provides one justification for my argument concerning authorial transparency. If the internet offers serendipitous discoveries whose algorithmic pathways nevertheless remain commercially hidden, then one compensatory move is for scholars to offer greater methodological self-reflection in other aspects of their research – as *Mooring the Global Archive* attempts to model.

By itself, this call for transparency is not entirely new. A recent literature on digital methodologies in history has argued for scholars to provide more reference information: on whether a newspaper article was accessed via a database, a microfilm or the original paper copy; on search strings – namely, the combinations of *yamashiro* and *steamship* and *1880s* that I no longer recall – and on the specialized databases through which we can run those searches.[64] The problem is, the assumption lying behind these arguments is that the digitized turn in history, including the new possibility to analyse millions rather than thousands of source pages, has rendered archival work exponentially more complex than it was in a predigital world. 'Historians' relationship to the archives used to be simple', we have been told; but with the digital age, 'Historians now

---

[61] On the archival principle of 'fonds', see Farge, *Allure of the Archives*, p. 4. See also Stoler, *Along the Archival Grain*, passim, and my Chapter 5.
[62] For an exegesis of this problem in the realm of race and gender studies, see Safiya Umoja Noble, *Algorithms of Oppression: How Search Engines Reinforce Racism* (New York: New York University Press, 2018).
[63] On the temporal inconsistencies to be found in archived webpages, see Niels Brügger, *The Archived Web: Doing History in the Digital Age* (Cambridge, MA: MIT Press, 2018), pp. 103–17.
[64] E.g. Milligan, *History in the Age of Abundance?*, pp. 59–60.

not only use but create, contribute to, and theorize collections of digital records, some at massive scale.'[65] Or equally, 'the stereotypical historian still remains resolutely tied to scholarly traditions – dust in the archives rather than bytes in the computer's memory'.[66] The straw man pervades such statements: if scholars in the old days can be represented as simply turning up to 'use' paper archives (trying not to sneeze too much from dust in the process), then new methodologies in digital history research appear even more innovative.

In digital as in global history, the appeal of the term 'unmooring' partly derives from this rhetoric of stasis, in which outdated methodologies are tied to analogue research traditions or national history pasts.[67] My contrasting emphasis on 'mooring' comes not from a place of nostalgia for those paper-filled days in national archives, but from a contention that the digitized turn has *not* rendered position and place irrelevant in the writing of history, especially global history. For sure, *Mooring the Global Archive* as a research project would have been dead in the water without the digitization of sources such as Mahlmann's *Reminiscences* or the *Daily Pacific Commercial Advertiser*. But the trap lay not just in the appeal of their accessibility or in their volume (and English-language bias), and the narrative consequences thereof. It also lay in the incalculable 'information cost' of what knowledge I would have overlooked without my pre-online memories of having first read microfilm copies of the *Advertiser* in the Periodicals Room of the Hawai'i State Library. Here, then, we arrive at a third archival trap, namely my assumption that historical context was primarily a matter of written text rather than material encounter.

---

[65] Itza A. Carbajal and Michelle Caswell, 'Critical Digital Archives: A Review from Archival Studies', *American Historical Review* 126, 3 (September 2021): 1102–20, here p. 1102.

[66] Crymble, *Technology and the Historian*, p. 1. Ian Milligan also offers a very simplified sketch of historians as 'users' of physical archives: *History in the Age of Abundance?*, p. 67. It's also true that historians have not shied away from writing about dust – but in ways that are anything but theoretically simple: Carolyn Steedman, *Dust* (Manchester: Manchester University Press, 2001), itself in extended conversation with Jacques Derrida, 'Archive Fever: A Freudian Impression', *Diacritics* 25, 2 (1995): 9–63.

[67] On metaphors of unmooring in digital history, see the Preface; in global history, see Renisa Mawani, 'The Politics of Empire: Minor History on a Global Scale', in Rita Dhamoon, Davina Bhandar, Renisa Mawani and Satwinder Kaur Bains, *Unmooring the Komagata Maru: Charting Colonial Trajectories* (Vancouver: University of British Colombia Press, 2019), pp. 280–9, on the need to unmoor the *Komagata-maru* from Canadian national histories (p. 284). For a counter view, positing the extent to which mobilities were conversely moored to port cities, see Lasse Heerten, 'Mooring Mobilities, Fixing Flows: Towards a Global Urban History of Port Cities in the Age of Steam', *Journal of Historical Sociology* 34 (2021): 350–74.

Trap 3: Fixation on the Written Word

The *Yamashiro-maru* does not survive. The board minutes of the Nippon Yūsen Kaisha (NYK), the enterprise formed in October 1885 from a merger of the KUK and Mitsubishi companies, record that the decision was taken in March 1908 to divest of 'obsolete and uneconomic' vessels, and both the *Yamashiro-maru* and the *Omi-maru* were sold for scrap eighteen months later.[68] A second-generation *Yamashiro-maru* would be constructed for the NYK in Kobe in 1912, the year of the Meiji emperor's death – but that story, with which Mori Arinori would surely have defended the notion that civilized nations build ships, must be for others to write.

Though the first *Yamashiro-maru*'s scrapping deprives me of a museum experience such as that offered by the Bristol-built *SS Great Britain* (launched in 1843), and thus of the chance to walk, touch and inhale the ship, there are other archival ways to grasp its materiality. This is because after historical vessels had been constructed through cutting, moulding, welding and hammering, they were then produced a second time: through adjectives, numerals, metaphors and iconography. Briefly examining some of these rhetorical constructions in Honolulu, first via New York, Millwall and Edo Bay, reveals a vocabulary of global encounter in the second half of the nineteenth century – while also highlighting the trap of our becoming too fixated on the written word alone.

When the *SS Great Britain* arrived for the first time in New York, for example, newspapers described it as a 'monster of the deep – this Megatherion [sic], or Megaplion, rather of the nineteenth century ... this mammoth'.[69] *Megaplion* simply meant 'great ship'; but *megatherium* (great beast) was the name that Georges Cuvier (1769–1832) had famously given to the huge fossil skeleton discovered in the 1790s in Spanish America, with which he proposed a theory of extinction and thereby a much longer history of the earth than Biblical time allowed. This kind of labelling, applied as it often was to mid nineteenth-century steamships, implied that the new technology was so revolutionary in shrinking global

---

[68] Nihon Kei'eishi Kenkyūjo 日本経営史研究所, ed., *Nippon Yūsen Hyakunenshi shiryō* 日本郵船百年史資料 [The NYK Centennial: Documents] (Tokyo: Nippon yūsen, 1988), p. 542. The ships were sold to Yamashina Marine Industries, founded by Yamashina Reizō 山科禮蔵 (1864–1930), later member of the House of Representatives and owner of the *Japan Times*. On the sale, *AS*, 31 October 1909 (accessed digitally through Kikuzo II Visual, https://database.asahi.com/help/jpn/about.html [subscription]).

[69] *Evening Post* (New York), 11 August 1845; *New York Herald*, 11 August 1845: both cuttings are displayed in Brunel's SS Great Britain museums (www.ssgreatbritain.org), which I visited in December 2013 and August 2018.

distance that, like the new disciplines of geology and palaeontology, it would 'burst the limits of time' (to use one of Cuvier's most memorable phrases).[70] Thus, the Millwall-built *SS Great Eastern* (launched in 1858) was similarly described by contemporaries as 'pre-Adamitic', a vessel 'to which even Noah's Ark must yield precedence'.[71] Half a century later, a newspaper correspondent looked back to the *Great Eastern* as a 'leviathan *born out of due time*, since even now she dominates the imagination of many'.[72]

Japanese commentators in the mid nineteenth century also constructed steamships rhetorically, but without the Biblical references. Like their European and North American counterparts, they offered their readers detailed technical descriptions. When, for example, Commodore Matthew Perry (1794–1858) arrived with a small squadron in Edo Bay in July 1853 to force the Tokugawa shogunate into agreeing trade treaties with the United States (see Chapter 6), one local artist framed his monstrous depiction of one of Perry's two steamships with a cartouche recording the alleged dimensions of the vessel: length 75 *ken* 間, breadth 20 *ken*, wheel 6.5 *ken*; three masts; distance from waterline to deck 2 *jō* 丈 5 *shaku* 尺; and so on (see Figure 1.4).[73] Encountering the squadron up close, local fishermen talked of ships 'as large as mountains' – a trope which was quickly taken up by writers as far away as Wakayama. (That there was already a word for 'steamship' in Japanese suggests that there may have been an element of hyperbole in these visual and verbal depictions.)[74] In June 1860, a diarist on the Tokugawa shogunate's

---

[70] On Cuvier, see Martin J. S. Rudwick, *Earth's Deep History: How It Was Discovered and Why It Matters* (Chicago: University of Chicago Press, 2014), pp. 103–14. On the shrinking of distance, see Yrjö Kaukiainen, 'Shrinking the World: Improvements in the Speed of Information Transmission, c. 1820–1870', *European Review of Economic History* 5, 1 (2001): 1–28.

[71] 'The Steamship Great Eastern', *South Australian Register*, 6 August 1857 (article syndicated from the *Times*, May 1857): available through https://trove.nla.gov.au (last accessed 29 June 2022).

[72] 'White Star Liners', *Auckland Star*, 19 January 1909, quoting an undated report in the *Daily Mail* by Frank T. Bullen (emphasis added): accessed through https://paperspast.natlib.govt.nz (last accessed 4 April 2021). The *Great Eastern* had originally been christened the *Leviathan*.

[73] This translated to 136 metres (length) and 36 metres (width). The largest of Perry's two steamships, the *Susquehanna*, was in fact only 78 metres long. We might read the measuring of monstrous-looking foreign ships as alluding to a genre of natural history in Japan that by the mid nineteenth century was drawing, mapping and measuring even monstrous creatures such as *kappa* (water goblins) so as to order them as objects of scientific knowledge: see Federico Marcon, *The Knowledge of Nature and the Nature of Knowledge in Early Modern Japan* (Chicago: University of Chicago Press, 2015), pp. 194–6.

[74] William M. Steele, *Alternative Narratives in Modern Japanese History* (London: Routledge, 2003), p. 6. For Wakayama, Sonoda Hidehiro 園田英弘, Seiyōka no kōzō: Kurofune, bushi, kokka 西洋化の構造：黒船・武士・国家 [Constructions of

Figure 1.4 'Depiction of a Foreign Ship' (Ikokusen-zu 異国船図). Courtesy of Nagasaki Museum of History and Culture.

aforementioned embassy to the United States used a similar analogy in New York, when the ambassadors' departure coincided with the arrival of the *Great Eastern* on its maiden transatlantic voyage: the British ship, he wrote, 'was like a mountain protruding from the sea'. Another of the mission's diarists inadvertently echoed the press coverage of the *Great Britain*'s arrival in New York fifteen years previously when he described the *Great Eastern* as a 'mammoth [*kyodai naru* 巨大なる] British merchant steamship'.[75]

To be clear, the *Yamashiro-maru* in the mid 1880s did not provoke such hyperbole. Its name notwithstanding – Yamashiro (山城) literally means 'mountain castle', referring to Japan's most important ancient province (see Chapter 4) – the vessel was no *Great Eastern*-like ship-mountain. But it did provoke considerable comment in Japan's English- and Japanese-language newspapers upon its post-launch arrival from

---

Westernization: Black ships, samurai, state] (Kyoto: Shibunkaku shuppan, 1993), pp. 56–7. For Sonoda's point about the Japanese word for 'steamship', pp. 52–4.

[75] Satō Tsunezō Hidenaga 佐藤恒蔵秀長 (1824–1905) and Muragaki Norimasa 村垣範正 (1813–80), respectively, in Ōtsuka Takematsu 大塚武松, ed., *Kengai shisetsu nikki sanshū* 遣外使節日記纂輯 [The diary collections of overseas embassies] (Tokyo: Nihon shiseki kyōkai, 1928), Vol. 1, pp. 484, 148.

Newcastle in July 1884, as if its much-noted interior electric lights embodied a level of enlightenment.[76] In another example of steamship anthropomorphism, a cartoonist working for the Yokohama-based *Japan Punch* newspaper even gave the *Yamashiro-maru* facial features (see Figure 1.5): the ship took on an appearance very close to that of the KUK's Robert W. Irwin, as the foreign press decried the deleterious competition between the KUK and Mitsubishi prior to the two companies' merger.[77] And in by far the most detailed written description I found during my years of research, the *Yamashiro-maru* was produced to have a different face, namely that of Japan.[78]

To understand how this rhetorical production of the ship as the face of Japan worked in Hawai'i, we need to return to the *Yamashiro-maru*'s arrival in Honolulu – the episode with which I began this chapter. During his perfunctory first inspection on the morning of 17 June, the government-appointed doctor had in fact missed all the classic symptoms of smallpox among a small number of passengers who were sick. Only thanks to a second inspection, after the ship had docked, was the disease discovered and the potential public health disaster of infectious passengers entering the archipelago avoided. Nevertheless, as Mahlmann had noted in his *Reminiscences*, 'The newspapers censured the port physician most severely for not knowing the difference between measles and smallpox, and had much to say about the probable dreadful consequences thereof'.[79] This comment gave me a new research lead. But if I wanted to know what these Hawaiian newspapers had actually written in the pre-digitized era of 2011, I needed to fly to Honolulu – and find the institutional sponsorship to do so.[80]

Once there, I started by retrieving some basic contextual facts on the smallpox incident from the government records of the time: the minutes of the Hawaiian Board of Health, for example, or those of the Board of Immigration. These survive in the Hawai'i State Archives, a rectangular, white-panelled building which squats among banyan trees in the southeast corner of the 'Iolani Palace grounds. (The palace had been completed in 1882 as a way of impressing Kalākaua's kingship upon both his

---

[76] *Japan Weekly Mail*, 26 July 1884; *HN*, 31 July 1884 (both accessed in paper form); *AS*, 30 July 1884.
[77] 'The Rivals', *Japan Punch* (Yokohama), January 1885 (accessed in paper form).
[78] On the 'national physiognomy' of ships, see Allan Sekula, *Fish Story* (Düsseldorf: Richter Verlag, 1995), p. 12.
[79] Mahlmann, *Reminiscences*, p. 187.
[80] For an acknowledgement of these resource inequalities in global history, see, for example, Dorothy Sue Cobble, 'The Promise and Peril of the New Global Labor History', *International Labor and Working-Class History* 82 (2012): 99–107, here p. 104.

Trap 3: Fixation on the Written Word 27

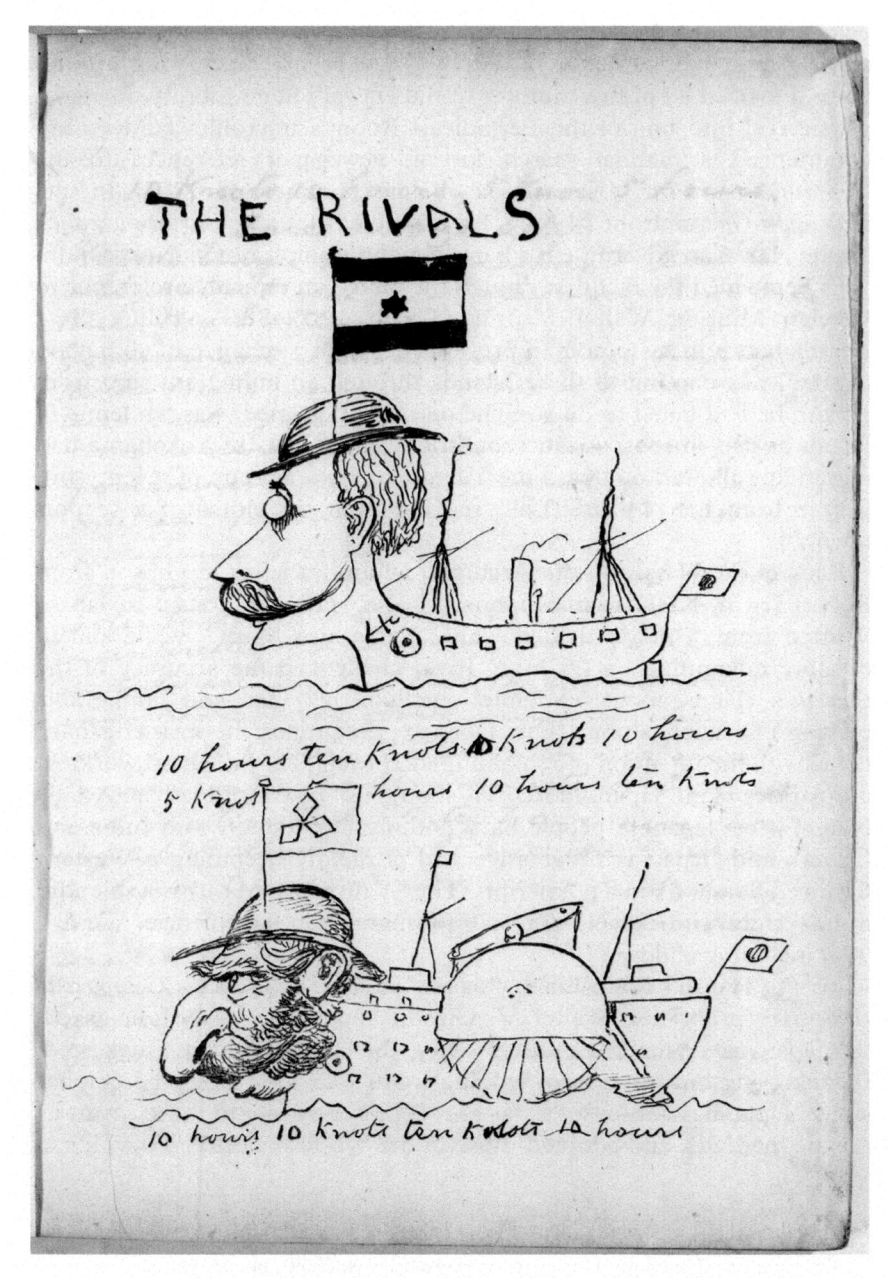

Figure 1.5 'The Rivals', *Japan Punch*, January 1885. (The *Yamashiro-maru* is the upper ship.)
Courtesy of Yokohama Archives of History Museum.

own people and the kingdom's increasingly powerful – and critical – sugar planter constituency.)[81] After a day or two burrowing around there, I walked all of five minutes to the Hawai'i State Library, loaded a plastic reel into one of the Periodicals Room's microfilm readers and commenced a manual search for all newspaper references to the *Yamashiro-maru* or to smallpox in the summer of 1885. In the *Hawaiian Gazette* from 24 June, for example, I found a blistering attack on the Hawaiian government's handling of the ship's original inspection. This bemoaned the fact that though the man – an unnamed reference to Foreign Minister Walter Murray Gibson (1822–88) – 'ruling these Boards had it in his power to prevent the slightest chance of contagion of small pox coming to these Islands through an immigrant ship from Japan', he had failed to do so. The disease, it claimed, was 'endemic in Japan, as it is in most Asiatic countries', and agents in Yokohama had regrettably allowed on board the *Yamashiro-maru* a group of seventy-five people from the city itself, all 'reeking from the slums of a seaport town'.[82]

Back in the Hawai'i State Archives, I found a letter to Gibson from Robert Irwin, KUK businessman and also Hawaiian consul to Japan. Written from 'On board Steamship "Yamashiro Maru"' while still in offshore quarantine on 25 June, Irwin challenged the accuracy of the *Gazette*'s claims about 'endemic' smallpox in Japan and immigrants reeking of seaport slums. 'Our Japanese Emigrants,' he insisted, 'have come with the intention of remaining in Hawaii. They are hard working, industrious men.' Japan, moreover, should not be considered 'an Asiatic Nation', for 'Japanese people have nothing in common with India and China', and 'Japan is progressive and is rapidly becoming a Western Civilized State'. (And a postscript: 'The "Yamashiro Maru" is a splendid iron steamer with capacity for 1,200 Emigrants in the steerage. We had 988, including children.')[83]

To the Hawai'i State Library again. In the *Daily Pacific Commercial Advertiser* (proprietor: Walter M. Gibson), an article on 29 June asked, 'Is Japan an Asiatic Country?' No, the correspondent suggested. Paraphrasing but not acknowledging Irwin's 25 June letter, he emphasized, 'Japan has cut loose, as far as it is presently safe to do so, from its Asiatic methods, and adopted those of the Western world'. To which, a

---

[81] Stacy L. Kamehiro, *The Arts of Kingship: Hawaiian Art and National Culture of the Kalākaua Era* (Honolulu: University of Hawai'i Press, 2009), pp. 55–76.
[82] *HG*, 24 June 1885. Accessed through microfilm.
[83] HSA, FO&EX 31, Immigration Matters (April to June 1885), Letter from Robert W. Irwin to Walter M. Gibson, 25 June 1885.

few weeks later, the *Gazette* responded with incredulity: 'If the Japanese are not Asiatics what are they? Let us have Professors from Harvard, Columbia, Oxford and Cambridge, to settle the point.'[84]

This to-and-fro, rhetorical as well as physical, offered two different ways to read the *Yamashiro-maru*. For critics of Japanese immigration to Hawai'i and sceptics of Meiji Japan's bona fide Westernization alike, it was no more than an 'immigrant ship'.[85] For defenders of the New Japan, on the other hand, it was a 'splendid iron steamer' which carried 'industrious' labourers.[86] In the words of the *Advertiser*'s correspondent, touring the ship after quarantine, it was 'a splendid specimen of marine architecture'. Indeed, his report, headlined, 'THE YAMASHIRO MARU – Description of this Fine Japanese Steamship – Constructed and Equipped as a Cruiser with Krupp Guns – Her Rate of Speed, and Other Interesting Details', appeared on 21 July, in the midst of the newspaper debate about whether or not Japan was 'Asiatic'. Thus, when the correspondent waxed lyrical about the ship's proportions, tonnage, engine size and consequent speed, about the reinforced main deck to support midship guns (should the *Yamashiro-maru* need to be converted for war service), about the electric lights of the Edison-Swan patent or the positioning of the compasses and steering mechanisms, the numbers were not neutral.[87] Rather, they gave empirical flesh to Irwin's argument that Japan was 'progressive' and (here the *Advertiser*) 'adopting [the methods] of the Western world'. Many miles from Newcastle, I was back at catch-up. The numbers produced the ship; the ship produced the face of Japan.

In Honolulu the archival trap was of a different nature, however. For a start, wherever I looked, the written sources constructed not only the ship but also the migrants on board. They were 'hard working'; they were 'Asiatic'; they were disease-ridden; and, after finishing quarantine on Sand Island, they were in the city and causing 'amusing scenes'.[88] But the 988 men, women and children remained unnamed: not for the *Advertiser* the 'interesting detail' that the one Japanese man to die of smallpox was Tanaka Kōji, aged thirty.[89] Moreover, these sources gave no insight into the multiple causes of the migrants coming to Hawai'i, including to work on the kingdom's burgeoning sugar plantations. In

---

[84] *PCA*, 29 June 1885; *HG*, 22 July 1885. Other aspects of Irwin's onboard letter were cited without acknowledgement in *PCA*, 7 July 1885.
[85] This trope dies hard in early twenty-first-century Europe: Jérôme Tubiana and Clotilde Warin, 'Diary', *London Review of Books* 41, 6 (21 March 2019), pp. 42–3.
[86] I analyse this term in Chapter 3. [87] 'The Yamashiro Maru', *PCA*, 21 July 1885.
[88] This phrase comes in a short paragraph, without headline, directly below the *PCA*'s long description of the *Yamashiro-maru* (21 July 1885).
[89] This 'detail' I found in Tokyo: DA 3.8.2.5–14.

other words, the nature of my archival fact retrieval rendered the *Yamashiro-maru* migrants silent – a silence that would be exacerbated by the post-digitized accessibility of the (English-language) *Advertiser* or the *Gazette*. The challenge would be to find a methodology to make them visible or audible – as I attempt, respectively, in Chapters 2 and 3.

But the main archival trap in Honolulu concerned the relationship between written words and their sites of preservation. Shuttling back and forth between the State Archives and the State Library, I was walking contemporary Hawai'i's statehood. The names of these institutions acknowledged the endpoint (in 1959) of a political history which came to the boil exactly in the years when the *Yamashiro-maru* transported migrants to Hawai'i: with the imposition by sugar planter interests of the so-called Bayonet Constitution on King Kalākaua in 1887, followed by their overthrow of his successor and sister, Queen Lili'uokalani (1838–1917), in January 1893. On the second floor of the 'Iolani Palace, where the deposed queen had been forcibly confined for eight months in 1895, was the Imprisonment Room. There visitors can today view a quilt sewed by Lili'uokalani while in captivity. The intricate patchwork was a very different kind of documentary evidence from the paperwork I was intent on retrieving. This was literal 'context', a weaving together (*con-texere*) of a past which coincided with the *Yamashiro-maru* but which it was all too easy to overlook if I stayed focused on rates of speed or other 'interesting details'. Indeed, the quilt's creation and survival constituted an act of archival resistance, into which Lili'uokalani threaded memories of her life, Hawaiian nationhood and her own short reign.[90] Thus, the royal-cum-state land across which I walked also constituted archival context – but of a material kind, crucial both to an understanding of the ship's nineteenth century world and to the kinds of 'tacit narratives' through which archives are constructed.[91]

In the era of digitized and born-digital sources, historians have become adept at reading metadata – that is, data about data (such as who digitized Mahlmann's *Reminiscences*, and when). But the 'Iolani Palace lands across which I walked must also be considered essential data about data: the grounds and sounds and colonial legacies right outside the Hawai'i State Archive's doors were at some level framing my reading of

---

[90] Joyce D. Hammond, 'Hawaiian Flag Quilts: Multivalent Symbols of a Hawaiian Quilt Tradition', *Hawaiian Journal of History* 27 (1993): 1–26.

[91] Eric Katelaar calls for these contexts to be made transparent in his article, 'Tacit Narratives: The Meanings of Archives', *Archival Science* 1 (2001): 131–41, here p. 137. See also Noelani Arista, *The Kingdom and the Republic: Sovereign Hawai'i and the Early United States* (Philadelphia: University of Pennsylvannia Press, 2019), pp. 12 and 230, for her argument, following J. G. A. Pocock, that language is context, not text.

the sources. It was a trap *not* to acknowledge this metadata, even if computer scientists have not (yet) found a way to annotate it. In falling into that trap, I risked overlooking both the historical protagonists whose migrant lives had tempted me to study the *Yamashiro-maru* in the first place – and the materially inescapable history of Native Hawaiian dispossession.

★ ★ ★

These were three archival traps: that I would anthropomorphize the ship at the time and place of its launch, turning its 'life' into a history of Japanese catch-up; that I would revel too much in the accessibility of digitized sources at the narrative expense of undigitized migrant actors; and that, in pursuing newspaper debates online, I would overlook crucial material metadata and its ongoing epistemological significance. My way out of these traps was to take time away from the archives, or from 'the archive' as I had imagined it to date – one comprising papers, microfilms and digitized sources. The credit for this goes to my wife Asuka, who convinced me that, enticing though the Hawai'i State Library collections were (open 'til late on Thursdays!), we should devote a few days to holiday not history – and we should do so at Hanalei, on the north-east coast of Kaua'i Island.

Kodama's Gravestone: A Mooring Berth

Of course, things are never that simple if you're married to a historian. To Asuka's demonstrable delight I proposed that on the way up to Hanalei we have the briefest of brief detours to Kapa'a. This is because I had worked out that one man whose name I had previously encountered in a Japanese village archive, during my PhD research, had also emigrated to Hawai'i on the *Yamashiro-maru* in 1889. A note from a village bureaucrat suggested that Fuyuki Sakazō had ended up in Kapa'a; thus, I sunnily assumed, it might be possible to find something of him in the town.

During my PhD, my earliest interest in Japanese overseas migrants had been triggered by the material traces many of them left in their rural home towns – in the form of commemorative stones recording their donations to the repair of temples and shrines, or to the construction of new schools. In the absence of the schools themselves, rebuilt again in the post-war years, the stones constituted a largely unread archive of lives lived abroad.[92] As such, they were also a *counter*-archive to the wide range

---

[92] Martin Dusinberre, 'Unread Relics of a Transnational "Hometown" in Rural Western Japan', *Japan Forum* 20, 3 (2008): 305–35.

of elite explanations as to the value of overseas migration. For example, in a December 1885 letter to the Meiji government's honorary consul in Tasmania, Foreign Minister Inoue Kaoru (1836–1915) wrote of his dismay at 'low and ignorant men' leaving Japan without official permission. (Like Mori Arinori, Inoue himself had left Japan clandestinely to study at University College London in the 1860s.) And yet, he continued, the government was loath to prohibit labourer mobility as this 'would not be consistent with the policy of promoting their progress by enlarging their knowledge of enterprise in the world'.[93] Here, the enlargement of knowledge was offered as a reason for which men sought work overseas. (No mention of women, as I explore in Chapter 5.) The fact that local institutions needed to be repaired or built from scratch, however, and that labourers were remitting money home, suggested that socioeconomic factors more than a thirst for 'knowledge of enterprise' lay behind the decision to emigrate. But where my earlier work had focused on the home town, for my new project I wanted to study the labourers' lives across the Pacific world, and to connect those transpacific histories through a ship.

In Kapaʻa we parked on the main street and, on nothing more than a whim, I entered the adjacent graveyard of the First Hawaiian Church. Already, I was doubting whether I would find any remains of Fuyuki, corporeal or otherwise; it would later transpire that the village bureaucrat in Japan had made a mistake, for Fuyuki never lived or worked anywhere near Kapaʻa. But after meandering for a few minutes, I stumbled across this untended headstone – and instantly knew that I'd had a stroke of incredible fortune:

> KEIJIRO, KODAMA
> ARRIVED
> HAWAII, NEI
> JUNE 18, 1885
> DIED
> KAPAA, KAUAI
> MEIJI XXIX
> JULY 9, 1896

By recording a date of arrival, the gravestone identified its subject as one of the nearly 1,000 migrants who had shipped to Honolulu on the *Yamashiro-maru*. No less importantly, it evoked a life lived between two

---

[93] Handwritten translation of a letter from Inoue Kaoru to Robert Beadon, 28 December 1885: DA 3.8.2.8.

worlds and the ambiguities arising therefrom. Thus, the comma on the first line indicated that the engraver – or, more likely, an unknown benefactor – was unsure whether the family name (Kodama) should take precedence or not. The comma on the third line suggested a similar cultural uncertainty with the Hawaiian phrase 'Hawaii Nei', or 'beloved Hawai'i'.[94] On the other hand, the inscriber knew enough to correctly translate the Gregorian calendar into that of imperial Japan (where 'Meiji XXIX' indicated the progression of Emperor Meiji's reign, with 1868 as Year I); and the positioning of imperial before Gregorian dates perhaps gave precedence to the temporal regime by which Kodama lived until his death.

Admittedly, I articulated few of these ambiguities on that morning in Kapa'a. And I missed entirely the inscription's error: according to all surviving archival accounts, the *Yamashiro-maru* arrived in Honolulu on 17 June. But working through both the gravestone's wrong date and its broader historical significance offered an escape from my previous archival traps. The simplest explanation for the mistake went as follows. Although the aforementioned International Date Line was agreed in an October 1884 treaty, its global synchronization was not simultaneous: Japan only harmonized in July 1886.[95] Thus, for anyone arriving in Honolulu from Yokohama in 1885, there may have been some confusion as to whether that morning was 17 or 18 June – a confusion exacerbated, more than a decade after the event, by the need to pinpoint a date for a gravestone inscription.[96] That said, there *was* no conventional need to record Kodama's date of arrival: no such information was listed on other immigrant graves I subsequently studied in Hawai'i (including several more on that 'holiday' weekend). This anomaly consequently raised a number of questions about Kodama himself.[97] Was the date so important in his memories that he repeatedly referenced it to friends? Did it signify for him the start of a new life, a new set of relationships to the

---

[94] As David A. Chang has pointed out, *nei* is 'a stylistic device rather than a grammatical necessity', one which locates the speaker and indicates 'the affection of the speaker for the place mentioned': *World and All the Things upon It*, p. 127.

[95] On these synchronizations, see Stefan Tanaka, 'History without Chronology', *Public Culture* 28, 1 (2016): 161–86, here p. 165.

[96] The surviving Spanish carrack from Magellan's circumnavigation of the world faced the reverse problem in 1522 when it arrived at the Cape Verde Islands on what its diarist believed to be 9 July: Ian R. Bartky, *One Time Fits All: The Campaigns for Global Uniformity* (Stanford, CA: Stanford University Press, 2007), pp. 9–10.

[97] On archival anomalies being the departure point for historiographic interventions, see Carlo Ginzburg, 'Our Words, and Theirs: A Reflection on the Historian's Craft, Today', in Susanna Fellman and Marjatta Rahikainen, eds., *Historical Knowledge: In Quest of Theory, Method, and Evidence* (Newcastle upon Tyne: Cambridge Scholars Publishing, 2012), pp. 97–119.

Hawai'i Nei? Did the gravestone's benefactor understand those feelings and acknowledge them by noting Kodama's date of arrival rather than his date of birth? Such questions were unanswerable. But at least to pose them reframed the problem away from my language of 'errors', 'mistakes' and 'wrong dates' – a vocabulary that reinscribed the idea of a standard base point against which all else must be measured, and that thus returned me to Trap 1. Instead, my questions suggested the necessity of positioning the labourers' experiences and imaginations at the heart of my story: their material histories, their language, their conceptions of time and space.

Though imperfectly, this narrative repositioning is one challenge I take up in *Mooring the Global Archive*: to trace the worlds of the Japanese migrants and the worlds seen by those migrants, and to connect these traces to broader historiographies of Meiji Japan's industrialization or the state's colonial ambitions. In so doing, I contribute to a new literature which argues that Japanese overseas migrants were central to the making of the imperial state – as central, indeed, as the better-known Chinese diaspora is considered to Qing and post-imperial state histories.[98]

---

[98] On transpacific Japan: Eiichiro Azuma, *In Search of Our Frontier: Japanese America and Settler Colonialism in the Construction of Japan's Borderless Empire* (Berkeley: University of California Press, 2019); Sidney Xu Lu, *The Making of Japanese Settler Colonialism: Malthusianism and Trans-Pacific Migration, 1868–1961* (Cambridge: Cambridge University Press, 2019); Mariko Iijima, 'Japanese Diasporas and Coffee Production', in David Ludden, ed., *The Oxford Research Encyclopedia of Asian History* (2019) (available online: https://oxfordre.com/asianhistory/). On Japanese migrations within East Asia: David R. Ambaras, *Japan's Imperial Underworlds: Intimate Encounters at the Borders of Empire* (Cambridge: Cambridge University Press, 2018); Hiroko Matsuda, *Liminality of the Japanese Empire: Border Crossings from Okinawa to Colonial Taiwan* (Honolulu: University of Hawai'i Press, 2019); Hannah Shepherd, 'Fukuoka's Meiji Migrants and the Making of an Imperial Region', *Japan Forum* 30, 4 (2018): 474–97. On China: Philip A. Kuhn, *Chinese among Others: Emigration in Modern Times* (Lanham, MD: Rowman and Littlefield, 2008); Shelly Chan, *Diaspora's Homeland: Modern China in the Age of Global Migration* (Durham, NC: Duke University Press, 2018). Key works in Japanese include: Araragi Shinzō 蘭信三, ed., *Nihon teikoku o meguru jinkō idō no kokusai shakaigaku* 日本帝国をめぐる人口移動の国際社会学 [An international sociology of population movement in the Japanese empire] (Tokyo: Fuji shuppan, 2008); Ishihara Shun 石原俊, '*Guntō' no rekishishakaigaku: Ogasawara shotō, Iōtō, Nihon, Amerika, soshite Taiheiyō sekai* 「群島」の歴史社会学：小笠原諸島・硫黄島、日本・アメリカ、そして太平洋世界 [A historical-sociology of 'islands': The Ogasawaras, Iwojima, Japan, America and the Pacific World] (Tokyo: Kōbundō, 2013); Shiode Hiroyuki 塩出浩之, *Ekkyōsha no seijishi: Ajia Taiheiyō ni okeru Nihonjin no imin to shokumin* 越境者の政治史：アジア太平洋における日本人の移民と植民 [A political history of border-crossers: Japanese emigrants and colonists in the Asia-Pacific] (Nagoya: Nagoya daigaku shuppankai, 2015); Hirai Kensuke 平井健介, *Satō no Teikoku: Nihon Shokuminchi to Ajia Shijō* 砂糖の帝国：日本植民地とアジア市場 [Official translation: Empire of Sugar: External Forces of Change in the Economy of the Japanese Colonies] (Tokyo: Tōkyō daigaku shuppankai, 2017).

But I go beyond this literature's primary focus on the Japanese metropole to examine how migrants became entangled in the colonial contexts of the polities in which they worked, and the historiographical implications thereof.[99] By focusing on passages and infrastructures, I also broaden that literature's assumptions about where migration histories might begin and end, and in what archival forms they might be found.

Indeed, my departure from the Kodama gravestone further entails a different way of writing about the historian's relationship to archives. Though paper-based archives and their digitized iterations remain central to this book, I try to avoid privileging their epistemologies over other kinds of archival assemblages for which search engines do not exist. Equally importantly, I bring to the fore oft-overlooked contexts in historical research, namely the 'metadata' of (in this case) a spousal escape to Kaua'i and improbable chance in a cemetery.[100] Such contexts raise important questions of privilege and transactional cost – visa regimes, institutional support, the carbon footprint, and not least time – which in most historical writing remains unacknowledged, or at best relegated to the Acknowledgements. I shall contend that what I call 'authorial metadata' is central to a historian's reading of the archives – not as a cursory first-person preface to the heavy intellectual lifting, but as constituent to that intellectual work itself.

In these ways, I take the Kodama gravestone as a berth, both for the histories I reconstruct in *Mooring the Global Archive* and for the methodologies by which I do so. Kodama does not appear in every chapter of the book, nor did my memories of Kapa'a prevent me from jumping head-first into other archival traps since 2011, as I shall show. But at some abstract level the gravestone informs all that now follows.

★ ★ ★

Chapter 2 departs from the temporal spaces implied in Kodama's 17–18 June discrepancy to consider what happened in the in-between spaces of the onboard. Here and in Chapter 3, I draw on John-Paul A. Ghobrial's observation that the study of global processes of movement 'obliges us to focus as much on the worlds that people left behind as the new worlds in

---

[99] See Andrew Zimmerman, 'Africa in Imperial and Transnational History: Multi-Sited Historiography and the Necessity of Theory', *Journal of African History* 54, 3 (2013): 331–40.

[100] For a rare acknowledgement of 'flukey pursuits' in archival practice, see Greg Dening, *The Death of William Gooch: A History's Anthropology* (Honolulu: University of Hawai'i Press, 1995), p. 74.

which they found themselves'.[101] The chapters offer microhistorical reconstructions of two *Yamashiro-maru* migrants and their home towns in the mid 1880s. In Chapter 2, this leads to a broader discussion of the archival juxtapositions necessary both to counter the documentary void of the transpacific journey, and to challenge dominant narratives of a homogenized 'Japanese' identity with which the labourers were labelled upon arrival in Hawai'i. Deconstructing these narratives in turn raises the problem of how the English- and Japanese-language historiography to date has excluded Native Hawaiian understandings of the new government-sponsored programme's significance in 1885. Building on this presence of Native Hawaiian voices (or, rather, their absence in the archives of Japanese transpacific migration), Chapter 3 addresses how the archival reading room's 'sounds in silence' can shape a historian's analysis of archival documents and the gaps therein.[102] The central problem addressed is one of linguistic commensurability: how Japanese canefield songs correlate with an oft-used vocabulary of 'circulation' in global history; and whether a language of 'industriousness' (*kinben* 勤勉) in English and Japanese brings historians closer to understanding migrant labourers' engagement in settler colonialism in Hawai'i.

Chapter 4 attempts to answer Paul Carter's questions, in his book *Dark Writing*: 'Can we live with our maps differently? Could we inhabit our histories differently?' Noting that 'these are questions that might be addressed to modernity generally', Carter contextualizes them by introducing the famous *Petitions of the Aboriginal People of Yirrkala*, two bark paintings dating from 1963 and collaboratively designed by Yolŋu artists in what colonial maps call the 'Northern Territory'.[103] I also examine Yolŋu bark paintings, in order to posit a different cartographic and archival approach from that embedded in the map at the chapter's heart – that is, an NYK company map which depicts its steamship routes across the Pacific world (including the Yokohama–Melbourne line, opened by the *Yamashiro-maru* in 1896). To the question of whether we could inhabit our histories differently, I reply in the affirmative, but with the caveat that any answer depends on who 'we' are, and what 'our' histories (and archives) are imagined to be.

Similar considerations of the first-person voice lie at the heart of Chapter 5. Interrogating the first-person testimony of a young Japanese woman, Hashimoto Usa, who left Nagasaki in June 1897 and ended up

---

[101] John-Paul A. Ghobrial, 'Moving Stories and What They Tell Us: Early Modern Mobility Between Microhistory and Global History', *Past & Present* 242, Supplement 14 (2019): 243–80, here p. 249.
[102] Dening, *Death of William Gooch*, p. 64.
[103] Paul Carter, *Dark Writing: Geography, Performance, Design* (Honolulu: University of Hawai'i Press, 2009), p. 19.

via Hong Kong in Thursday Island, I explore the gendered construction of the archival trail between Tokyo and Brisbane, and the concomitant difficulty in accessing the voices of female migrants. But part of the problem is my unfortunate use of verbs such as 'interrogate': thus, while I acknowledge Lisa Yun's point that testimonial statements generated by state-led agendas are 'not impervious to appropriation from below' and may be 'seized upon by subaltern agendas', I also reflect upon the (male) historian's archival interventions in the reading of female voices.[104] Finally, in Chapter 6, I step back – and below – to consider the fuel infrastructures of transpacific Japanese migration. This chapter focuses on a different kind of journey: that of a piece of coal from seam to ship. In so doing, it radically expands the scale of the temporal regimes that frame Kodama's gravestone. But while I thereby make a small nod towards 'big' or 'deep' history, my interest remains anthropocentric. Like Timothy J. LeCain, I see the danger that very large scales of history can conversely lead to historical materiality being overlooked in favour of aggregate phenomena. Like mine, his interests lie in 'the smaller scale lived phenomena of individual embodied human beings trying to warm their frosty fingers by tossing a few extra lumps of coal on the fire'. My chapter merely attempts to specify which coal, which fire and which human beings.[105]

This has been a messy book in the making. Unlike a long and distinguished literature which has addressed 'the world' through the history of single ships, *Mooring the Global Archive* boasts no single textual genre through which to chart its course: no onboard journal, collection of poems, log book, popular travel account or legal case in the aftermath of a crime or mutiny.[106] My stories are disorderly and often out of chronological order – as demonstrated by my new interpretation of

---

[104] Lisa Yun, *The Coolie Speaks: Chinese Indentured Laborers and African Slaves of Cuba* (Philadelphia, PA: Temple University Press, 2008), p. 54.

[105] Timothy J. LeCain, *The Matter of History: How Things Create the Past* (Cambridge: Cambridge University Press, 2017), p. 13; on big histories, see David Christian, *Maps of Time: An Introduction to Big History* (Berkeley: University of California Press, 2004).

[106] Michael Wintroub, *The Voyage of Thought: Navigating Knowledge across the Sixteenth-Century World* (Cambridge: Cambridge University Press, 2017); Robert Harms, *The Diligent: A Voyage through the Worlds of the Slave Trade* (New York: Basic Books, 2000); Edyta M. Bojanowska, *A World of Empires: The Russian Voyage of the Frigate* Pallada (Cambridge, MA: Harvard University Press, 2018); Renisa Mawani, *Across Oceans of Law: The Komagata Maru and Jurisdiction in the Time of Empire* (Durham, NC: Duke University Press, 2018); Dening, *Mr Bligh's Bad Language*; Marcus Rediker, *The Amistad Rebellion: An Atlantic Odyssey of Slavery and Freedom* (London: Verso, 2013); Verene A. Shepherd, *Maharani's Misery: Narratives of a Passage from India to the Caribbean* (Kingston: University of the West Indies Press, 2002); Johan Heinsen, *Mutiny in the Danish Atlantic World: Convicts, Sailors and a Dissonant Empire* (London: Bloomsbury, 2017). See also Boyd Cothran and Adrian Shubert, 'Maritime History, Microhistory, and the Global Nineteenth Century: The Edwin Fox', *Global Nineteenth-Century Studies* 1, 1 (2022): 73–80.

Commodore Perry's engagement with Tokugawa Japan in 1853–4, addressed in the book's final chapter.[107] To moor the reader, each of my chapters begins with a primary source and concludes with a methodological reflection, such that each may also be considered a stand-alone essay.[108] *Mooring the Global Archive* also includes images of people and places pertinent to the discussions – with the exception of Chapter 5, where, given the ways that migrating Japanese women were framed as 'unsightly', I have tried to avoid adding to these visual stereotypes through stock contemporary depictions of 'Japanese ladies' or the like. Given my arguments about the complex epistemologies inherent in cartography, I have equally refrained from including any custom-made maps and hope, for the most part, that the reader can follow my narrative routes through the historical maps in question.

---

[107] If my book reads at times like a montage, then I blame Jordan Sand, 'Gentleman's Agreement 1980: Fragments for a Pacific History', *Representations* 107 (2009): 91–127. On disorder, see Florence Bernault, 'Suitcases and the Poetics of Oddities: Writing History from Disorderly Archives', *History in Africa* 42 (2015): 269–77.

[108] The chapter conclusions are partly inspired by ch. 8 in Linda Tuhiwai Smith, *Decolonizing Methodologies: Research and Indigenous Peoples*, 3rd edn (London: Zed Books, 2021 [1999]).

2 Between the Archives

A Painting

One fun-filled afternoon early in April 2011, as I sparred once more with the Hawai'i State Library microfilm readers, my eye picked up the word 'Yamashiro' in an unusual context. Limiting my search period to June–July 1885, I had been browsing the *Daily Pacific Commercial Advertiser*, owned by then-Hawaiian minister for foreign affairs, Walter M. Gibson. The pages were grainy on the screen, my control of the scrolling speed shaky. I registered a headline, 'HAWAIIAN ART', and then, at the end of the article, paused on the sentence: 'Mr. Irwin, His Majesty's Charge d'Affairs [sic] in Japan, takes the picture with him to Japan on the Yamashiro Maru.' I rewound, zoomed in, waited for the machine to focus – and then commenced reading.

The article announced a 'Handsome Present from His Majesty the King to the Emperor of Japan': a 'fine picture', approximately 60 inches wide by 30 inches high (152cm by 76cm), by the artist J. D. Strong, depicting a scene 'on Maui, where Mr. Strong took many elaborate sketches':

> In the foreground stands a strong, fine looking Japanese man, with his hands resting on his hips and his feet apart, gazing good-naturedly out of the pictures [sic]. By his side sit two women, also unmistakably Japanese, who are giving a little baby a drink of water out of a bowl. [...] In the middle distance is Spreckelsville and a glimpse of the sea, with a final background of lofty mountains, topped by floating clouds.[1]

In other words, nothing to concern myself with. More out of duty than genuine interest, I inserted a quarter into the microfilm machine, cropped and printed the article, and scrolled on.

Some months later, I did an internet search for Strong – Joseph Dwight Strong (1853–99) – and Spreckelsville, and, much to my surprise, found the painting on Wikipedia with the title, 'Japanese Laborers

---

[1] *PCA*, 8 July 1885.

on the Sugar Plantation in Spreckelsville, Maui'. I realized I had seen the image before, at least a detail of it: the man, two women and child appear on the front cover of a book published in 1985 to commemorate the centenary of Japanese government-sponsored immigrants first arriving in Hawai'i. I had bought a Japanese-language copy of the book at the Bishop Museum during my 2011 fieldwork in Honolulu.[2] And now I *was* genuinely interested, for in the meantime, I had discovered that Kodama Keijirō had himself worked on the Spreckelsville plantation after his arrival in 'Hawaii Nei' in June 1885. If I wanted to write about Kodama, I needed to see the picture – ideally, in the flesh. But the Wikipedia copy, uploaded by the contributor Wmpearl in October 2007, merely noted that the painting was owned by a 'private collection (Taito Co, Tokyo)'.[3] What were my hopes of identifying that company, let alone gaining access to the collection?

What happened next is a salutary tale in how not to conduct research. I moved jobs, I procrastinated, I wrote about the painting in passing – and I asked one of my new Zurich colleagues, Hans B. Thomsen, an expert in Japanese art, about 'Taito Co'. He got to work with his customary generosity, and within a couple of weeks suggested that the company might possibly be Taitō – that is, the post-war incarnation of the Taiwan Sugar Company (Taiwan Seitō Kabushiki Kaisha 台湾製糖株式会社, itself often abbreviated to Taitō 台糖 in Japanese). In fact, to save him time, I could have simply looked at the back cover of the 1985 centenary publication, where the painting's corporate owner is spelled out loud and clear – but I'd failed to do so (and Hans still doesn't know).[4] Either way, all we now had to do was contact the present-day successor to Taiwan Sugar, the Mitsui Sugar Co. Which is how, on a spring morning almost exactly eight years after I first read about Strong's 'fine picture' in Honolulu, I found myself in Tokyo, in the Mitsui Sugar president's office, standing in front of what one art historian has called a

---

[2] Odo Franklin 王堂フランクリン and Sinoto Kazuko 篠遠和子, *Zusetsu Hawai Nihonjinshi, 1885–1924* 図説ハワイ日本人史 1885–1924 [A pictorial history of the Japanese in Hawai'i, 1885–1924] (Honolulu: Bishop Museum, 1985).
[3] For the revision history of the Wikipedia entry over the years, see https://bit.ly/3Jd2HKh (last accessed 4 August 2021).
[4] The real sleuth in this story appears to have been the late Sinoto Kazuko, co-author of the 1985 centenary book and employee of the Bishop Museum. According to *AS*, 27 March 1986, it was Sinoto who in the early 1980s tracked down the Strong painting to Taitō, thus enabling the painting to be reproduced on her book's front cover in 1985. As a consequence, the painting was publicly displayed for the first time in Japan in 1986.

Figure 2.1 Joseph Dwight Strong, 'Japanese Laborers on the Sugar Plantation in Spreckelsville, Maui', 1885. Courtesy of Mitsui Sugar Co, Ltd, Japan.

'monumental genre painting [...] virtually unparalleled in Hawaiian art of the period' (see Figure 2.1).[5]

In fact, this wasn't my first unmediated encounter with the painting, but it was the first time I'd seen it *in situ*. Most striking to the eye was a feature which didn't appear on the internet, nor on the cover of the 1985 book, namely the work's massive gold and plush frame. Almost a work of art in itself, it was grand, fussy in its intricately carved geometries, and above all extremely heavy. (At fifty-nine kilograms, it probably weighed about the same as the Japanese man depicted in the painting's foreground – assuming, like Chapter 3's Fuyuki Sakazō, that he was just under five feet tall.) Made to order by the Honolulu-based King Bros, it was a frame fit for a monarchical gift.[6] And yet the 'handsome present' self-evidently had not ended up in the Japanese imperial household. Hanging in private collections, it had seemingly not accomplished its object, according to the original *Advertiser* article, 'of giving the Mikado a correct and pleasant idea of the new home and employment of his countrymen'.

Where Strong's painting had instead been hung, and how it ended up here in the office of the Mitsui Sugar president, were partly explained by a small wooden inscription screwed into the King Bros. frame:

明治拾八年於にける
布哇砂糖耕地の状景
アルイン夫人寄贈

(In Year 18 of Meiji
A sugar plantation scene in Hawai'i
The gift of Mrs Irwin)

If Mrs Irwin, née Takechi Iki,[7] bequeathed Strong's work to Taiwan Sugar sometime in the wake of her husband Robert's death in 1925, then this would suggest that after arriving with the painting in Japan on the *Yamashiro-maru* in August 1885, Irwin kept it in his private residence for forty years – for reasons I shall later speculate.

---

[5] David Forbes, *Encounters with Paradise: Views of Hawaii and Its People, 1778–1941* (Honolulu: University of Hawai'i Press, 1992), p. 177.
[6] The frame's maker was revealed during a restoration of the Strong painting undertaken by Mitsui Sugar in 2017. Cf: 'Kings' illuminated gold frames, with internal borders of plush, are works of art themselves': *Daily Bulletin* (Honolulu), 22 December 1884. Accessed online through https://chroniclingamerica.loc.gov.
[7] The Takechi household, into which Iki had been adopted as a child, consented to her marriage with Irwin in 1870, but official recognition in Japan and the United States took another twelve years: Irwin Yukiko アーウィン・ユキコ, *Furankurin no kajitsu* フランクリンの果実 [The offspring of Franklin] (Tokyo: Bungei shunjū, 1988), pp. 11–13.

At any rate, by the early 1930s Strong's painting was hanging in the offices of Taiwan Sugar, a company which Irwin had co-founded with businessmen connected to the Mitsui conglomerate in 1900. The company's president after 1927 was fellow co-founder Takechi Tadamichi (1870–1962) – who was also a relation by marriage to Irwin himself.[8] And there, fifty years after its composition, the work acquired a set of different associations from its (alleged) original object. On the one hand, it reminded Takechi 'of the period in his youth that he spent in Hawai'i' as a student at Oahu College in the mid 1880s – a period which had begun with his passage there on the *Yamashiro-maru* in June 1885.[9] On the other hand, its very location spoke to the history of Taiwan Sugar, one of colonial Japan's most important corporations. Indeed, just as the painting had been used to frame a centenary success story of Japanese immigration to Hawai'i in 1985, so, in 1990, it was reprinted at the beginning of Taitō's ninety-year company history. Juxtaposed to a preface penned by then-president Takechi Fumio (Tadamichi's son), in which Taiwan Sugar was celebrated as having transformed a 'disease-ridden primitive land' (*mikai shōrei no chi* 未開瘴癘の地) into a site of modern sugar production, Strong's work took on a set of colonial and neo-colonial associations across the twentieth century.[10] In short, the painting I was gazing at in Tokyo had acquired multiple new meanings in its passage from Hawai'i to Japan.

This chapter explores such histories of meaning changing in passage. Indeed, what was true of Strong's painting was also true of the subjects depicted therein: as I shall first argue, the Japanese men, women and children who crossed to Hawai'i on the *Yamashiro-maru* – or any other migrant-carrying ship during this period – experienced the world differently as a consequence of their transit between Yokohama and Honolulu. To study these quotidian transformations is important because the significance of ships as historical arenas in their own right has often been overlooked, as historians interested in global migrations start their

---

[8] Both Takechi Iki and Tadamichi were adopted children from the Hayashi household. One scholar in the 1930s claimed that Iki was Tadamichi's biological aunt, meaning that Robert Irwin was his uncle by marriage: see Kōno Shinji 河野信治, *Nihon tōgyō hattatsu-shi: Jinbutsu-hen* 日本糖業発達史：人物篇 [A developmental history of the sugar industry in Japan: People] (Kobe: Nihon tōgyō hattatsu-shi hensanjo, 1934), p. 272.

[9] 'Iminsen de raifu shi, ima kokoku zaikai no kyotō' 移民船で来布し、今故國財界の巨頭 [Arrived in Hawai'i on an immigrant ship, now a leading figure in the old country's financial world], *Nippu jiji* 日布時事, 12 December 1933. Available through https:// hojishinbun.hoover.org (last accessed 5 August 2021).

[10] Taitō Kyūjūnen Tsūshi Hensan Iinkai 台糖90年通史編纂委員会, *Taitō kyūjūnen tsūshi* 台糖90年通史 [A ninety-year history of Taitō] (Tokyo: Taitō kabushiki kaisha, 1990), frontmatter.

analyses in place A and continue them in place B, irrespective of what happened in-between. Some scholars have even gone so far as to argue that transoceanic migrant voyages 'will be short, at least in memory, because nothing of interest is being recorded. What for mariners is a sea-lane, for a rural or urban migrant is an empty expanse.'[11]

Such claims of the passage as empty of meaning derive partly from the surviving source genres. Alongside Robert W. Irwin and Takechi Tadamichi, Fujita Toshirō (1862–1937) was another first-class passenger on the *Yamashiro-maru* in June 1885. As his later autobiography makes clear, his crossing to Hawai'i opened a new chapter in his life, marked by his transformation from employee at the KUK (owner of the ship) to his first assignment as budding diplomat – a career which would eventually take him to San Francisco, Mexico, Singapore and beyond.[12] And yet he described this transpacific journey in only one half-sentence: 'I became a clerk in the Foreign Ministry on 29 May, Meiji 18 [1885]; five days later I boarded the *Yamashiro-maru* and began my assignment in Honolulu'. Fourteen days at sea is compressed into a change of verb, from 'boarding' (*tōjō* 搭乗) to 'beginning of assignment' (*funin* 赴任).[13] We can be sure that had pirates attacked, or the *Yamashiro-maru*'s crew mutinied, or perhaps even had the ship's engines conked out mid-journey, Fujita would have written more. For an elite actor writing from a retrospective position of having travelled the world, however, the passage seemed narratively

---

[11] Dirk Hoerder, 'Migrations and Belongings', in Emily S. Rosenberg, ed., *A World Connecting, 1870–1945* (Cambridge, MA: Harvard University Press, 2012), pp. 435–589, here p. 470. For a counter-proposition on the significance of transit in global history, see Martin Dusinberre and Roland Wenzlhuemer, 'Being in Transit: Ships and Global Incompatibilities', *Journal of Global History* 11, 2 (2016): 155–62. Meanwhile, scholarship on Japanese overseas migration in particular has almost entirely overlooked the period of passage. For examples of its absence, see Alan Takeo Moriyama, *Imingaisha: Japanese Emigration Companies and Hawaii 1894–1908* (Honolulu: University of Hawai'i Press, 1985); Yukiko Kimura, *The Issei: Japanese Immigrants in Hawaii* (Honolulu: University of Hawai'i Press, 1992); Doi Yatarō 土井彌太郎, *Yamaguchi-ken Ōshima-gun Hawai iminshi* 山口県大島郡ハワイ移民史 [A history of emigration to Hawai'i from Ōshima county, Yamaguchi prefecture] (Tokyo: Matsuno shoten, 1980). The key exception is Yamada Michio 山田迪生, *Fune ni miru Nihonjin iminshi:* Kasato-maru *kara kurūzu kyakusen e* 船にみる日本人移民史：笠戸丸からクルーズ客船へ [Japanese emigration history as seen through ships: From the *Kasato-maru* to passenger cruise liners] (Tokyo: Chūkō shinsho, 1998).

[12] On Fujita in Mexico, see Lu, *Making of Japanese Settler Colonialism*, p. 84; Bill Mihalopoulos, *Sex in Japan's Globalization, 1870–1930: Prostitutes, Emigration and Nation-Building* (London: Pickering & Chatto, 2011), pp. 109–10. See also Nicholas B. Miller, 'Trading Sovereignty and Labour: The Consular Network of Nineteenth-Century Hawai'i', *International History Review* 42, 2 (2020): 260–77.

[13] Fujita Toshirō 藤田敏郎, *Kaigai zaikin shihanseiki no kaiko* 海外在勤四半世紀の回顧 [Reminiscences of a quarter-century of overseas postings] (Tokyo: Kyōbunkan, 1931), p. 3.

unimportant. But if historians equally view transoceanic time as 'nothing of interest', we risk silencing the key actors in histories of migration, namely the migrants themselves. By seeking to reconstruct processes of transit from other genres of sources, this chapter offers new understandings of the migratory lives of labourers such as those in Strong's plantation painting.

My second interest lies in how men and women similar to Strong's subjects were ascribed new meanings during their period(s) of transit by a range of powerful actors. For example, in my lukewarm excitement at having found a brief mention of the *Yamashiro-maru* in the microfilmed pages of the *Advertiser*, I had overlooked a key example of such ascriptions. Only some years later, retracing my steps with the aid of the text-searchable Chronicling America database, did I digest the whole 8 July issue in peace and quiet. I first noted the fact that directly under some self-puffery ('The Weekly P. C. Advertiser is the best and most complete paper published in the Kingdom', etc.), the page in question had printed the wrong date (7 July). And then, below this and to the left of the 'Hawaiian Art' article, I noticed the headline, 'Japanese Friendship'.[14] This recorded the granting of a Japanese imperial decoration to Walter M. Gibson, observing:

[T]he honor conferred upon the Hawaiian Foreign Minister possesses more than ordinary meaning, and augurs well for the success of that industrial partnership, as it were, between the two countries, which is expressed so potentially by Japanese immigration. We have room and verge enough for tens of thousands of Japanese families on these Islands, and we hope to see them established here, in thrift and comfortable independence, under our equal and humane laws.[15]

Here was a pregnant set of expectations: that the newly initiated government-sponsored migration programme would eventually expand to an 'industrial' scale;[16] that this would be a positive outcome for what the article earlier called 'the well-being and progress of this Kingdom'; and that there was space for tens of thousands of migrants. No less than the King Bros' golden carvings, this was also a frame for Strong's painting: according to this interpretation, the man, women and child stood for those anticipated thousands of Japanese families and their potential contributions to the Hawaiian nation.

[14] Some scholars have suggested that the digitization of newspapers will lead to 'keyword blinkers' – that is, where scholars ignore the wider context of a defined search result. My experience was the opposite: given the time pressures inherent in microfilm browsing, I was more likely to miss the page context during on-site research. See Bob Nicholson, 'The Digital Turn: Exploring the Methodological Possibilities of Digital Newspaper Archives', *Media History* 19, 1 (2013): 59–73, here p. 61.
[15] *PCA*, 8 July 1885. Accessed online through https://chroniclingamerica.loc.gov.
[16] On 'industry', see Chapter 3.

But was this how the migrants themselves understood their arrival as they began new lives in Hawai'i? And, if not, how can historians counter such narratives of the decorated and the [s]trong? The answers to these questions lie partly in how the space of the in-between – that is, the passage between Fujita's two verbs, or between the 17 and 18 June dates on Kodama's gravestone – can be archivally reconstructed. My dream archive of the in-between would be the *Yamashiro-maru* itself.[17] But in the absence of the ship, the challenge is one of framing: of bringing together archives at both ends of the journey in order to make educated guesses about the meanings of the passage for the labourers who slept one deck below Irwin, Takechi or Fujita.[18] And the challenge is also of *un*framing: of using the archives, and their gaps, to identify the complex agendas which coalesced in visual and textual representations of 'unmistakably Japanese' subjects. Only in these ways, I will argue, is it possible to offer some kind of narrative corrective to what the *Advertiser*, describing Strong's painting, suggested was a 'fine representation of a sunny, thriving, hard-working plantation scene'.

Ship as Plantation Boot Camp

The *Advertiser* newspaper offered the male protagonist of Joseph Strong's painting a basic humanism: he was 'fine looking' and he gazed 'good naturedly' outwards. In an ideal world, I would like to go one step further and determine his name. In an ideal world, indeed, I would like to reveal him as Kodama Keijirō, just arrived from Japan on the *Yamashiro-maru* and now adjusting to his new life in Spreckelsville.

The place to start such a quest – ultimately futile though it will be – is the Diplomatic Archives of the Ministry of Foreign Affairs in central Tokyo. This is because Kodama and the other Japanese who crossed to Honolulu in 1885 were part of a new, government-sponsored emigration programme (*kan'yaku imin* 官約移民) between Japan and Hawai'i which was trialled that year after much lobbying of the Meiji government by Hawaiian Consul Robert W. Irwin. As usually explained in the secondary literature, the programme was pitched as beneficial to both sides. On the one hand, the sugar-planting lobby in Hawai'i, which had become increasingly influential in the two decades since the end of the US Civil

---

[17] Or alternatively diaries: for one such reconstruction of onboard 'in-between-ness', see Paul Ashmore, 'Slowing Down Mobilities: Passengering on an Inter-war Ocean Liner', *Mobilities* 8, 4 (2013): 595–611, here p. 596.

[18] My thinking on framing in this chapter is influenced by Robert M. Entman, 'Framing: Toward Clarification of a Fractured Paradigm', *Journal of Communication* 43, 4 (1993): 51–8.

War (1861–5), would be guaranteed a supply of new labour for the plantations; on the other, Japanese farmers, impoverished by the land tax reform of the early 1870s and especially by the so-called Matsukata deflation (1881–5), would have a new income stream – and in a valued foreign currency.[19] The Mitsui Bussan trading company, whose founder, Masuda Takashi (1848–1938), was close friends with both Irwin and Japan's foreign minister Inoue Kaoru, helped organize recruitment.

The first shipment of 945 labourers, arriving in Honolulu on 8 February 1885, was testament to this confluence of business, politics, and diplomacy in mid-Meiji Japan. More than a third of the labourers came from Inoue's home prefecture of Yamaguchi, in the west of Japan; and they travelled on the specially chartered *City of Tokio*, a steamship owned by the Pacific Mail Steamship Company – for whom Irwin had worked when he initially came to Japan in 1866. After the *City of Tokio* sank in June 1885, Irwin chartered the Pacific Mail's *City of Peking* for the third dispatch of labourers, in February 1886. In the meantime, the *Yamashiro-maru*, chartered for the second group, was owned by the KUK, one of whose principal shareholders was the Mitsui Bussan company's Masuda Takashi.[20] (As we have seen, Mitsui interests, along with those of Irwin, also lay behind the establishment of the Taiwan Sugar Company in 1900.)[21]

In the Foreign Ministry archives, four thick volumes name the post-1885 government-sponsored departees from Japan, with volume one listing every migrant on the *City of Tokio*, the *Yamashiro-maru*, and the *City of Peking*.[22] The lists are vertically compiled and divided into sections according to the male labourer's home prefecture. At the top of each page appears the administrative subdivision one level below prefecture, namely county (*gun* 郡); and then come the migrant's town or village, his detailed address, his status and profession, and, at the very bottom of the page, his – or his wife and child's – name and age. All of the *Yamashiro-maru* migrants in 1885 were 'commoner' apart from three

---

[19] Moriyama's *Imingaisha*, pp. 1–10, offers such an explanation.
[20] For a full list of the KUK's founding shareholders, see Shibusawa Eiichi denki shiryō kankōkai 渋沢栄一伝記資料刊行会, *Shibusawa Eiichi denki shiryō daihakkan* 渋沢栄一伝記資料第8巻 (Shibusawa Eiichi: Biographical sources, Vol. 8) (Tokyo: Ryūmonsha, 1956), p. 57.
[21] For a list of Taiwan Sugar's original shareholders, see Masuda Takashi 益田孝 and Nagai Minoru 長井実, *Jijo Masuda Takashi-ō den* 自叙益田孝翁伝 [Autobiography of Masuda Takashi, Esq.] (Kanagawa: private publication, 1939), p. 344. Masuda even served as interim Hawaiian consul to Japan while Irwin was in Hawai'i for an extended sojourn from February 1886: HSA 404-15-252a (Hawaiian Officials Abroad Japan 1886), Irwin to Inoue Kaoru, 1 February 1886.
[22] DA 3.8.2.5–14, Vol. 1.

'samurai', and all of the commoners were recorded as 'farmers'. If the Strong painting was one medium by which the labourers became (or were intended to become) *visible* to Japanese government elites, then these Foreign Ministry volumes rendered them *legible* – similar to the exhaustive passenger lists of sixteenth-century New World migrants produced by Seville's Casa de la Contratación.[23] Moreover, in this structuring of the archival page, both the compiler and the future reader were conditioned to frame each of the volume's nearly 3,000 individuals by their provenance; and this, in turn, gives us some sense of what motives lay behind a young man wanting to move to Hawai'i for work.[24]

The concentration of departees from particular villages reveals the vicissitudes of Japan's changing engagement with the outside world across the nineteenth century. For example, Hiroshima prefecture accounted for nearly the greatest number of migrants on board the *Yamashiro-maru* in June 1885 (390, or nearly 40 per cent). Within Hiroshima, Saeki county accounted for the greatest number of migrants (239); and, within Saeki, the village of Jigozen, which supplied thirty-seven migrants aged between twenty and thirty-eight, constituted the largest sending community. Like many of the migrant-sending villages from neighbouring Yamaguchi prefecture, Jigozen is located on the coast of the Seto Inland Sea. In the eighteenth century and up to the mid nineteenth, shipping lanes through the Inland Sea were crucial elements in the transport infrastructure by which western and northern domains shipped both their tributary taxes and their produce eastwards to the Tokugawa 'kitchen' of Osaka. There, they traded in commodities which they shipped back to distant ports via Shimonoseki, at the Inland Sea's western extreme. As domestic trade increased through the eighteenth century, so too did the number of long-distance ships sailing east and west through small ports such as Jigozen; indeed, the village was one of many coastal communities between Osaka and Shimonoseki whose economies began to grow in this period at the expense of hitherto more

---

[23] Bernhard Siegert, 'Ficticious [sic] Identities: On the interrogatorios and *registros de pasajeros a Indias* in the Archivo General de Indias (Seville) (16th century)', in Wolfram Nitsch, Matei Chihaia and Alejandra Torres, eds., *Ficciones de los medios en la periferia: Técnicas de comunicación en la ficción hispanoamericana moderna* (Cologne: Universitäts- und Stadtbibliothek Köln, 2008), pp. 19–30. I thank Frieder Missfelder for this reference.

[24] Women could not emigrate unless they accompanied their spouses, although Hawai'i-bound labourers sometimes found creative ways to manipulate the category of 'wife': Yukari Takai, 'Recrafting Marriage in Meiji Hawai'i, 1885–1913', *Gender & History* 31, 3 (2019): 646–64.

established market and castle towns.[25] This, we must assume, lay behind the near-doubling of the population between the 1820s and 1881, when the village was recorded as having 2,300 residents.[26]

In turn, such a demographic transformation throws light on the nominal 'farmer' status of the later *Yamashiro-maru* migrants. In fact, by the 1860s, only 40 per cent of Jigozen's households were landowners – meaning that 60 per cent of the village's population somehow made a living without owning land. Most likely, they survived on by-employments connected with the Inland Sea's increased volume of trade, on coastal fishing, and also on work in the household industries that were renowned in this part of Japan, particularly cotton production. But these survival strategies made non-landed households particularly vulnerable to new infrastructures of interregional trade which were established in the wake of the 1868 Meiji revolution.[27] In addition, falling agricultural yield in Jigozen in the 1880s, and the opening of a new mill by the Hiroshima Cotton Spinning Company in Saeki county in 1883, created a perfect storm of problems for 'farmers' – many of whom had for a generation or two *not* worked exclusively in agriculture.[28]

No wonder that a large group of working-age men – all men – sought to escape Jigozen in 1885: these were desperate times. A one-line entry on an emigrant list in Tokyo will never do more than hint at the complex motivations which spurred Jigozen villagers to up roots and cross the Pacific; but for a middle-aged man such as the thirty-seven-year-old Wakamiya Yaichi, there were perhaps already half a lifetime of employment disappointments tied up in such a decision. Perhaps personal disappointments, too: if he was married and already had children, he would not see his family again for the minimum three-year period he would be contracted in Hawai'i. On the other hand, the draw of the new government-sponsored programme was substantial: a guaranteed,

---

[25] Thomas C. Smith, *Native Sources of Japanese Industrialization, 1750–1920* (Berkeley: University of California Press, 1988), pp. 15–49.

[26] For these and other population figures, see Hatsukaichi-chō hen 廿日市町編, *Hatsukaichi chōshi* 廿日市町史 [Hatsukaichi town history] (Hiroshima: Hatsukaichi-chō, 1988), Vol. 7, p. 323; Vol. 6, pp. 870–81, 885–8.

[27] I detail the impact of these changes on by-employments in Chapter 3.

[28] On falling agricultural yield in Jigozen in the 1880s, see Ishikawa Tomonori 石川友紀, 'Hiroshima wangan Jigozenson keiyaku imin no shakai chirigakuteki kōsatsu' 広島湾岸地御前村契約移民の社会地理学的考察 [A social and geographic study of contract emigration from Jigozen village, Hiroshima bay], *Jinbun chiri* 19 (1967): 75–91, here, p. 88. On the cotton mills, whose numbers nationwide increased from three in 1877 to twenty-three in 1886, see Yuji Ichioka, *The Issei: The World of the First Generation Japanese Immigrants, 1885–1924* (New York: Free Press, 1988), pp. 43–4; and Edward E. Pratt, *Japan's Protoindustrial Elite: The Economic Foundations of the Gōnō* (Cambridge, MA: Harvard University Asia Center, 1999), p. 65.

unfluctuating wage of nine US dollars a month on a sugar plantation (equivalent to 10.6 yen in 1885), plus room and board, was almost three times what Wakamiya could earn as a day-labourer in Jigozen.[29] Fuelling these expectations of economic independence and even prosperity, he would have read – or, more likely, have been read – a message from his prefectural governor on 25 May, the day when the migrants left Hiroshima for transit to Yokohama. Work hard, it said, using an idiom of triumphant homecoming, 'that you may gain the distinction of one day returning to your home town dressed in brocade'.[30]

There were nearly a thousand similar stories to Wakamiya's on the *Yamashiro-maru* as it steamed out of Yokohama on 4 June. Such is the imbalance of historical sources in favour of the programme's backers and organizers that a single entry in the Mitsui Bussan company diary reveals more about the departure than anything I will find in records relating to the migrants: to wit, the fourth was a rainy day, but Mitsui Bussan founder Masuda Takashi nevertheless went to wave the ship off from the pier.[31] I know hardly anything about Wakamiya Yaichi on board the *Yamashiro-maru* at that moment, and even less about Kodama Keijirō – who, unlike Wakamiya, was the only departee from his small village of Orisaki, in the county of Tamana, in the west of Kumamoto prefecture. In Orisaki, there was no group exodus by which a historian might hypothesize a motivation for departure, no chain reaction of transpacific migration such as that which would lead to early twentieth-century Jigozen becoming known as 'America village' for its high rate of overseas workers.[32] If I want to understand Kodama's background, I will need a different archival strategy.

That said, the paper trail generated by the *Yamashiro-maru*'s botched arrival in Honolulu offers an initial clue as to the transformation that the ship's migrants underwent while onboard. As soon as the 988 surviving

---

[29] Income figures based on Ishikawa, 'Hiroshima wangan Jigozenson', p. 85. The US$9 salary (US$6 for women) was on top of a monthly allowance for food (US$6 for men and US$4 for women).

[30] Hiroshima kenritsu monjokan 広島県立文書館, *Hiroshima-ken ijūshi: Shiryō-hen* 広島県移住史資料編 [A migration history of Hiroshima prefecture: Sources] (Hiroshima: Hiroshima-ken, 1991), p. 10. See also Jonathan Dresner, 'Instructions to Emigrant Workers, 1885–1894: "Return in Triumph" or "Wander on the Verge of Starvation"', in Nobuko Adachi, ed., *Japanese Diasporas: Unsung Pasts, Conflicting Presents and Uncertain Futures* (Abingdon: Routledge, 2006), pp. 52–68.

[31] My thanks to Koba Toshihiko of the Mitsui Archives, who shared with me extracts from an unpublished draft transcript of the Mitsui Bussan diaries for 1885 (Vol. 12, 23 October 1884 – 22 September 1886). Only brief extracts of the diaries from 1876–8 have been published to date, in the Archive's in-house journal, *Mitsui bunko ronsō* 三井文庫論叢, issues 41 (2007) to 43 (2009).

[32] Ishikawa, 'Hiroshima wangan Jigozenson', pp. 78–9.

men, women and children were released from quarantine, and just before they were dispersed to plantations throughout the kingdom, the men's names were entered in the 'Laborer Contract Book', today kept in the Hawai'i State Archives. Each name has been transliterated into the Roman alphabet, but instead of providing vertical information on provenance, the book lists them horizontally, next to a number: Kodama is #1146, Wakamiya, #1405. This was the *bango*, an individual number engraved on a metal disk and hung around the migrant's neck like the dog tags later worn by soldiers. (Women, absent in the 'Laborer Contract Book', went by their husbands' *bango*.)[33] Such numerical labelling made it easier for employers and government officials to discuss individual cases without dealing with what they clearly regarded as the encumbrance of Japanese names. For example, correspondence from Kaua'i's Kekaha plantation regarding Takiguchi Jinta, who arrived on the *Yamashiro-maru* in 1885 but died eighteen months later at the age of thirty-six, simply referred to 'the death of Japanese #863', as if discussing an account-book entry.[34]

By juxtaposing the Tokyo and the Honolulu archives, historians can therefore frame a small but significant transformation in how the labourers were officially identified. On their departure from Yokohama, Wakamiya Yaichi, Kodama Keijirō or Takiguchi Jinta were individuals with names, but on their arrival in Honolulu they were objects with numbers. If later testimony is anything to go by, this shift from name to number was a source of considerable grievance. 'The [overseers] never call a man by his name,' one Japanese migrant recalled. 'Always by the bango, 7209 or 6508 in that manner. And that was the thing I objected to. I wanted my name, not the number.'[35] In this sense, my desire to give the male protagonist in Strong's painting an individual name is anachronistic. To the overseer on horseback, and possibly even to Strong himself, this 'fine looking' man and his presumed wife were no more than a shared number in a ledger book.

And if we dig further into the moment of the *Yamashiro-maru*'s arrival, it becomes clear that a second, more existential transformation occurred in the migrants' lives between embarkation in Japan and disembarkation in Hawai'i. For Wakamiya, Kodama and Takiguchi did not simply step off the ship and dally into port. Rather, following the outbreak of

---

[33] For examples of how female *bango* were used, see HSPA, KAU PV Vol. 7, *passim*.
[34] HSPA, KSC 19-13, letter from the Bureau of Immigration to the manager of Kekaha Sugar Co. (Kaua'i), 10 January 1887.
[35] Ronald Takaki, *Pau Hana: Plantation Life and Labor in Hawaii* (Honolulu: University of Hawai'i Press, 1983), p. 89.

smallpox among a dozen labourers during the *Yamashiro-maru*'s passage, the migrants were bundled off to the isolation of Honolulu's Sand Island quarantine station. There, in what later became known among the Japanese as the *sennin-goya*, or 'thousand-person huts',[36] they and their compatriots spent more than a month, surrounded by high paling and a watchtower, and guarded by as many as ten men during the daytime.[37] (The Japanese reportedly 'kept their quarters and the grounds beautifully clean', with 'their own police [guarding] against any nuisance being committed anywhere near the quarters'.)[38] These cramped conditions offered migrants a foretaste of the minimal accommodation on some of the sugar plantations, where the wooden bunks of similarly named 'thousand-person huts' could be stacked three or four high.[39] For Wakamiya Yaichi as for the others, then, this was an existential transformation in the sense that his physical freedom of movement was considerably curtailed in Hawai'i compared to his old life in an Inland Sea port. In the quarantine station, it was curtailed by high paling and guards; on the plantation, by a strict labour regime which was laid out in the contract each migrant had signed and then enforced through overseers and managers, kingdom officials and Japanese consular staff, and, in the worst-case scenarios, through the Hawaiian courts.

That such adjustments to time regimes and curtailments of freedom could lead to outbreaks of conflict between the labourers and their overseers was unsurprising.[40] A different folder in the Japanese Foreign Ministry Archives contains dozens of pages of written testimony detailing the problems that some ex-*City of Tokio* migrants faced within a few weeks of having arrived – problems corroborated by records in Hawai'i. From Pā'ia in central Maui, for example, came complaints of 'rough handling, insufficient medical attendance, compelling men to work who are sick, and bringing men to court for refusal to work', as the Hawaiian Board of Immigration's special agent reported in April. Moreover, 'On Paia plantation, about the middle of March, a native Hawaiian, a bullock driver, had a dispute or rather fight, with a Japanese, the Japanese received a scalp wound in the forehead.' After the subsequent court case, 'all the Japanese, except those on the sick list, [...] refused to work and

---

[36] Moriyama, *Imingaisha*, p. 112.
[37] For the quarantine station, see *PCA*, 25 June 1885. I have calculated the number of guards from HSA, Vol. 519 (*Yamashiro-maru*, 1892).
[38] *PCA*, 7 July 1885 (accessed through Chronicling America).
[39] Odo, *Voices from the Canefields*, p. 51.   [40] On plantation time regimes, see Chapter 3.

arming themselves with knives and sticks made threatening demonstrations along the highway'.[41]

The Board of Immigration's president, in a soothing letter to the Japanese Consul in Honolulu at the end of May, acknowledged these accounts but explained that on Pāʻia and the neighbouring plantation of Haiku, 'immigrants of the farming class, of simple habits, came into a strange country, [and] the people who received them were unaccustomed to their habits, and ideas, and did not make sufficient allowance'.[42] Although he promised that Pāʻia and Haiku would henceforth be given a 'trial' status in the government-sponsored programme, bureaucrats in Tokyo were sufficiently alarmed to arrange for a special commissioner to accompany the programme's second shipment of labourers in June. Inoue Katsunosuke, the adopted son of Foreign Minister Inoue Kaoru, was to report back to the ministry on plantation working conditions, with the threat – not quite spelled out – that if he were unhappy with what he observed, the government-sponsored programme would be suspended or abandoned. Even in late June, however, as Inoue saw out his own quarantine in the considerably more salubrious conditions of the offshore *Yamashiro-maru*, ex-*City of Tokio* labourers on Pāʻia were still complaining of horseback-mounted *lunas* (overseers) beating them with cane stalks, spitting on them, kicking them in the head, lassoing their necks with the horse's whip, and depriving them of drinking water during working hours.[43]

To a newly arrived Japanese labourer, therefore, the basic composition of Strong's painting would have been all wrong. In light of the Pāʻia complaints, the bullock cart and the mounted *luna* would have brought very different associations. The overseer would always have been at the *fore*ground of their daily consciousness. And it seems very unlikely that the male protagonist, or indeed any other labourer, would have found (or been granted) time during the working day, especially during the cane-cutting season, to have a cup of tea with his wife and child, let alone gaze good naturedly over his place of work.

Admittedly, such maltreatment of men and women with 'simple habits' lay at the far end of a spectrum of migrant experiences in 1885 Hawaiʻi. No labourer could have expected kicking and spitting and

---

[41] W. Austin to Charles Gulick, 25 April 1885, in DA 3.8.2.7. Austin had been appointed special agent at a Board of Immigration meeting on 6 April 1885, and his report was discussed at a Board meeting on 27 April: HSA Government Records Inventory Sheets, FO&EX, Interior Department, 522 Vol. 1 (Board of Immigration Minutes, 1879–1899).
[42] Gulick to Nakamura, 30 May 1885, in DA 3.8.2.7.
[43] Letter from Nakagawa Nisuke and four others to the Japanese consulate in Honolulu, 26 June 1885: DA 3.8.2.7.

beating, especially in light of pre-departure visions of brocade. On the other hand, the labourers cannot have been entirely surprised by the change of habits they were forced to experience upon arrival. This is because, in material ways, the shipboard passage had already habituated them to a new way of experiencing the world. First-class passengers might well enjoy the 'fine smoking room' to the aft of the *Yamashiro-maru*'s central funnel, or a sheltered promenade along the ship's stern railings; they could commune, immediately below the smoking room, in a 'handsome' dining saloon which was 'well lighted with electric lights of various descriptions', or in the music room; and they could relax in 'large, lofty, and well ventilated' cabins, each containing two berths and a bell to summon the steward. By contrast, the 940 male labourers, thirty-five women and fourteen children on the government-sponsored emigration programme spent the majority of their days packed into two rooms, one deck below first-class.[44] The floors on which the migrants slept were supplemented by large wooden bunks built inwards from the *Yamashiro-maru*'s port and starboard sides (compared by some migrants to silkworm shelves).[45] Here, each migrant had an individual sleeping area of a little over 0.9 square metres, or approximately 163 by 55 centimetres, most probably with about 80 centimetres to sit up and/or change clothes. Coffin-like accommodation this was not, in comparison to so-called 'coolie' labourers transported across the Pacific and Indian Oceans in the mid nineteenth century.[46] Moreover, the *Yamashiro-maru*'s newness marked it out from vessels typically used in the contemporary Melanesian forced-labour trade, many of which became human transporters only *after* they were no longer fit for inanimate cargo.[47] But, sleeping head-to-foot and probably three people deep on either the

---

[44] For the fullest description of the *Yamashiro-maru*, see *PCA*, 21 July 1885. For other elements of my reconstruction, see *PCA*, 19 June 1885; *Morning Bulletin* (Rockhampton, Queensland), 14 February 1898. My calculations of sleeping space are explained more fully in Martin Dusinberre, 'Writing the On-board: Meiji Japan in Transit and Transition', *Journal of Global History* 11, 2 (2016): 271–94, here pp. 279–81. On the spatial divisions of British-built steamships during this period, see Douglas Hart, 'Sociability and "Separate Spheres" on the North Atlantic: The Interior Architecture of British Atlantic Liners, 1840–1930', *Journal of Social History* 44, 1 (2010): 189–212.

[45] See the interview with Kame Okano (born in 1889 in Yamaguchi prefecture) in Ethnic Studies Oral History Project, *A Social History of Kona*, Vol. 1 (Honolulu: Ethnic Studies Program, University of Hawai'i, Manoa, 1981), pp. 591–626, here p. 601 (Okano is the family name).

[46] Evelyn Hu-DeHart, 'La Trata Amarilla: The "Yellow Trade" and the Middle Passage, 1847–1884', in Emma Christopher, Cassandra Pybus and Marcus Rediker, eds., *Many Middle Passages: Forced Migration and the Making of the Modern World* (Berkeley: University of California Press, 2007), pp. 166–83, here p. 173.

[47] Laurence Brown, '"A Most Irregular Traffic": The Oceanic Passages of the Melanesian Labor Trade', in Emma Christopher, Cassandra Pybus and Marcus Rediker, eds., *Many*

deck's floor or the elevated wooden bunks, using futons or ship canvasses as mattresses and any blankets they themselves had brought,[48] it seems unlikely that Wakamiya and his fellow villagers would have enthused – as had Osaka residents viewing the *Yamashiro-maru* for the first time in 1884 – about the ship's 'lofty 'tween-decks'.[49]

Thus, just as the 'thousand-person huts' at the Sand Island quarantine station prepared the migrants for later accommodation on the sugar plantations, so the ship played a crucial role in socializing Wakamiya and his compatriots for the physical confinements of their new lives. Not for nothing did one Hawaiian planter offer a casual analogy about plantation living conditions in the mid 1880s: 'Dwellings for plantation laborers are furnished free of rental by the plantations. The rooms are generally about twelve square feet, and for unmarried men contain bunks, *as in ships*.'[50] Moreover, when Irwin decreed, five days out of Yokohama, that the migrants must take three hours of daily exercise on the upper deck of the *Yamashiro-maru* (safely screened off from the fourteen first-class passengers), Wakamiya experienced for the first time the intervention of a white man in his daily routines and bodily regimes.[51] This would be a precedent both for the mass disinfecting showers which the migrants would be forced to take in the quarantine station, and for the racial hierarchies of their lives on the plantations. Even the auditory sensations of the ship – the bridge bell, sounding every half-hour and then eight times on the fourth hour to mark a change of watch, or the constant rumble and grind of the engine – prepared the migrants for the new time regimes they would experience on the plantations, and for the non-stop clatter of the sugar mill. Archivally framed in this way, the ship can be seen for its partial function: not just a mode of transportation, but a boot camp for the plantation.

That said, ignorance was also an aspect of the in-between. One of my favourite photographs from Hawai'i has nothing to do with the *Yamashiro-maru*: rather, it depicts government-sponsored

---

Middle Passages: Forced Migration and the Making of the Modern World (Berkeley: University of California Press, 2007), pp. 184–203, here pp. 191–4.

[48] I take these details from Consul Andō Tarō's description of the *City of Peking*, 13 February 1886, in Hiroshima kenritsu monjokan, *Hiroshima-ken ijūshi*, p. 35.

[49] *HN*, 31 July 1884.

[50] *PM*, VI, 9 (December 1886), p. 242 (emphasis added). While some migrants called the shipboard bunkbeds silkworm shelves, others did the same for the plantation accommodation: see the interview with Usaku Morihara (born in 1884 in Yamaguchi prefecture), Ethnic Studies Oral History Project, *Social History of Kona*, Vol. 1, pp. 841–84, here p. 855 (Morihara is the surname).

[51] HSA, FO&EX 31, Immigration Matters (April–June 1885), Robert W. Irwin to Walter M. Gibson, 25 June 1885.

Figure 2.2 Japanese immigrants landing. Honolulu, c. 1893. PP-46-4-005. Courtesy of Hawai'i State Archives.

migrants from the *Miike-maru*, circa 1893, crossing a long wooden walkway across the beach from ship to land (see Figure 2.2). The men are laden down with luggage – with rolled-up bedding, bamboo-woven trunks, shoulder-bags stuffed with clothes, pots and pans and other packages, all slung over their backs and balanced on the backs of their necks.[52] They glance towards the strange sight of photographic paraphernalia as they approach shore, and the foremost two men offer a smile. Even in the stillness of the celluloid, there seems to be a spring in the migrants' step. Arriving in Hawai'i, the men cannot know how their new lives will unfold. The photograph thus captures them in an extended moment of landfall, a moment which arguably began as soon as they left their home towns and villages in rural Japan.[53]

---

[52] I take these details from the exhibits on display at the Japanese Cultural Center of Hawai'i Honolulu, which I visited in 2011.

[53] Here I depart from Joseph Conrad, who argues that a landfall is a particular temporal moment (a cry of 'Land ho!'), while a departure is a technical act, namely, the pencilled

The Nation Cheek by Jowl

The photograph of labourers arriving in mid-1890s Hawai'i also takes us into a different aspect of the migrants' daily lives, namely their visual framing as 'Japanese'. To comprehend one making of that ascribed identity, a short detour is necessary: to explain why, in 1885, a German doctor was present in the kingdom.

Of all the new phenomena visited upon nineteenth-century Hawaiian society, arguably the single most important was disease – acute infectious disease on an unprecedented scale. When one of the *ali'i* (chiefs) of Kaua'i island, Kā'eokūlani, had a group of men paddle out to engage with the newly arrived foreign ships in what those foreigners called January 1778, there were perhaps 500,000 or more Kānaka Maoli (Native Hawaiians) living on the islands as a whole. But among the gifts bestowed by Captain Cook's men in that first visit were syphilis, gonorrhoea and almost certainly tuberculosis as well. Thus began a century of Native decimation by illnesses which came later to include also mumps, smallpox, measles, influenza and dysentery. By the late 1870s, the islands had lost at least 70 per cent of their Indigenous population, if not 90 per cent.[54]

In Strong's 1885 painting, particular details spoke to wider ecological and epidemiological transformations in the history of Hawai'i. For example, the oxen and the overseer's horse were both animals imported at the turn of the nineteenth century, with massive unanticipated consequences for questions of enclosure and therefore land ownership; and the newly cut cane reminded the viewer of sugar's post-1830s emergence as the archipelago's key commodity.[55] But the most important detail,

---

cross on a track-chart after the final sight of land (even though the ship, while still in sight of the coast, may actually 'have been at sea, in the fullest sense of the phrase, for days'). My reconstruction of the shipboard passage reverses this argument, instead to posit landfall as a process which started days before the migrants physically approached the pier: Joseph Conrad, *The Mirror of the Sea*, 10th edn (Edinburgh: Methuen, 1906), pp. 1–2.

[54] I take these figures from R. D. K. Herman, 'Out of Sight, Out of Mind, Out of Power: Leprosy, Race and Colonization in Hawai'i', *Journal of Historical Geography* 27, 3 (2001): 319–37, here p. 320; and Appendix B in Seth Archer, *Sharks upon the Land: Colonialism, Indigenous Health, and Culture in Hawai'i, 1778–1855* (Cambridge: Cambridge University Press, 2018). On the first engagement by Native Hawaiians with Captain Cook's ships, see Chang, *World and All the Things upon It*, pp. 25–30.

[55] On the significance of horses and especially cows in Hawai'i, see John Ryan Fischer, *Cattle Colonialism: An Environmental History of the Conquest of California and Hawai'i* (Chapel Hill: University of North Carolina Press, 2015), pp. 30–3, 165–94. On the environmental transformation of the islands due to sugar production, see Carol A. MacLennan, *Sovereign Sugar: Industry and Environment in Hawai'i* (Honolulu: University of Hawai'i Press, 2014).

whether intentional or not, was the almost complete absence of Kānaka Maoli in Strong's work. In a painting set in Hawai'i, there were no Native Hawaiians – at least at first sight. Absence-by-disease was a history weighing upon the scene like the clouds hanging over the painting's background mountains; and absence explained why imported labour from Asia, the Pacific Islands and even Europe was necessary in the first place.

By the mid 1880s, leprosy had joined the list of diseases afflicting Native Hawaiians – although, as historians have subsequently shown, its discursive impact was in some ways more significant on Hawaiian society than its death count. In a throwback to the practices of twelfth-century Europe, foreign doctors in Hawai'i peddled the association of leprosy with indolence and filth, and thus insisted on segregating Native patients from the general population. One Strasbourg- and Breslau-trained dermatologist, Eduard Arning (1855–1936), who was appointed government resident physician by the Hawaiian Board of Health in 1883, claimed that sufferers were 'dangerous' and 'a hot bed of contagion'.[56] Reinforcing the association of leprosy with immorality, Arning arranged in 1884 for the death sentence of a convicted Native Hawaiian murderer, forty-eight-year-old Keanu, to be commuted so that the doctor might suture leprous tissue into the prisoner's arm. The aim, as Arning explained in a letter to King Kalākaua, was to conduct experiments 'in relation to the possibility of inoculating leprosy on healthy subjects'. Though he declined to 'dwell here on the propriety of these experiments',[57] they attracted much comment in the *British Medical Journal* in a period when, in the words of one historian, 'Hawai'i was coming to be seen as the imperial world's leprosy laboratory'.[58] (Keanu died on the so-called leper colony in Molokai in 1892.)

When not treating patients, Arning took photographs as a hobby. His lens roved widely, exploiting the access to ordinary Hawaiian homes that he enjoyed as a doctor. As to be expected from a European male working

---

[56] Cited in Herman, 'Out of Sight', p. 328. The comment itself dates from 1886, the year that Arning left Hawai'i. For a brief biographical overview, see Adrienne Kaeppler, 'Eduard Arning: Hawai'is ethnografischer Fotograf/Ethnographic Photographer of Hawai'i', in Wulf Köpke and Bernd Schmelz, eds., *Blick ins Paradies / A Glimpse into Paradise* (Hamburg: Museum für Völkerkunde Hamburg, 2014), pp. 86–103.

[57] Letter from Eduard Arning to King Kalākaua and the Privy Council, 13 August 1884, HSA FO&EX Chronological Files 1850–1900, Box 31, 'Miscellaneous: Local, Jul-Dec 1884'.

[58] Rod Edmond, *Leprosy and Empire: A Medical and Cultural History* (Cambridge: Cambridge University Press, 2006), p. 91.

in the late nineteenth-century Pacific region, Arning's depictions of human subjects have at times a voyeur quality: here he lines up four lightly clad New Hebridean labourers next to their (three-piece-besuited) Caucasian helmsman; there he positions a small group of half-naked Melanesian workers, the women's waists covered with dried-grass skirts.[59] Doubtless the doctor would have defended his compositions as 'authentic' and also of medical–ethnographic interest – a corporeal and cultural study, in which the accompanying props (spears, coconuts, clothing) were allegedly revealing of differences between Pacific Islander communities. As such, it was unsurprising that Arning was among the visitors to the Honolulu immigration depot on 11 February 1885, when the city's great and good gathered to welcome, and to gawk at, a new group of islanders, namely the very first group of Japanese labourers recently arrived on the *City of Tokio*. According to the *Advertiser* newspaper, the 'representatives of the various [Japanese] provinces' offered King Kalākaua and members of his government 'an exhibition of wrestling that was very interesting and amusing'. As if anticipating Arning's own physiological interests, the *Advertiser*'s correspondent continued:

Those who were to take part in the wrestling wore nothing but a band of cloth passed between their legs and then wound around the waist. Their naked bodies showed every degree of muscular development, some being without any superfluous flesh, but wilh [sic] plenty of sinew, while others were clothed with an abundance of solid brawn, and a few were inclined to fatness.[60]

Arning was on hand to record these wrestlers for posterity, and nine of the images he took that day survive. They capture a variety of poses: groups of families gathered around rice pots; a woman playing the shamisen next to her husband and child; migrants seated or lying on thick blankets; a reader, a smoker and their companions observed by two Caucasian men; a bathing scene in which the women expose their breasts and a toddler stands naked; and, of course, the much-observed bout of sumo. They also include a group shot, of eleven adults and a backward-facing child, which seems designed to capture all the variety in *yukata* (summer kimono) design that one might expect from a large, diverse group: the cottons worn are variously plain dyed, striped, checked, dark-coloured and light (see Figure 2.3). One man, on the second-right of the

---

[59] See Wulf Köpke and Bernd Schmelz, eds., *Blick ins Paradies / A Glimpse into Paradise* (Hamburg: Museum für Völkerkunde Hamburg, 2014), pp. 319 and 363 respectively.
[60] *PCA*, 12 February 1885 (accessed by microfilm).

Figure 2.3 Ex-*City of Tokio* migrants in Honolulu, February 1885. Photograph by Eduard Arning, Inv. No. 2014.8:20. © Museum am Rothenbaum (MARKK), Hamburg.

back row, wears his *yukata* somewhat unnaturally over a collarless, buttoned shirt; another, squatting on the front row, turns his back to the camera as if deliberately to display the Chinese character on his back. That this and all the scenes were staged, for technical as well as compositional reasons, does not diminish their historical value. In the bodies on display, as well as in the material culture of pots, pans, bedding, clothing and luggage, Arning's photographs offer scholars a more vibrant snapshot of Japanese rural life in the mid 1880s than any descriptions of the quotidian I have been able to find in the prefectures whence the migrants originally came.

Arning's photographs were also a visual manifestation of a written trope pervasive in all contemporary descriptions of the *City of Tokio* and later *Yamashiro-maru* arrivals: the migrants as *Japanese*. English-language newspaper readers in Honolulu were not only informed of 'Japanese sports' being performed at the immigration depot; they could also educate themselves – by reading the reprint of a long public lecture delivered by the recently departed US consul-general to Japan – about the working conditions of the 'Laborer in Japan'. One of the consul's express hopes was that the Japanese would 'prove themselves industrious, capable, temperate, amiable, obedient to law, and ready to identify themselves with your progress and your prosperity'.[61] Yet Japaneseness in 1885 was a claim as much as an empirical reality. To the migrants themselves, the fact that they came from 'various provinces' would have loomed as large in their consciousness as any labelling about their life in Japan. Indeed, until they left their home towns to come to Hawai'i, many of the migrants may never have met men and women from different provinces. For this reason, our ability to imagine the shipboard passage between Yokohama and Honolulu is important in terms of discourses of nationhood. For not only was the ship a preparation for the plantation; it was also a space of nascent nation-making.[62]

The transformation of scale in a migrant's sense of imaginative belonging, from village to nation, began with the bureaucracy of the government-sponsored programme itself. When Wakamiya Yaichi applied for his passage to Hawai'i in late April 1885, for example, he addressed his papers – including a pledge of good behaviour, a request for passage assistance, and a statement from his guarantor (usually an older relative) – to the head of the Jigozen village office.[63] In a community of 2,000 people, this bureaucrat, who was also a neighbour, would have been a familiar face in mediating Wakamiya's interactions with the Meiji state.[64] In such a role, village elites would have dealt on Wakamiya's behalf with officials in the Saeki county office; they, in turn, would have dealt with officials in the Hiroshima prefectural office; and prefectural officials would finally have dealt with bureaucrats in Tokyo. By contrast, once the *City of Tokio* and *Yamashiro-maru* migrants arrived in Honolulu and were dispersed to their individual plantations, this familiar local face of the bureaucratic state no longer existed. Instead, the migrants communicated with a direct representative of Tokyo in the form of the Japanese consul and his deputies in Hawai'i, or with Japanese inspectors employed by the consulate. Compared to the familiar mediation on offer in Jigozen, the Meiji state became more impersonal in

---

[61] Lecture by Thomas B. Van Buren (1824–89), reprinted in the *PCA* on 10, 12, 19, 20, 21 and 23 February 1885; citation from 12 February. Van Buren had also travelled on the *City of Tokio* to Honolulu.
[62] For the argument that migrants did not necessarily arrive possessing a national identity, see Hoerder, 'Migrations and Belongings', p. 482. Indeed, here I follow Hoerder's argument that the nation-state should not be the historian's default framework in analyzing long-distance migrations in the late nineteenth century. Yet in calling the transoceanic voyage an 'empty expanse' (ibid., p. 470), Hoerder also overlooks the ship as a key site in the formation of national self-identifications.
[63] I have extrapolated such a relationship from documents in Hiroshima kenritsu monjokan, *Hiroshima-ken ijūshi*, pp. 7–10.
[64] On the multiple bureaucratic and community roles that local elites played in Meiji Japan, see Martin Dusinberre, *Hard Times in the Hometown: A History of Community Survival in Modern Japan* (Honolulu: University of Hawai'i Press, 2012), pp. 53–80.

Hawai'i – and yet, in terms of bureaucratic layers, conversely less distant. From Wakamiya's new plantation, and indeed from his moment of embarkation on the ship, Tokyo was figuratively closer than it had ever been in Jigozen.[65]

Again, this process started from before the moment of embarkation, when, in the aforementioned written instructions from the governor of Hiroshima prefecture, Wakamiya was explicitly warned 'not to disgrace the nation' (*kokujoku o ukezaru* 国辱ヲ受ケサル) during the period of his contract. Such an admonition echoed the wider state campaigns of moral suasion in Meiji Japan – but the material space of the ship also played a key role in helping prepare migrants for their new figurative proximity to the nation-state.[66] For example, if we think back to the lists in the Japanese Foreign Ministry archives, the provenance of individual migrants was read vertically down, from prefecture to county to village: in the case of Wakamiya, from Hiroshima to Saeki to Jigozen. From the perspective of a bureaucrat in Tokyo, 'Japan' was so obvious a label as to be left unwritten. But my guess is that as Wakamiya left Jigozen on 25 May to begin his long journey to Honolulu, he would have ranked the relative importance of those names in reverse order. That is, Jigozen would have offered him a primary sense of belonging which was reinforced by the presence of thirty-six fellow villagers on the road to Hiroshima. But in the port of Ujina, he might have begun to feel lost among the crowd of 389 other migrants from Hiroshima prefecture; and onboard the *Yamashiro-maru* for the first time, en route to Yokohama, he was thrust into the same space as 276 migrants from Kumamoto and 149 from Fukuoka – two other key prefectures from which the government-sponsored emigrants hailed. True, as a native of an Inland Sea port town, Wakamiya would at the very least have previously seen people from other parts of Japan, and perhaps even conversed with them. But in the steamship, then in the Nagaura quarantine centre near Yokohama, and then during the passage to Hawai'i, nominal compatriots were suddenly cheek by jowl.

---

[65] For a similar argument on the relation of Wakayama pearl divers to the Arafura Sea, see Manimporok Dotulong, '*Hyakushō* in the Arafura Zone: Ecologizing the Nineteenth-Century "Opening of Japan"', *Past & Present* 257, 1 (November 2022): 280–317.

[66] Admonition from the governor of Hiroshima prefecture, 25 May 1885, in Hiroshima kenritsu monjokan, *Hiroshima-ken ijūshi*, p. 10. Such appeals can be traced back at least as far as the Meiji government's initial instructions to passport holders in 1869: see Takahiro Yamamoto, 'Japan's Passport System and the Opening of Borders, 1866–1878', *Historical Journal* 60, 4 (2017): 997–1021, here p. 1009. On domestic moral suasion in the Meiji period, see Sheldon Garon, *Molding Japanese Minds: The State in Everyday Life* (Princeton, NJ: Princeton University Press, 1997).

In the absence of an onboard archive, the historian can only speculate as to what Wakamiya made of this physical proximity. For purposes of comparison, we know from the scholarship of Naoko Shimazu that long railway journeys could serve as a catalyst to new self-identifications.[67] For example, conscript soldiers called up during the Russo-Japanese War (1904–5) first embarked on what Shimazu terms a 'journey of life' from their respective home towns to the aforementioned Ujina port in Hiroshima, whence they would subsequently ship to the Asian frontline. As they travelled by train, the soldiers were regularly greeted by cheering crowds, whose support helped young men from otherwise diverse backgrounds begin to feel a sense of connection to 'the nation'; they also passed key landmarks of 'national' culture such as the Akashi Straits, Himeji Castle, and especially – for those coming from the south-west of the archipelago – the floating shrine at Itsukushima (itself close to Jigozen). Shimazu writes that 'the internal journey from their home town to Hiroshima played a key role in expanding [the conscripts'] geographical space of what constituted "Japan" and, in the process, effortlessly integrated these soldiers from disparate parts of the country into the common national landscape of the homeland'.[68]

Transpacific crossings played a similar role for labour migrants in expanding the geographical space of what constituted 'Japan'.[69] For the women on board the *Yamashiro-maru* in 1885, and for those men who had avoided compulsory military service (of whom there were many in the early 1880s), this may have been the first opportunity in their lives to inhabit the same space as other 'Japanese'.[70] We may thus assume that the *Yamashiro-maru*'s cramped onboard conditions facilitated cross-prefectural communication. As Michael Ondaatje's evocation of a 1950s shipboard passage in *The Cat's Table* (2011) suggests, children were perhaps central to one aspect of this communication.[71] The antics of Nakano Tatsuzō, Nakamura Keitarō, Katō Yohei and Shiina Tatsuzō,

---

[67] I speak of 'identification' rather than 'identity' in light of Frederick Cooper, *Colonialism in Question: Theory, Knowledge, History* (Berkeley: University of California Press, 2005), pp. 71–3.

[68] Naoko Shimazu, *Japanese Society at War: Death, Memory, and the Russo-Japanese War* (Cambridge: Cambridge University Press, 2009), p. 76. See also Tamson Pietsch, 'A British Sea: Making Sense of Global Space in the Late Nineteenth Century', *Journal of Global History* 5, 3 (2010): 423–46.

[69] See Noah McCormack, '*Buraku* Migration in the Meiji Era: Other Ways to Become "Japanese"', *East Asian History* 23 (2002): 87–108.

[70] In addition to the more than 800 migrants from Hiroshima, Kumamoto and Fukuoka prefectures, the *Yamashiro-maru* carried labourers from Kanagawa (12), Niigata (37), Chiba (8), Shiga (74), Gunma (10) and Wakayama (33).

[71] Michael Ondaatje, *The Cat's Table* (London: Jonathan Cape, 2011).

all boys aged three, may have provided a common point of conversation for their parents, who respectively came from Fukuoka, Kanagawa and Chiba prefectures. The mothers Matsuda Tsui (Hiroshima) and Kobatake Kita (Wakayama), both aged twenty-three, perhaps bonded over their baby daughters, aged seven months and twelve months respectively. More generally, the three hours of daily deck-exercise that Irwin ordered midway through the passage would have provided other opportunities for cross-prefectural communication, as would cards and *shogi* (Japanese chess) games in the lower deck.[72]

Just as the Atlantic slave ships were a site of ethnogenesis for an 'African' slave community, the mid-Meiji migrant ships furthered the genesis of national self-identification among the 'Japanese' passengers. For bonded people on the slave ships, Marcus Rediker argues, 'broader similarities suddenly began to outweigh local differences', such that cultural and linguistic commonalities became 'crucial to cooperation and community'.[73] In a similar process, although very different physical conditions, the experience of transit may have served as a precedent for the label of 'Japanese' that the labourers were exposed to upon their arrival in Honolulu and then on the plantations – and that they subsequently themselves appropriated. One migrant would later recall her passage to Hawai'i on 'a Japanese ship'. She was in fact referring to the *Yamashiro-maru*'s sister ship from Newcastle upon Tyne, the *Omi-maru*, and the memory may simply refer to the kind of labelling that became a daily accompaniment to her life in Hawai'i.[74] Or it may obliquely reference a process of *becoming* Japanese which intensified on the transpacific passage. Either way, the shipboard experience prepared the migrants for the textual tropes of 'Japan' articulated in the *Advertiser* after the *Yamashiro-maru*'s arrival in June 1885, or for visual tropes such as Arning's photographs of the *City of Tokio*'s cohort in February.

Yet the ship also remained an ambivalent space of nation-making. The migrants continued to be divided by prefecture for administrative purposes – for example, while being transported from the Japanese quarantine station at Nagaura back to the *Yamashiro-maru* before departure from Yokohama. According to the very few oral histories which discuss shipboard life, the migrants tended to sleep and socialize in their prefectural groups during the passage to Honolulu – and, given the

---

[72] DA 3.8.2.5-14, Vol. 1; HSA, FO&EX 31, Immigration Matters (April-June 1885), Robert W. Irwin to Walter M. Gibson, 25 June 1885.
[73] Marcus Rediker, *The Slave Ship: A Human History* (London: John Murray, 2007), p. 118.
[74] Doi, *Hawai iminshi*, p. 114, referring to an 1889 emigrant's later recollections.

absence of a large dining room on board the ship, most probably ate in shifts with their prefectural compatriots.[75] Moreover, as many historians have pointed out, local differences remained central to the Japanese migrants' daily lives on the Hawaiian plantations, as expressed particularly in dialect and diet.[76]

How, then, should we read Arning's photographs from February 1885 and the 'national' pastimes that they depict? Was what the *Advertiser* called an *exhibition* an amusing spectacle for the Honolulu hosts, and for Arning, who saw a chance to add to his nominally ethnographic visual repertoire? In an age when Meiji Japan used world exhibitions to project a certain vision of 'Japaneseness' internationally, was it a performance of nationhood encouraged by the Tokyo officials on board the *City of Tokio*, themselves conscious that the performance's date, 11 February, was a recently inaugurated national holiday to celebrate the mythical founding of the Japanese nation? Did these Japanese government officials also hope that a celebration of wrestling would foster a sense of national belonging which the migrants were otherwise lacking in their daily lives? We cannot know for sure. But we should also not rule out that the migrants themselves may have been engaged in a moment of play. In both of Arning's sumo photographs, the bout's referee, whom the *Advertiser* refers to as announcing the result 'with a waive [sic] of his fan', is actually raising, with dramatic effect, a cast-iron frying pan. Does the pan for the fan thereby undermine the supposed seriousness of the exhibition or the patriotic celebrations of the participants?

Such ambiguities abound in the photographic archive – which, in Arning's case, is to be found in Hamburg, Germany.[77] To acknowledge them is better to understand the artifice of the migrants' reception and representation upon arrival in Honolulu. And they are also important because of the closing sentences of the *Advertiser*'s report of the 11 February festivities. Having noted that there had been 'a fine display of muscle, pluck and good nature', the newspaper recorded: 'Mr. J. D. Strong took some instantaneous negatives, besides securing some other fine studies.' In other words, Strong was as active as Arning in the immigration depot on 11 February. And, though it required a sharp-

---

[75] For an example of one government-sponsored emigrant (in 1888) remembering spending most of his passage with fellow Hiroshima labourers, see Moriyama, *Imingaisha*, p. 161. On Nagaura, see Consul Andō's report from the *City of Peking*, 13 February 1886, in Hiroshima kenritsu monjokan, *Hiroshima-ken ijūshi*, p. 34.
[76] Y. Kimura, *Issei*, pp. 22–32.
[77] The Museum am Rothenbaum – Kulturen und Künste der Welt (MARKK), previously the Museum für Völkerkunde Hamburg, holds 237 of Arning's glass plate photographs.

Figure 2.4 Photographic models for Strong (see also Figures 2.1 and 2.3).

eyed student to point this out to me, three of the figures who also appear in Arning's aforementioned group photograph are undoubtedly the models for the foreground family in Strong's Spreckelsville painting. They are the standing man, hands on hips; the seated woman with partially exposed breasts; and the small boy whose cropped hair is rather a blur (Figure 2.4).[78]

Nobody should be surprised that painters use models, nor that they apply some artistic licence in departing from those models. The point here, to use an anachronism, is rather that Strong's effective 'photoshopping' of his models into a Maui context was a deliberate attempt to gloss over the emerging archival record about the aforementioned maltreatment of ex-*City of Tokio* labourers in the Hawaiian Islands. Consider the public relations timeline. The self-proclaimed architects of the government-sponsored programme, Walter Gibson and Robert Irwin, imagined immigration on an 'industrial' scale and the transformation of

---

[78] My immense thanks to Christina Wild for this insight during a University of Zurich BA seminar in the autumn of 2015. The crouched woman on the foreground right of Strong's painting may be based on a reverse pose of the aforementioned squatting man (front row, left) in Arning's photograph.

the kingdom by 'tens of thousands of Japanese families'. ('Certainly no public man in this Kingdom has labored more assiduously to make Japanese immigration a success than His Excellency Mr. Gibson', the *Advertiser* claimed.)[79] True, not everyone in Hawai'i felt so sanguine about this prospect, as the spat between the *Advertiser* and the *Hawaiian Gazette* over the 'Asiaticizing' of the islands demonstrated.[80] But if anything were likely to kill the programme in its infancy, it would be the lack of supply from Japan rather than the opposition of certain anti-government constituencies in Hawai'i. And so, only a few weeks after he had accompanied the *City of Tokio* labourers to Hawai'i in February 1885, Irwin seems to have commissioned Strong to paint the newly arrived Japanese as a gift to the Meiji emperor. We can only guess at his motivations, but presumably if he could offer the emperor a visual manifestation of the extent to which Japanese subjects were contented in the kingdom, then he might hope for an increased flow of labourers. Thus, the consul and the painter, together with Strong's studio partner, the equally renowned Jules Tavernier (1844–89), toured Maui in early March.[81] They visited the Wailuku, Waikapu, Pā'ia and Spreckelsville plantations, and upon their return to Honolulu, Strong publicly displayed – at a dinner given by Gibson in honour of Irwin on 11 March – several pre-studies, including 'a sketch of a picture, of Japanese at work in the cane fields at Spreckelsville'.[82]

But the problem with this report was that no ex-*City of Tokio* Japanese had been posted to Spreckelsville. The first government-sponsored labourers to work there would be the ex-*Yamashiro-maru* migrants – in fact, the whole 276-strong cohort from Kumamoto prefecture (275 men, one woman, and no children, exposing the fallacy of Strong's composition). They would be picked up from Honolulu on 21 July 1885, nearly two weeks *after* the *Advertiser*'s article on Strong's completed painting.[83] So Strong did not and could not have sketched any Japanese on

---

[79] *PCA*, 8 July 1885.   [80] See Chapter 1.
[81] On Strong's pre-Hawaiian career, see 'California Artists', in *Overland Monthly* 27, 161 (May 1896): 501–10.
[82] *Daily Bulletin* (Honolulu), 12 March 1885, which includes details of the painting's then commission. See also *PCA*, 12 March 1885, for the suggestion that the sketch 'shows a group of Japanese at work in the cane-fields of Spreckelsville, with the mountains of West Maui in the distance'.
[83] The *PCA* reported, on 20 July 1885, that Spreckelsville's manager had arrived in Honolulu on 19 July to oversee final arrangements for the transportation of 275 men to Maui (the one woman in the Kumamoto contingent was overlooked). The report implies that the *Yamashiro-maru* group constituted the plantation's first experience of Japanese labour: 'Should the experience with this large body of Japanese laborers prove satisfactory at Spreckelsville, arrangements will be made to employ at least 800 men.'

Spreckelsville. Most likely, given his recognizable if somewhat romanticized depiction of the Maui landscape (the sketches do not survive), Strong may have studied the Japanese at work in the cane fields of Pāʻia, which neighboured Spreckelsville.[84]

If Irwin or Gibson or anyone else in the Hawaiian government had been hoping to appeal to Japan to send more labourers, however, then Pāʻia was not the place to paint. As we have seen, disputes there about 'rough handling' were already beginning in March 1885 – disputes which would lead to a Hawaiian government investigation of the labourers' complaints in April. Indeed, reports of maltreatment in Pāʻia, in Haiku and in numerous other plantations beyond Maui were arriving at the Japanese consulate in Honolulu and from there being forwarded to top a growing pile of paperwork in Tokyo. All the more urgent, then, that the Meiji government be presented with a 'fine representation of a sunny, thriving, hard-working plantation scene'. Without question, the plantation represented could not be Pāʻia, given the troubles there – and also given that Pāʻia was owned and managed by Samuel Thomas Alexander (1836–1904), son of a first-generation New England missionary and active in opposition politics to King Kalākaua. But Spreckelsville, owned by the king's close ally, Claus Spreckels (1828–1908), would do nicely.[85] Spreckels would get – to use another anachronism – 'product placement' for what would, by the early 1890s, be the biggest sugarcane plantation in the world.[86] And the king – who, if the *Advertiser*'s July report is to be believed, seems to have taken over the painting's commission from Irwin – would have a visually striking means of appealing to the Japanese emperor and his government for more labourers.

We've come a long way from the actual experiences of those labourers – of men such as Kodama Keijirō, who started working on Spreckelsville in July 1885. But that, it would seem to me, was exactly the point of the painting: it should distract the viewer from the realities of plantation life

---

[84] Knowing that Strong published occasional sketches in *Harper's Weekly*, my assistant David Walter Möller searched all issues from 1885 but could find no works by Strong.

[85] On the financial entanglements between King Kalākaua and Claus Spreckels, see Jacob Adler, *Claus Spreckels: The Sugar King in Hawaii* (Honolulu: University of Hawaiʻi Press, 1966), p. 183. For more recent scholarship on Spreckels, see Uwe Spiekermann, 'Das gekaufte Königreich: Claus Spreckels, die Hawaiian Commercial Company [sic] und die Grenzen wirtschaftlicher Einflussnahme im Königtum Hawaii, 1875 bis 1898', in Harmut Berghoff, Cornelia Rauh and Thomas Welskopp, eds., *Tatort Unternehmen: Zur Geschichte der Wirtschaftskriminalität im 20. und 21. Jahrhundert* (Berlin: de Gruyter, 2016), pp. 47–67. Strong had originally come to Hawaiʻi in 1882 on a commission from Claus's son John D. Spreckels (1853–1926), whom he knew from San Francisco.

[86] *Paradise of the Pacific* (September 1893), pp. 133–4.

for the first groups of government-sponsored Japanese in Hawai'i. It should divert our interests away from the evidence accumulating in the archives that all was not as equal or as humane as it might seem.

As one archival counterpoint to these complex political agendas, we may note that Spreckelsville itself became the focus of worker ire within a month of Irwin's returning with the painting to Japan. Unfortunately, there survive only the reports generated by the authorities: for example, a court case in September 1885 against seven Kumamoto workers, named and numbered in the court record. Here, in response to the labourers' claims that they were sick, a Japanese doctor testified that they were not, and that they could go back to work; the Japanese were fined US$3.75 each. Another court summary from October 1885 details the case brought against twenty Spreckelsville Japanese who were accused of gambling.[87] And, a month later, reports received by the Board of Immigration described 'trouble arising between Japanese Immigrant laborers on the Spreckels Plantation and their employers'. The latter were investigated by the Board's secretary, Mr Cleghorn, who instead reported from Spreckelsville of labourers 'up at night gambling, long after the regulation hour of nine o'clock, at which time lights are ordered put out'. Cleghorn's interlocutor and translator at this time, as also in the Hawaiian courts in the previous months, was a Japanese immigration inspector called Itō. Channelling Itō, Cleghorn reported that 'the Japanese laborers on Spreckelsville come from a district in Japan where there was a good deal of trouble in 1877' – that is, the Satsuma Rebellion against the Meiji government, fought partly in Kumamoto prefecture.

And so we are back at the problem of framing: Itō's disdain for the class and regional background of the Spreckelsville workers framed Cleghorn's reports, which then constitute the main surviving written record of Japanese life on the plantation. I'm not sure which is more problematic for the historian: Strong's commissioned fiction or Cleghorn's reported facts. But I am sure that, in trying to position the Spreckelsville labourers between the poles of alleged contentment and demonstrable recalcitrance, we are no closer to understanding how Kodama gazed out at the world.[88]

Meanwhile, a second archival counterpoint to the framing of 'Japanese Laborers on the Plantation in Spreckelsville' became possible in

---

[87] HSA 255-52: District Court of the Second Circuit Court, Minute Books: Wailuku Police Court Minute Book, March 1885 – January 1886. I am very grateful to Noelani Arista for summarizing these cases from the original Hawaiian.
[88] On illness and slow work as demonstrations of recalcitrance on the Hawaiian plantations, see Takaki, *Pau Hana*, pp. 129–32.

2017 thanks to the launch of Stanford University's Hoji Shinbun Digital Collection. Among the many overseas Japanese newspapers digitized in the collection is the Honolulu-based *Nippu jiji*, which in February 1935 published a bilingual supplement to celebrate the 'golden jubilee' of Japanese immigration to Hawai'i. This, too, engages in its own framing of Japanese and Hawaiian history: the first page's subheading, 'They Till the Soil, and Out of Their Sweat a New Territory Is Born', rings of the pioneer imagination of settlement in the Pacific which was so prevalent in expansionist Japanese discourse by the 1930s (and which lived on in the Taitō ninety-year history).[89] But for me the most interesting part of the supplement is the brief life histories of surviving *City of Tokio* and *Yamashiro-maru* migrants. We learn, for example, that five of the original Kumamoto contingent to Spreckelsville were still alive and working on the islands in 1935: as builders, coffee growers, pineapple labourers or simply raising their own vegetables. There are photos of these five men, all in their seventies, all in formal jackets and ties. Their hair is grey, their faces lined and tanned after years working in the sun. Back in Hawai'i in 2011, I had assumed I would never find photos of any of the *Yamashiro-maru* migrants. But now they gaze out of the pictures and out of my computer screen. These men were the real protagonists – and survivors – of the history embedded in Strong's painting.

(Re)framing

When Robert W. Irwin accompanied Strong's large oil painting and the King Bros' even larger frame back to Yokohama on the *Yamashiro-maru* in July–August 1885, he may already have known that his intended framing had failed. Not in the sense of the government-sponsored programme: to the contrary, its future was in a better place than it had been on the outward voyage. For after visiting several plantations, Inoue Katsunosuke had placed several formal demands on Gibson, including that 'no overseer (*luna*) will be allowed under *any* circumstances to put his hands in *any* way on *any* Japanese for *any* purposes whatsoever'. When Gibson agreed, and also established a Bureau of Inspection under the Board of Immigration (the very bureau which would later send Itō to Spreckelsville), the course was set for formalizing the programme through the Hawaiian–Japanese Labor Convention of January 1886.[90]

---

[89] 'Panorama of Japanese in Hawaii', *Nippu jiji*, 16 February 1935, available through https://hojishinbun.hoover.org; see also Azuma, *In Search of Our Frontier*.

[90] Letter from Inouye [Inoue] Katsunosuke to Walter M. Gibson, 18 July 1885 (emphasis added); and Precis of a Conversation between Inoue and Gibson on 18 July, including

Rather, the failure of the Strong painting concerned how it positioned Japan in the world. The whole tenor of the younger Inoue's diplomatic mission to Hawai'i had been set by a letter he carried in June from his adopted father, the foreign minister Inoue Kaoru, for delivery to Gibson. Welcoming the likely future expansion of Japanese emigration into the kingdom, Inoue senior sought to raise various matters of concern, including the need for more Japanese interpreters on the islands. But the main thrust of the letter concerned Chinese immigration to Hawai'i. In short, he stated, Japanese emigration would be dependent on the Hawaiian government restricting Chinese immigration. This was because 'His Imperial Majesty's Government [Japan] are not inclined to regard with favor the association of Japanese and Chinese. In other places such association has been a fruitful source of embarrassment'.[91] Here, in the polite cursive script of diplomatic missives, was the sharp end of a mid-Meiji discourse of redefining 'civilization' away from the hitherto centrifugal power of China and framing it instead within tropes of Euro-American 'progress'. The doyen of such 'civilization' debates was the journalist Fukuzawa Yukichi (1835–1901), whose popular newspaper had indeed published an essay with the title 'Casting Off Asia' (*Datsu-A ron* 脱亜論) in March 1885, arguing that 'the spirit of [Japan's] people has already moved away from the old conventions of Asia to Western civilization'.[92] Irrespective of whether Irwin himself had read the essay, he channelled its spirit in his onboard letter to Gibson of 25 June 1885 (see Chapter 1), in which he claimed that 'Japanese people have nothing in common with India and China'.

But Strong's painting undermined this claim – firstly through the figure of the seated child. 'Excellent' though the *Advertiser* suggested the 'little baby' [sic] was, its 'shaved head and side-tufts of black hair' identified it as having a 'Chinese-boy' (*karako* 唐子) haircut. As David Ambaras has shown, popular sensitivities about children were acute in the Meiji period in light of reports about the abduction of Japanese children for sale in China.[93] Thus, whatever the reason for Strong's artistic licence in adapting his model's original immigration depot pose, there could be no denying the fact that the painting's foreground child

---

Appendix to the Precis: both HSA 403-16-250 (Foreign Officials in Hawai'i; Japan; 1885).

[91] Letter from Inoue Kaoru to Walter Gibson, 2 June 1885: HSA, FO&EX 31 (Immigration Matters, April–June 1885).

[92] There is some debate as to whether Fukuzawa himself wrote the essay, as was long assumed. See Pekka Korhonen, 'Leaving Asia? The Meaning of *Datsu-A* and Japan's Modern History', *Asia-Pacific Journal* 12, 9 (3 March 2014).

[93] Ambaras, *Japan's Imperial Underworlds*, pp. 29–72.

embodied exactly the kind of associational 'embarrassment' which the Japanese foreign minister sought to avoid. This, I would suggest, is one reason why Strong's painting never made it to the Meiji emperor, either as a 'handsome present' from King Kalākaua or as a gift from Irwin – and one reason why Irwin never displayed it publicly after 1885.[94]

Another reason for Irwin's likely sense of failure was the foreground woman's exposed breasts. Assuming Strong took negatives of the same group which Arning photographed (or that Strong based his protagonists directly on Arning's image), then we are confronted once again with the question of visual performance. Bearing in mind Arning's other image of half-naked Japanese women waiting to bathe, the doctor may have staged the exposed mother in order to frame eroticism within the genre of ethnographic observation.[95] Equally, it is possible that the women in both photographs presented themselves 'naturally', behaving according to the social mores of rural Japan in which the exposure of breasts during public bathing or indeed the performance of manual labour was no source of shame (see also Figure 6.3). That public nudity persisted in the contemporaneous Japanese countryside was confirmed by the Victorian traveller Isabella Bird (1831–1904), who noted in the late 1870s that 'the Government is doing its best to prevent promiscuous bathing' in rural areas.[96] And yet Bird's language reveals exactly the problem that Irwin confronted as he carried the painting on the *Yamashiro-maru*: nudity was 'promiscuous', and it was associated in Europe and North America – as also by the New England missionaries in 1820s Hawai'i – with 'uncivilized' Indigenous peoples.[97]

---

[94] One painting *was* delivered from King Kalākaua to the Emperor Meiji in 1885: it is mentioned in a letter from the king to the emperor as 'a token of the friendship and esteem with which We shall ever regard you' – but this was a portrait of Kalākaua, and indeed registered as such (*shōzōga* 肖像画) in the imperial household register of gifts in August 1885: see Letter from Kalākaua to Mitsuhito, 24 July 1885 (HSA Executive Correspondence (outgoing) TS Kalakaua 1884–85) and Letter from J. S. Webb to R. W. Irwin, 24 July 1885 (HSA 410 v. 100); also *AS*, 27 March 1986.

[95] This was a defence which scholars have characterized as 'respectability by association': see Philippa Levine, 'The Mobile Camera: Bodies, Anthropologists, and the Victorian Optic', *Nineteenth-Century Contexts* 37, 5 (2015): 473–90, here p. 474 and particularly pp. 481–2 for a comparable defence in 1879 London.

[96] Isabella Lucy Bird, *Unbeaten Tracks in Japan: An Account of Travels in the Interior including Visits to the Aborigines of Yezo and the Shrine of Nikkô and Isé*, Vol. 1 (London: John Murray, 1880), p. 205.

[97] For Hawai'i, see Jennifer Thigpen, *Island Queens and Mission Wives: How Gender and Empire Remade Hawai'i's Pacific World* (Chapel Hill: University of North Carolina Press, 2014), p. 50. For Bird in Japan, Joohyun Jade Park, 'Missing Link Found, 1880: The Rhetoric of Colonial Progress in Isabella Bird's *Unbeaten Tracks in Japan*', *Victorian Literature and Culture* 43 (2015): 371–88.

Thus, Strong's painting undermined Irwin's own claim, written from on board the ship in June 1885, that 'Japan is progressive and rapidly becoming a Western Civilized State'. Indeed, in an interview which the president of Taiwan Sugar, Takechi Tadamichi, gave in the early 1930s for a new book on the history of the Japanese sugar industry, he recalled that 'during his lifetime, Irwin would look at the painting, see the Japanese woman with her breast exposed, and feel it was shameful [*haji* 恥] to the Japanese people'. For this reason, Takechi requested that the painting not be reprinted in the book.[98]

There may also have been a third reason for Irwin's discomfort, one which additionally accounts for the painting disappearing from view for more than forty years after arriving in Japan. When Mitsui Sugar commissioned the work's restoration in 2017, it became clear that the man and nursing woman's faces were *not* 'unmistakably Japanese'. Compared to the original Arning photograph, they both featured slightly wider eyes, higher and more rounded cheeks, fuller lips and more pronounced noses. Perhaps such judgements lie as much in the beholder's eye as in the painter's brush. But the facial ambiguity of Strong's protagonists, who might as equally have been Native Hawaiians as Japanese, does speak to a final problem for Irwin and a final framing for us. For Irwin, any hint that the painting's future viewers – *any* viewer in *any* circumstances, not merely the Mikado or his ministers – could possibly have construed 'the Japanese' as Pacific Islanders would have profoundly undermined Meiji Japanese claims to a higher (European) civilizational status. According to Fukuzawa Yukichi, for example, the history of the 'Sandwich Islands' only began with their 'discovery' by Captain Cook in 1778.[99] By this logic, Native Hawaiians were allegedly a people without history prior to their interactions with Euro-American 'civilization'. If the nominal Japanese depicted by Strong might in any way be construed as synonymous with such people, then the image would fundamentally undermine Meiji intellectuals' claims to 'progress' – claims embodied by the *Yamashiro-maru* itself.

Given these ambiguities, perhaps we may conclude that Native Hawaiians were not completely absent from Strong's work after all. This is important because the overlooking of Native Hawaiian history, and the marginalization of Native Hawaiian voices, were not just

---

[98] Kōno, *Nihon tōgyō hattatsu-shi*, pp. 237–8.
[99] Fukuzawa Yukichi 福沢諭吉, *Sekai kuni zukushi: Taiyōshū kan no 5, 6* 世界国盡：大洋洲巻之五六 [All the countries of the world: The Pacific] (n.p., 1871 [1869]), digitized by the National Diet Library, Japan: http://dl.ndl.go.jp/info:ndljp/pid/993094 (last accessed 8 August 2021).

discursive projects pushed with ever greater intensity by would-be colonialists in the 1880s and 1890s. They are also trends which continue in secondary scholarship: less so in histories of Hawai'i's relationship with the United States, which have begun to redress the long historical bias towards English-language sources, but rather in historical accounts of Asian immigration to the archipelago.[100] The ambiguity inherent in Strong's key protagonists – that is, the difficulty in ascribing them 'Japanese' or 'Hawaiian' characteristics, let alone 'unmistakable' ones – thus points to the historian's need to find yet more archival starting points, thereby to reframe the complex histories depicted in this painting.[101]

One alternative archive is the huge collection of nineteenth-century Hawaiian-language newspapers which have now been digitized. My own language deficiencies have precluded my taking the lead in conducting such research, but an assisted trawl of newspapers from 1885 suggested that there is much work to be done in understanding how different constituencies within Native Hawaiian society debated the inauguration of the new government-sponsored programme. In a February 1885 leader for the Honolulu-based *Ka Nupepa Kuokoa*, for example, the unknown writer begins by framing the arrival of the *City of Tokio* Japanese with reference to an earlier, much smaller migration from 1868. This was the group commonly known by its ex post facto Japanese name, the Gannenmono, referring to the 'first year' (*gan'nen* 元年) of the new Meiji regime. The Gannenmono, comprising fewer than 150 labourers, are generally considered to be a failed first experiment in mass migration, one which explains why Meiji leaders waited almost twenty more years before sanctioning a new Japanese–Hawaiian programme in 1885.[102] Yet for the *Ka Nupepa Kuokoa* author, the *City of Tokio* labourers were a

---

[100] Noelani Arista offers an overview of the changing field of Hawaiian–US research in the opening pages of *Kingdom and the Republic*, pp. 1–18. One article which does (partly) discuss Chinese immigration to Hawai'i with the help of Hawaiian-language sources is David A. Chang, 'Borderlands in a World at Sea: Concow Indians, Native Hawaiians, and South Chinese in Indigenous, Global, and National Spaces', *Journal of American History* 98, 2 (2011): 384–403.

[101] My thinking here is influenced by Linda Tuhiwai Smith's discussion of 'reframing' as 'about taking much greater control over the ways in which Indigenous issues and social problems are discussed and handled': L. Tuhiwai Smith, *Decolonizing Methodologies*, p. 175.

[102] On the Gannenmono, see Masaji Marumoto, '"First Year" Immigrants to Hawaii & Eugene van Reed', in Hilary Conroy, ed., *East Across the Pacific: Historical and Sociological Studies of Japanese Immigration and Assimilation* (Santa Barbara, CA: American Bibliographical Center–Clio Press, 1972), pp. 5–39; John van Sant, *Pacific Pioneers: Japanese Journeys to America and Hawaii, 1850–1880* (Urbana: University of Illinois Press, 2000), pp. 97–116.

reminder 'of the Japanese workers who first arrived here in Hawai'i. The uniting of these peoples with our own people was pleasant, and the generation that emerged from the mixing with Hawaiians possesses fine strength.' In other words, the arrival of more than 900 new Japanese in February 1885 was an opportunity to 'help perpetuate the population of the Hawaiian Islands, at its previous level, through intermixing with the true people of this land'.[103]

Here, then, was a vision of Japanese–Hawaiian 'intermixing' (*awiliwili*) which arguably found its visual counterpart in the faces of Strong's nominally 'Japanese' labourers. Moreover, *Ka Nupepa Kuokoa*'s hopes for the new programme grew out of its insistence that Japanese immigration was part of a well-formulated Native political agenda for the kingdom, one that would help 'the true people of this land' (*me ka lahui ponoi o ka aina nei*). Immigration was related to King Kalākaua's policy of 'increasing the nation' (*hooulu lahui*).[104] Referring to the 'carefree season of death' that continued to blight the Native population, the newspaper argued that the king, queen and all the chiefs had sought new ways to strengthen the nation:

Due to the shadow that persistently covers the Hawaiian nation and the lack of resurgence of the people proper [*lahui ponoi*], it is as if the thought to increase has grown, through mixing with those belonging to the outside. That is how we think now, upon the arrival of this new people from the islands of Japan.

Though it be a single article, the *Ka Nupepa Kuokoa* leader offers rich departure points for a reframed analysis of the government-sponsored programme. First, it suggests that the traditional historiographical view – that the main Hawaiian motivation for the programme was to address labour shortages in the sugar plantations – needs revision. Instead, the article claims that the main reason for inviting the Japanese was to repopulate the decimated Native population.[105] True, repopulation was

---

[103] 'Na Iapana [The Japanese]', *Ka Nupepa Kuokoa*, 14 February 1885, accessed through www.papakilodatabase.com (last accessed 6 March 2019). I am grateful to Ami Mulligan and Cameron Grimm, who translated this article for me under the supervision of Noelani Arista at the University of Hawai'i–Mānoa. Following the original text, I leave all diacritical markings out from the Hawaiian transliteration.

[104] See also Leah Caldeira, 'Visualizing Ho'oulu Lāhui', in Healoha Johnston, ed., *Ho'oulu Hawai'i: The King Kalākaua Era* (Honolulu: Honolulu Museum of Art, 2018), pp. 11–35.

[105] Christine Skwiot has argued, in passing, that 'a nationalist Hawaiian government sought to thwart U.S. imperial ambitions in Hawai'i by seeking assistance from Japan in revitalizing and strengthening the native people and independent Kingdom', but she provides no source evidence for this claim: Skwiot, 'Migration and the Politics of Sovereignty, Settlement, and Belonging in Hawai'i', in Donna Gabaccia and Dirk Hoerder, eds., *Connecting Seas and Ocean Rims: Indian, Atlantic, and Pacific Oceans*

not mutually exclusive with the sugar planters' needs. But historians of Japanese–Hawaiian migration should not assume that the planters' interests were synonymous with an undifferentiated Hawai'i: there were multiple different agendas at stake, including those of Native Hawaiian actors. Thus, secondly, the article calls for different protagonists to be foregrounded in the history of Japanese–Hawaiian relations from those on whom I have focused thus far. As we have seen, the *Advertiser* would state in July that 'no public man in this Kingdom has labored more assiduously to make Japanese immigration a success than His Excellency Mr. Gibson'. But such claims, according to the *Ka Nupepa Kuokoa*, were nothing less than the 'grand misidentification of the people responsible for this work'. The real protagonist of the government-sponsored programme, 'the father who sought, who strove until success', was King Kalākaua himself.

★ ★ ★

My other attempt to reframe the archival history of the *Yamashiro-maru* and its migrant passengers in 1885 was, like the Hawaiian newspaper translation project, a group effort. In 2013, a British man called Graham Corkhill contacted me out of the blue to find out more about my interest in the *Yamashiro-maru*, and eventually to offer the long-term loan of a constructor's model of the ship. Also built by Armstrong-Mitchell in 1884, the nearly two-metre-long gleaming hull, encased in glass, suddenly made it possible to understand why port newspapers in Kobe or Honolulu or later Australia so often labelled the *Yamashiro-maru* 'handsome'. Spurred by the ship's presence in Zurich, the then-director of the Johann Jacobs Museum, Roger M. Buergel, suggested we try to loan the Strong painting as well (first we needed to find it!), and some reproductions of the Arning photos, and perhaps a plantation labourer's *yukata* or two – and gradually the idea for an exhibition took shape.

Opening in February 2018, 'Ein Bild für den Kaiser' (A Painting for the Emperor) displayed Strong's painting, frame and all, in public for the first time since 1986 and for the first time out of Japan since July 1885.[106] The painting stood in one of the small museum's ground-floor rooms, accompanied by a pair of late nineteenth-century rice-straw sandals that a Japanese labourer once wore in the Hawaiian canefields. Downstairs, in

---

and China Seas Migrations from the 1830s to the 1930s (Leiden: Brill, 2011), pp. 440–63, here p. 450.

[106] 'A Painting for the Emperor: Japanese Labourers on Sugar Plantations in Hawai'i', Johann Jacobs Museum, Zurich, 8 February – 31 May 2018: http://johannjacobs.com/en/formate/a-painting-for-the-emperor/ (last accessed 8 August 2021).

(Re)framing

the basement exhibition rooms, we juxtaposed the ship model with the Arning photographs, with plantation working clothes, and with subterranean coal paintings by Yamamoto Sakubei (e.g. Figure 6.3). Roger Buergel also commissioned three contemporary artists to reflect on the themes of migration and belonging: one, Jürgen Stollhans, composed a charcoal rendering of the pier-crossing Japanese (Figure 2.2) as a wall mural. This would be, or so I hoped, a different kind of archival space in which to reflect on historical passage and landfall. We invited visitors to walk between image and text, painting and photography, song and silence; and especially between black coal and white sugar.

The exhibition was the closest I ever got to a physical manifestation of the in-between archive I have been exploring in this chapter – but there was someone still missing. And so, on a pre-planned family trip to Japan in the middle of the exhibition period, I took a day to go to Kumamoto, hired a car, and from there drove up the Ariake Sea coast to the tiny hamlet of Orisaki.

As soon as I arrived, I was struck by the folly of what had, to that point, seemed like a really good plan. Said plan was to cold-call one, or possibly all three, of the present-day Kodama households in Orisaki, households I knew existed from a land registry map I had consulted in Tokyo a few years previously. To try and delay the inevitable failure I suspected was coming my way, I first strolled around the local shrine, noting in passing the name of a Kodama Chōmei on a *torii* (ceremonial gate) dating from 1915. Following a narrow path up towards a cluster of houses, I noticed that one of the Kodama addresses had a small office annexe in its spacious garden – and before I knew it, a twinkly-eyed man in his early sixties was standing before me, turning my photos of a Hawaiian graveyard in his hands.

My name is Kodama, he says almost apologetically, and with that the cogwheels of rural Japan grind into glorious gear.[107] Within a couple of minutes, Mr Kodama has called someone I think is his brother, an older man who, though looking somewhat less enamoured, nevertheless advises that I do really need to speak to 'Fusa-chan'. And so we are off, back down the footpath past the Tenmangū shrine, to another Kodama household. There, said Fusa-chan's wife, Mrs Kodama, quickly produces a biographical dictionary from 1932 that has an entry on her father-in-law. I skim the half-page of text – this man was the first son of Kodama Chōmei, whose name I'd seen as a donor on the shrine *torii* from 1915 – while a conversation continues in the background

---

[107] I have changed some names in these paragraphs.

(a neighbour has dropped by). Yes, a long time ago there was a Kodama from this household in America and in Brazil. But was that the same person as this Kodama Keijirō who died in Hawai'i, asks Mr Kodama, reading my thoughts exactly. That's the question, Mrs Kodama says. And then they decide that there's really only one way to find out: we must drive down to the Nagasu-town municipal office and ask to inspect her husband's household register.

I feel exultant. If they were ever opened to historians, household registers would be a gold mine of information about family life and thus the decision to emigrate. But they are closed by law in order to protect private citizens from unscrupulous researchers who might – as was often the case until the 1960s – dredge up unsavoury facts about a history of family illnesses or 'outcaste' origins, and then use this information for discriminatory purposes during marriage negotiations or job applications.[108] The only way you can access the register is if a family member accompanies you in person to the relevant municipal office – and that is what Team Kodama is now doing, enthusiastically brandishing my photo of the Kapa'a gravestone and a copy of the relevant emigrant list from the Ministry of Foreign Affairs archives in Tokyo. An official listens calmly. Tall and middle-aged, she is the kindly face of Japanese bureaucracy, a woman caught between the personal desire to help us and the legal responsibilities she holds as a town employee. She has indeed found a record for someone called Kodama Keijirō, she says after returning from another room. She asks me his date of birth, and when I say sometime during the Ansei period (1854–60), she nods and says it's a match. But there's a problem: neither Mr Kodama nor Mrs Kodama are Keijirō's direct descendants, by which she means children or grandchildren. How could that be possible, I ask: surely the Kodama in Kapa'a did not have children? Indeed not, she says, but she could only release further information to direct descendants of his siblings. And so we are in a Catch-22: the Kodamas cannot access Keijirō's register because neither of them are direct descendants, but we cannot know who the direct descendants are without accessing the register. This is also the archive of the in-between: between a rock and a hard place.

A long discussion ensues, with cousins' names thrown back and forth, all suffixed with the diminutive and affectionate -*chan*. I zone out and try to read between the lines of what we have learned. It's clear that Keijirō was a second son: that much I should have known already, given that the

---

[108] For an overview of these issues, see David Chapman, 'Geographies of Self and Other: Mapping Japan through the *Koseki*', *Asia-Pacific Journal* 9, 29 (18 July 2011), https://apjjf.org/2011/9/29/David-Chapman/3565/article.html (last accessed 8 August 2021).

second character of his given name means 'two'. Thus, he would not have expected to inherit land from his father – and he did not have children. I think back to Orisaki, to a site behind the Tenmangū shrine about equidistant between the three Kodama addresses marked on the map. Even if nobody knows quite from which branch household Keijirō came, this was certainly his milieu as a boy. It's a quiet scene. At midday in early May, the month Keijirō left Japan, all I can hear are the pigeons cooing, a couple of ducks holding forth, the clatter of plates being stacked in a nearby kitchen, a child laughing. There would have been many more children back in the early 1880s, of course, and no sound of motorcars or tractors occasionally passing by. Orisaki is flat, rice-farming country: from this small rise behind the shrine, there's no mountains to see, no rice fields stretching into the distance. It's just houses and trees. To a certain type of man, the horizon might feel stultifying.

In the meantime, it has been decided that the person who should help me is a cousin in Fukuoka. Yes, he must be here in person to access the register. So Mr Kodama and Mrs Kodama debate whether it wouldn't somehow be possible to get this cousin, some 100 kilometres distant, to come and help me.

All in aid of what?, I suddenly ask myself. The possibility to read a one-line note in a household register explaining that a son called Keijirō one day left the Kodama household and never came back? Despite our wild goose chase, I have spent several unexpected hours in the company of a Mr Kodama and a Mrs Kodama, both of whom are somehow distantly related to the *Yamashiro-maru* labourer whose gravestone I encountered in Kaua'i. If that chance encounter was the beginning of an extended archival detour, then here, in rural western Kumamoto, is where the journey finally ends. While Mrs Kodama goes upstairs for a quick chat with the Nagasu-town mayor, I thank Mr Kodama and marvel aloud at the generosity one encounters in rural Japan.

'Really?' he asks. 'I don't know about Japan's good points because I've never been abroad.'

3 Outside the Archive

A Transcript

Tsutsumi Otokichi was called. He stated: – I was employed doing work on board the Yamashiro-maru. On the night of the collision I was forward beside the port bow rail. I cannot remember who was with me, but I was standing there looking. I do not know how many people were there. I remained there about half an hour. I have no idea what time it was.
THE PRESIDENT Was it daylight or had darkness set in?
WITNESS It was after darkness had set in.
THE PRESIDENT In that position, what did you see?
WITNESS I was expecting to see Yokohama.
THE PRESIDENT But what did you see?
WITNESS Nothing, but the lights of fishing boats.[1]

Tsutsumi Otokichi appears nowhere else in documents I have gathered concerning the *Yamashiro-maru*'s career. It's probable, indeed, that he would have remained a nameless actor in this history had it not been for the events of Tuesday, 21 October 1884. On a dark evening, with rain threatening – this according to the testimony of Ishikawa Shinobu, second mate to the captain[2] – the *Yamashiro-maru* ploughed at full speed into the starboard side of an iron-hulled, three-mast sailing ship, the *Sumanoura-maru* (715 tons), as the former approached the entrance to Tokyo Bay.[3] Fatally breached with a gash of up to thirty-five feet (10 m) in length, the *Sumanoura-maru* was steered into the shallow waters of nearby Kaneda Bay, where it sank without loss of life. The *Yamashiro-maru* was damaged and would be temporarily decommissioned.

That the *Sumanoura-maru* was owned by Mitsubishi – in an earlier life, as the Stockton-on-Tees-built *Bahama*, the ship had been a blockade

---

[1] *HN*, 5 November 1884.   [2] *HN*, 1 November 1884.
[3] For details of the *Sumanoura-maru*, including its cargo (which I discuss in Chapter 5), see Mitsubishi gōshi kaisha 三菱合資会社, *Mitsubishi shashi* 三菱社誌 [Mitsubishi company history], Vol. 12 (Tokyo: Mitsubishi, 1980), pp. 334–45.

runner for Confederate forces during the US Civil War[4] – only added to the drama of the collision. In the autumn of 1884, Mitsubishi was engaged in a battle almost to the death with the KUK, owners of the *Yamashiro-maru*, over which company could offer the fastest and cheapest passage between Kobe and Yokohama – the route that the *Yamashiro-maru* had been steaming on the evening of the crash.[5] For this reason, I assumed, the surviving transcript of the subsequent proceedings in the Marine Court of Inquiry, opening six days later on 27 October, would offer revealing insights into a business rivalry which had entertained the press and concerned the government in equal measure (see Figure 1.5). Indeed, the fact that the proceedings had been meticulously transcribed and printed in the Kobe-based *Hiogo News*, today preserved in the Kobe City Archives, indicated the high level of interest the case had generated among the foreign merchant community in the city.

I was wrong in those particular assumptions: little of intrigue or rivalry was revealed in the court of inquiry's transcript. But two other points did emerge from the columns and columns of tiny print. First, the source offered the rarest of brief insights into the daily lives of the ship's working crew or temporary contractors – men like Ishikawa Shinobu and Tsutsumi Otokichi respectively. Here, even in a few sentences, was a genre I had never accessed for the Wakamiyas and Kodamas of the *Yamashiro-maru*'s steerage decks, namely a mini ego-document with the first-person singular at its heart. Here lay a possibility, even momentarily, to hear beyond the 'official' voice of the ship, as would later be represented by Chief Engineer Mr Crookston when he acted as interlocutor for the *Daily Pacific Commercial Advertiser* reporter in Hawai'i (see Chapter 6).

These, for example, are the opening words spoken by one Kawashima Sukekichi, an ordinary seaman:

I have been on board the *Yamashiro* from the 16th inst. [16 October] I joined her at Yokohama. I have been only one voyage in the *Yamashiro*. I have been at sea since the 15th year of Meiji.[6]

---

[4] www.teesbuiltships.co.uk (last accessed 16 October 2017). See also Arthur Wyllie, *The Confederate States Navy* (private publication, 2007), pp. 22, 28 (last accessed through Google Books, 16 October 2017).

[5] Just six weeks before the crash, the *Yamashiro-maru* was reported to have set a new speed for the journey from Yokohama to Kobe of twenty-six hours, twenty-five minutes: *AS*, 6 September 1884. On the KUK–Mitsubishi rivalry, see Sekiguchi Kaori 関口かをり and Takeda Haruhito 武田晴人, 'Yūbinkisen Mitsubishi Kaisha to Kyōdō Un'yu Kaisha no "kyōsō" jittai ni tsuite' 郵便汽船三菱会社と共同運輸会社の「競争」実態について [On the 'competitive' state between the companies, Yūbinkisen Mitsubishi Kaisha and Kyōdō Un'yu Kaisha], *Mitsubishi Shiryōkan ronshū* 11 (2010): 13–48.

[6] *HN*, 5 November 1884. The Marine Court of Inquiry was held in the Ministry of Agriculture and Commerce.

It's not much to go on, admittedly. But we may presume from this autobiographical record that Kawashima was one of the 1,570 seamen employed by the KUK in 1883–4 through the agency of the Seafarers' Relief Association (Tokyo);[7] that he had worked for the company since its founding in 1882 (Meiji 15); and that his transfer to serve as an ordinary seaman on the *Yamashiro-maru*, then the KUK's flagship steamer, therefore marked something of a promotion in his fledgling career.

As for his actual testimony, Kawashima stated:

On the night in question I did not see either the barque [Sumanoura] or her lights. I was standing at the starboard rail forward, looking towards the sea. I did not see anything. I did not see anything after the collision, as I went aft to get the boats ready.

Such denials were to be expected: those on board the *Yamashiro-maru*, including especially the ship's captain, Mr Steedman, claimed to have seen nothing on the night of the crash. This reinforced Steedman's insistence that the fault must lie squarely with his *Sumanoura-maru* counterpart, Mr Spiegelthal, who, he claimed, had failed to properly illuminate his vessel's port and starboard lights. Whether or not Kawashima saw anything is therefore unclear; but in toeing the company line under legal caution, he was also proving himself to be a loyal employee of the KUK.

The second point which emerged from the *Hiogo News* transcript concerned the nature of record-keeping. Shorn of their courtroom context, the testimonies of Kawashima, Ishikawa or Tsutsumi offer no indication as to what language the three men were speaking. Only when we note the names of the court's officers – Mr Geo. E. O. Ramsay, Esq. (President), Captain J. F. Allen (commanding the Lighthouse Department steamship *Meiji-maru*) and Mr E. Knipping, Esq. (Meteorological Department, Tokyo) – does it become clear that the testimony of the Japanese actors had to be translated into English for the benefit of the principal players. Thus, the role of the unnamed Japanese-to-English interpreter was key to the production both of the court record and of the transcript I was reading in the English-language newspaper.

Yet the interpreting abilities of this key linguistic broker were questionable.[8] One of the principals to raise particular objections was Robert

---

[7] *Kansenkyoku dai-sanji nenpō* 管船局第三次年報 [Third annual report of the marine bureau] (1884), p. 61, available from JACAR (www.jacar.go.jp) (reference code A07062251700) (last accessed 15 May 2021).

[8] I take the language of brokerage from Simon Schaffer, Lissa Roberts, Kapil Raj, and James Delbourgo, eds., *The Brokered World: Go-Betweens and Global Intelligence, 1770–1820* (Sagamore Beach, MA: Science History Publications, 2009). According to the *Japan Weekly Mail*, translation problems at times turned the court of inquiry's proceedings 'into something very like a farce' (8 November 1884).

W. Irwin, future owner of Joseph Strong's Spreckelsville painting, who stood before the court in his capacity as foreign manager for the KUK.[9] Two years previously, Irwin's marriage to Takechi Iki had been the first non-Japanese/Japanese union to be officially recognized by the Meiji government. Irwin seems to have communicated with his wife at least partly in Japanese.[10] It was presumably on the basis of this ability that he challenged the court of inquiry's interpreter during crucial evidence from a witness who had been aboard neither the *Yamashiro-maru* nor the *Sumanoura-maru*, and who might therefore be expected to speak with a higher degree of impartiality. President Ramsay had previously ruled that the interpreter be left uninterrupted in his work, but now Irwin sought clarification:

MR. IRWIN I understood you to say at that time that you would permit a written memorandum.
THE PRESIDENT Yes, passed in silence, but I think it was arranged that there would be no interruption, because the work is very distressing to the interpreter of the Court. He does his best, and for myself I am satisfied with it.
MR. IRWIN But, take for instance, a serious question of mis-interpretation?
THE PRESIDENT Then the point will be this. I do not think any difficulty will arise; because, although this enquiry has been exhaustive, at the present day it remains in a small space. It is simply in reference to the [Sumanoura's] lights – and the lights only.[11]

The exchange is at one level banal – the type of procedural question about the admissibility of evidence played out in courts across the world and across the centuries. But that banality is exactly the point. Irwin was seeking to confirm the accuracy of the interpretation and thereby the precision of the recorded facts; together with the president and the interpreter, he was co-crafting the factual record and thus engaged in the first moment of what Michel-Rolph Trouillot terms 'the process of historical production'. This moment of fact creation, or the making of *sources*, is followed by three others, to which I shall return: fact assembly, fact retrieval, and retrospective significance – or, respectively, the making of *archives*, the making of *narratives*, and '"the making of *history*" in the final instance'.[12]

---

[9] *Japan Directory for the Year 1884* (Yokohama: Japan Gazette, 1884), p. 100.
[10] When I visited the Hawai Ōkoku Kōshi Bettei ハワイ王国公使別邸 [Villa of the minister to the kingdom of Hawai'i] in Ikaho town, Gunma prefecture, in September 2016, there was an undated letter on display from Iki to Irwin, written in phonetic katakana. This suggests Irwin's listening and speaking abilities in Japanese were better than his reading skills. On Takechi Iki, see Chapter 2.
[11] *HN*, 12 November 1884.
[12] Trouillot, *Silencing the Past*, p. 26 (emphasis in the original).

The question of interpretation was also raised at a more abstract level. In his cross-examination of Tsutsumi Otokichi, President Ramsay asked if the witness had seen any coloured light:

WITNESS I had not seen any coloured light. I did not see the form of any foreign built ship.
THE PRESIDENT Had a coloured light appeared, would you have noticed it?
WITNESS I do not know any light at all – or rather I do not know such light. Except small boats' lights I did not see any lamp lights.
THE PRESIDENT What was the colour of those small boat lights.
WITNESS All small, red lights. All the lights burning in fishing boats were small, red lights.

Thus far, the testimony reads as we might expect: Tsutsumi denied that he had seen anything resembling the green starboard light of the *Sumanoura-maru*, or indeed the looming shape of a foreign-built ship. But at this point the *Yamashiro-maru*'s captain intervenes and asks an apparently bizarre question, one which the interpreter – in a rare moment of recorded speech – feels necessary to explain:

CAPTAIN STEEDMAN Will you ascertain what is this man's idea of colour?
THE INTERPRETER You must understand that Japanese call all lights at a distance red, even though they may be only a yellowish white – not by any means scarlet.

The President tested the witness by giving him red and white scraps of paper to separate, the witness selecting the red pieces.[13]

The exchange seems tangential at best to the issue of why two ships collided.[14] But the point here is not whether 'Japanese' *did* actually perceive colours differently;[15] rather, it's that the court's president found a quick way to dismiss the 'idea of colour' as an explanatory factor in Tsutsumi's testimony. If, for the purposes of a thought experiment, we were to consider this 'idea' an example of Indigenous knowledge, then the court transcript records a process in which such knowledge was measured against an apparently objective scale – red and white scraps of paper – and then made to be commensurate.[16] That is, 'red' was

---

[13] *HN*, 5 November 1884.
[14] The court of inquiry eventually found against the *Yamashiro-maru*'s captain, and KUK was forced to pay a fine of 20,000 yen to Mitsubishi: Mitsubishi gōshi kaisha, *Mitsubishi shashi*, Vol. 12, pp. 344–5.
[15] On the significance of blue and red in mid nineteenth-century Japan, see Henry D. Smith II, 'Hokusai and the Blue Revolution in Edo Prints', in John T. Carpenter (ed.), *Hokusai and His Age: Ukiyo-e Painting, Printmaking, and Book Illustration in Late Edo Japan* (Amsterdam: Hotei Publishing, 2005), pp. 234–69.
[16] Wendy Nelson Espeland and Mitchell L. Stevens, 'Commensuration as a Social Process', *Annual Review of Sociology* 24 (1998): 313–43.

defined according to the standardized norms of an English-language courtroom, such that the nuances both of the vernacular language and of vernacular ways of seeing were edged out of the historical record. The witness himself, in being forced to make a binary choice in silence, was rendered voiceless.

In this chapter, I explore such edges of the historical record, and the silences produced in their recording. I question the commensurability of apparently similar concepts across very different historiographical contexts. I try to interpret from scraps of paper. But most of all, I am interested in the view and the sounds of the outside – in what can be seen from the bow rails, and what historians might miss in the archival dark.

Outside (1): Hawai'i State Archives

The retrieval of facts from the archive, or what Trouillot calls the third moment of silences entering the production of history, demands a level of scholarly alertness that is sometimes difficult to maintain while battling jetlag. Such, at least, was my experience during a two-week stay in Hawai'i in March 2013. On this particularly somnolent Friday morning, I am trying to retrieve more facts about how plantation life may have been experienced by the labourers themselves. I have a hunch that the career of a man called Fuyuki Sakazō may help me in this endeavour.[17] Fuyuki – he of my initial trip to Kapa'a (Chapter 1) – left for Hawai'i on the government-sponsored programme's ninth crossing, in September 1889. As I begin to size up his life, I would like to imagine him standing on the *Yamashiro-maru*'s forward decks, looking towards the open seas as his pre-migration life receded into the distance. Ideally, though, I would like to do more than imagine: I am here in the Hawai'i State Archives looking for any scraps of paper which might figuratively reveal his own 'idea of colour', his own way of seeing his new world. But, once again, the only traces I can find have been authored by the bureaucrats, the agents, the inspectors.

I have on the desk yet another handwritten letter from Robert W. Irwin. This one, marked 'confidential', is dated 8 May 1890 and addressed to Interior Minister Lorrin A. Thurston (1858–1931). Irwin begins by reporting on the incoming Japanese government's seemingly perennial complaint about the categorizations of East Asia labourers: 'the new men [that is, ministers] have formed the opinion that there is a

---

[17] Fuyuki is a pseudonym, for reasons I shall later explain.

tendency in Hawaii to treat the Japanese from a Chinese standpoint, and to class Japanese and Chinese together'.[18] He cites the new Hawaiian Constitution of 1887 (the so-called Bayonet Constitution, forced upon King Kalākaua by Thurston and others) as an object of Tokyo's concern, in particular the articles limiting the suffrage to male residents 'of Hawaiian, American or European birth or descent'.[19] He describes the 'soreness' of some officials 'over the exclusion of the Japanese from the [Hawaiian] electoral franchise', and his worry that this might negatively affect the emigration programme. In other words, Irwin argues that the Bayonet Constitution's bracketing of Japanese and Chinese as equally ineligible for the franchise (and thus, by implication, equally uncivilized) might provoke the Meiji government into reviewing a programme which Irwin took to be self-evidently in Hawai'i's interests. But then he closes on an optimistic note – albeit with a comically awkward turn of phrase: 'I believe that I can take care of this political question and can have it postponed; and considered hereafter upon it's [sic] own merits; leaving the emigration a purely industrial question to stand upon it's [sic] own bottom.'[20]

Grateful to have been jolted from my torpor by anything remotely scatological, I make a pencilled note of an adjective I have now seen more than once in the context of Japanese migration, namely *industrial*. The 'industrial partnership' hailed by the *Daily Pacific Commercial Advertiser* in July 1885 flickers at the back of my mind, as does a proprietary claim Irwin would make in 1893, when, in the wake of the Hawaiian monarchy's overthrow, he called the government-sponsored programme 'our great industrial Emigration Convention'.[21] On the one hand, the word gives historians a sense of the scale of Irwin's and the planters' ambition, namely that sugar would transform Hawai'i as it already had the Caribbean islands. (While on this trip, I have been reading Sidney Mintz's *Sweetness and Power*, with its description of the Caribbean sugar plantation as 'an industrial enterprise'.)[22] But when set alongside the history of the Hawai'i-bound emigrants from Japan, the adjective 'industrial' also offers a different perspective on a long-running historiographical debate about the so-called preparedness of the mid

---

[18] For a similar articulation, from San Francisco in 1890, see Azuma, *In Search of Our Frontier*, p. 44.
[19] The relevant articles were 59 and 62; for the constitution in full, see *HG*, 7 July 1887.
[20] HSA Interior Box 16, Irwin Correspondence 1890.
[21] *PCA*, 8 July 1885 (see Chapter 2); HSA FO&EX Box 404-16-253e, Letter from Robert W. Irwin to Sanford B. Dole, 27 April 1893.
[22] Sidney W. Mintz, *Sweetness and Power: The Place of Sugar in Modern History* (New York: Viking, 1985), p. 50.

nineteenth-century Japanese economy for the country's subsequent industrialization.

One key argument, articulated in a 1969 essay by Thomas C. Smith (1916–2004), focused on the 'readying' of the rural population for the transition from agriculture to industry through the practice of part-time, non-agricultural work. The essay began:

> By-employments, one may suppose, tend to ready preindustrial people for modern economic roles since they represent an incipient shift from agriculture to other occupations, spread skills useful to industrialization among the most backward and numerous part of the population, and stimulate ambition and geographical mobility.[23]

To flesh out these general observations, Smith offered a granular study of one 'county' (*saiban* 宰判) in the south-east of the Chōshū domain, itself located just west of Hiroshima and today known as Yamaguchi prefecture. Based on an extraordinary economic survey conducted by domain officials in 1842, Smith identified Kaminoseki county as having been characterized by a particularly high level of by-employments, ranging from salt-making in Hirao village to the income-generating opportunities offered by the marine transportation industry in Befu village. Meanwhile, in the eponymous port-town of Kaminoseki, where the Inland Sea narrows to a fast-flowing corridor around 100 metres in breadth, trade accounted for a very high proportion of non-agricultural income, and the same was true on the opposite side of the Kaminoseki straits in the port-town of Murotsu.

When, at the beginning of my doctoral studies, I had first read Smith's essay, my interest had been spurred by the coincidence of my having worked and lived in what is today Kaminoseki town – that is, Kaminoseki and Murotsu ports, plus some outlying villages and islands. The town's obvious late twentieth-century stagnation spoke to one general critique of Smith's speculative 'connection between the development of by-employments in the eighteenth century and modern economic growth' – namely, that there was often no straight line connecting proto-industrial growth with industrial growth.[24] Perhaps, in general terms, an argument could indeed be made that 'Japan's industrial labor force expanded in

---

[23] Thomas C. Smith, 'Farm Family By-Employments in Preindustrial Japan', *Journal of Economic History* 29, 4 (1969): 687–715, here p. 687.

[24] T. C. Smith, 'Farm Family By-Employments', p. 711. Later scholars abandoned the teleological language of *pre*-industrial in favour of *proto*-industrial, partly in order to make exactly this critique: see Kären Wigen, *The Making of a Japanese Periphery, 1750–1920* (Berkeley: University of California Press, 1995), and Pratt, *Japan's Protoindustrial Elite*. On the application of 'proto-industrialization' from European to Japanese historiography, see David L. Howell, 'Proto-Industrial Origins of Japanese Capitalism', *Journal of Asian Studies* 51, 2 (1992): 269–86.

large part by the recruitment of workers from farm families who, thanks to by-employments, brought to their new employment usable crafts, clerical skills, and even managerial skills'; but this wasn't the story in the shrinking villages and towns of Kaminoseki county itself.[25]

Moreover, Smith's hypothesis that by-employments stimulated 'ambition and geographical mobility' focused only on the phenomenon of domestic migration within Japan. It thus overlooked the most interesting aspect of Kaminoseki's late nineteenth-century history, namely overseas migration on an extraordinary scale. And this, in short, was why I was engaged in a soporific search for any details which might facilitate a basic narration of Fuyuki Sakazō's life. That Fuyuki came from Murotsu, in the same Kaminoseki county studied by Smith, suggested that his employment history, spanning Japan and Hawai'i, might offer new insights into the hitherto understudied transpacific dimension of Japan's emerging transition from agriculture to industry across the nineteenth and early twentieth centuries. I hadn't yet articulated it in this way, but on that slow morning in the state archives, these were a few of the thought associations provoked by the adjective 'industrial'.

Abruptly, my daydreaming is broken by brass chords and the voice of a female singer. Looking up from Irwin and Thurston and bottoms, I remember that on Friday lunchtimes the Royal Hawaiian Band performs for tourists.[26] So I down tools, leave the archives' air-conditioned reading room for the warmth of an overcast day, and stroll past the rear of 'Iolani Palace to where the musicians are playing.

The band's members, all in white, are arrayed under the canopy of a great monkeypod tree, while around seventy tourists, mostly middle-aged and dressed in shorts and tucked-in T-shirts, sit on metal fold-up chairs. After a set or two the MC, a Native Hawaiian man wearing a scarlet Aloha shirt, again takes to the microphone to explain that the next song dates from the very darkest chapter of Hawaiian history. The overthrow of the Hawaiian monarchy in January 1893, he says, was plotted by the sons of missionaries with the connivance of the then-US minister. Deprived of their queen, their land, their very nationhood, the Hawaiian people protested, and in that moment of protest, the composer Eleanor Kekoaohiwaikalani Wright Prendergast (1865–1902) wrote 'Kaulana Nā Pua' for the Royal Hawaiian Band sitting here today. The band, which the leaders of the coup tried to disband, had refused to be cowed, and so the very playing of Prendergast's song constituted an act of resistance.

---

[25] T. C. Smith, 'Farm Family By-Employments', p. 712.
[26] I attended the Royal Hawaiian Band's lunchtime concert on 15 March 2013.

Kaulana nā pua aʻo Hawaiʻi
Kūpaʻa mahope o ka ʻāina
Hiki mai ka ʻelele o ka loko ʻino
Palapala ʻānunu me ka pākaha ...

I don't have a translation of Prendergast's song to hand. I will find one later that evening, in Haunani-Kay Trask's essay, 'From a Native Daughter':

> Famous are the children of Hawaiʻi
> Who cling steadfastly to the land.
> Comes the evil-hearted with
> A document greedy for plunder.[27]

But as the singer begins to perform, a man in the audience quietly rises to his feet, doffs his cap and holds it to his chest. Standing behind him, I cannot see what his gesture may represent – regret? an apology? a sign of respect? – but I find it unexpectedly moving.

Walking back to the state archives past great banyan trees re-rooting themselves into the land, I am unsure whether and to what extent a migrant labourer such as Fuyuki Sakazō might be pertinent to this history of monarchical overthrow. That he may have been imbricated in the historical context was implied by the May 1890 letter still on my desk: Fuyuki was one of thousands recruited by Irwin; Irwin was selling the emigration programme to Thurston as in the interests of the Hawaiian government; and Thurston, in addition to having agitated for the imposition of the 1887 Bayonet Constitution, would also be a rebel ringleader during the 1893 coup.

In the meantime, the act of leaving my desk to hear a song had revealed something more fundamental about historical production. The traditional 'sound of the archive', as Wolfgang Ernst has suggested, is silence – an absence of voices, a negative sound which conversely becomes part of the archive. The scribbling pencil, the nasal snort, the rustle of turning pages: these para-archival elements may be taken to constitute what he calls the reading room's 'sonosphere'.[28] There are no songs in this sonosphere. Yet the melodies of the Royal Hawaiian Band drifting in from outside highlighted an act of exclusion embodied in the archive. Here, in the enveloping quiet, I could retrieve facts which helped

---

[27] Haunani-Kay Trask, *From a Native Daughter: Colonialism and Sovereignty in Hawaii* (Honolulu: University of Hawaiʻi Press, 1999 [1993]), pp. 118–20.

[28] Wolfgang Ernst, 'History or Resonance? Techno-Sonic Tempor(e)alities', *Journal of Visual Culture* 14, 1 (2015): 99–110. On silence in the archives, see also Farge, *Allure of the Archives*, pp. 53–78.

me reconstruct Irwin's narrative of the world: *his* idea of plantation labour as an 'industrial' project, for example. But if I could not do the same for Fuyuki, this was because I was looking in the wrong place, hindered by the second moment in Trouillot's analysis of historical production, namely the moment of fact assembly (or the making of *archives*).[29] Of course there would be nothing revealing of Fuyuki's worldview here. The narrative colours were predefined by the agendas of the actors I was reading: actors who spoke to and for Fuyuki, thus rendering the migrants' choices and decisions silent.

To make amends for the gaps in the particular fact assembly that had given rise to this set of records on my desk, I would figuratively have to step outside: not to abandon the written records per se, but to read them according to a different set of definitions, ones articulated by the labourers themselves. Inspired by the genre if not at that point the meanings of Prendergast's composition, I decided to look in more detail at the words which the plantation labourers sang in their transplanted work songs from western Japan. The canefield songs, I shall argue in this chapter, did more than express the workers' frustrations, their shattered expectations, their wry observations on conditions at individual plantations such as Spreckelsville. They also voiced a vernacular worldview no less significant to historians' understanding of nineteenth-century economic transformations than Robert W. Irwin's (or, indeed, Thomas C. Smith's) understanding of 'industry'. In particular, two images in the lyrics – the human body and the idea of circulation, itself a pregnant but understudied metaphor for global historians[30] – spoke to the intellectual and physical landscapes from which a migrant like Fuyuki Sakazō had departed. Stacking up a series of meanings associated with the term 'circulation' in nineteenth-century Japan, I ask how these landscapes, or more accurately seascapes, shaped Fuyuki's understanding of labour.[31] How might he have conceptualized his own place in a world of circulating goods, ideas and people? And how might historians interpret up from these scraps of songs to frame the historiographies of 'industry' and the related term of 'industriousness' in new ways?

---

[29] Trouillot, *Silencing the Past*, p. 26.
[30] Kapil Raj, 'Beyond Postcolonialism ... and Postpositivism: Circulation and the Global History of Science', *Isis* 103 (2013): 337–47; Stefanie Gänger, 'Circulation: Reflections on Circularity, Entity, and Liquidity in the Language of Global History', *Journal of Global History* 12, 3 (2017): 303–18.
[31] On the practice of *helu*, or the stacking and listing of words in order to produce a web of meaning in the Hawaiian language, see Arista, *Kingdom and the Republic*, pp. 15, 232.

To answer these questions, I must shortly depart the *Yamashiro-maru*. Without the ship sailing transpacific sea lanes, Fuyuki's career would have been impossible. But to make sense of that career, we need other sounds, other sources, and other archival starting points.

Labouring Bodies in Circulation

Following the *Yamashiro-maru*'s initial passage to Hawai'i in 1885, the ship did not return to the kingdom for another four years. Instead, after the KUK and Mitsubishi merged to become the Nippon Yūsen Kaisha (NYK) in October 1885, it ran the more profitable Kobe–Yokohama line – during which time it sped the young Yanagita Kunio off to his adult life (see Preface). Only in September 1889 did the ship resume carrying migrants on the government-sponsored programme. Over the next three years, it crossed to Honolulu eleven times in total, transporting more outgoing Japanese than any other NYK vessel. On the passage back from Hawai'i, too, the NYK ships carried Japanese labourers, though in lower numbers. These were men and women who had either completed their three-year contract or who were returning to Japan after a second plantation contract. Included in the latter group was Wakamiya Yaichi, who departed Honolulu on the *Yamashiro-maru* for his home village of Jigozen, Hiroshima prefecture, on 6 December 1892.[32]

By that time, some of the work melodies from the migrants' pre-Hawaiian lives had become part of the plantation soundscape. Reaching their hands into the cane plant's one-to-two metre long, painfully sharp leaves (*holehole* in Hawaiian) to pick out dead matter, the labourers kept their spirits up with songs (*bushi* in Japanese). Like the largest number of government-sponsored migrants, the melodies of these *holehole bushi* ホレホレ節 came from Hiroshima, perhaps from the songs that farmers sang as they hulled rice.[33] By contrast, the lyrics grew out of the labourers' new lives on the islands and expressed the full gamut of emotions about the plantations' often lamentable working conditions – punning, for example, on the words for cane (*kibi*) and harsh (*kibishii*).[34] One such first-generation *holehole bushi* reads:

---

[32] DA 3.8.2.5–13, Vol. 1. Wakamiya was one of thirty-six original *Yamashiro-maru* migrants who returned to Japan in 1892: DA 2.8.2.5–5 (thirty-four men and two women).

[33] Odo, *Voices from the Canefields*, pp. xx–xxii: the genre of song is *momisuri-uta* 籾摺り歌.

[34] Fujii Shūgorō 藤井秀五郎, *Shin Hawai* 新布哇 [New Hawai'i] (Tokyo: Taiheikan, 1900), p. 644: digitized by the National Diet Library (https://dl.ndl.go.jp/info:ndljp/pid/767370).

Ikkai, nikai de yō –	After one or two contracts
Kaeranu yatsu wa	The poor bastards who don't go home
Sue wa Hawai no	End up in Hawai'i
Kibi no koe	Fertilizer for the sugar cane.[35]

Here punning on the homonym *koe*, the song's last line can mean '*fertilizer* for the cane' but also '*voices* of the cane [fields]'. The singer thus articulates a fear that they will die without ever returning to Japan, and that their body will end up as fertilizer, their voice silent in the earth. And yet, the words were performed, not read: depending on speed, gesture and other paralingual elements in harmony with the music, they could be humorous, regretful, salutary or angry. Whichever way, to sing was to defy the fate of silence.

As these lyrics demonstrate, the labouring body offered migrants one framework for interpreting their Hawaiian experiences. Here, the meanings were rendered especially earthy by the fact that *koe* refers to night soil – to fields fertilized by human urine and faeces. Such a relationship between the body and work appears in another *holehole bushi* sung in the 1890s and published by a Hawaiian-based Japanese journalist in 1900:

Kibi wa furomu de	The cane drifts down the flume
Mīru e nagare	To the mill.
Wagami wa doko e	As for my body –
Nagaru yara	Where will it drift?[36]

Here the key word is 'drift' (*nagaru* 流る), a character whose left-hand radical denotes water. The meanings of *nagaru* range from 'flow', to 'pour' (including the transitives, *namida o nagasu*, literally 'to pour tears', or *ase o nagasu*, 'to pour sweat'), to – in combination with other characters – 'current' or 'circulation'. And it is in this imagination of the circulating, drifting, sweating and even crying body that we can posit one vernacular interpretation for how migrant labourers crossing from Japan to Hawai'i might have imagined their place in the world.[37]

In fact, the relationship between work and circulation in mid nineteenth-century Japan had been visualized a generation prior to the

---

[35] Odo, *Voices from the Canefields*, p. 87.

[36] Odo, *Voices from the Canefields*, p. 84. This is a *dodoitsu* poem (in a 7-7-7-5 syllable pattern), printed in Fujii, *Shin Hawai*, p. 643. I follow Fujii's transcription rather than Odo's (which has the particle *ni* in the second line). *Wagami* わが身 is usually translated 'myself', but Odo's rendering brings to the fore its corporeal sense.

[37] See, for example: 'Hawai'i, Hawai'i / I came, chasing a dream / Now my tears flow (*nagasu namida* 流す涙) / In the cane field'. Or 'Drained so much sweat (*Ase o nagashite* 汗を流して) / For this bounty / Today we cut the cane / Time to celebrate': Odo, *Voices from the Canefields*, pp. 84, 88.

government-sponsored programme in a popular woodblock print by Utagawa Kunisada 歌川国貞 (1786–1864). Entitled 'Rules of Dietary Life', it depicted a portly, seated man in cross-section, thus offering the viewer a glimpse of the body's internal organs at work (see Figure 3.1).[38] And work was the operative term. In the print, dozens of miniature male labourers, dressed in blue uniforms, busy themselves stoking the fires under the spleen's huge cooking pot, or shovelling mushy food into wooden barrels which they then carry from the warehouse of the stomach to the millstone of the liver. As they work, they chat in a patois that the print visualizes in the native hiragana script, in contrast to the more formal medical explanations written in Chinese characters. Parallel to the oesophagus, for example, four labourers are waving huge fans marked with the character 'breath' in order to aerate the lungs. One, bent exhausted over his fan, complains to his co-worker that he is at breaking point. His observation puns on the word *hone*, referring both to the fan's ribs and to the labourers' own bones:

'I'm beat! Shouldn't we take a short break?'

'Let's keep giving it our best,' his co-worker says, punning once more on *hone* by using the idiom 'great effort' (*hone oru* 骨折る), 'and *then* we can rest.'

In the body's other lung, two colleagues, still fanning with all their might, grumble to each other, 'What're we gonna do if this guy doesn't work?'

As if nineteenth-century Oompa Loompas in the body's astonishing factory, the four men know that theirs is part of a bigger effort. If they do not work, the heart will not pump; if the heart does not pump, the food will not circulate; if the food does not circulate, the body will not function. Thus, circulation was key to good health, as Japanese doctors had begun to argue from the late seventeenth century onwards. This belief was a departure from Chinese medicine, which maintained that poor health was caused by depletion of vitality (Ch. *qi*, Jp. *ki* 気) from the body, and that such depletions could be minimized by avoiding wasteful effort. Instead, as Shigehisa Kuriyama has argued, Japanese doctors came to see the problem of ill health not in terms of depletion *from* the body but rather the stagnation of vitality *in* the body. Stagnated vitality, in the form of impeded internal circulation, would cause 'congestions, congelations, accumulations, hardenings, knots'.[39]

---

[38] The print was one half of a pair by Utagawa: the other, depicting a smoking woman similarly dissected and worked upon by internal female labourers, was entitled 'Rules of Sexual Life' (*Bōji yōjō kagami* 房事養生鑑).

[39] Shigehisa Kuriyama, 'The Historical Origins of Katakori', *Japan Review* 9 (1997): 127–49, here pp. 131–2.

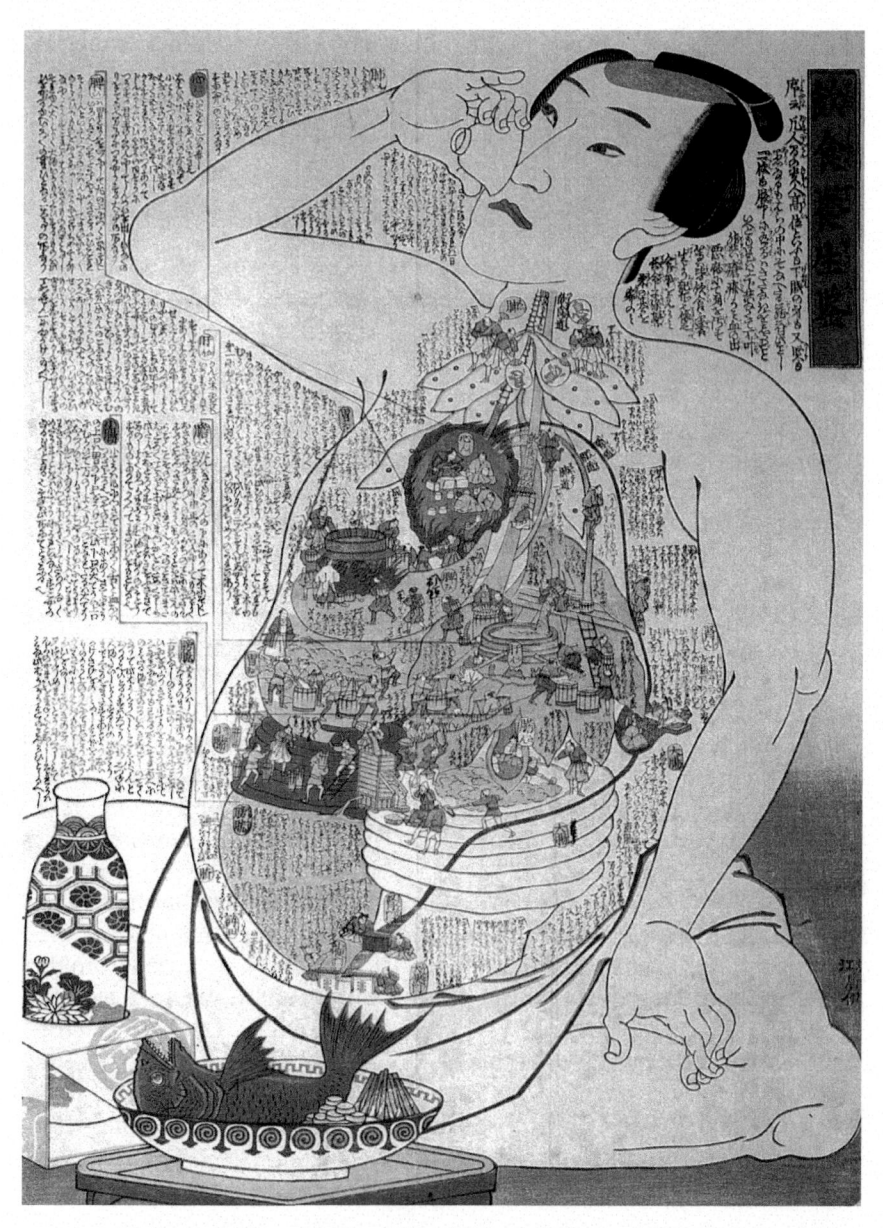

Figure 3.1 Utagawa Kunisada, 'Rules of Dietary Life' (*Inshoku yōjō kagami* 飲食養生鑑), c. 1850. Courtesy of University of California San Francisco (UCSF) Archives and Special Collections.

What was true of the corporeal realm applied also to the economic. In *Principles for Nourishing Life* (*Yōjō kun* 養生訓, 1713), the Confucian scholar Kaibara Ekiken 貝原益軒 (1630–1714) had argued that the stagnation of wealth was to be avoided at all costs:

> If the flow of material force (*ki*) through heaven and earth is stopped up, abnormalities arise, causing natural disasters such as violent windstorms, floods and droughts, and earthquakes. If the things of the world are long collected together, such stoppage is inevitable. In humans, if the blood, vital ether (*ki*), food and drink do not circulate and flow, the result is disease. Likewise, if vast material wealth is collected in one place and not permitted to benefit and enrich others, disaster will strike later.[40]

By the mid nineteenth century, this idea that collection would lead to disaster was commonplace. In the aftermath of the Ansei Edo earthquake (1855), for example, one popular print depicted an unsympathetic catfish – long a symbol of seismic activity in Japan – forcing a merchant to vomit gold coins onto gleeful labourers gathered below him.[41] The print was a visualization of Kaibara Ekiken's broader argument within the specific context of the shogun's capital: stagnated flow, or the Edo merchants' unnatural hoarding of money, had caused a natural disaster.[42] Other intellectuals in late-Tokugawa Japan similarly made the case for the relationship between circulation and economic health. The words used for 'circulation' differed by author, but the reasoning was always the same: the flow of money generated by commerce was as important to economic prosperity as the flow of blood to human well-being.[43]

---

[40] Cited in Mark Metzler and Gregory Smits, 'Introduction: The Autonomy of Market Activity and the Emergence of Keizai Thought', in Bettina Gramlich-Oka and Gregory Smits, eds., *Economic Thought in Early Modern Japan* (Leiden: Brill, 2010), pp. 1–19, here p. 14.

[41] See Gregory Smits, *Seismic Japan: The Long History and Continuing Legacy of the Ansei Edo Earthquake* (Honolulu: University of Hawai'i Press, 2013), p. 23.

[42] Here, we may also consider the medical vocabulary of 'panic' and 'depression' being applied to economic crises in Europe in the same period: see Daniele Besomi, 'Crises as a Disease of the Body Politick: A Metaphor in the History of Nineteenth-Century Economics', *Journal of the History of Economic Thought* 33, 1 (2011): 67–118.

[43] In *Admonitions Regarding Food Consumption* (*Hoju shokuji kai* 保寿食事戒, 1815), Takai Ranzan 高井蘭山 wrote of circulation (of blood, *ki*, and food) using *shūryū* 周流: see Michael Kinski, 'Admonitions Regarding Food Consumption', *Japonica Humboldtiana* 7 (2003): 123–78, here p. 167. In the economic sphere, Ogyū Sorai 荻生徂徠 (1666–1728) spoke in *Master Sorai's Teachings* (*Sorai-sensei tōmonsho* 徂徠先生答問書, 1724) of *ryūtsū* 流通: see Samuel Hideo Yamashita, *Master Sorai's Responsals: An Annotated Translation of Sorai Sensei Tomonsho* (Honolulu: University of Hawai'i Press, 1994). In the same decade, Yamashita Kōnai 山下幸内 wrote of *yūzū* 融通 to describe the importance of money circulating (my thanks to David Mervart for this reference), a term used also by Osaka financier Kusama Naokata 草間直方 (1753–1831) (see Metzler and Smits, 'Introduction', p. 15). Scholars of Tokugawa Japan echo these associations in their

This association of flowing commerce with economic prosperity would have made good sense to anyone growing up in Fuyuki's home town of Murotsu.[44] Located in the south-eastern tip of the Chōshū domain, Murotsu was a key regional port by the 1840s – second in importance only to Kaminoseki, on the other side of the straits. Murotsu's importance and success were reflected in the occupational and income profile of its households. In what Chōshū administrators termed the 'port district' (*ura-kata* 浦方), there were 228 households in 1842, almost double the number from the mid eighteenth century. Ninety-eight per cent of these port households were non-farmers and the district's reported income was entirely non-agricultural. Thus, to an even greater extent than in Wakamiya Yaichi's home town of Jigozen, a day's sail further east, the residents of Murotsu's port district made their money not from farming-related activities but rather from the growing importance of interregional trade in mid–late Tokugawa Japan (trade accounted for 72 per cent of the port-district's reported income). Located on the Inland Sea's main east–west shipping route, Murotsu's port district was where the richest and most politically powerful merchant households were located: where most houses boasted the status-symbol of a tiled roof, and where the most successful wholesalers enjoyed privileges normally reserved for the samurai, including surnames and walled gardens.

At the heart of these merchants' activities was a complex money-making system that depended on both collection and circulation. Suppose, in 1842, that you were the captain and owner of a small cargo ship sailing eastwards through the Inland Sea. Your ship carries up to 1,000 *koku* (approximately 5,000 bushels) of newly harvested rice from your home domain of Kaga, in north-east Japan – a cargo which you have purchased on the Kaga market for x silver *monme*, and which you therefore want to sell at profit in Osaka. You have arrived in the Kaminoseki straits after a long day's sail from Shimonoseki,[45] and you anchor at Murotsu to stock up on fresh water. When a rowboat from one of the port's teahouses draws up alongside your ship, some of your

---

descriptions of, for example, water routes constituting 'the true arteries of the circulation system', or 'the towns, roads, and seaways [being] the nodes and arteries of economic life': see, respectively, Wigen, *Making of a Japanese Periphery*, p. 33, and Andrew Gordon, *A Modern History of Japan: From Tokugawa Times to the Present*, 3rd edn (Oxford: Oxford University Press, 2014), p. 27.

[44] The following paragraphs are a reworking of Dusinberre, *Hard Times in the Hometown*, pp. 20–36.

[45] Shimonoseki 下関 literally means 'lower gate' and Kaminoseki 上関 'upper gate', referring to their older functions as customs posts (*sekisho* 関所) on the Inland Sea trading routes. There was a Nakanoseki 中関 (middle gate) too, otherwise known as Mitajiri 三田尻.

six-strong crew hop in, planning to spend a night carousing with the establishment's young women (and occasional young men).

But the next morning, the strong westerlies which hastened the previous day's passage from Shimonoseki have turned into an easterly breeze. With such a headwind, it will be impossible to tack against the tidal currents rushing through the straits. So you summon one of the many rowboats milling around in the port – here and in Kaminoseki, there are more than 100 cargo ships at overnight anchor, to which the rowboats hawk their business – and go ashore to pay a courtesy call to one of Murotsu's most important merchant dynasties, the Yoshida household. (Unlike you, they carry a surname.) As you step off the sturdy stone dock, you fall into conversation with a fellow captain waiting for a rowboat back to his ship. He is making haste for departure, wanting to use the easterly to sail towards Shimonoseki. He was in Osaka ten days ago, he says, and the price of rice was dropping like a stone in an empty well. Perhaps it will have recovered by the time you arrive in approximately a week – depending on the winds – but perhaps it will continue to fall. If it drops anything below *x monme*, you'll be carrying a loss-making cargo and have no capital to buy the tea and sugar you intended to ship back for sale in Kaga.

So when you enter the Yoshida grounds – there is a roofed gate in the wall that surrounds the property – you have a deal on your mind. Crossing the Yoshida's small but immaculate garden, you pass a two-storey warehouse where servants are stacking small barrels of sake and soy sauce. In the reception room of the household's large main building, you are greeted by eighth-generation household head Yoshida Bunnoshin, and you begin a formal negotiation.[46] He offers to store your potentially loss-making cargo and sell it on commission; you prefer him to buy the rice outright. He haggles down the price before agreeing, and he summons more servants to prepare the unloading of your ship. In the meantime, he suggests you partake of lunch together – bream, rice, *wakame* soup, pickled plums all the way from the Kii peninsula. Sated, you drop into a bathhouse on the way back to the waterfront for a scrub

---

[46] The Yoshida household, thought to have been built at the beginning of the nineteenth century, survives in the Shōtōen museum 松濤園 in Shimo-Kamagari, Kure city, Hiroshima prefecture. Yoshida Bunnoshin 吉田文之進 (? – 1862) became household head upon the death of his adoptive father, Kisuke 喜助, in 1834. Kisuke, for his part, devoted himself to infrastructural investment in order to improve the port-district's shipping facilities, including the building of a stone dock which lasted until the first decades of the twentieth century: Shibamura Keijirō 芝村敬次郎, *Yamaguchi-ken Kaminoseki Yoshida-ke shiryō to Yoshida-shi* 山口県上関吉田家資料と吉田氏 [The Yoshidas and the Yoshida household of Kaminoseki, Yamaguchi prefecture] (Hiroshima: Shimo-Kamagari-chō, 2000), p. 101.

and a soak. You will be up early tomorrow to buy an alternative cargo for transportation to the Osaka markets (Yoshida has made a couple of suggestions, based on intelligence passing through the port); but perhaps tonight you might also visit a teahouse.

Fundamentally, the port economy reconstructed here depended on circulation: of goods, information, money, and naturally the ships that channelled these things. Contrary to a popular stereotype of staid village life, Murotsu and other Inland Sea ports were worlds constantly in flux. But such circulation would have been impossible without the constant heartbeat of labour. The captain's transactions alone depended on the manual labour (in order of previous appearance) of the water carriers, the rowboat oarsmen, the teahouse women, the stevedores, the servants, the fishermen, the cooks, the bathhouse maids and the wood cutters – and this was for just one of hundreds of daily interactions between port residents and visiting ships. To borrow the lexicon of Utagawa Kunisada, such workers were the fanners, the stokers, the shovellers and the millers through which circulation was enabled; to borrow the lexicon of the 2010s and 2020s, they were the labourers in a gig economy.

But these men and women did not – could not – live among the established denizens of the port district itself. Instead, many of them lived in what Chōshū administrators termed the 'inland district' (*jikata* 地方), which included both the port's hillside suburbs and also farming hamlets located several kilometres up the Murotsu peninsula. These were poorer communities, where the cost of living was cheaper. In terms of reported income in 1842, that of the inland district constituted only a third of the port's, while the houses here were smaller and only had thatched roofs. Yet between the 1730s and the 1840s, the number of households in this district almost quadrupled, to 232. Most significantly, 88 per cent of these households owned no land – an even higher percentage than in Wakamiya's home village of Jigozen (see Chapter 2).

Such a demographic transformation in Murotsu's poorer, inland districts only makes sense if we assume that the port acted as an economic magnet for the region as a whole. That is, the quadrupling of inland district households, which outstripped the accompanying population increase in the same period,[47] suggests that there was considerable inward migration from the mid eighteenth to the mid nineteenth centuries. If you felt moved to establish a new household in Murotsu's inland district during this period, you were unlikely to be acting on the prospect

---

[47] The population itself rose from 350 to 1,190 people between the 1730s and the 1840s.

of empty farm land waiting to be exploited. Instead, you were probably planning to engage in subsistence farming and otherwise earn cash by working in the port – as a carrier or oarsman or stevedore.[48] And if you didn't own land, then so be it: your port-based by-employment would hopefully offer your household enough security.

This was something like the world into which Fuyuki Sakazō was born, in approximately 1868. Although the Fuyuki address later listed in the Japanese Ministry of Foreign Affairs paperwork is impossible to trace to an exact street, his inland district household would have lain in walking distance of the port district. Most likely, the port's prosperity would therefore have generated by-employments for the household's previous generations – even if, on paper, Fuyuki's ancestors were classified as 'farmers' (*nōnin* 農人).[49]

But by Fuyuki's teenage years, the types of circulations on which the port economy depended had been profoundly disrupted: first by Japan's reengagement with international trade in the late 1850s; then by the transformations to domestic trade which accompanied the Meiji revolution and the subsequent abolition of the domains;[50] and, perhaps most importantly, by the gradual introduction, after 1872, of the telegraph to Japan. This is because the instantaneous communication of price information across the national realm rendered obsolete the system of regional price betting on which merchant households such as the Yoshida made their money. The shippers might still come to port – although with the eventual introduction of steam technology to the Inland Sea routes, even this was no longer a given, as winds and tides would no longer delay speed-conscious captains. But if there were no longer demand either for transactions involving unknown price differentials or for the storage of commodities in transit, then there were consequently fewer profits for the merchants to make. Such were the factors

---

[48] This is an oversimplification of a complex and much debated transformation in the wider Tokugawa economy. On the relationship between rural industry and population increase, see Osamu Saito, 'Population and the Peasant Family Economy in Proto-industrial Japan', *Journal of Family History* 8 (1983): 30–54.
[49] For Fuyuki's listed address at the time he first emigrated to Hawai'i: DA 3.8.2.5–14, Vol. 3 (25 September 1889). Only two 'Fuyuki' households appear in Murotsu 1891 tax records: see Sonkaigian 村会議案 (1891), hereafter MYM 95. One was ranked in the top 13 per cent of Murotsu's 538 household taxpayers; the other ranked just below median. My guess is that Sakazō came from the latter household, whose head was a woman (perhaps indicating that his mother was a widow).
[50] On the collapse of the local marine transportation industry in nearby Befu, see Kimura Kenji 木村健二, *Zaichō Nihonjin no shakaishi* 在朝日本人の社会史 [A social history of the Japanese in Korea] (Tokyo: Miraisha, 1989), pp. 37–43.

behind a petition which several Murotsu merchants addressed to the village mayor in 1894:

> The fact is, despite us being called the most prosperous port in the [western Japan] region, world conditions have been transformed: the domains have been replaced by the prefectural system; the coming and going of official ships has stopped; most shipping has become steam-powered; goods are being transported directly to meet demand; and both commercial shipping and merchants are no longer coming.[51]

The reduced circulation of ships, goods and capital had thus severely affected the port district by the early 1890s, half a century after Chōshū officials enumerated all the hallmarks of a booming economy.

But the structures of Murotsu's mid nineteenth-century economy dictated that the impact of such transformed world conditions actually fell first – and hardest – on the poorer inland communities, for fewer profits in the ports translated into fewer by-employments for inland residents. Even back in 1842, domain administrators had been concerned by the demographic fragility of the Murotsu inland district, describing rice production as insufficient for people's needs, and dry fields cultivated to the crests of the ridges and the depths of the valleys. In other words, overpopulation and cramped land were socioeconomic realities even before there existed a Malthusian rhetoric which officialdom could deploy to conceptualize the problem.[52]

Although the circumstances of port decline were particular to Murotsu, here as elsewhere in late nineteenth-century Yamaguchi, new domestic industries offered an outlet for the newly impoverished to find employment. Young women could go to the silk mills in places such as Tomioka, far to the east; young men and women could go work in the coal mines of Fukuoka prefecture in Kyushu (see Chapter 6).[53] But by

---

[51] MYM 112 (Kaimu ni kansuru ikken tsuzuri 会務ニ関スル一件綴, 1895); Kaminoseki Chōshi Hensan Iinkai 上関町史編纂委員会, *Kaminoseki chōshi* 上関町史 [Kaminoseki town history] (Kaminoseki: Kaminoseki-chō, 1988), p. 450.

[52] Malthusian ideas were first debated in Japanese in the late 1870s: Sidney Xu Lu, 'Colonizing Hokkaido and the Origin of Japanese Trans-Pacific Expansion, 1869–1894', *Japanese Studies* 36, 2 (2016): 251–74, here pp. 255–6.

[53] On a group of Yamaguchi women going to work in Tomioka in 1873, see E. Patricia Tsurumi, *Factory Girls: Women in the Thread Mills of Meiji Japan* (Princeton, NJ: Princeton University Press, 1990), p. 30. By 1920, of all Yamaguchi-born labourers engaged in (domestic) out-migration work, the majority were employed in the Fukuoka coal mines: see Kimura Kenji 木村健二, 'Senzenki Nihon ni okeru kaigai imin: Yamaguchi-ken no jirei o chūshin ni' 戦前期日本における海外移民：山口県の事例を中心に [Overseas emigration in pre-war Japan: The case of Yamaguchi prefecture], in Komai Hiroshi 駒井洋, Chin Tenji 陳天璽 and Kobayashi Tomoko 小林知子, eds., *Higashi Ajia no diasupora* 東アジアのディアスポラ [East Asian diasporas] (Tokyo: Akashi shoten, 2011), pp. 126–51, here p. 137.

the late 1880s, overseas migration in particular offered a potential panacea to the troubles of the inland district's nominal farmers. 'Murotsu is by far the most impoverished village', a village official wrote to his county counterpart in November 1888. Most probably with the inland district in mind, he explained: 'There is [high] population relative to the amount of land, such that our economy could not survive without out-migration labour; we are in great hardship.'[54] Already the village had received approximately 150 applications to the new government-sponsored emigration programme, but to date, no one from Murotsu had actually crossed to Hawai'i. The implication was clear: Murotsu, as also Kaminoseki and other villages in Kumage county, had been unfairly treated in comparison to neighbouring Ōshima, whence hundreds of Hawaiian migrants had departed since the programme's first crossings in 1885.

Whether by coincidence or as a direct consequence of the official's appeal, thirty-eight Murotsu villagers were accepted onto the emigration programme's seventh crossing, in December 1888. Among their number was Fuyuki's first cousin, Kōchiyama Kanenoshin (also born c. 1868), who, according to Fuyuki's granddaughter, must have written home early in 1889 – or had someone write for him – to encourage other villagers to emigrate.[55] These were the kinds of circulatory information networks which Irwin had in mind when he wrote to Lorrin Thurston in October 1889, the month that Fuyuki and fifty-two more Murotsu villagers arrived in the kingdom:

'[t]he Japanese immigrants now in Hawaii have sent highly favorable reports to their families and friends, and the Emigration is very popular in Yamaguchi and Hiroshima [...] I personally sent my Secretary, Mr. Onaka, to every district in Yamaguchi and Hiroshima, which he visited between September 21st and October 11th.[56]

If ever a name was apt for a pun, this is it: in addition to being a surname, *onaka* – with different characters – is a generic term for 'stomach' in Japanese. Thus, in the style of Utagawa's 'Rules of Dietary Life', Mr Stomach shovels young Murotsu men on their way to the mills and fields of Hawai'i. And yet the body metaphors are transmuted in this reading:

---

[54] Kaminoseki Chōshi Hensan Iinkai, *Kaminoseki chōshi*, p. 461.
[55] Author's private correspondence with Murakami Tomoko (2011).
[56] Letter from Robert W. Irwin to Lorrin A. Thurston, 21 October 1889: HSA, Interior, Box 16. The secretary was Onaka Naozō, who had worked with Irwin since at least 1885: DA 3.8.2.5–5 (Letter from Irwin to Inoue Kaoru, 16 August 1885). On the role of agents in the recruitment of government-sponsored Hawaiian emigration, see Moriyama, *Imingaisha*, pp. 20–2.

whereas at the beginning of the 1850s the Fuyuki household and its neighbours had been the figurative fanners and beaters in the circulatory port economy, by the end of the 1880s they had themselves become the objects of circulation, herded and carried and beaten – literally, by some *luna* – as crucial raw materials of the sugar plantation economy.

This, then, was the world of the *holehole bushi* lyrics: 'The cane drifts down to the flume / To the mill. / As for my body – / where will it drift?' And, in the very different context of international diplomacy, it was also the world depicted by the official diarist of the Iwakura Mission to North America and Europe (1871–3). Reflecting in one entry on the nature of international trade, he described London, Marseilles, Amsterdam, Hamburg and many European ports 'whose names are heard less frequently' in terms of 'how the world's products circulate [*ryūtsū* 流通]':

[Raw materials] are carried along the sea-lanes and unloaded at the main ports. They make their way overland to the factories of every region, and the [subsequent] manufactured goods are then sent from the main inland hubs back to the ports [*gyakuryū* 逆流]. This is like the flow [*ryūnyū* 流入] of a hundred rivers or the pulsing of blood through the arteries. And, like the ebb of the tide or the flow of blood back along the veins, the goods in the ports flow back [*tōryū* 倒流] to every region [of the world].[57]

The character *ryū* 流 is also read *nagareru*: it is the same character used by late-Tokugawa intellectuals in their explanations of economic principles, and the same verb used to conjure up flowing bodies in the plantation song.

We need not assume that the Japanese labourers toiling in Hawai'i had read Tokugawa tracts, perused the Iwakura Mission's diaries, or even seen Utagawa's popular woodblock print when they lifted a terminology so laden with theoretical baggage for their songs. Indeed, it's unlikely that a Murotsu migrant would have narrated the port's history with the language I have just used, even if my story's general flow would have been recognizable. And yet at some level it seems justified to assume that the language of 'drifting' was not entirely devoid of historical meaning and memories in the *holehole bushi*. Indeed, by-employments in the particular context of Murotsu may have strengthened a worldview in which the natural order of things was characterized by circulation. In turn, this may have facilitated the labourers' understanding of their own mutation into commodified bodies which circulated – which, in the

---

[57] This is a modified translation of Kume Kunitake, *The Iwakura Embassy 1871–73: A True Account of the Ambassador Extraordinary & Plenipotentiary's Journey of Observation through the United States of America and Europe*, Vol. 5, trans. Graham Healey and Chushichi Tsuzuki (Richmond: Curzon Press, 2002), pp. 175–6.

words of the *holehole bushi*, drifted down to the mill. And if that mill happened to be in Hawai'i and not Japan, and if it happened to refine cane rather than weave cotton or silk, then the industrial project for which Murotsu-based by-employments might be said to have 'prepared' migrant labourers was the Maui sugar factory or plantation field. To return to Thomas C. Smith, by-employments indeed constituted a 'connection' from an agricultural to an industrial history – but one that traversed the Pacific. By this logic, the *holehole bushi* are as much an archival departure point for what Smith called 'speculations' about the nature of nineteenth-century Japanese economic transformations as the surveys compiled by Chōshū officials in Kaminoseki.

Outside (2): Kaminoseki Municipal Archives

If songs from the Hawaiian canefields offered a different historical inflection on statistics from Kaminoseki, then the next step in exploring the nature of transpacific 'circulations' was to see if the reverse were true – namely, if and how sources from rural Japan might offer a new lens through which to consider transformations in late nineteenth-century Hawai'i. For this, the archival departure point was the Kaminoseki Board of Education, with its view over the straits to Murotsu port and beyond to the regal slopes of Mount Ōza (527m), literally the 'emperor's seat' (皇座). Here, local legend claims that during the epochal late twelfth-century struggle between the rival Minamoto and Heike clans, the boy emperor Antoku (1178–85) scanned the Inland Sea for the white sails of the despised Minamoto ships – in contrast to his own Heike red.[58]

The Board of Education, on what the Japanese called the second floor of a nondescript concrete building also housing the Chamber of Commerce, was the closest that Kaminoseki had to a municipal archive, to a repository of records documenting the individual villages and islands – Murotsu, Yashima, Iwaishima, Kaminoseki itself – which had administered the everyday lives of local people until the town merger in 1958. The narrow office that the head of education kindly offered me was the equivalent to an archival reading room. By contrast, the 'stacks' were downstairs, left out of the main entrance, a hop down the town's seafront road, another left into a sheltered alley, and then a right into a large wooden warehouse – which in 2007 had seen better days and within a few years would be demolished entirely.

---

[58] The Heike would eventually be defeated by the Minamoto in the Battle of Dannoura, in today's Shimonoseki city, in the spring of 1185.

I had first been brought here in the spring of 2007 by the Board of Education's Kawamura Mitsuo, an archival gatekeeper whose enthusiasm for The History of Japan was unrivalled if somewhat dilatory. Then a stocky man in his late fifties, with tousled greying hair and uneven outgrowths of stubble, the late Mr Kawamura's greatest passion was the stone wall architecture of Iwaishima island, where he'd insisted on taking me for a study-morning. ('Mi-chan's tour', my father-in-law had chuckled, using the affectionate nickname by which Kawamura-san was known to most townspeople.) On the ferry ride back, I broached not for the first time the topic of the warehouse – in the whole town, only Mr Kawamura seemed to have a set of keys – while he regaled me with more tall wall tales. At the end of the day, he pressed further reading material into my hands – this time, a thick official report which until my next bout of insomnia lay unopened at home – and agreed to unlock the warehouse the following Thursday.

What we found that Thursday morning, in an unlit rear room and under the cover of tarpaulin, were some eighty cardboard boxes containing mainly Murotsu village documents from the 1870s to the 1958 merger. This was my first encounter with serious archival dust – and damp, and the occasional louse – and it made me drunk on the possibilities of the handwritten document.[59] For subsequent months on end, I opened and sniffed through boxes we had decanted from the stacks to the reading room, only occasionally interrupted by Mr Kawamura and his curious colleagues. For reasons I have trouble fathoming some fifteen years later, I used my digital camera only rarely. Instead, unconsciously adhering to an older paradigm of archival research as a period of reading not photographing, I spent my time transcribing texts and entering households into ever more unwieldy Excel spreadsheets. The name of Fuyuki Sakazō did not immediately leap out from the pages, but it recurred enough for me to know that I might one day attempt a short biography – and, in an act of great generosity which also underlined the town's dense social networks, Mr Kawamura would later put me in touch with one of Fuyuki's surviving granddaughters in Osaka.

Each unpacked box helped fill out Fuyuki's story. From the tax records, I could calculate the relative prosperity of Murotsu's two Fuyuki households in 1891, eighteen months after his departure. From pupil lists, I knew some of his children had been enrolled in the elementary school in the 1910s. From fundraising appeals, I read that he had

---

[59] Steedman, *Dust*, ch. 2.

pledged significant donations towards a new school hall in 1914.[60] And in the village's land registers – which I accessed in a neighbouring town – I discovered that in 1913 he had purchased three properties in the port district of Seto, just across the straits from the Board of Education.[61] This chronology was at first confusing: only after Fuyuki's granddaughter wrote to me did it become clear that Sakazō returned to Murotsu in the late 1890s to marry his first cousin, Kōchiyama Sumi (quite possibly the younger sister of Kanenoshin, who had preceded Fuyuki to Hawai'i by a few months in 1889); that the first of their eight children was born in Hawai'i in 1901; that the last two children were born in Japan in the 1910s, after Sumi emigrated back to Murotsu; that most of the children attended school in Japan; and that Sakazō himself also spent some time in Murotsu in the 1910s – coinciding with his purchase of new property – before returning to Kaua'i. His was also a life of flow along the post-1880s artery which connected Yamaguchi to the Hawaiian archipelago.

At the most basic level, the school donations and property acquisitions were all individual markers of how the early twentieth-century material culture of Fuyuki's home town had been transformed by the Japanese diaspora community: they were indications that 'the global' was walked even in the everyday lives of people who stayed at home.[62] Indeed, the volume of paperwork on my reading room desk testified to the extent that village officialdom needed to think and write in newly expansive ways by the 1910s compared to just forty years earlier, as harried record keepers tried – and, in the case of mistakenly placing Fuyuki in Kapa'a, often failed – to keep accurate track of who was residing where in the Asia-Pacific world. In the Foreign Ministry archives in Tokyo, the story was the same, but on a bigger scale. In addition to enumerating comings and goings, for example, ministry officials gathered reports in 1891 from emigrant-sending prefectures on the post-return employment of the *City of Tokio* and *Yamashiro-maru* labourers (although many, such as Wakamiya Yaichi and Kodama Keijirō, did not return after a single contract). Of particular interest was how the migrants had spent the 25 per cent of their Hawaiian wages which they had been obliged to save while working in the canefields. As Fuyuki would later do, many migrants reportedly bought land or property with this money, which

---

[60] MYM 95; MYM 919 (Gakureibo 学齢簿, 1907–9) and MYM 920 (Gakureibo 学齢簿, 1910–12); MYM 773 (Bei-Ha-kan kenchiku ikken kenchiku kifu mōshikomi-sho kifu hōmeibo 米布館建築一件建築寄附申込書寄附芳名簿, 1914–15).
[61] Legal Affairs Bureau, Ministry of Justice of Japan, Yanai branch, *Tochi daichō*.
[62] See Dominic Sachsenmaier, *Global Entanglements of a Man Who Never Traveled: A Seventeenth-Century Chinese Christian and His Conflicted Worlds* (New York: Columbia University Press, 2018).

officials in Yamaguchi and Kumamoto respectively labelled *kinben cho-chiku* 勤勉貯蓄 and *kinbenkin* 勤勉金 – that is, 'industrious savings' and 'industrious remittances', themselves the consequence of 'industrious work' (*kinben rōdō* 勤勉労働).[63]

This language of industrious Japanese was equally echoed in Hawaiian government documents. In the same year of 1891, a Bureau of Immigration official wrote to the minister of interior that local authorities in Japan only allowed the overseas migration of 'men of good character, and those who are law abiding and industrious'.[64] Back before the government-sponsored programme was even established, the bureau's president had anticipated that Japanese labourers would constitute 'an industrious and law-abiding addition to the [Hawaiian] nation'.[65] Irwin himself, in his letter from onboard the *Yamashiro-maru* while in quarantine in June 1885 (see Chapter 1), had praised the Japanese as 'hard working, industrious men', while the *Daily Pacific Commercial Advertiser* claimed a few months earlier: 'These people are intelligent, self-respecting, faithful to engagements, and very industrious. Many bring their wives and children with them, transferring to these islands the home life of rural Japan.'[66]

The apparent linguistic alignment of *kinben* and 'industrious' in sources spanning the Pacific Ocean was fortuitous: like Irwin's labelling of the government-sponsored emigration programme as 'industrial', it offered an overlooked Hawaiian entry point into another key historiographical debate concerning Japan's nineteenth-century transformations, namely the 'industrious revolution' (*kinben kakumei* 勤勉革命). This was a term coined in the 1970s by the economic historian Akira Hayami (1929–2019). In his analyses of demographic data from central Japan, Hayami argued that a supply-side labour transformation had occurred in eighteenth-century Japan, in which the rural population had increased, the amount of capital investment (as measured in farm livestock) had declined – and yet the standard of living, far from falling, had actually risen. He explained this apparent conundrum by emphasizing an

---

[63] DA 3.8.2.5–5. In Tokyo as in Murotsu, the paperwork was generated by officials 'keeping track, and keeping track of keeping track': Thomas Richards, *The Imperial Archive: Knowledge and the Fantasy of Empire* (London: Verso, 1993), p. 3.

[64] Paul Neumann to Charles N. Spencer, 18 March 1891: cited in Moriyama, *Imingaisha*, p. 18.

[65] Chas T. Gulick, 'Report of the President of the Bureau of Immigration to the Legislative Assembly' (Honolulu), 9 June 1884, p. 6.

[66] HSA, FO&EX 31, Immigration Matters (April to June 1885), Letter from Robert W. Irwin to Walter M. Gibson, 25 June 1885; *PCA*, 2 March 1885. See also *PCA*, 22 April 1885 ('[The Japanese] are an eminently desirable class, cleanly and industrious').

intensification of rural labour practices in the period from the 1670s to the 1820s, such that 'human power replaced livestock power'; and it was this labour-intensive model of structural change he characterized as an 'industrious revolution'.[67]

In ways that Hayami could hardly have anticipated back in the 1970s, the 'industrious revolution' continues to be debated to this day, both within Japan and especially without.[68] The phrase was adopted and adapted by European historians in the 1990s to describe a slightly different phenomenon in eighteenth-century European history, whereby rural household labour intensified in order both to meet consumer demand (that is, in response to the market) and also to facilitate agricultural households themselves participating in the consumer revolution.[69] More recently, historians have attempted to sketch a global typology of industriousness – in which they cite Thomas C. Smith's work on the Murotsu peninsula, itself quoting official descriptions of by-employments from the 1840s, in order to demonstrate the nature of household labour division in rural Japan.[70] Meanwhile, the aforementioned Shigehisa Kuriyama has argued that the dozens of toiling workers in Utagawa's 'Rules of Dietary Life' comprise a mid nineteenth-century visualization of the labour-intensive industrious revolution.[71]

And so the expectant language of government officials and newspapermen in mid-1880s Hawai'i seemed to promise an additional reading of the industrious revolution – one in which, in allegedly 'transferring to these [Hawaiian] islands the home life of rural Japan', the government-sponsored

[67] These arguments are summarized in English in Akira Hayami, *Japan's Industrious Revolution: Economic and Social Transformations in the Early Modern Period* (London: Springer, 2015).
[68] For an overview, see Osamu Saito, 'An Industrious Revolution in an East Asian Market Economy? Tokugawa Japan and Implications for the Great Divergence', *Australian Economic History Review* 50, 3 (2010): 240–61.
[69] Jan de Vries, 'The Industrial Revolution and the Industrious Revolution', *Journal of Economic History* 54 (1994): 249–70; see also Jan de Vries, *The Industrious Revolution: Consumer Behaviour and the Household Economy, 1650 to the Present* (Cambridge: Cambridge University Press, 2008).
[70] See Kaoru Sugihara and R. Bin Wong, 'Industrious Revolutions in Early Modern World History', in Jerry H. Bentley, Sanjay Subrahmanyam and Merry E. Wiesner-Hanks, eds., *The Cambridge World History*, Vol. 6: *The Construction of a Global World, 1400–1800 CE* (Cambridge: Cambridge University Press, 2015), pp. 282–310. On p. 300, Sugihara and Wong cite Thomas C. Smith, himself citing the Chōshū domain's report on salt-making by-employments in Hirao ('Farm Family By-Employments', p. 697), thereby drawing attention to the kinds of rural management experience which, according to Smith, had 'prepared' villages on the Murotsu peninsula for subsequent industrialization.
[71] Shigehisa Kuriyama, 'The Travel of Anxieties: Rethinking Western Medicine in Edo Japan', public lecture at the Heidelberg Center for Transcultural Studies, 22 January 2015.

programme facilitated the circulation of industrious labour from Japan to Hawai'i and industrious remittances back.

Except, there were two problems with this reading. First, it was not evident that labour-intensive Japanese modes of working *did* 'transfer' to Hawai'i. Behind some of the worker-management disputes I mentioned in the previous chapter, for example, lay a different conception of working time. As early as July 1885, the Yamaguchi-based *Bōchō shinbun* newspaper reported on the first group having to learn to keep an eye on the clock at their work stations.[72] This was partly to protect the labourers from unscrupulous *luna* – the type who hurried their charges on between tasks, not counting walking time as work time, and who, when faced with recalcitrance, prosecuted the Japanese and testified to the court: 'I told [the defendants] that they must hurry up as I did not want them to take half a day in going from one field to another and if they did not hurry up I should dock them [pay] and also report them to the Boss.'[73] Yet overzealous overseers aside, the Yamaguchi newspaper equally noted that the working day in rural Japan, with its frequent breaks for tea or tobacco or lunch, was very different to the plantation expectations in Hawai'i. Consequently, it had taken the *City of Tokio* labourers 'some effort to comply, and the working hours felt very long'.

The idiom of effort – *hone o oru*, literally 'to break one's bones' – was the same as that used by the exhausted fan-bearers in Utagawa's 'Rules of Dietary Life'. It appeared elsewhere – for example, in the instructions issued to the third group of government-sponsored labourers in 1887 ('Article 1: The attitude of working with *great effort* required of the migrant workers'), and in the explanation that plantation labour followed set working times without breaks.[74] In other words, if Utagawa's conscientious workers were indeed visualizations of the industrious revolution, then the repeated exhortation in official documentation for the Hawai'i-bound migrants to expend 'great effort' implies that Japanese working practices did *not* transfer well to a canefield setting.[75] In Hawai'i, too, the inspector general of immigration publicly suggested in 1886 that:

---

[72] *Bōchō shinbun* 防長新聞, 1–3 July 1885, cited in Doi, *Hawai iminshi*, p. 100.

[73] HSA Court Records CIVIL A 115 (Second Judicial Circuit), *W. Y. Horner* vs. *Miamoto* [sic] *et al.*, 4 December 1888. The charge was for 'Deserting Contract Service', and eventually served against sixteen labourers on the Horner plantation in Lahaina, Maui.

[74] 'Dekasegi-nin no kokoroegaki' 出稼人の心得書 (1887), in Hiroshima-ken, *Hiroshima-ken ijū shiryōhen*, pp. 10–16, here p. 10 (also printed, but undated, in Doi, *Hawai iminshi*, pp. 76–82).

[75] Here I build on Thomas C. Smith's important argument – itself a critique of E. P. Thompson's imagination of 'pre-industrial' time – that the intensity and complexity of early modern Japanese village life in fact facilitated the transition from 'peasant' to

Great allowances should be made for [the Japanese] at first, as their manner of work (though industrious people) is quite different in their own country, from what it is here; as I am informed, that in Japan, they work a short while and rest, then proceed with their work, so on through the day, whereas, here, they have to work continuously the day through. In a short time, they will be familiar with our mode of work.[76]

All of which suggested a second problem: the 'industriousness' for which the Japanese were repeatedly praised in Hawai'i was not the linguistic equivalent of the labour-intensive modes of work implied in Hayami's 'industrious revolution'. Red in one setting was not commensurate with the same idea of colour elsewhere.[77] Rather, the term 'industrious' in Hawai'i was laden with an ideological baggage of colonial power and the dispossession of Indigenous land – as we shall shortly see. For men like Fuyuki to be praised as 'industrious', and for him to contribute to the material culture of his home town by engaging in 'industrious remittances', was for him to carry this imposed baggage, too.

In this light, the view across the straits from the Kaminoseki Board of Education to the Murotsu district of Seto, where Fuyuki purchased three properties in 1913, raised new questions. Thanks to the land registers, I knew from *whom* he had bought the land, but the real point was *how* he had been in a position to do so.[78] At whose expense were his 'industrious' remittances earned? And thus, just as workers like Fuyuki had been rendered voiceless by the nature of fact assembly in the Hawai'i State Archives, whose histories had been written out of the Kaminoseki town archives?

'Invaded by the Industrious'

Arriving in Honolulu on the *Yamashiro-maru* on 1 October 1889, Fuyuki Sakazō was deployed to the Hāna plantation, in eastern Maui, where his *bango* was 8051 (see Figure 3.2). In November 1897 he boarded the *SS Belgic* and returned to Japan, eventually to marry his cousin Sumi.[79] After

---

'factory' time in Meiji Japan: the evidence from the sugar 'factories' of Hawai'i suggests that the transition was far from smooth. See Thomas C. Smith, 'Peasant Time and Factory Time in Japan', *Past & Present* 111 (1986): 165–97, and E. P. Thompson, 'Time, Work-Discipline and Industrial Capitalism', *Past & Present* 38 (1967): 56–94.

[76] A. S. Cleghorn, 'Report of the Inspector-General of Immigrants' (Honolulu), May 1886, p. 256.

[77] On this problem, see Chakrabarty, *Provincializing Europe*, pp. 72–96.

[78] All three properties were purchased from members of the Kōchiyama household – perhaps from the father, or brother, of Fuyuki's cousin, Kōchiyama Kanenoshin, and his cousin/wife, Kōchiyama Sumi (see previous two sections).

[79] DA, Hawai imin 3.

110   Outside the Archive

Figure 3.2 Hāna plantation, Maui, c. 1885. PP-106-9-018. Courtesy of Hawai'i State Archives.

Hawai'i was annexed by the United States in 1898, incoming passenger records also noted the traveller's physical appearance: thus, in his transpacific circulations over the next twenty years, Fuyuki was described as being between four foot ten inches and five feet tall, with a dark complexion and black hair even into his fifties. He had a scar on the index finger of his left hand and a mole on his forehead.[80]

A few months before Fuyuki completed his contract in Hāna, the *Paradise of the Pacific* newspaper ran an article noting that '[t]he district of Hana is one of the least known to the general public of any of the districts on the islands'. One day, the correspondent predicted, it will 'awake out of sleep', just like the districts of Kona and Puna on Hawai'i Island itself – the former 'now full of the busy hum of industry', the latter also 'no longer the dreary, uninhabited waste it used to be'. The article went on to describe the landscape north-west of the Hāna plantation in lyrical terms:

[80] Honolulu Passenger and Crew Lists, 22 May 1914 and 4 June 1922, digitized by www.ancestry.com (last accessed 24 October 2013).

The country is broken by deep gulches, the sides of which run anywhere from 400 to 900 feet, while the plateauxs [sic] between rise to 1200 feet above the sea-level. [...] The scenery is magnificent – the finest, by far, on the islands. Roaring cascades dash down steep terraces, finally forming deep streams that waste their waters in the sea. The forests are thick and tangled; wild bananas, ohias and various native fruits grow in luxuriance.[81]

And then the author's most troubling claim: 'at present, the whole stretch of territory is practically unused. Some of these days the district will be invaded by the industrious, and the scene will be changed.'

As we have seen, the adjective 'industrious' was widely used in late nineteenth-century Hawai'i as a marker of positive attributes. In the 1880s and 1890s, Japanese labourers were one sub-section of the archipelago's population – or anticipated population – especially identified in this way, although such labelling was not reserved exclusively for the Japanese, nor was it unambiguously positive.[82] But behind these allegedly positive connotations lay also a negative evaluation. For the argument that Hawai'i was ripe for the 'invasion' of industrious labourers also constituted an implicit critique of the Native Hawaiian population that itself stretched back to the earliest days of the New England Congregationalist mission in the 1820s. Indeed, the imagination of Hawai'i as a land calling to be 'possessed' and covered with 'fruitful fields and pleasant dwellings' – thereby to raise 'the whole people to an elevated state of Christian civilization' – even predated the departure of the first American Board of Commissioners for Foreign Missions (ABCFM) expedition for the islands in October 1819.[83] As Noelani

---

[81] *Paradise of the Pacific* 10 (March 1897).

[82] In a *PCA* article under the headline, 'Spreckelsville: Visit to the Largest Sugar Plantation in the World', the plantation's Chinese labourers are described as 'industrious and thrifty people', as are the Japanese ('industrious, facile, companionable, quick to take in the customs of civilization') and the Portuguese ('the men are on the whole temperate and industrious'): 5 June 1886 (last accessed through Chronicling America, 27 January 2021). Isabella Bird also described the Chinese labourers as 'quiet and industrious' in *The Hawaiian Archipelago: Six Months among the Palm Groves, Coral Reefs, and Volcanoes of the Sandwich Islands* (London: John Murray, 1875), p. 117. But in the Deep South, the labelling of Chinese 'coolie' labourers as 'industrious' was also a way of depriving them of their humanity and imagining them instead as 'the ideal industrial machine': Matthew Pratt Guterl, 'After Slavery: Asian Labor, the American South, and the Age of Emancipation', *Journal of World History* 14, 2 (2003): 209–41, here p. 230. On labels of Portuguese industriousness as euphemisms for racial categorization, see Cristiana Bastos, 'Portuguese in the Cane: The Racialization of Labour in Hawaiian Plantations', in Sofia Aboim, Paulo Granjo and Alice Ramos, eds., *Changing Societies: Legacies and Challenges*, Vol. 1: *Ambiguous Inclusions: Inside Out, Outside In* (Lisbon: Imprensa de Ciências Sociais, 2018), pp. 65–96, here p. 79.

[83] ABCFM, *Instructions to the Missionaries about to Embark for the Sandwich Isles* (delivered by Rev Dr Samuel Worcester in Boston on 15 October 1819 and subsequently published

Arista has shown, such tropes were part of the rhetorical production of Hawai'i and of Hawaiian subjects for a US-American audience. The handful of already converted Hawaiian boys in New England were presented in pamphlets and sermons as 'industrious, faithful, and persevering', in contrast to the 'heathen' masses whose Christian salvation would be the mission's *raison d'être*.[84] Post-arrival ABCFM missionaries continued to compare their influence on 'Owhyhee' to 'a perennial stream whose gentle flow shall fertilize the barren waste'.[85]

The *Paradise of the Pacific*'s 1897 article on Hāna demonstrates that these rhetorical productions were still blooming at the end of the nineteenth century – as seen in the description of 'practically unused' territory, and in the casual suggestion that the streams 'waste their waters in the sea'. But the intellectual roots of such claims were not merely missionary. Claus Spreckels, whose Spreckelsville plantation had only been made possible through the diversion of mountain 'waste' water to the previously dry plains of north-central Maui, similarly characterized 'these islands' as 'very rich lands' where there nevertheless remained 'a great deal' of wasteland.[86] Given Spreckels's animosity towards the many planters who were descended from the ABCFM missionaries and who had agitated for the overthrow of the Hawaiian monarchy, his imagination of Hawaiian 'waste' may have drawn less consciously on missionary rhetoric than on a John Locke-inspired justification for colonial acquisition that had animated America's westward expansion – and which had made Spreckels's prior business successes in San Francisco possible. It was Locke, after all, who had favourably compared a well-cultivated farm in Devonshire with 'the wild woods and uncultivated wast [sic] of America'; it was Locke who had argued that 'common and uncultivated' land should be given over to 'the Industrious and the Rational', and who – in an intellectual justification for English colonial

---

in 1823), cited in Arista, *Kingdom and the Republic*, p. 96. On the trope of 'possession', see ibid., pp. 79–83.

[84] The Hawaiian boy Honoli'i (John Honoree), who had arrived to be schooled in New England in 1815, was described as 'industrious' in *Narrative of Five Youth from the Sandwich Islands: Published by Order of the Agents Appointed to Establish a School for Heathen Youth* (New York: J. Seymour, 1816), p. 30 (downloadable from the HathiTrust Digital Library, www.hathitrust.org). On rhetorical production more generally, see Arista, *Kingdom and the Republic*, chs 2–3.

[85] *Journal of the Sandwich Islands Mission*, 12 April 1820, cited in Arista, *Kingdom and the Republic*, p. 118.

[86] *53rd Congress, House of Representatives: Appendix II: Foreign Relations of the United States 1894, Affairs in Hawaii* (Washington, DC: United States Government Printing Office, 1895), 'Interview with Claus Spreckels, June 5, 1893' [by Mr Blount], pp. 973–81, here p. 974. On the irrigation of Spreckelsville, see Adler, *Claus Spreckels*, pp. 33–51.

acquisition – suggested that 'subduing or cultivating the Earth, and having Dominion', were two sides of the same coin.[87]

In other words, the adjective 'industrious' was imbued with deep historical meaning in Hawai'i by the time it came to be used as a descriptor for the Japanese in the mid 1880s: it connoted both the archipelago's missionary settlement and the wider colonial expansion of Europe into the New World. We can only speculate as to what it may have meant in the hands of particular authors. The president of the Board of Immigration in 1884, for example, was Charles T. Gulick (1841–97), scion of a missionary dynasty in Hawai'i. When he wrote that Japanese labourers would constitute 'an industrious and law-abiding addition to the [Hawaiian] nation', he may have been drawing on an ABCFM trope from the 1820s; he may also have been influenced by reports from his cousins, Orramel Hinckley Gulick (1830–1923) and John Thomas Gulick (1832–1923), then leading the ABCFM mission in Kobe and Osaka respectively.[88] Either way, to imagine the Japanese as 'industrious' was not merely to express hopes for the government-sponsored migration programme; it was also to bind the new arrivals into a discourse which for decades had presented Hawai'i as a wasteland, unused, ripe for colonial development – and Native Hawaiians as heathen, indolent and worthy of invasion.[89]

This is important because Fuyuki was no mere bystander in a story of 'invasion'. For a start, he was a labourer in Hāna during a period of profound change: under the new management of the California-registered Grinbaum & Co. since September 1887,[90] the number of plantation workers was in the process of more than doubling, from 175 to 454, by the time that Fuyuki had completed his second year of work. At the beginning of 1890, almost two-thirds of the labour force was

---

[87] John Locke, *Two Treatises of Government*, ed. Peter Laslett (Cambridge: Cambridge University Press, 1988), pp. 291–4 (Second Treatise, chapter V, paragraphs 37, 34 and 35 respectively). On the relationship between Locke and colonialism, see David Armitage, 'John Locke, Carolina, and the *Two Treatises of Government*', *Political Theory* 32, 5 (2004): 602–27; Kris Manjapra, *Colonialism in Global Perspective* (Cambridge: Cambridge University Press, 2020), pp. 50–2. On Locke and concepts of wasteland, see Judith Whitehead, 'John Locke, Accumulation by Dispossession and the Governance of Colonial India', *Journal of Contemporary Asia* 42, 1 (2012): 1–21.

[88] *Japan Directory for the Year 1884*, p. 103. Both of these Gulicks were sons of one of Hawai'i's most distinguished ABCFM families: see Clifford Putney, *Missionaries in Hawai'i: The Lives of Peter and Fanny Gulick, 1797–1883* (Amherst: University of Massachusetts Press, 2010).

[89] On the dissemination of these ideas in Hawaiian-language Christian textbooks from the 1830s onwards, see Chang, *World and All the Things upon It*, pp. 118–21.

[90] Grinbaum & Co bought Hāna from its Danish owner and co-founder in the 1860s, Oscar Unna, for US$103,000: *PM*, VI, 9 (September 1887), p. 389.

generation political or entrepreneurial ascendancy, as 'made possible by the continued national oppression of Hawaiians, particularly the theft of our lands and the crushing of our independence'.[96]

One problem with such arguments is that they tend to be ex post facto: that is, subsequent successes and settlement in mid twentieth-century Hawai'i in and of themselves rendered the original migrant labourer a 'colonist', even if he – almost always a male protagonist – at first harboured intentions merely to serve his contract and remit what he could to his household in Japan.[97] This is why the February 1897 application in Murotsu is so unusual and revealing, for it shows Fuyuki Sakazō actively recruiting new labourers on behalf of 'the American Mōrison'. Indeed, when I use keyword searches to contextualize the 1897 document a little further, Fuyuki's potential 'complicity' (Trask's word) in a story of Native Hawaiian dispossession is rendered more visible. 'The American Mōrison' was not, in fact, American: Hugh Morrison was born in 1844 in Aberdeen and, as he told a newspaper interviewer in January 1896, a proud 'Scotch'.[98] Nor was he ever an employer at Hāna: having come to Hawai'i in 1879 and initially worked at the Hakalau plantation, he served as the manager of Spreckelsville from 1887 to 1891 and then, until his death in 1901, as the manager of the new Hawaiian Sugar Company plantation at Makaweli, Kaua'i.[99] Given the distance between

---

[96] Haunani-Kay Trask, 'Settlers of Color and "Immigrant" Hegemony: "Locals" in Hawai'i', *Amerasia Journal* 26, 2 (2000): 1–24, here p. 4. Trask's essay appeared in a special issue of *Amerasia*, the essays from which were revised and republished as Candace Fujikane and Jonathan Y. Okamura, eds., *Asian Settler Colonialism: From Local Governance to the Habits of Everyday Life in Hawai'i* (University of Hawai'i Press, 2008). Her framework has proved inspirational for others: see, for example, Eiko Kosasa's claim that Japanese immigrants to Hawai'i, by adapting and in many cases succeeding in a 'colonial space', 'are therefore not "immigrants" in a "nation of immigrants," but settlers in a colony like all other foreigners and their descendants in the islands': Kosasa, 'Ideological Images: US Nationalism in Japanese Settler Photographs', in Candace Fujikane and Jonathan Y. Okamura, eds., *Asian Settler Colonialism: From Local Governance to the Habits of Everyday Life in Hawai'i* (University of Hawai'i Press, 2008), pp. 209–32, here p. 211.

[97] To this problem, Candace Fujikane argues that 'it is not colonial *intent* that defines the status of Asians as settlers but rather the historical context of US colonialism of which they unknowingly became a part': Candace Fujikane and Jonathan Y. Okamura, eds., *Asian Settler Colonialism: From Local Governance to the Habits of Everyday Life in Hawai'i* (University of Hawai'i Press, 2008), 'Introduction', pp. 1–42, here p. 20 (emphasis added).

[98] On Morrison's birth, *Honolulu Republican*, 16 May 1901. The interview is printed in *HG*, 10 January 1896. These and all other biographical details concerning Morrison – except for the *Planters' Monthly* (fn 99) – were accessed through the Chronicling America database.

[99] For Morrison's appointment at Spreckelsville, see *PM*, VI, 6 (June 1887), p. 245. Under his management, Spreckelsville recorded its largest annual production to date:

Maui and Kauaʻi, Fuyuki is unlikely to have been personally acquainted with Morrison; but he probably knew of him through his own manager on Hāna until 1897, David Center, another Scot, whose brother was also Morrison's brother-in-law.[100] Thus, in passing news of Morrison's recruitment drive on to his cousin Hiraki in Murotsu, Fuyuki was advancing the interests of a group of managers whose networks encompassed both Hāna in Maui and Makaweli in Kauaʻi. (Given that Fuyuki himself eventually ended up living in the neighbouring Kauaʻi town of Eleele, he may also have been setting up a relationship from which he would later benefit.)[101]

In the aforementioned newspaper interview, Morrison was asked by the American journalist Kate Field (1838–96) to speak to the 'political principles' of the planter class. 'We are determined that there shall be no more monarchy,' he answered. 'A large majority of us want a settled government. We need it for our peace of mind as well as for our pockets.' Contrasting the alleged 'orgies' of the late King Kalākaua's rule to the 'admirable' men running the post-overthrow Republic of Hawaiʻi, Morrison looked to the future: 'Though a British subject, I realize, as every one must, that these islands are to all intents and purposes American. They owe their prosperity to the United States, and we are ready for annexation.'[102]

Recall now the image of the 'evil-hearted' in Prendergast's 'Kaulana Nā Pua', and the lament – from the third stanza – that 'Annexation is wicked sale / Of the civil rights of the Hawaiian people'. If Morrison fitted

---

PCA, 4 May 1891. Makaweli was the name of the *ahupuaʻa* (traditional land unit); today the district is known as Kaumakani.

[100] *Daily Bulletin*, 16 November 1891; on David Center, see *Honolulu Star*, 3 January 1901 (both accessed through Chronicling America). This connection through the Scottish expatriate network, and through family ties, and also through Spreckelsville – David Center had first come to Hawaiʻi through Claus Spreckels's invitation, and his brother Hugh would succeed Hugh Morrison as the manager of Spreckelsville in 1891 – makes me convinced that the Murotsu application, though mistaken in some details, is fundamentally correct in claiming that Fuyuki knew about Morrison's recruitment drive.

[101] I am grateful to Marylou Bradley of the Kauaʻi Historical Society for her generous assistance concerning Fuyuki's life in Eleele, in particular her finding a reference to Fuyuki in *Polk-Husted's Directory and Handbook of Honolulu and the Territory of Hawaii* (Honolulu: Polk-Husted Directory Company, 1922). Although Fuyuki rose to the position of clerk at the McBryde Sugar Company's Eleele store, I could find no record of him among the company's lists of contracts and salaried employees from the years either side of 1900, when he and Sumi first moved to Kauaʻi: HSPA: MSC 1/2-9 Labor Contracts 1899 and MSC V.1-7 Cash Books 1899–1939, vol. 2 (for the McBryde Sugar Company); MSC PV. 21 Labor Contracts 1899 (for the Eleele Plantation Company).

[102] *HG*, 10 January 1896. Field died in Honolulu only a few months after this interview.

If I look up from my Zurich desktop, in my mind's eye I can look across the straits from the Kaminoseki Board of Education to that narrow strip of land where Fuyuki's houses once stood, where the sea meets the steep slopes of Mount Ōza. I think: land is central to the concept of settler colonialism, but the acquisition of land need not be a story situated only in the colony.[105] Given that Fuyuki could buy houses in Seto thanks to money he made in Hāna and Eleele, and given that the system which enriched him there was founded on the denial of Native Hawaiian rights, then at some level land acquisition in Japan was also a story of land dispossession in Hawai'i. In this sense, just as Hawaiian plantations should be considered in relation to Japanese histories of industrialization, so Japan-bound remittances should be considered in relation to Hawaiian histories of settlement.

But of course, Fuyuki's plantation labour did not simply fund his own family's prosperity. In the mid 1910s, as Europe tore itself apart in war, he was a cheerleader in raising funds from more than thirty members of the Murotsu diaspora community in Hawai'i and North America to construct a new building for the village elementary school. That building was completed in January 1916, and Fuyuki's third daughter Mitsuyo, born in Hawai'i in 1906, would have been one of the hundreds of pupils to perform the 'Song of Celebration' upon its ceremonial opening:

> In the middle of the playground,
> Looking up from beside the willow tree,
> Our eyes are astonished by the America-Hawai'i Hall.
> This beautiful structure was built
> with the pure fortunes
> of people living in America and Hawai'i:
> 'May the home town for which we yearn
> become yet better,' they hoped.
> So every day, in this building,
> where we learn of people's toils,
> let us with one heart
> Work, apply ourselves, and unfailingly become
> good Japanese
> As a token of our gratitude.[106]

I can read these lyrics on the page in Kaminoseki or on screen in Zurich; but without a melody, they do not disturb the archival sonosphere.

---

[105] Wolfe writes of 'the insatiable dynamic whereby settler colonialism always needs more land', pointing also to the ways in which John Locke was used to justify colonial agricultural expansion: 'Settler Colonialism', p. 395.

[106] MYM 773.

The lack of music is not the only silence in the song, however. If historians are to interpret land acquisition in Murotsu as part of a settler narrative in Hawai'i, then we must critically investigate at whose expense the migrants' allegedly 'pure fortunes' (*kiyokizai* 清き財) were made.

And, if the sources permit, the next set of questions should focus not just on interpreting the multifaceted histories of the toiling settler migrants but also on ways of archival seeing amongst the Indigenous communities on the ground. Re-routing, like the *Yamashiro-maru*, from the colonial context of 1890s Hawai'i to 1890s Australia, this will be the challenge for Chapter 4.

4   Archival Country, Counterclaims

> As an indication of improving trade between the colonies and the East, the inauguration of a new steamship service under the auspices of the Japanese Mail Steamship Company is an event to be welcomed, and in the Yamashiro Maru, the pioneer vessel, which arrived here yesterday, the proprietors of the service have presented a steamship which should at once commend itself to the travelling public.
>
> *Argus* (Melbourne), 12 November 1896

> And in that water lies our sacred Law.
> Not just near the foreshore. We sing from the shore to where the clouds rise on the horizon.
>
> Lanani Marika, 'Declaration', 1999[1]

A Map

In its heyday, the *Yamashiro-maru* was known not only for having transported thousands of Japanese labourers to Hawai'i but also for having opened the NYK's monthly service to Australia. Beginning in October 1896 and in rotation with two other company ships, it steamed from Yokohama to Melbourne via Hong Kong every three months until the end of 1898, when it was replaced on the route by a newer, bigger vessel.

In my initial online research for this period of the ship's life in 2012, I came across a man who took early advantage of the new Japan–Australia line, possibly after reading reports of its official opening in the Japanese newspapers.[2] Hasegawa Setsutarō was born in the Hokkaido port of Otaru in 1871 and trained as a schoolteacher. Having applied for a passport at the end of 1896, he arrived in Australia on the *Yamashiro-*

---

[1] Lanani Marika, 'Declaration', trans. Raymattja Marika, in Buku-Larrngay Mulka Centre, *Saltwater: Yirrkala Bark Paintings of Sea Country: Recognising Indigenous Sea Rights* (Neutral Bay, NSW: Jennifer Isaacs Publishing, 2003 [1999]), p. 19.
[2] A number of articles about the new NYK line to Australia appeared in the *Yomiuri shinbun* in October 1896, including a description of the tiffin and fireworks that accompanied the *Yamashiro-maru*'s departure from Yokohama on 3 October: *YS*, 4 October 1896.

maru in February 1897, travelling in steerage with one other Japanese and nine Chinese passengers. According to oral history interviews given by his daughter-in-law in the mid 1980s, he came to Melbourne to learn English, lodging at the residence of a certain Colonel Tucket as a 'houseboy'. But having allegedly been badly treated by his employer, Hasegawa ended up in Geelong, where he became one of four Japanese laundry owners. Marrying Australia-born Ada Cole in 1905, he and Ada brought up three sons before divorcing in 1914. After his attempt to open an import–export company failed during the First World War, Hasegawa returned to the laundry business, where he worked until his internment as an enemy alien in December 1941. During the war, two of his sons permanently adopted their mother's maiden name in an attempt to avoid anti-Japanese discrimination.

Upon his death in 1952, Hasegawa left his family a collection of documents, objects and clothes, which they later donated to Museums Victoria.[3] Among the surviving possessions which he brought from Japan in 1897 was a Ministry of Education-approved textbook of English lessons by Reverend D. A. Murray, then head of a commercial school in Kyoto. The book speaks to Hasegawa's training as a teacher, to his hopes for a new life in Melbourne – and to a rote-based mode of teaching English still prevalent a century later in Japan. Structured according to the 'Style of Sentence', for example, Lesson 1 was entitled: 'This is a book'. And Lesson 2: 'This is a book *and* a pen'.[4]

★ ★ ★

---

[3] Moya McFadzean (2009), 'Setsutaro Hasegawa, Japanese Migrant, 1897–circa 1952', in Museums Victoria Collections, https://collections.museumsvictoria.com.au/articles/2935 (all links in this footnote were last accessed on 8 May 2021); McFadzean incorrectly notes Hasegawa's date of birth as 1868. Since my initial internet searches in 2012, more information about Hasegawa has come online, including Andrew Hasegawa, 'Story of Hasegawa Family', *Nikkei Australia: Japanese Diaspora in Australia*, 6 October 2014, www.nikkeiaustralia.com/story-hasegawa-family/, 'Interview with Ida Hasegawa', 31 August 2020, www.nikkeiaustralia.com/interview-with-ida-hasegawa-on-hasegawa-family-history/, and various posts by Andrew Hasegawa (Setsutarō's great-grandson) on *Untitled.Showa: With Love from Australia*, https://untitled.showa.com.au. The historian Yuriko Nagata conducted her own interview with Setsutarō's daughter-in-law, Ida, in August 1987, which she references several times in her 'Japanese Internment in Australia during World War II' (unpublished PhD thesis, University of Adelaide, 1993). For details of Hasegawa's arrival on the *Yamashiro-maru*, see the microfilms 'Brisbane Inwards 1892–97 Rolls 5 and 6', National Archives of Australia (Brisbane) J715.

[4] Rev. D. A. Murray, *Inductive English Lessons; Japanese Text*, 3rd edn (Osaka: Osaka kokubunsha, 1892); https://collections.museumsvictoria.com.au/items/1556835 (last accessed 8 May 2021) (emphasis in the original).

128 Archival Country, Counterclaims

mini-exhibition centred on ten bark paintings composed by Yolŋu artists and activists in the north-east of Arnhem Land, in today's Northern Territory. Five of the paintings, it was explained, had been used as evidence in a 2008 high court case which focused on the 'ownership' of coastal waters. In the years following that encounter, I began to realize that although the NYK map's claims per se were important, the institutional settings in which those claims were preserved and could be researched must also be acknowledged. Those settings had framed not merely my knowledge of what I understood to be the 'Japan–Australia line' but also the positionality from which I approached its history: they were the museums, the university libraries, the state and national archives where I felt most at home, and even the infrastructures of digitization which had led me to a man such as Hasegawa Setsutarō. I explore these ideas in the section entitled 'Archival Directionality'.

But an archive need not necessarily comprise books, words or maps, all to be measured for their empirical truths against other paper sources: for paper can simply be thrown away, as the Japanese historian Minoru Hokari learned from his mentor Jimmy Mangayarri of Daguragu.[15] Instead, 'Saltwater Visions' alerted me to something that my historical training in the universities of Britain and Japan had rarely allowed (in all senses of the word): that the material basis for historical claims need not only be paper and a pen. The sand could be the book; the bush, the university.[16] That is, the archive was as equally situated in Aboriginal country as in the modern state's institutions of knowledge.[17] 'Country', as many scholars have pointed out, is a spatially fluid concept whose meanings may partly be read in contradistinction to the bordered sovereign entity of the colonial state (the etymological roots of 'country' lie in *contra-*).[18] Thus, if the earthy and watery materiality of the country could as equally be considered sites of archival knowledge as museums or

---

[15] Minoru Hokari, *Gurindji Journey: A Japanese Historian in the Outback* (Sydney: University of New South Wales Press, 2011 [2004]), pp. 122, 134.

[16] Samia Khatun, *Australianama: The South Asian Odyssey in Australia* (London: C. Hurst & Co, 2018), especially ch. 6 ('The Book of Sand'). The phrase 'bush university' was used by Djambawa Marawili in 'Gapu-Moṉuk: Saltwater', a promotional video to accompany the Australian National Maritime Museum's much bigger exhibition of its Saltwater Collection, which ran from 9 November 2017 to 17 February 2019: www.sea.museum/saltwater (last accessed 10 May 2021). For more on Djambawa Marawili, see the 'Delineating' section later in this chapter.

[17] My thinking on sites of knowledge is influenced by Christian Jacob, *Qu'est-ce qu'un lieu de savoir?* (Marseille: Open Edition Press, 2014), http://books.openedition.org/oep/423 (last accessed 11 May 2021); and David N. Livingstone, *Putting Science in Its Place: Geographies of Scientific Knowledge* (Chicago: Chicago University Press, 2003).

[18] Timothy Neale and Stephen Turner, 'Other People's Country: Law, Water, Entitlement', *Settler Colonial Studies* 5, 4 (2015): 277–81, here p. 280.

university libraries, then the question arose: what counterclaims could be enunciated through this archive? I offer one answer to that question in the chapter's final section.

As I say, I did not begin to imagine the archives in this way until my last day in Australia. My 'stepping outside' to that point had been less intellectually demanding, limited as it was to a two-day road trip to Queensland's northernmost sugar-farming town of Mossman, where in 1898 a group of Japanese labourers arrived to work after their passage on the *Yamashiro-maru* to Port Douglas. Given these oversights, I planned in June 2020 to revisit the far north of Queensland – Mossman, Port Douglas and Thursday Island – in order to explore the basis by which historians might reconstruct alternative archival claims concerning the arrival of the ship and its passengers. The Covid-19 pandemic put paid to that trip, and in any case an additional two weeks would probably have been insufficient time to think through the lessons of Yolŋu saltwater visions for how the Kuku Yalanji peoples of Mossman might have understood the arrival of Japanese sugar labourers in their country in the late nineteenth century. Consequently, what follows in the chapter's final third is less a reconstruction of the specific moment of the *Yamashiro-maru*'s arrival as seen from Kuku Yalanji perspectives than a broader challenge to the historical directionality both represented by the NYK map and embodied in the archival institutions of libraries, museums and universities. My argument here is for historians, as part of our archival practices, to acknowledge country-derived counterclaims to sources such as the NYK map as empirical interventions in our reconstructions of the past.

Claim 1: Lines Away from the Sinosphere

When a ship sailed, what did it carry? Goods and people, of course; but a ship also carried a set of associations which went beyond its cargo or physical appearance and crossed into the realm of the imagination. One entry point into this imaginative space was the ship's name. It mattered, for example, that some functionary in the British Admiralty chose to rename the *Earl of Pembroke*, the Whitby-built collier that Captain Cook would command while observing the transit of Venus from Tahiti in 1769, the *Endeavour*. The ship could have as conceivably been called the *Racehorse* or the *Carcass* – both names, Nicholas Thomas quips, 'which would rather have diminished the mythic potential of Cook's voyage, one feels'.[19]

---

[19] Nicholas Thomas, *Discoveries: The Voyages of Captain Cook* (London: Penguin Books, 2018 edn), p. 19.

So it was with the *Yamashiro-maru*: no records survive to indicate whether a KUK employee or an Imperial Navy bureaucrat chose the name for the 2,500-ton vessel launched from Low Walker yard 467 on a cold morning in January 1884 – but in Newcastle upon Tyne as elsewhere in late nineteenth-century Europe, an appellative strategy was clearly at work.[20] Yamashiro was the most important province of ancient Japan. The imperial capital had been moved there from Nara in 784 (that is, exactly 1,100 years before the *Yamashiro-maru*'s launch), and then again in 794 to another of Yamashiro's settlements, Heian – later known as Kyoto, where the capital remained until the Meiji 'restoration' of 1868.[21] Meanwhile, the *Yamashiro-maru*'s sister ship, the *Omi-maru*, was named after a neighbouring province and site of one of the ancient court's summer palaces (Ōmi 近江), while the fourteen other British-built steamships of the KUK fleet each carried province- or place-names that connoted Japan's seventh-century Ritsuryō state.

Such referencing of the distant past for the transformative present was standard fare in mid–late Meiji Japan, as demonstrated by the rhetoric of the 1868 revolution as a 'revival of ancient kingly rule' (*ōsei fukko* 王政復古). Modern innovations were regularly embellished in the language and iconography of the ancient, as in (to name but one of countless examples) the new paper notes of the new national currency, which were released in 1873 and whose ten-yen issue featured the legendary Empress Jingū (169–269 CE) on her conquest of the Korean peninsula.[22] In many cases, moreover, such uses of the past also had spatial and not merely temporal dimensions. In 1869, Meiji officials renamed the large island to the north of Honshu from Ezo to Hokkaidō (北海道), literally 'northern sea circuit'. This looked back to a spatial ordering of the aforementioned Ritsuryō state known as the 'five provinces, seven circuits' (*goki-shichidō* 五畿七道) – except that Hokkaido now implied an eighth circuit, as if the island had been part of a Japanese territorial imagination from time immemorial.[23]

---

[20] For naming strategies in the German and British imperial navies in the late nineteenth century, see Jan Rüger, *The Great Naval Game: Britain and Germany in the Age of Empire* (Cambridge: Cambridge University Press, 2007), pp. 147–59, 165–82. The naming of the KUK fleet is unfortunately absent from Richard Ponsonby-Fane, *The Nomenclature of the N. Y. K. Fleet* (Tokyo: Nippon yusen kaisha, 1931), which nevertheless explains the NYK naming rationale for later classes of steamships.

[21] Ellen van Goethem, *Nagaoka: The Forgotten Capital* (Leiden: Brill, 2008).

[22] On these tensions, see Mark Ravina, 'Locally Ancient and Globally Modern', in Robert Hellyer and Harald Fuess, eds., *The Meiji Restoration: Japan as a Global Nation* (Cambridge: Cambridge University Press, 2020), pp. 212–31. As Ravina points out, the ¥10 note was in fact modelled on the US$10 National Bank note from the 1860s.

[23] Ravina, *To Stand with the Nations of the World*, p. 174.

A ship named *Yamashiro*, after one of those five central provinces, therefore made explicit reference to the spatial logic of ancient Japan. Indeed, in cartographic terms it recalled a schematic type of provincial map, used even into the nineteenth century, in which Yamashiro was marked as the 'centre of the imperium' and distances were indicated in the time it took to travel 'up' to the imperial capital and back 'down' – that is, to and from Kyoto.[24] Such temporal schemata were a far cry from the mid-1920s 'N. Y. K. Line' map, which offered a representation of space apparently divorced from time, with Japan rather than Kyoto at its folded centre. But as the infrastructures were put in place from the mid 1880s onwards to realize this NYK vision of Japan's place in the maritime world, the *Yamashiro-maru*'s early status as the fleet's primus inter pares made the ship symbolically central to mid-Meiji Japan in a way presumably intended to reference the historical province's analogous centrality to the ancient state. In this sense, to adapt Kären Wigen's apt phrase, the ship constituted a 'province of the mind'.[25]

In fact, however, the NYK map *can* also be read through a temporal lens. As we have seen, the bold red lines emanating from Japan glossed over the geopolitical realities of the 1920s, namely that white walls had been or were being erected in the Pacific Anglosphere to keep Japanese immigrants out. Yet such contestations notwithstanding, the drawing of thick connections across the Pacific was itself indicative of a major historical transformation. Throughout the Tokugawa period, Japanese world maps had presented an ocean untraversed by shipping lines. Moreover, in Nagakubo Sekisui's (1717–1801) famous 'Complete Illustration of the Globe, All the Countries, and the Mountains and Oceans of the Earth' (c. 1790), the great uncoloured space at the centre of the world was not even marked the 'Pacific' (see Map 2). It was instead labelled both the 'small eastern sea' and the 'large eastern sea', in which 'small' (it has been argued) suggested *nearby* or *familiar* and 'large' *faraway* or *fearful*, thereby reflecting a profound Japanese ambivalence towards the distant Pacific world before the mid nineteenth century.[26] By contrast, Nagakubo's colour scheme, whereby all of South, Southeast and East Asia (including Japan) were marked in red, unambiguously

---

[24] Kären Wigen, *A Malleable Map: Geographies of Restoration in Central Japan, 1600–1912* (Berkeley: University of California Press, 2010), pp. 33–7. See also Nobuko Toyosawa, *Imaginative Mapping: Landscape and Japanese Identity in the Tokugawa and Meiji Eras* (Cambridge, MA: Harvard University Asia Center, 2019), especially pp. 88–144.
[25] Wigen, *Malleable Map*, p. 2, in turn adapting John R. Gillis, *Islands of the Mind: How the Human Imagination Created the Atlantic World* (New York: Palgrave Macmillan, 2004).
[26] Marcia Yonemoto, 'Maps and Metaphors of Japan's "Small Eastern Sea" in Tokugawa Japan, 1603–1868', *Geographical Review* 89, 2 (1999): 169–87.

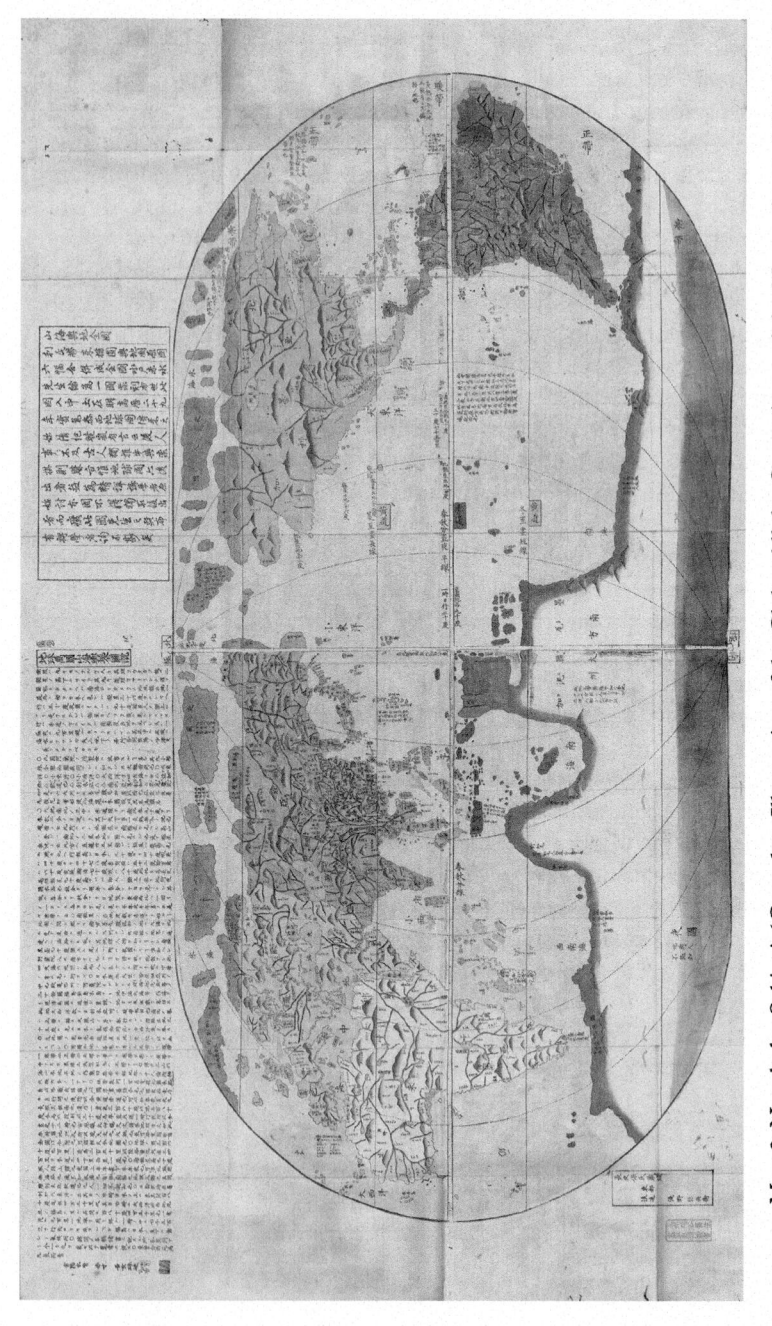

Map 2 Nagakubo Sekisui, 'Complete Illustration of the Globe, All the Countries, and the Mountains and Oceans of the Earth' (*Chikyū bankoku sankai yochi zenzusetsu* 地球萬國山海輿地全圖説), c. 1790. Call number G3201 .C1 1790z N2. Courtesy of University of British Columbia Library, Rare Books & Special Collections.

posited Japan as part of the continental Sinosphere – a positioning reinforced by the fact that the cartographic inspiration for Nagakubo's map had been published in Beijing in 1602 and entered Nagasaki, via Jesuit conduits, soon thereafter.[27]

This contrast in representations of Asia and the Pacific reveals that the claim in the NYK map was not simply *for* Japan's post-1868 centrality to the Pacific world; it was therein also a claim *against* the hitherto defining role that the Sinosphere had played in Japanese cultural and intellectual life for many centuries.[28] In the map's colour scheme, imperial Japan's deep red now stood in marked contrast to China and Mongolia's yellow. Even the graticule delineation of longitude and latitude reinforced the map's message of new world centres away from China, with zero degrees longitude anchored at the Greenwich meridian.[29]

Steaming towards Australia in October 1896 and thereby establishing one of the subsequent NYK map's linear claims, the *Yamashiro-maru* was emblematic of Japan's transformed temporal relationship to the Sinosphere. On the one hand, the ship's name referenced the Ritsuryō state, itself modelled closely on Tang China (618–907). On the other, after being requisitioned by the Japanese Imperial Navy in June 1894, the ship had been active in the conflict which brought China's long claim to wider cultural and intellectual influence in East Asia decisively to an end, namely the Sino-Japanese War (1894–5).[30] True, the *Yamashiro-maru* was never feted for its wartime service in the Japanese press like its NYK counterpart, the *Saikyo-maru*, which famously fought in the heat of the Battle of the Yalu River.[31] Rather, from July 1894 to the end of the war in April 1895 and even

---

[27] On the Chinese-language 1602 map by the Italian Jesuit Matteo Ricci (1552–1610), see Yasuo Endō, 'The Cultural Geography of the Opening of Japan: The Arrival of Perry's Squadron and the Transformation of Japanese Understanding of the Pacific Ocean during the Edo Period', *Acta Asiatica* 93 (2007): 21–40, here pp. 25–9.

[28] Joshua Fogel, *Articulating the Sinosphere: Sino-Japanese Relations in Space and Time* (Cambridge, MA: Harvard University Press, 2009).

[29] On Greenwich-centred standardization, see Chapter 1.

[30] The *Yamashiro-maru* was one of ten NYK ships requisitioned for military or supply purposes (*goyōsen*) on 4 June 1894: Nihon Kei'eishi Kenkyūjo hen, *Nippon Yūsen Hyakunenshi shiryō*, p. 456. The ship's service during the war (including Map 3) is detailed in The National Institute for Defense Studies, Ministry of Defense, *Meiji 27/8-nen kaisenshi fuki: Tokubetsu kanteitai kiryaku (Dai issetsu: Yamashiro-maru)* 明治27・28年海戦史附記：特別艦艇隊記略（第1節：山城丸）[Supplement to the naval war history: Outline of the special ship squadron, 1894–5: *Yamashiro-maru*], available from JACAR (http://www.jacar.go.jp/) (reference code C08040561900) (last accessed 15 May 2021).

[31] On the ways in which the requisitioned ships carried not just supplies but also crucial information on the progress of the war back for the Japanese press, see Catherine L. Phipps, *Empires on the Waterfront: Japan's Ports and Power, 1858–1899* (Cambridge, MA: Harvard University Asia Center, 2015), pp. 189–216 (on the *Saikyo-maru*, p. 201).

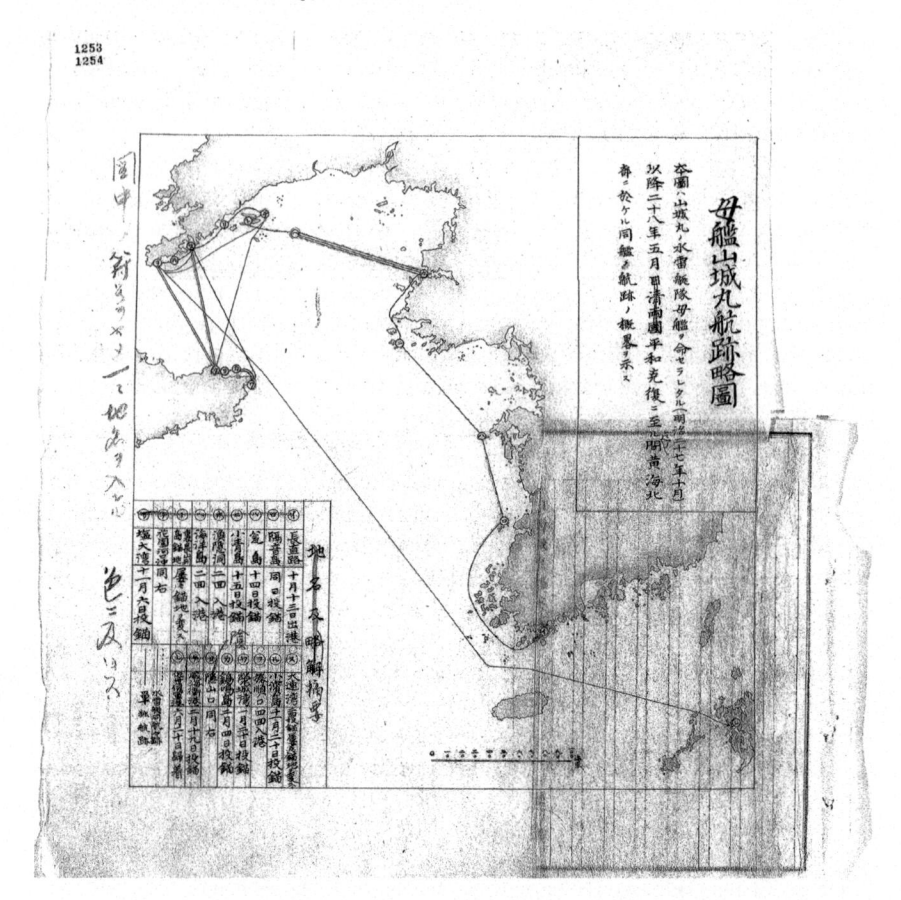

Map 3 'Chart of the Mother-Ship *Yamashiro-maru*'s Routes' (Bokan Yamashiro-maru kōseki ryakuzu 母艦山城丸航跡略図), 1894–5. Courtesy of Japan Center for Asian Historical Records (Holding institution: National Institute for Defense Studies, Center for Military History), Ref. C08040561900.

into the first months of peace, the *Yamashiro-maru*'s role was to deliver torpedoes to the imperial navy's battleships, and to supply coal to those ships as they were engaged across the Yellow Sea (see Map 3). But such logistical support from the NYK commercial fleet was nevertheless vital in bringing to fruition Fukuzawa Yukichi's desire for Japan to 'cast off Asia'.[32]

---

[32] During the Sino-Japanese War, NYK ships carried 59 per cent of Japan's requisitioned tonnage, 83 per cent of its military personnel and 75 per cent of its horses: Wray, *Mitsubishi and the N. Y. K.*, p. 361; Kuwata Etsu 桑田悦, 'Nisshin sensō ni okeru yusō, hokyū' 日清戦争における輸送・補給 [Transportation and supply in the Sino-Japanese War], in *Kindai Nihon sensō* 近代日本戦争 [Japan's modern wars] (Tokyo: Dōdai keizai konwakai, 1995), pp. 251–68, here pp. 260–1. On Fukuzawa, see Chapter 2.

Claim 1: Lines Away from the Sinosphere 135

Thus, while the *Yamashiro-maru*'s name conjured up a seventh-century imagination of spatial order in Japan and in East Asia, its Australia-bound navigations looked to a post-Sinosphere future and to a new cartographic representation of Japan's place in the world. That the 'great prospects' for this new route had been enhanced by victory in the Sino-Japanese War – that the *Yamashiro-maru*'s service to the southern hemisphere was inseparable from its supply missions in the Yellow Sea – reminds historians of two oft-overlooked truisms: first, that conflict was a key form of connection in the modern world; and second, that the power of maps ultimately derives from the force – legal, bureaucratic and in this case military – which lies behind their representation.[33]

These were just some of the ideas borne by the *Yamashiro-maru* in 1896. And while no Australian newspaper could have been expected to know the finer details of the ship's career or its historical references, NYK company officials and Meiji bureaucrats would nonetheless have purred at some of the press coverage triggered by the *Yamashiro-maru*'s arrival. The Melbourne *Argus* remarked upon the ship's 'exciting exploits' during 'the late war between China and Japan, in which she acquitted herself with credit'; the Rockhampton *Morning Bulletin* (Queensland) alleged that due to the ship's design, the 'peaceful trader' could in merely twenty minutes metamorphose into a 'virulent wasp of war'.[34] But of especial note were the *Morning Bulletin*'s opening sentences, which offered a volley of pleasing tropes – Japan's 'aptitude', its 'spirit of progress' and 'intellectual powers' – like a cruiser firing a salute:

Japan is the coming nation. Since it doubled up the Chinese forces and fleets in the late war it has been praised and admired by the western nations. Not so much a revival of something that had formerly been in active existence, but a great demonstration of the possession of intellectual powers and capabilities, and manifestation of a spirit of progress have raised it to a prominent place among

---

[33] Daniel A. Bell, 'This Is What Happens When Historians Overuse the Idea of the Network', *New Republic*, 26 October 2013; see also the concluding remarks in Jürgen Osterhammel, 'Arnold Toynbee and the Problems of Today', 2017 Toynbee Prize Lecture, *Bulletin of the GHI Washington* 60 (2017): pp. 69–87, especially p. 86. On representational force, see Wood, *Rethinking the Power of Maps*, pp. 2, 137.

[34] 'A New Steamship Service to the East', *Argus* (Melbourne), 12 November 1896; *Morning Bulletin* (Rockhampton), 11 November 1896: available through https://trove.nla.gov.au (last accessed 18 May 2021). Unless otherwise stated, all the Australian newspapers in this chapter were accessed through NLA Trove. When the *Yamashiro-maru* first arrived in Japan, the ship's potential for military adaptation was duly noted: 'In the event of her being required for transport duties two thousand troops could be easily carried for a short run, and she is fitted with two 17-centimetre breech-loading Krupp guns, for which ports are provided on the main deck amidships'. See 'New Japanese Steamers', *Japan Weekly Mail*, 12 July 1884.

the powers of the earth. Among other things it is displaying an aptitude and a desire for engaging in trade and commerce. Of this we have had practical evidence by the appearance on the Queensland coast of the pioneer steamer of the Nippon Yusen Company.

Claim 2: Points of Contact

If the first of the NYK map's claims lay in its delineation of 'routes', then its second lay in its representation of 'ports of call': that is, of precise points where the lines met the land. The ships docked, business was conducted and then the ships moved on – or so the map's reader is led to believe.

In my case, the simple clarity of this representation was bolstered by the archival port of call I had made in the early pre-fieldwork stages of my Australian research, namely to the National Library of Australia's database of historic newspapers. There, a basic search with the keyword 'Yamashiro' for the year 1896 had uncovered such gems as the Rockhampton *Morning Bulletin*'s characterization of Japan as 'the coming nation'. More broadly, it had revealed a genre of article which had been generated from a particular place: not the dock (which I'll return to shortly) but rather the ship's saloon. For when the *Yamashiro-maru* called at port, this 'handsome apartment' in the vessel's stern, most probably lit by small chandeliers and filled with a long dining table at its centre, itself became a port of call: for local businessmen, politicians and newspapermen, who gathered to laud and report on the ship's arrival.[35] We can join them in Brisbane on the summer evening of 3 November 1896, an auspicious day, when, 'it being the Japanese Emperor's birthday[,] the ship was going dressed with all her bunting, which attracted great attention' in the city.[36] Captain James Jones has invited more than twenty local dignitaries to dinner. Glasses tinkle, cutlery clinks, men's voices rise, the sun sets – and then a hush descends upon the 'commodious and airy' saloon.[37]

The first to speak is the Honourable Thomas J. Byrnes (1860–98), attorney-general of Queensland. Dark hair brushed high on his forehead,

---

[35] Suppositions based on a photograph of the interior of the aforementioned *Saikyo-maru* (see fn 31), constructed in London in 1888, and briefly discussed in Nippon Yūsen Kaisha, *Yōjō no interia II* 洋上のインテリアII/ *The Interiors of Passenger Ships II* (Yokohama: Nippon yūsen rekishi hakubutsukan, 2011), p. 3. 'The saloon is a handsome apartment': 'Nippon Yusen Kaisha: New Japanese Mail Line', *Australian Town and Country Journal*, 21 November 1896.

[36] 'The New Mail Line from Japan', *SMH*, 7 November 1896.

[37] 'New Steamship Service to the East', *Argus*, 12 November 1896.

Byrnes is a precocious young man, his fulsome beard giving him an older appearance than his thirty-six years. His erudition in history and his skills as a barrister make public speaking second nature, and his three years to date as a legislative assemblyman for Cairns mark what will be his rapid ascent to the colony's premiership by 1898.[38] We do not know Byrnes's direct words, only – from the paraphrasing of the *Brisbane Courier*'s correspondent – that he celebrates the *Yamashiro-maru*'s arrival as the first time a steamer flying the Japanese mercantile flag has come up the Brisbane River. 'It [is] a fine thing for Queensland to have direct communication with rising Japan,' he says of the new NYK line, and indeed inevitable that 'the Eastern countries' would seek new markets for their commercial enterprise. On the occasion of the emperor's birthday, and 'looking at things from the broad standpoint of progressive humanity', Byrnes suggests that they (the Japanese? the assembled gentlemen?) 'ought to be proud of the strides made by the Japanese nation, and he trusted the Emperor would be spared to see his people make still further advancement.'[39]

The speeches continue: Captain Jones on behalf of the Nippon Yūsen Company; Mr Thynne, postmaster general, proposing a toast to the NYK's Queensland agents, Burns, Philp & Co. (in whose archives I found the map); Mr Robert Philp (1851–1922), responding on their behalf, but also present as Queensland minister for railways and mines; and various other toasts, including to 'The Health of the Queensland Ministry' and 'Long Life to the Mikado'.[40] Indeed, it was the same story as the *Yamashiro-maru* steamed southwards: celebratory luncheons in Sydney and Melbourne; newspapers commenting on how 'the inauguration of a new and well-subsidised mail service with a distant country is felt to be an event in a nation's history'; more onboard toasts as the ship returned northwards; and all this couched in the trope of the *Yamashiro-maru* as a 'pioneer' steamer – a word redolent with meaning in a white settler society.[41]

---

[38] On Byrnes's erudition, see 'Immigration of Coloured Aliens, 16 July 1896', *QPD*, vol. 75 (Legislative Assembly, 1896), pp. 304–17. These debates are now available online (www.parliament.qld.gov.au/work-of-assembly/hansard), but in 2013 I accessed them through paper copies in the State Library of Queensland, Brisbane.

[39] 'The Yamashiro Maru', *BC*, 4 November 1896.   [40] *BC*, 4 November 1896.

[41] On the Melbourne celebrations, 'Australia and Japan', *Age* (Melbourne), 14 November 1896. On 'the inauguration', *SMH*, 7 November 1896. On the celebrations as the *Yamashiro-maru* returned north: *SMH*, 21 November 1896, and *BC*, 21 November 1896. On 'the pioneer steamer', *SMH*, 4 November 1896 and *SMH*, 7 November 1896; on 'the pioneer boat', *Mercury* (Hobart), 9 November 1896, and *Northern Territory Times and Gazette*, 13 November 1896; on 'the pioneer vessel', *Australian Town and Country Journal*, 14 November 1896.

What was the 'commercial enterprise' that Byrnes and others had in mind? On the *Yamashiro-maru*'s maiden voyage to Australia, the ship carried a cargo which included fish oil, bamboo blinds, camphor, curios, matting, silk, rice and fire crackers.[42] The last item excepted, this was not a list of goods likely to ignite an immediate boom in bilateral trade. Instead, the Kobe-based Kanematsu Shōten (Kanematsu Trading Company), which from 1890 had been the leading Japanese company involved in the Australia trade, was merely exploring what shape the future Japanese export market might take.[43] For, as Captain Jones explained in a lengthy interview with the *Daily Telegraph* (Sydney), '[The Japanese] say they have not found out yet exactly what the Australian people will purchase from them, but they are making inquiries on this subject, and hope in time to get in touch with the Australian markets.'[44]

More likely, then, Byrnes and company were excited about the Japanese market for Australian goods. Already in December 1896, the *Yamashiro-maru* returned to Japan with a cargo including 500 bags of crushed cattle bone, plus more bones, sinews and hooves – in other words, the raw materials of fertilizer for the Japanese agricultural sector. By one of the *Yamashiro-maru*'s final return trips, leaving Australia in August 1898, the ship's cargo included more than 500 tons of fertilizer, plus 1,031 bags of bones, hooves and other component parts of bonemeal. To be sure, 1898 was an exceptional year: processed fertilizer accounted for more than 40 per cent of the total value of Australian imports to Japan, whereas during the first fifteen years of bilateral trade, the most important cargo by value was generally sheep's wool.[45]

---

[42] *BC*, 5 November 1896; *SMH*, 7 November 1896.

[43] On Kanematsu's early trade with Australia, see Amano Masatoshi 天野雅敏, 'Senzen ni okeru Nihon shōsha no Gōshū shinshutsu ni tsuite: Kanematsu Shōten to Mitsui Bussan no jirei o chūshin ni shite' 戦前における日本商社の豪州進出について：兼松商店と三井物産の事例を中心にして [Concerning the pre-war advance of Japanese trading firms into Australia: With a focus on the examples of Kanematsu Shōten and Mitsui Bussan], in Andō Sei'ichi 安藤精一, Takashima Masaaki 高嶋雅明 and Amano Masatoshi 天野雅敏, eds., *Kinsei kindai no rekishi to shakai* 近世近代の歴史と社会 [The history and society of the early modern and modern] (Tokyo: Seibundō shuppan, 2009), pp. 260–89.

[44] 'A Chat about Japan', *Daily Telegraph* (Sydney), 7 November 1896.

[45] I take the *Yamashiro-maru*'s cargoes in December 1896 and August 1898 from the surviving Kanematsu papers 兼松商店資料, preserved in Kobe University's Research Institute for Economics and Business Administration 神戸大学経済経営研究所, especially Honten kanjō 本店勘定 (II), Gaikoku yunyū shōhin 外国輸入商品 (24), Gaikoku yunyū shōhin kanjōchō 外国輸入商品勘定帳 (1), vols. 1 (July 1894 – December 1897) and 2 (December 1897 – December 1900). For an overview of imports and their values, see Amano, 'Senzen ni okeru Nihon shōsha no Gōshū shinshutsu,' pp. 268–9. For general context, see David Sissons, 'Japan and the Australian wool industry, 1868–1936', in Arthur Stockwin and Keiko Tamura, eds.,

(As Captain Jones also explained to the *Telegraph*, 'The Japanese, whose clothing has hitherto been cotton, imported from India, are taking to wearing wool.')

Either way, the export of wool and fertilizer from Australia to Japan placed this new trading relationship at the heart of a wider ecological transformation of the Pacific world. In Japan, German-trained soil experts in the mid 1890s had calculated that the archipelago had a serious phosphate deficit: the search was on for new sources of agricultural fertilizer, including both guano deposits and domestic bonemeal. The import of Australian bonemeal was thus one element of a wider concern for Japanese phosphate production, a concern which led both to the entrepreneurial exploitation of islands in the western Pacific and to the large-scale import of soybean cake from Manchuria.[46] Moreover, as Gregory Cushman has argued, the fact that nineteenth-century colonialists had successfully turned much of Australia into – in terms of livestock production – a 'mirror image' of the British Isles was itself a development dependent on fertilizer, and thus on the destruction of several tropical islands in the Pacific in the name of guano imports.[47]

The advent of the Japanese mercantile flag coming up the Brisbane River and trading in cow and sheep products was therefore a story of the Australian colonies' own economic engagement with and exploitation of the Pacific Ocean. This may explain the expansionist vision expounded by saloon speakers at the *Yamashiro-maru*'s other ports of call. In Sydney, for example, Mr James Burns, managing director of Burns, Philp & Co, declared that his city 'was destined to become the London of the southern seas'. There were good prospects for direct services from Sydney to Manila, Dutch Java, German New Guinea and beyond. 'Altogether, everything pointed to expansion. Sydney, from its natural position, should command the whole of the trade of Greater Australia, embracing the rich and fertile groups of islands that stretched from our shores to China and Japan, and east to North and South America.'[48] By this logic, the NYK's lines from Japan to Australia were just part of a story in which Sydney would be connected to other strategic points in the Pacific world.

Bridging Australia and Japan, Vol. 1: *The Writings of David Sissons, Historian and Political Scientist* (Acton, ACT: Australian National University Press, 2016 [1978]), pp. 311–18.

[46] Paul Kreitman, *Japan's Ocean Borderlands: Nature and Sovereignty* (Cambridge: Cambridge University Press, 2023), pp. 130–1.

[47] Gregory T. Cushman, *Guano and the Opening of the Pacific World: A Global Ecological History* (Cambridge: Cambridge University Press, 2013), pp. 109–35, citation from p. 135. See also Ben Daley and Peter Griggs, 'Mining the Reefs and Cays: Coral, Guano and Rock Phosphate Extraction in the Great Barrier Reef, Australia, 1844–1940', *Environment and History* 12 (2006): 395–433.

[48] 'Luncheon on the Japanese Mail Steamer', *SMH*, 21 November 1896.

This was an outward-looking imagination of 'Greater Australia' (itself a term which perhaps drew on contemporaneous Anglophone discourses of Greater Britain or Greater America) – as if ports, being departure points for exports, were sites primed towards the sea and not the land. Perhaps Burns's views were momentarily shaped by their articulation in the extraterritorial space of the ship.

Even in the saloon, however, inward-looking anxieties wisped among the invitees. They were to be sensed in the denials. Queensland Attorney-General Byrnes: 'He did not view the new [Japanese trading] venture with apprehension at all, but a needless amount of alarm had been expressed about it. He believed the Anglo-Saxon race would hold its own.' Mr Philp: 'He was not afraid of the Japanese coming to Australia and flooding them out. [...] He did not think there was the slightest fear that the Japanese would come here in greater numbers than Queensland would care to receive.'[49] And in Sydney, the former premier of New South Wales, Sir George Dibbs (1834–1904): 'Australians were not afraid of the Japanese.'[50]

And yet, as these keen politicians knew, many Australians felt differently. In Brisbane, the *Worker* newspaper had for the past three years warned of a 'Jap deluge', of 'A Plague of Japs', of 'JAPANESE DANGER' (this in a letter from an enraged 'Anglo-Saxon'), and of 'Japs Colonising Queensland'.[51] The assembled gentlemen could hardly have been surprised, therefore, by the *Worker*'s visual representation of the *Yamashiro-maru*'s arrival, a few days after the celebratory onboard dinner (see Figure 4.1). Under the headline, 'AUSTRALIANS, HOLD YOUR OWN!' (itself a phrase used by Byrnes), a cartoon depicted a large steamship, its Rising Sun flag fluttering in the breeze as its cargo is manifested on the quayside. The ship is a hive of activity: an officer stands on a soapbox directing operations as two Asian-looking men manoeuvre a large crate marked MACHINERY; behind them appear other boxes and containers, all labelled with a popular nickname referring to Sir Thomas McIlwraith (1835–1900), the former premier of Queensland and leading figure in the colony's politics.[52] Meanwhile, in the cartoon's foreground an East Asian sailor grapples with a swarthy Caucasian worker, wrapping his claw-like hands around the worker's

---

[49] 'New Line of Japanese Steamers', *Mercury* (Hobart), 9 November 1896. The two men's apprehensions were not reported in the *BC*, to my knowledge.
[50] *SMH*, 21 November 1896.
[51] *Worker* (Brisbane), 4 March 1893, 8 July 1893, 27 October 1894, 11 May 1895.
[52] 'Australians, Hold Your Own!' *Worker* (Brisbane), 7 November 1896. McIlwraith had defended 'alien labour' in Queensland in 1893: 'Motion for Adjournment, 28 June 1893: Japanese Immigration', *QPD*, vol. 70 (Legislative Assembly, 1893), pp. 136–44.

Claim 2: Points of Contact 141

Figure 4.1 'AUSTRALIANS, HOLD YOUR OWN!' *Worker: Monthly Journal of the Associated Workers of Queensland* (Brisbane), 7 November 1896. Courtesy of the National Library of Australia.

throat. All this is observed by a multitude of unemployed men – IRON FOUNDER, BOOT MAKER, [C]ARPENTE[R] – whose numbers press back into one of two large warehouses on the dock.

As the *Worker*'s title made clear, the newspaper's particular gripe was with the perceived threat of cheap Japanese labour, which would allegedly undercut the working man's wages and even render him unemployed. Here, the dock rather than the saloon was the key point of contact between the ship and the shore, and the antagonism expressed in the *Worker*'s 1896 cartoon therefore belied the NYK map's later representation of lines cleanly intersecting with the land. Indeed, the New South Wales politician and secretary of the Sydney Wharf Labourers' Union in the late 1890s, William 'Billy' Hughes (1862–1952), made anti-Asian labour campaigns central to his emerging career. Two decades later, as Nationalist Party prime minister of Australia, Hughes and US president Woodrow Wilson (1856–1924) agreed to deny Japan's campaign for a 'racial equality' clause at the Paris Peace Conference – thereby undermining the NYK map's fiction of untrammelled transpacific connections.[53]

Perhaps most striking of all, the anxieties present in the *Yamashiro-maru*'s saloon were revealed by the disconnect between the private celebrations of politicians who supped at the NYK's expense, and their statements of a very different tenor for the official public record. In Queensland, for example, the Legislative Assembly had first debated the issue of Japanese immigration in June 1893, partly prompted by a brief report in the Sydney *Daily Telegraph* to the effect that 500 Japanese labourers had recently arrived to work in the northern Queensland sugar plantations.[54] Thereafter, in increasingly heated annual debates on the issue, politicians of all persuasions – even those, such as Byrnes, who argued that the solution to immigration concerns was to increase the number of white immigrants to Queensland rather than worrying about the Japanese – used the language of 'invasion' to describe the alleged problem. This drew on a longer discourse both in the colonies and in the British metropole concerning the numerous perceived threats from Russia, China or latterly Japan – or a combination of all three. In Australia it found particular expression in the popular literature of the time, such as the 1895 novel by New South Wales-born Kenneth Mackay

---

[53] Naoko Shimazu, *Japan, Race and Equality: The Racial Equality Proposal of 1919* (London: Routledge, 1998); Lake and Reynolds, *Drawing the Global Colour Line*, pp. 149–50, 293–7.

[54] *QPD*, vol. 70 (1893), pp. 136–44; 'Japanese Labor for Queensland', *Daily Telegraph* (Sydney), 23 June 1893.

(1859–1935), entitled, *The Yellow Wave: A Romance of the Asiatic Invasion of Australia.*[55]

Indeed, as if prompted by the language of 'waves', many Queensland assemblymen also drew on metaphors of water. In the first debate on Japanese immigration, one spoke about 'the new importation [of Japanese] with which we are about to be *deluged*' (the *Worker* had used the same term three months earlier).[56] Albert James Callan (1839–1912), member for the constituency of Fitzroy and invitee to the *Yamashiromaru* in November 1896, announced the danger that 'this country, and especially the Northern portion of it, will be *inundated* with Japanese'. In 1897, he suggested that 'one of the most grievous dangers Queensland has to face is the possibility of an *influx* of Japanese' – a word used almost as frequently as 'invasion'.[57] Such was the power of the water metaphor that Robert Philp, whose business interests were so entwined with the NYK, was forced to deny in his onboard speech the prospect of 'the Japanese coming to Australia and *flooding them out*'.[58]

Thus, at the very point where the line met the land, be that the saloon or the dock, anxieties about labour and race threatened to muddy the vision of an outward-facing Australia and an expansive Japan connected across the seas. The latter was an optimistic vision which would later justify the cartographic claims of the 'N. Y. K. Line' map in the mid 1920s. But, as suggested by the language of inundation, flooding and tides, it was also an inherently unstable imagination of the world.[59] Such instabilities were particularly pertinent for the cargo unmentioned in the

---

[55] D. Walker, *Anxious Nation*, pp. 98–112 (on Mackay, pp. 105–7). See also Cees Heere, *Empire Ascendant: The British World, Race, and the Rise of Japan, 1894–1914* (Oxford: Oxford University Press, 2019), pp. 8–45.

[56] *QPD*, vol. 70 (1893), p. 138 (emphasis added): the speaker was John Hoolan (Labour) (1842–1911).

[57] 'Asian and African Aliens, 30 August', *QPD*, vol. 73 (Legislative Assembly, 1895), pp. 770–89, here p. 779; 'Motion for Adjournment, 20 July 1897: Continued Immigration of Japanese', *QPD*, vol. 77 (Legislative Assembly, 1897), pp. 343–60, here p. 357 (emphasis added). Callan, an independent whose constituency neighboured Rockhampton, had visited Japan between February and April 1893 (*QPD*, vol. 70, p. 138) but was unabashed in expressing his 'dislike [for] the notion of Japanese being brought here [...] because they will take the work from men of our own race': 'Motion for Adjournment, 31 August 1894: Influx of Japanese', *QPD*, vol. 71 (Legislative Assembly, 1894), pp. 400–6, here p. 402.

[58] *Mercury* (Hobart), 9 November 1896 (emphasis added). The government resident of Thursday Island, John Douglas (see also Chapter 5), acknowledged in an interview in 1897 the 'fear that we were going to be inundated with Japanese': 'Hon. John Douglas', *Telegraph* (Brisbane), 13 December 1897.

[59] Sir James Dickson (1832–1901), ministerialist and premier of Queensland between 1898 and 1899, told the Legislative Assembly during this period, 'I am determined as far as possible to resist the tide of Japanese invasion', as reported in 'The Japanese Question', *BC*, 13 May 1899.

'Ex Yamashiro Maru' lists of goods and wares, namely the Japanese men and small numbers of women who travelled on the NYK ships – migrants who were largely poorer and less educated than Hasegawa Setsutarō. As we shall see, for Japanese male labourers disembarking in the far north of Queensland as for white working-class readers of the *Worker* in Brisbane, blots rather than clean points would have been a more realistic graphic by which to represent Japanese–Australian entanglements.[60]

Claim 3: Uniform Colours

Though Japan may well have been 'the coming nation' for the Rockhampton *Morning Bulletin* in November 1896, it was not the only one. In fact, the exact same phrase had been used in the Queensland Legislative Assembly's first debate on Japanese immigration in June 1893 – but with reference to Australia. 'In the name of the coming nation,' exclaimed John Dunsford (1855–1905) at the end of his speech, 'I call upon the Premier and this House to assist in making this a white man's country, and [in] conserving the welfare of the coming Australian nation.'[61]

The NYK map's colour scheme was problematic for the monochrome claims of uniformity it made about this alleged white man's country.[62] At a first level, these claims were a question of the implied umbilical cord between Britain and its Australian dominions (both coloured the same shade of pink). In fact, that cord had been under increased strain since July 1894, when Britain led the world in concluding a new Treaty of Commerce and Navigation with Japan, thereby replacing the 1858 'unequal' treaty (see Chapter 6). The new agreement, to come into force in 1899, included the promise of 'full liberty' for both Japanese and British subjects 'to enter, travel, or reside in any part of the dominions and possessions of the other Contracting Party' (Article I). That is, Japanese people would be free to live and work in the dominions of Australia – if, within a two year period, the Australian colonies agreed to adhere to the treaty's provisions. But if they did not agree, then the colonies would equally not enjoy 'the reciprocal freedom of commerce and navigation' between the contracting parties (Article III), including

---

[60] Billy Hughes himself described Japanese and Chinese immigration as a 'blot' on Australia's national destiny in 1901: cited in Lake and Reynolds, *Drawing the Global Colour Line*, p. 149.
[61] *QPD*, vol. 70 (1893), p. 143.
[62] Cf. Lauren Benton, *A Search for Sovereignty: Law and Geography in European Empires, 1400–1900* (Cambridge: Cambridge University Press, 2010), p. 2 on the 'monochrome shading of imperial maps'.

protection from unequal import tariffs (Articles V and VI) and the mutual right to transport goods to port without depending on each other's merchant navies (Articles VIII and IX). In these ways, the treaty was central to the vision of an expansive, Pacific-facing Australia articulated on the *Yamashiro-maru* by James Burns, with Sydney as the 'London of the southern seas'. And yet, as the Queensland premier confidentially telegrammed his Victoria counterpart in April 1895, 'it may be found necessary to legislate for restriction of [Japanese] immigration into Queensland in which case adhesion to Treaty would cause difficulty at the time such legislation was initiated'.[63]

The dilemma that the British–Japanese treaty thus forced upon the Australian colonies, between the promise of free trade and the peril of free entry, was epitomized in Queensland by the contradictory voices emerging from Rockhampton. As we have seen, the town's newspaper lauded the opening of the new NYK line in November 1896, including Japan's 'desire for engaging in trade and commerce'. Twelve months earlier, however, the Rockhampton Chamber of Commerce had also passed a resolution arguing that 'it will be very injudicious for these Colonies to accept the Imperial Commercial Treaty with Japan of 1894 and thereby grant a free and unrestricted entry of the Japanese into this and the adjoining colonies'. In case the message was unclear, the Chamber's secretary explained to the Queensland premier that the treaty 'carries with it the very objectionable risk of *flooding* our country with an undesirable alien race'.[64]

If anything, the arrival of the *Yamashiro-maru* in 1896, at a time when the colonies' adherence or otherwise to the treaty was still an open question, was therefore a reminder of Australia's relative impotence concerning its relations to Asia's coming nation. As the aforementioned honorary consul of Japan, Alexander Marks, provocatively noted in his saloon speech upon the ship's arrival in Melbourne, '[t]he Governments of Australia should understand that they were parts of the British Empire. Britain had made treaties with foreign nations, and those treaties must be

---

[63] Telegram from Sir Hugh Nelson to Sir George Turner, 2 April 1895: QSA, Item ID ITM861853 (top number 95/03738). On the QSA system of top-numbering, see Chapter 5.

[64] Letter from Rockhampton Chamber of Commerce to Sir Hugh Nelson, 18 November 1895, QSA, Item ID ITM861853 (top number 95/14011) (emphasis added). A public meeting in Mackay in September 1894 similarly passed a motion bemoaning the 'repeated influx of Japanese' as 'a menace to the white workers of this place and neighbourhood as they are undesirable colonists': Letter from the Mackay Town Hall (writer illegible) to James Chataway, 24 September 1894, QSA, Item ID ITM861850 (top number 94/10020).

observed. Of course Australia had no "sovereign rights".'[65] Others were less sanguine about this reality. A month earlier, an editorial in the *Maitland Weekly Mercury* (New South Wales) obliquely referenced Cinderella when it complained:

Our right of self-government is a mockery, unless it includes power to regulate the components of our population. [...] And, if we are threatened with a gradual, an insidious, but none the less certain and menacing irruption of [Chinese, Japanese] and other peoples whom we do not desire for the purposes of admixture with our own, the mother-country must help us. She must see that it is an essential part of Imperial policy that she should help us. She is no mother at all, but only a cruel stepdame, if she does not.[66]

As for Queensland, by the time of the Legislative Assembly's 1897 debate on the 'Continued Immigration of Japanese', the metaphors connoted less pantomime than power abuse, with one member objecting 'to the British Government practically holding up a revolver to our heads'. Hence the proposal, in Queensland and elsewhere, that if '[w]e are all agreed that the Japanese should not be allowed to flow into this colony', then '[t]he great remedy is for Australia to become united under one Federal Government.' Or, as the Rockhampton representative phrased it, 'I have no more desire to cut the bonds that bind us to the old country than the [previous speaker] has, but if the only way by which I could save Australia from an Asiatic invasion was by cutting those bonds I would do it to-morrow.'[67]

In portraying the Australian continent as a single political entity in the mid 1920s, the NYK map sanitized a history of excision between the 'old' or 'mother' country and the colonies. In fact, the perception of a Japanese influx had been one stimulation for the federated Australia that the map now depicted, an act of fundamental disconnection from Britain. At this first level, therefore, the conformity of pink across the map's British empire offered a rose-tinted interpretation of metropole–colony relations during the period of the new NYK line to Australia.

---

[65] 'Australia and Japan', *Age* (Melbourne), 14 November 1896. Marks's critique was perhaps particularly directed at Victoria, whose protectionist policies stood in contrast to the more free-trade instincts of Sydney's politicians: D. Walker, *Anxious Nation*, p. 73. But he had also been banging this drum elsewhere, as when he wrote to the Queensland government warning the Australian colonies that they should 'not take upon themselves a sovereign right, so as to cause complications with the Mother Country, unless the peace and safety of their colony is threatened': Letter from Alexander Marks to illegible addressee in Brisbane, 12 April 1894, QSA, Item ID ITM 861850 (top number 94/3720).

[66] 'Exclusion of Coloured Races', *Maitland Weekly Mercury* (NSW), 17 October 1896.

[67] *QPD*, vol. 77 (1897), respectively p. 348 (George Jackson, Labour), p. 354 (Robert Harrison Smith, Ministerialist), and pp. 357–8 (William Kidson, Labour).

The second way in which the map's colours corralled the colonies' recent past was in their conformity of pink across the huge area of Queensland – as if political control was evenly distributed from Brisbane, in the south, to Thursday Island, more than 2,000 kilometres to the north (comparable to the distance between London and Saint Petersburg). In the eyes of Australia's late nineteenth-century opinion makers, such control was more de jure than de facto. Editorializing on the new British-Japanese treaty, the *Sydney Morning Herald* argued that Australia's relations with Japan must be considered differently from those of England, America and the nations of Europe, for '[n]o other has vast unoccupied territories exposed to an influx of people'. Australia's choice, the paper claimed, 'will have to be taken between exclusion from a share in the coming trade of Japan and the possibility of our unoccupied territories being overrun by an alien "inferior race"'.[68] In other words, the colonies' legal claim to 'territory' was undermined in practice by the fact that so much of Australia was allegedly 'unoccupied'.

In the case of Queensland, this tension found expression in the trope of the 'empty North', and one site at which its contours were rendered visible was the small town of Mossman, some 1,500 kilometres north of Brisbane.[69] In the mid 1890s, Mossman was the northernmost outpost of the Australian sugar industry, as it remains today. But Mossman had never been unoccupied. The wide river valley was, and is, known as Wikal. Manjal Dimbi, at the valley's western rim, is the 'mountain holding back', representing in turn Kubirri, the 'good shepherd' who restrains the flesh eater, Wurrumbu, and thereby protects the people.[70] And the people, speaking Kuku Yalanji, had lived off this land for many thousands of years before European gold prospectors and loggers began to encroach in the early 1870s and impose their own placenames.

Among the arrivistes was a certain Daniel Hart, who described himself as a British subject and 'native of the West Indies'. This presumably made him familiar with the Caribbean sugarcane economy, and indeed in an 1884 petition to the governor of Queensland, Hart described an exploration he undertook in June 1874 from Cooktown to the area around the Mossman River, where he and his small party discovered an

---

[68] *SMH*, 6 December 1894.
[69] For a discussion of this trope in the 1900s and 1910s, see D. Walker, *Anxious Nation*, pp. 113–26.
[70] On the name Wikal: http://pandora.nla.gov.au/pan/144049/20170330-1816/queenslandhistory.blogspot.com.au/2011/03/far-north-queensland-place-names-mo-my.html (last accessed 7 November 2017); 'Manjal Dimbi: Kuku Yalanji Origin Story, Mossman Gorge, Australia', www.youtube.com/watch?v=wUQzIQ7cQMM (last accessed 23 July 2021).

'abundance of cedar and excellent sugar land'. Hart reiterated how his own subsequent clearances and the arrival of other loggers fully endorsed 'his repeatedly expressed opinion as to [the land's] value for sugar growing'. (In the petition, Kuku Yalanji people appear only offstage, when Hart mentions that two men from another party 'were speared and conveyed to hospital by Your Petitioner'.)[71]

But the gap between Hart's sugarcane vision and the reality on the ground was substantial. At the very least, the land must be cleared, a mill built, the cane cultivated, and the crop harvested at speed – that is, transported to the mill for juice extraction and purification in the forty-eight hour window before the cut cane would begin to rot. All this required capital and labour. Further south in Queensland, where the sugar industry had been developed since the mid 1860s, the labour had been provided partly by Chinese immigrants who had previously crossed to Australia in successive gold rushes, and partly by Pacific Islanders, whom the white settlers derogatorily referred to as 'kanakas' – that is, labourers often transported to Australia against their will and in horrific conditions.[72] (A key motivation for one of the *Yamashiro-maru*'s first captains, John J. Mahlmann, to pen his later autobiography was to deny his involvement in this 'blackbirding' trade in the late 1860s: see Chapter 1.) But such was the weight of liberal opinion against the importation of Pacific Islanders that legislation banning the trade was passed in 1885 – just as Hart was imagining a sugar future in the Mossman River valley. Though not effective immediately, both the ban and simultaneous restrictions on Chinese immigration were two factors, along with a decline in sugar prices, which resulted in the contraction of the Queensland sugar industry in the late 1880s.[73]

---

[71] 'The Petition of Daniel Hart', 13 December 1884, QSA, Item ID ITM847142, but reprinted in *Queensland Heritage* 3, 2 (1975): 21–8, and accessed online through the University of Queensland, https://espace.library.uq.edu.au. The context for Hart's petition was the rapid sale of agricultural land in the far north of Queensland in the early 1880s – land partly purchased by speculators from Victoria, who hoped to form sugar plantations: Peter D. Griggs, *Global Industry, Local Innovation: The History of Cane Sugar Production in Australia, 1820–1995* (Bern: Peter Lang, 2011), pp. 49–50. The settlement was named after Hugo Mosman (1843–1909), whose Aboriginal servant, Jupiter Mosman (1861–1945) is credited with finding gold at Charters Towers in 1871.

[72] It is estimated that 62,500 Pacific Islanders were shipped to Queensland after their introduction by businessman Robert Towns (founder of Townsville) in 1863: Emma Christopher, 'An Illegitimate Offspring: South Sea Islanders, Queensland Sugar, and the Heirs of the British Atlantic Slave Complex', *History Workshop Journal* 90 (2020): 233–52; Brown, '"Most Irregular Traffic"', pp. 184–203.

[73] Griggs, *Global Industry, Local Innovation*, pp. 52–3, 86, 191. Writing under the name 'North Queenslander, Mosman [sic] River' and drawing on his experience in Jamaica, Hart proposed the importation of 'coolie' labour: '[I]f Queensland is to compete in the

That a newly constructed mill was nonetheless to be found in Mossman less than a decade later was due in no small part to the Queensland government's attempts simultaneously to stimulate the sugar industry, to encourage white settlement in the colony, and thereby to fill the 'empty North'. One legislative mechanism to do so was the Sugar Works Guarantee Act (1893), by which public loans were pledged to finance the construction of expensive sugar mills. This, it was hoped, would increase the financial viability of small, family-managed sugar farms – which would in turn attract white settlers as far north as places like Mossman.[74] (In this way, the Queensland sugar model was very different to that of Hawai'i, where mills were privately owned and required major investment, leading to the consolidation of the industry in the hands of major capitalists.) Under the Act, therefore, a group of settler-farmers formed the Mossman Central Mill Company in December 1894 and borrowed £66,300. The mill crushed its first cane in August 1897, and within a decade had almost quadrupled its tonnage. In a 1904 newspaper report, it was considered 'to be in a good position financially'.[75]

So much for the problem of capital. But the problem of labour remained, despite the presence of several hundred Chinese and Pacific Island workers in the Mossman district.[76] And this labour shortage explains the arrival of 100 Japanese men at Port Douglas on the afternoon of 12 August 1898 – labourers who were contracted to work at the Mossman Central Mill Company.[77]

---

world's market with these commodities she must have suitable labourers on something near the same terms as other sugar-producing countries, and then I feel sure that Queensland will become in a few years one of the principal, if not *the* principal, sugar producers of the world': 'The Tropical Labour Question', *Queenslander* (Brisbane), 10 March 1883.

[74] On this logic, see Jodi Frawley, 'Containing Queensland Prickly Pear: Buffer Zones, Closer Settlement, Whiteness', *Journal of Australian Studies* 38, 2 (2014): 139–56, here p. 140. On the legislation, see Griggs, *Global Industry, Local Innovation*, pp. 100–2. Mossman was one of ten government-funded sugar mills built between 1891 and 1901.

[75] 'The Mossman River and District', *Queenslander* (Brisbane), 24 December 1904; on the increase in output from 27,905 tons crushed in 1897 to 103,291 tons in 1906 (an unusually good year), see John Kerr, *Northern Outpost* (Mossman: Mossman Central Mill Co, 1979), p. 151.

[76] There were 'about five hundred Chinese and three hundred kanakas in the Mossman district' in August 1898: 'Queensland (By Telegraph)', *North Queensland Register* (Townsville), 17 August 1898. See also Christopher Anderson and Norman Mitchell, 'Kubara: A Kuku-Yalanji View of the Chinese in North Queensland', *Aboriginal History* 5, 1/2 (1981): 20–37, here pp. 27–8.

[77] The directors G. L. Rutherford, W. H. Buchanan and Thomson Low were delegated with 'obtaining a supply of Japanese' in 1898: Kerr, *Northern Outpost*, p. 45.

The men who stepped off the *Yamashiro-maru* that afternoon knew none of this context. Like their compatriots in Hawai'i, they had left Japan in search of better wages and perhaps the possibility of a new life. Like Wakamiya Yaichi and Kodama Keijirō, they hailed from Hiroshima and Kumamoto prefectures respectively; indeed, sixteen of their number came from Hiroshima's Saeki county alone (see Chapter 2).[78] There was, however, one structural difference with their migration from that of their earlier Hawaiian counterparts: the Mossman men travelled under the auspices not of the state but rather through the mediation of a private emigration enterprise, the Tōyō Imin Gōshi Gaisha (Oriental Emigration Company). Co-founded under a different name in 1891 by a Tokyo businessman and the vice-president of the NYK, the Oriental Emigration Company shipped more than 10,000 Japanese overseas in the period 1891–1917, including to New Caledonia, Fiji, Guadeloupe and Brazil. Along with dozens of other private migration companies which were founded in the years after the replacement of the Hawaiian government-sponsored programme in 1894 by a system of 'free' emigration, the Oriental Emigration Company thereby contributed significantly to an expansive vision of the Japanese empire articulated in the mid 1890s by a coalition of Tokyo-based politicians, journalists, intellectuals and businessmen.[79] The Mossman Japanese were the foot soldiers of this transpacific vision – though this, too, they were not to know.

Although this imagination of a 'Greater Japan' (*Dai-Nihon*) had many ideological reference points, one of its key tenets was a Malthus-inspired discourse of domestic demographic explosion – and, so the thinking went, a concomitant need to identify overseas destinations for Japan's surplus population.[80] And although Queensland's politicians were far from attuned to the nuances of the Japanese-language debates in Tokyo, population considerations were also central to their anti-treaty (and anti-Japanese) rhetoric. Thus, against the 'scattered population of North Queensland' was contrasted '*the teeming population* of Asiatic countries

---

[78] For a full list of these migrants and their addresses, see DA 3.8.2.83, vol. 2. The ship carried around fifty-nine other labourers who were contracted to work for three different companies in Mackay.

[79] Azuma, *In Search of Our Frontier*, pp. 81–90 (Oriental Emigration Company figures on p. 84). The Oriental Emigration Company was called the Nihon Kissa Imin Gōshi Gaisha until 1897. This company shipped the first group of Japanese contract labourers to Queensland in 1892, and over the next four years organized five further crossings: Kodama Masaaki 児玉正昭, 'Shoki imingaisha no imin boshū to sono jittai' 初期移民会社の移民募集とその実態 [The conditions and recruitment strategies of the first emigration companies], *Hiroshima kenshi kenkyū* 3 (1978): 20–44, here pp. 20–7.

[80] Lu, *Making of Japanese Settler Colonialism*, passim.

that are close within reach of our ports'.[81] The aforementioned Mr Callan was typical in his articulation of the problem, in August 1895:

> You cannot bounce the Japanese. They have had their turn at war now, and have done remarkably well, and if they once turn their attention to Queensland, I do not know that there is anyone here capable of keeping them out unless measures for the purpose have been taken beforehand. It is ridiculous to talk about stopping the Japanese without England to back us. We [Queensland] have a population of about 400,000, or about the population of a third or fourth class European city, and Japan has a population of 40,000,000. What could we do unless we put the case before those who are able to protect us, and say we do not want the Japanese to come here?[82]

Yet by the winter months of mid 1898, Queensland's range of possible 'measures' had narrowed considerably. Having joined the 1894 Anglo-Japanese Treaty of Commerce and Navigation on the expectation that a separate protocol on the immigration of labourers and artisans, agreed in March 1897 with Tokyo, would also be accepted by London, Brisbane's politicians were dismayed to be disabused of that notion by the mother country in August 1897.[83] (This was the context for the 'revolver' complaint.) A year later, as ships continued to discharge Japanese men and women at Thursday Island in their dozens, the *Townsville Daily Bulletin* furiously observed that 'this peaceful invasion will prove so disastrous to Queensland's interests ultimately that Thursday Island will be in fact an "appanage of the Mikado's kingdom"'.[84] And thus, in the absence of legislative options, the new premier of Queensland, Thomas J. Byrnes (who had led the celebratory speeches onboard the *Yamashiro-maru* in November 1896), decided to strengthen the administration of immigration control, by decreeing that any Japanese without valid passports for Queensland would not be permitted to land in the colony. In the meantime, however, the *Yamashiro-maru* had already left Japan for Australia, carrying among its passengers the 100 Mossman-bound labourers – and thus prompting a flurry of telegraphs between various agencies about the legal status of those on board.[85]

---

[81] Respectively: *QPD*, vol. 71 (1894), p. 401 and vol. 73 (1895), p. 780 (emphasis added). On Australia's own declining birth-rate: D. Walker, *Anxious Nation*, p. 101.

[82] *QPD*, vol. 73 (1895), p. 779.

[83] The protocol was signed between Britain's minister in Tokyo, Ernst Satow (on behalf of Queensland), and the Japanese foreign minister, on 16 March 1897: QSA, Item ID ITM861853. Queensland ratified the 1894 treaty in June 1897: QSA, Item ID ITM 861851 (top number 97/10112).

[84] *Townsville Daily Bulletin*, 20 July 1898. This is not available on NLA Trove; rather, the article had been clipped out by Japanese consulate officials in Townsville and forwarded to Tokyo: DA 3.8.2.33, vol. 2.

[85] *NGB* Meiji 31 (1898), vol. 2, 107, 114–15.

These were the circumstances in which the Mossman Japanese disembarked in Port Douglas in August 1898: a diplomatic wrangle over passports – a wrangle itself reflective of wider geopolitical tensions over the position of the Australian colonies in Britain's new relationship with Japan – tensions themselves prompted by anxieties about the 'scattered' settler population in the otherwise 'unoccupied' North – anxieties themselves suggestive of the concomitant need to encourage further Anglo-Saxon colonization through state subsidies for the emerging sugar industry. If the labourers detected a chill in the air, it had nothing to do with the winters, which are mild this far north. Instead, it had to do with the 'public feeling' in Port Douglas that 'runs very high against the importation of Japanese'.[86] And it had to do with the accusation that the contracting of Japanese to work at Mossman ran against the intent of the 1893 Sugar Works Guarantee Act – as articulated by the Rockhampton-based *Capricornian* newspaper:

> When the central mills scheme was launched by the Government, and Parliament agreed to invest such a large sum in the venture, the great inducement held out was that by this means black labour would be shut out of the colony, and at the same time the sugar industry would be saved from destruction. But now the Government which put forward this argument is itself sanctioning the introduction of Japanese for one of these very central mills, built by Government money for the purpose of establishing the sugar industry on a white instead of a black man's basis.[87]

In this Manichean world view, the Queensland sugar industry was strategically important not just for its economic value but because, through the provision of central mills, 'black labour would be shut out of the colony'. In this way, 'white sugar' was not just a descriptor of the end product but also an aspirational marker of the labour involved in its production. Conversely, any labourer who was not white – be they 'black' or Japanese – contaminated this vision of white product and white production.[88] To complain about the 'introduction of Japanese' in Mossman was another way of calling the Japanese racially impure: their presence in the mill would undermine the coming nation's imagination of its own refined future.

Thus, at the point of Port Douglas, where 100 Japanese disembarked from the new NYK line, the colonial polity imagined by Brisbane

---

[86] 'Queensland (By Telegraph)', *North Queensland Register* (Townsville), 17 August 1898.
[87] 'Stray Notes', *Capricornian* (Rockhampton), 20 August 1898.
[88] On this point, see Stefanie Affeldt, 'A Paroxysm of Whiteness: "White" Labour, "White" Nation and "White" Sugar in Australia', in Wulf D. Hund, Jeremy Krikler and David Roediger, eds., *Wages of Whiteness and Racist Symbolic Capital* (Berlin: Lit Verlag, 2011), pp. 99–130.

politicians could never merely be a colour on the map: it was also a question of the colour of skin and the colour of the product, and thus a question of who would be free to enter and who would be shut out.[89]

Archival Directionality

One of the most detailed surveys of the northern Queensland sugar industry at the turn of the twentieth century survives not in Brisbane, Sydney or Canberra but in Tokyo. Written by Townsville consul Iijima Kametarō on the basis of a three-week tour he took in July and August 1900, the ninety-one-page handwritten report describes the location, labour force, acreage, working conditions and production output of the planting districts at – travelling north from Townsville – Macknade, Ripple Creek, Victoria, Goondi, Mourilyan, Hambledon and Mossman; and, just to the south of Townsville, Kalamia and Pioneer (see Figure 4.2). This itinerary was determined by the distribution of Japanese sugar labourers throughout the northern part of the colony, ranging from the 57 employed at Ripple Creek to the 137 working at Victoria, and numbering 839 in all. At Mossman, Iijima wrote of only 70 Japanese labourers – not two years after 100 had arrived on three-and-a-half year contracts. The reason for this was that in March 1900 (he explained), the Japanese there had gone on strike. Broken only after the intervention of the Townsville consulate, one result of the unfortunate incident was that the main instigators were repatriated to Japan.[90] Iijima was suitably vague on this point, but contemporary newspaper reports suggested that 140 'rebellious Japs' downed tools in Mossman, implying both that more labourers had arrived subsequent to those in August 1898, and that approximately half the Japanese workforce had proved 'troublesome' enough to be 'sent back to their own land'.[91] Similar to the Japanese consular staff dealing with complaints from the Spreckelsville

---

[89] For comparison, see Jonathan Hyslop, 'The Politics of Disembarkation: Empire, Shipping and Labor in the Port of Durban, 1897–1947', *International Labor and Working Class History* 93 (2018): 176–200. On the ways in which the site of immigrant disembarkation framed subsequent archival imaginations of race and class in Canada, see Lisa Chilton and Yukari Takai, 'East Coast, West Coast: Using Government Files to Study Immigration History', *Histoire sociale / Social History* 48, 96 (May 2015): 7–23.

[90] Iijima Kametarō 飯島亀太郎, 'Kita Kuinsurando chihō junkai hōkokusho' 北クインスランド地方巡回報告書 [Report of a tour around the Northern Queensland area], 25 September 1900: DA 6.1.6.29. A few years after I first accessed this report, it was digitized and is now available from JACAR (www.jacar.go.jp) (reference code B16080742300) (last accessed 15 May 2021).

[91] *North Queensland Register*, 26 February 1900: the strike occurred in February, not March. For further (unfootnoted) details, see Kerr, *Northern Outpost*, pp. 45–6.

154   Archival Country, Counterclaims

Japanese and trucks loaded with cane.

Figure 4.2 'Japanese and trucks loaded with cane', Hambledon Mill, near Cairns, c. 1890.[92] Image Number APU-025-0001-0010. Courtesy of John Oxley Library, State Library of Queensland.

labourers in 1885 Hawai'i, Iijima's unsympathetic opinion of the Mossman agitators is suggested both by his report failing to discuss the strike's origins – allegedly a labourer being struck by one of the cane-transporting rail trucks – and by his condescending descriptions of the labourers in Queensland as 'Japanese boys'.[93]

The generation and preservation of reports such as Iijima's in Tokyo was indicative of the professionalization of the Japanese overseas diplomatic service in the late nineteenth century, with the Foreign Ministry sending trained officials to Townsville in 1896 to take over consular

---

[92] Although the date is given as c. 1890, a photo from the same series on display in the Australian Sugar Heritage Centre, in Mourilyan, offers a date of c. 1898 – which seems more likely to me.

[93] E.g. the private letter from K. Iijima to Henry Dutton, Under Secretary, Chief Secretary's Office, 20 August 1900, QSA, Item ID ITM861853 (no top number).

duties which had previously been carried out from afar – and in English – by Melbourne-based Alexander Marks. Iijima's report thus typifies the multilingual and transnational archival traces by which historians might reconstruct the complex history of the Queensland sugar industry in the late 1890s. Moreover, it hints at new ways through which to globalize that history. A few weeks before he embarked on his tour, for example, Iijima had contacted one of the most senior officials in the new colonial government of Taiwan, Gotō Shinpei (1857–1929), to suggest that the experience Japanese sugar labourers had acquired in Queensland might be of use to the recently established Taiwan Sugar Company. Perhaps one motivation for Iijima's subsequent tour of northern Queensland was therefore the labour-relations and land-ownership lessons to be learnt for the future development of colonial Taiwan. If so, his report speaks to the more general history of transplanted sugar knowledge, personnel and capital which was occurring across and between Japanese diasporic communities in the Pacific Ocean at the turn of the twentieth century.[94]

Yet for all the ways in which the Tokyo archives complexify the history of Queensland's sugar-producing areas, the paperwork therein shared in two important ways a basic worldview with that of the Queensland politicians and newspapermen I have cited to this point. For a start, the Aboriginal peoples of northern Queensland were as absent in Iijima's report as they were in colonial imaginations of an 'unoccupied territory'. Of Chinese, 'Kanakas', 'Malays' and Europeans, and of their relations to Japanese labourers, Iijima had plenty of observations; of, say, the Kuku Yalanji people of Mossman, he wrote not a word. (And even if he had discussed them, he would certainly have used the generic word *dojin* 土人 in the Japanese parlance of the time, literally meaning 'earth people', rather than naming individual Aboriginal countries.)[95] Second, like the politicians with whom he was in regular contact (including Robert Philp, since December 1899 the premier of Queensland), Iijima interpreted the

---

[94] See Martin Dusinberre and Mariko Iijima, 'Transplantation: Sugar and Imperial Practice in Japan's Pacific', *Historische Anthropologie* 27, 3 (2019): 325–35. On Iijima's letter, see Miki Tsubota-Nakanishi, 'The Absence of Plantations in the Taiwanese Sugar Industry', *Historische Anthropologie* 27, 3 (2019): 385–409, here pp. 385–6. The letter itself is in DA 3.5.2 and is also available from JACAR (www.jacar.go.jp) (reference code B11091025600) (last accessed 15 May 2021).

[95] It was not until the onset of Japan's hostilities with Great Britain (1941) that Aboriginal groups in northern Australia were considered potential collaborators for the expanding empire – leading to the terminology changing from *dojin* 土人 to *genjūmin* (原住民, literally 'original inhabitants'): Shuji Iijima, 'Australian Aboriginal Studies in Japan, 1892–2006', *Japanese Review of Cultural Anthropology* 7 (2006): 51–70, here pp. 53–4. My reading of silence in Iijima's report is influenced by Samia Khatun's discussion of Muhammad Bux's memoirs in Khatun, *Australianama*, pp. 79–80.

undeniable tensions in the north in terms of 'the mutual relations of both countries'. In other words, in the nation-state imagination of the world for which he had been trained, northern Queensland constituted a borderland between the expansive interests of Japan and the exclusionary anxieties of Australia.[96]

This co-production of northern Queensland as a remote border region was, like the NYK map, a beguilingly simplistic way of seeing the world – and one which I myself bought into during my archival research in Australia. For, after a few days in the Burns Philp Collection and also at Canberra's National Library of Australia, I returned to Sydney by bus and flew north to Iijima's old stomping ground of Townsville. Of a mild Saturday evening, I strolled around the historical downtown, whose colonial-era buildings have themselves been colonized by nightclubs and cocktail bars. (The historical plaque on the former Burns, Philp & Co Building, erected in 1895, noted that in the late nineteenth century the company 'was the largest exporter of Queensland cedar – "red gold"'. A sign hanging near the building's main entrance, displaying the graphic of a white pole dancer against a black background, promised a different currency: 'Gold Santa Fe: Showgirls of Style, Dancers of Pleasure'.) The following morning, I hired a car and began the drive some 420 kilometres up to Mossman. Although I had not read Iijima's report at that point, I was inadvertently tracing his route north: within an hour or two I was passing through the cane country of Ingham (site of the Macknade, Ripple Creek and Victoria mills); then Mourilyan, home of the Australian Sugar Heritage Centre museum; Innisfail (Goondi) and Edmonton (Hambledon) before, after an overnight stay in Cairns, I took the Captain Cook Highway first to Port Douglas and then on to Mossman.[97]

There, at the small town library on Mill Street, a stone's throw from the working mill, I asked about any possible Japanese graves in the area. Staff showed me a book of oral histories which included the testimony of

---

[96] Private letter from K. Iijima to R. Philp, Premier of Queensland, 20 August 1900, QSA, Item ID ITM861853 (no top number). Iijima's nation-state imagination of the world may be judged from one sentence in the letter: 'Each nation has its own "amour-propre" as well as its national prejudices, the latter being, no doubt, the direct cause of the agitation against the Japanese labourers in this Colony.' On the applicability of the borderland framework to northern Queensland, see Maria Elena Indelicato, 'Beyond Whiteness: Violence and Belonging in the Borderlands of North Queensland', *Postcolonial Studies* 23, 1 (2020): 99–115.

[97] My reconstruction of what Paul Carter calls the '*running hither and thither*' is to demonstrate, as he suggests, the materiality and the physical 'moving across ground' which lies behind knowledge construction: Carter, *Dark Writing*, pp. 20–1 (emphasis in the original).

Archival Directionality 157

the late Walter Mullavey, born in 1914 and interviewed in 2006. His stories meandered through the byways of his memory: they featured Jack, his gold-prospector-turned-cattle-farmer grandfather from Ireland; another Jack – 'Jack the Kanaka' – who'd come from the Solomon Islands and had flog marks like 'grooves in his back'; the Chinese prostitutes who'd come up from Sydney during harvest season; and, out of the blue:

> When the Japanese died up at the mill, they were the workers and the whites told them what to do, I forget what year it was, my father took them all out with a dray. You couldn't get to Port or anywhere in the wet and he said you only dug a grave that deep and it was full of water. They were buried opposite the Rex's cemetery, towards the mountain. They died of Mossman Fever. Dad said four or five every night. Where Rupert Howe lived, there was the Jap hospital in the mill yards. But I've an idea it's gone. It was a good old building too.[98]

On the basis of this lead, one of the librarians, Judy Coulthard, generously drove me a short way north to Rex's cemetery – in reality the extended family plot of Richard Owen Jones (1852–1914), a Welsh immigrant and one of the area's first settlers (his home was called The Cedars). From there we headed west through verdant cane fields to a site where, as the result of some phone calls, Judy had a hunch the Japanese graves might have been moved.

In the end we found nothing. And in any case, the idea of four or five Japanese successively dying each night of Mossman Fever – the local name for typhus – seemed unlikely, at least without corresponding records in Tokyo.[99] As did the story of Chinese sex labourers making a trek more than 2,500 kilometres north for work. (Did they come from Cairns instead?) As did a boast that Mullavey made about avenging 'the blacks', who allegedly murdered a Mossman River selector in March 1885. In the wake of the murder, he recalled, the settlers and the police, aided by 'a lot of black trackers', chased the Aboriginal people 'right up onto Rifle Creek. And they said they shot 112, the whole tribe.' There was undoubtedly some basis for Mullavey's claims, but unlike the widespread newspaper coverage concerning the white victim, there was very little public information on the massacre – which would have counted as one of the biggest in Queensland's blood-soaked history.[100] As I headed

---

[98] Pam Willis Burden, *Raindrops and Sugar Crops: Tales from South of the Daintree* (Port Douglas, QLD: Douglas Shire Historical Society, 2010), pp. 59–63, citation from p. 60.
[99] On 'Mossman Fever', see John Pearn, *Outback Medicine: Some Vignettes of Pioneering Medicine* (Brisbane: Amphion Press, 1994), p. 101.
[100] On the original murder, 'Port Douglas, March 14', *Queenslander* (Brisbane), 21 March 1885, which noted, 'The impression is that Barnard was murdered and carried away. It is reported that the native troopers are to leave the Johnstone River today. The blacks

down south, to spend several days in the more familiar territory of Brisbane's Queensland State Archives, I was left with the impression that empirical truths might be unknowable in the borderlands: that here even more than elsewhere, historical facts must compete with boasts and blindspots, hunch and hearsay.

Which, I would later realize, was an entirely unoriginal observation and one reinforced by what we might call the archives' directionality – that is, their position in the south, looking towards the north. In his magnum opus on the Mediterranean, Fernand Braudel described a similar directionality in terms of the upland mountains and the lowland plains:

> The history of the mountains is chequered and difficult to trace. Not because of lack of documents; if anything there are too many. Coming down from the mountain regions, where history is lost in the mist, man enters in the plains and towns the domain of classified archives. Whether a new arrival or a seasoned visitor, the mountain dweller inevitably meets someone down below who will leave a description of him, a more or less mocking sketch.[101]

In other words, the archival descriptions of mountain dwellers were generated by those 'down below'. In late nineteenth-century Queensland, too, descriptions of the north were plentiful – exacerbated, if anything, by the alleged absence of inhabitants. But such sketches were imbued with the physical and imaginative distance that separated the speaker's (or writer's) audience from the realities on the ground. In the resultant empirical mist, authority had to be claimed on the basis of experience. 'Any man who travels about the colony – and especially in the North – must see the large numbers of Japanese who are now engaged in every line of business,' argued W. H. 'Billy' Browne (1846–1904), in opening the Legislative Assembly's 1895 debate on 'Asiatic and African Aliens'. Browne himself had worked extensively in the north, and he represented the northern constituency of Croydon; and thus his long speech was peppered with claims – *I have seen, I have worked,*

---

are bad all through the district.' The incident is not discussed in Timothy Bottoms, *Conspiracy of Silence: Queensland's Frontier Killing Times* (Sydney: Allen & Unwin, 2013), nor is it recorded in the 'Colonial Frontier Massacres in Australia, 1788–1930' database, https://c21ch.newcastle.edu.au/colonialmassacres/ (last accessed 10 June 2021) – which doesn't mean that it did not occur. The most detailed online reference I could find was in the Queensland government's 'Communities' section, www.qld.gov.au/atsi/cultural-awareness-heritage-arts/community-histories/community-histories-m/community-histories-mossman-gorge (last accessed 10 June 2021), itself citing the *Queensland Figaro*, 4 April 1885 (not available online).

[101] Fernand Braudel, *The Mediterranean and the Mediterranean World in the Age of Philip II*, trans. Sian Reynolds (London: Harper & Row, 1972 [1966]), p. 44.

I have been, and therefore *I know* – which implied his colleagues had *not* seen, worked or been in the north, and therefore did *not* know about 'the large numbers of Japanese'. If only Browne's colleagues would travel north from the urban settlements of the south, they would know.[102]

Time and again, Queensland's politicians used a language which spoke to a popular imagination of the distant north – even if they themselves represented northern areas. Mr Hamilton, member for the vast northern constituency of Cook, asked Mr Browne if 'the hon. Member require[d] to go *as far as* Thursday Island' to find evidence of Japanese 'Yokohama' red-light districts (see Chapter 5). Mr Ogden, representing Townsville, reminded the assembly 'that this matter affects North Queensland more than the South, and that the North is practically made an experimenting ground for these cheap classes of labour, and in the North we have to suffer the whole of this'. Browne talked of 'a lot of communications [which] *came down* from the north-west about the Chinese coming across from the northern territory', while Mr Archer (Rockhampton) simply spoke of the 'danger of an influx of Japanese [...] *up North*'.[103] This rhetorical distance of the North from the seat of government served also to reinforce claims about northern Queensland's proximity – 'within a few days' sail' – to Asia, and its concomitant 'position of danger'.[104]

Thus, the *distant North* was foundational to the claim of the *empty North*. Distance pervaded the archival reports coming from the far northern offices of Burns, Philp & Co to its Sydney headquarters; it was there in every bulletin transmitted 'by telegraph' to Townsville-, Rockhampton- or Brisbane-based newspapers; it was present in Iijima's preface, noting that one of the three weeks he had been away from Townsville was simply for travel; and it remains in the title of the company-sponsored history of Mossman, *Northern Outpost*. In a similar way to Iijima, my memories of driving *all the way up* to this outpost formed a lens through which I approached the Queensland State Archives upon arrival in Brisbane. The action was up there; I was reading it from down here.

---

[102] *QPD*, vol. 73 (1895), pp. 771–6 (quotation about the Japanese on p. 772). Browne represented Labour.
[103] *QPD*, vol. 73 (1895), quotations respectively on pp. 784, 787, 773, 779 (emphases added). Hamilton (1841–1916) was a member of the governing Ministerialist party; Ogden (1866–1943) a member of Labour; and Archer (1820–1902) was an independent.
[104] *QPD*, vol. 73 (1895), p. 780. The speaker was James Drake (1850–1941), an opposition politician.

This was history from the south writ large: an Anglo-Celtic imagination of Australia, according to Regina Ganter, in which the national narrative started in 1788 with the arrival of the First Fleet in Sydney Cove and worked its way upwards.[105] And without realizing it, mine was also an imagination which took for granted the finished map of post-1901 Australia as the natural territorial conclusion of that settler history. My archival research had started in Canberra, a capital city which would not have existed other than for the fact of federation. Like the NYK map I found there, I imagined a country with its land borders at the northern Queensland coast – thereby overlooking the fact that the Australia of the 1920s was not the inevitable outcome of historical contingencies in the 1890s. Moreover, as if following the *Yamashiro-maru*'s route down from those distant borderlands to the civilized urban centres of the south, my return archival itinerary took me from Port Douglas to Brisbane and finally to Sydney – the 'London of the southern seas'. There, in the Darling Harbour constituency once represented by Billy Hughes, I visited the National Maritime Museum of Australia. Like other tourists on the day and no doubt over the years, I stooped my way through the unfathomably cramped quarters of the replica *Endeavour*. The ship in many ways frames the museum, as if the national maritime story can only begin with Captain Cook and sail its way north.

But what, Ganter asks, 'if we start to write Australian history from north to south, instead of the other way round, and chronologically forward instead of teleologically backward'? Straightaway, she argues, historians must 'give up the idea of Anglo-Celts at the centre of the Australian universe'. This is a suggestion whose archival implications are left unmentioned.[106] But to the question of where, archivally, we might begin such a reverse-directional history, one credible answer was hanging in the museum's Tasman Light Gallery. It challenged the notion of a maritime narrative which must by default be national. It also drew attention to two common critiques of the 'borderlands' framework which in my mind I had posited to this point: namely, that 'a nation-state focus in borderlands history risks obscuring the histories of Indigenous peoples whose lands had been colonized or were at risk of colonization'; and that it focuses too much on *land*.[107]

My archival departure point was a bark painting by Djambawa Marawili (born 1953), entitled 'Baraltja'.

---

[105] Regina Ganter, 'Turning the Map Upside Down', *History Compass* 4, 1 (2006): 26–35.
[106] Ganter, 'Turning the Map', p. 33.
[107] Chang, 'Borderlands in a World at Sea', pp. 384, 393.

Delineating

'Baraltja' demonstrates that the most fundamental claim of the 'N. Y. K. Line' map concerned neither the shipping routes nor the land colours, but rather the idea that the land and the sea are separate entities which can be representationally divided by a line. In arguing against such an apparently 'natural' boundary, Djambawa Marawili's work, and that of his fellow Yolŋu artists, makes an important contribution to the historian's conception of the archive. I'll return to this shortly – but first it's worth reflecting on the epistemological roots of the linear division of land from sea.

Some scholars have argued that such lines are based on a 'European cultural disposition to draw boundaries where land meets sea'.[108] Whether it is in fact appropriate to apply a single cultural explanation to a spatial entity as historically and linguistically diverse as 'Europe', even as scholars call for greater sensitivity to the historically and linguistically diverse histories of 'Australia', is a separate debate.[109] But it is true that from the seventeenth century onwards, a body of theory was produced in Europe concerning the alleged distinction between the land and the sea, which in turn offered the justification for a set of legal frameworks defining the 'ownership' of the former and the fundamental 'freedom' of the latter (themselves both terms loaded with European theory).[110] In their representations of these frameworks through devices such as lines, European imperial maps appeared to offer non-indexical interpretations of the world: that is, they claimed a set of truths which were allegedly independent of local context and were thus universal. But despite presenting the 'truth' of such boundaries as transcending indexicality and being globally applicable, European imperial maps were not in fact autonomous of the local theoretical context in which they were produced. They instead reflected and 'can only be read through the myths that Europeans tell about their relationship to the land'.[111]

---

[108] Monica E. Mulrennan and Colin H. Scott, '*Mare Nullius*: Indigenous Rights in Saltwater Environments', *Development and Change* 31 (2000): 681–708, here p. 681. S. E. Jackson similarly writes of 'the European cultural distinction between land and sea': 'The Water Is Not Empty: Cross-Cultural Issues in Conceptualising Sea Space', *Australian Geographer* 26, 1 (1995): 87–96, here p. 87.

[109] Such a debate has taken many forms: see, for example, Frederick Cooper's critique of Dipesh Chakrabarty's *Provincializing Europe* for not provincializing Europe enough: Cooper, *Colonialism in Question*, pp. 113–49.

[110] On the complex processes by which imperial legal regimes were established at sea, see Benton, *Search for Sovereignty*, pp. 104–61.

[111] Turnbull, *Maps Are Territories*, Exhibits 4, 7, and quotation from Exhibit 9.

Thus, in drawing on this imperial European cartographic tradition, the 'N. Y. K. Line' map must be read as advancing both a set of specific claims about Japan and Australia in the late nineteenth century *and* a more fundamental imperial ontology – namely, the boundary between land and sea.

Djambawa Marawili's 'Baraltja' exposes this myth as indexical and therefore inapplicable to the saltwater country in which he grew up. A brief historical overview of that country helps contextualize how he does so – and underlines Ganter's call to turn the Australian map upside down. Marawili is a senior leader of the Maḏarrpa clan in the Yirritja moiety, which, along with the Dhuwa moiety, constitutes half the world of the Yolŋu people, in what settler maps call north-eastern Arnhem Land (Northern Territory). Taking its name from a Dutch city via a Dutch East India Company ship which navigated the so-called Gulf of Carpentaria in 1623, 'Arnhem Land' nods to a history of European maritime contact with northern Australia that predates the British by more than 150 years. Indeed, the word for 'White person' or 'European' in many Yolŋu languages is *balanda* – a clear reference to Hollanders.[112]

But linguists have actually shown that *balanda* derives from the Makassarese and Buginese word *Balanda* (Holland). Along with Yolŋu verbs such as *djäma* (to work, make, do; Makassarese/Buginese, *jaäma*, to build, do, work; touch, handle) or *djäka* (to care for, look after; *jaäga*, to watch, look out), or indeed the noun *lipalipa* (canoe-dugout; *lepa*), these words point to a long history of interactions between Yolŋu people and trepang (bêche-de-mer) fishers from Makassar and its South Sulawesi environs – people who themselves called the northern coast of Australia *Marege'*.[113] Analysis of trepang exports from Makassar to the Dutch administrative centre of Batavia and then on to the Chinese market suggests there was a sudden increase in exports in the late eighteenth century. Read against a famous encounter in 1803 between the British navigator Matthew Flinders (1774–1814), on his

---

[112] A number of language groups comprise 'Yolŋu Matha' (literally the 'words/speech' [matha] of 'man'). These include Dhuwala, spoken by Djambawa Marawili's Maḏarrpa clan (see his 'Declaration', fn 125). For an overview, see 'N230: Yolngu Matha', in the online 'Austlang' database of the Australian Institute of Aboriginal and Torres Strait Islander Studies, https://collection.aiatsis.gov.au/austlang/about (last accessed 23 June 2022).

[113] C. C. Macknight, *The Voyage to Marege': Macassan Trepangers in Northern Australia* (Melbourne: Melbourne University Press, 2017 edn [1976]), pp. 89–90; John Greatorex, *Yolngu Matha Dictionary* (2014): https://yolngudictionary.cdu.edu.au (last accessed 2 June 2021). See also Alan Walker and R. David Zorc, 'Austronesian Loanwords in Yolngu-Matha of Northeast Arnhem Land', *Aboriginal History* 5 (1981): 109–34.

Delineating   163

circumnavigation of Australia, and Pobassoo, a Bugis 'old Commander' of the trepanging fleet, some scholars have dated the first sustained engagements between Makassarese fishermen and Yolŋu peoples to around 1780.[114] Until trepanging from Makassar to the Northern Territory was effectively prohibited in 1906, thereby 'islanding' northern Australia from Southeast Asia, the impact of these engagements was profound: it can be traced not only linguistically but also archaeologically, and in Yolŋu ritual practices and rock art.[115]

This Yolŋu–Makassar history is important because it refutes the stereotype of an isolated, static, 'traditional' Aboriginal past set against the dynamism of the post-European encounter – as if Aboriginal/non-Aboriginal history only began with Captain Cook. Yolŋu peoples were actively engaged with the world of today's Southeast Asia from before the arrival of the First Fleet, and probably from before the arrival of the Dutch in the early seventeenth century, in a historical relationship which also changed across time. The line which divides the nation-state of 'Australia' from Southeast Asia is thus a historical anachronism – even if it continues to determine the infrastructures of travel in the region. Moreover, as the anthropologist Ian McIntosh argued with reference to the early 2000s, contemporary memories of Yolŋu encounters with Makassar across this anachronistic border affirmed the identity and authority of Yolŋu people as landowners and as claimants in a battle for sea rights.[116]

---

[114] Campbell Macknight, 'The View from Marege': Australian Knowledge of Makassar and the Impact of the Trepang Industry across Two Centuries', *Aboriginal History* 35 (2011): 121–43, here pp. 133–4. This is a revision of Macknight's earlier suggestion (see fn 113) that the trade began in the late seventeenth century. By contrast, fishers from Makassar may have reached the Kimberley coast a few decades earlier. On the act of interpretation between Flinders and the trepangers, see Paul Thomas, 'Interpreting the Macassans: Language Exchange in Historical Encounters', in Marshall Clark and Sally K. May, eds., *Macassan History and Heritage: Journeys, Encounters and Influences* (Canberra: Australian National University E-Press, 2013), pp. 69–93.

[115] On islanding, see Sujit Sivasundaram, *Islanded: Britain, Sri Lanka, and the Bounds of an Indian Ocean Colony* (Chicago: University of Chicago Press, 2013). For an overview of the literature on Yolŋu-Makassar mutual influences (and its points of disagreements), see Stephanie Mawson, 'The Deep Past of Pre-Colonial Australia', *Historical Journal* 64, 5 (2021): 1477–99, here pp. 1493–8.

[116] Ian S. McIntosh, 'Unbirri's pre-Macassan legacy, or how the Yolngu became black', in Marshall Clark and Sally K. May, eds., *Macassan History and Heritage: Journeys, Encounter and Influences* (Canberra: Australian National University E-Press, 2013), pp. 95–105, here pp. 95, 103–4. On the revival of Yolŋu-Makassar engagements since the 1980s, see Regina Ganter, 'Remembering Muslim Histories of Australia', *La Trobe Journal* 89 (2012): 48–62, here pp. 59–62.

Which brings us to Djambawa Marawili's evocation of 'Baraltja' (see Figure 4.3).[117] In settler geographical terms, Baraltja refers to the northern anabranch of the Koolatong River as it discharges into Jalma Bay, which itself forms part of the big, shallow Blue Mud Bay in eastern Arnhem Land. Nine Yolŋu clans claim estates in Blue Mud Bay – four from the Dhuwa moiety and five from the Yirritja, including Marawili's own Maḏarrpa clan. But whereas the word 'estates' may conjure up an image of land units, Yolŋu estates traverse the boundary of land and sea, as Marawili's bark painting demonstrates. In its simplest form, 'Baraltja' depicts fresh water (the vertical lines at the bottom of the painting) from the inland part of the Maḏarrpa estate flowing into the estuary at Baraltja.[118] There, before the fresh water meets the clan's body of saltwater (known as Muŋurru, which further from the shore is shared with two other Yirritja moiety clans), it mixes with another body of Maḏarrpa clan water, the Wiḏiyarr – a brackish mixture of salt and fresh water (represented by the horizontal lines). The brackish waters in Baraltja are the ancestral home of the lightning serpent Burut'tji, who is central to Maḏarrpa creation stories.[119] Here taking the form of a sandbar perpendicular to the horizontal brackish lines, Burut'tji is so excited by the flushing freshwater that he stands and, like other snakes associated with the brackish waters, spits lightning towards the painting's upper reaches. There we see the Waŋupini ancestral storm cloud, two terns flying in her winds, while other, smaller thunderclouds appear as triangles at the very top of the painting. Meanwhile, the brackish water flows from shallow

---

[117] For a general introduction to Marawili's work, see Kimberly Moulton, 'Djambawa Marawili AM: Change Agent', to accompany Marawili's collaboration, *where the water moves, where it rests*, with the Kluge-Ruhe Aboriginal Art Collection, University of Virginia, 1 August 2015 – 24 January 2016, downloadable from https://kluge-ruhe.org/collaboration/djambawa-marawili/ (last accessed 31 May 2021). One of the Marawili paintings commissioned by the Kluge-Ruhe, 'Journey to America', later won the NATSIAA award for 2019: www.theguardian.com/artanddesign/2019/aug/09/natsiaa-2019-djambawa-marawili-wins-for-bark-painting-written-in-my-soul-and-in-my-blood (last accessed 31 May 2021).

[118] The following description is based on *Saltwater*, pp. 34–5; Howard Morphy and Frances Morphy, 'Tasting the Waters: Discriminating Identities in the Waters of Blue Mud Bay', *Journal of Material Culture* 11, 1–2 (2006): 67–85, here pp. 70–3; Frances Morphy and Howard Morphy, 'The Blue Mud Bay Case: Refractions through Saltwater Country', *Dialogue* 28 (2009): 15–25, here pp. 20–1; Marcus Barber, 'Where the Clouds Stand: Australian Aboriginal Relationships to Water, Place, and the Marine Environment in Blue Mud Bay, Northern Territory', unpublished PhD dissertation, Australian National University (2005), pp. 169–74. The fresh water is known as Gularri.

[119] Muŋurru is the Yirritja moiety name for deep saltwater; the Dhuwa moiety clans call it Balamumu. The Wiḏiyarr is owned by both the Maḏarrpa and the Dhaḻwaŋu clans. The lightning serpent is also known as Mundukul'.

Delineating 165

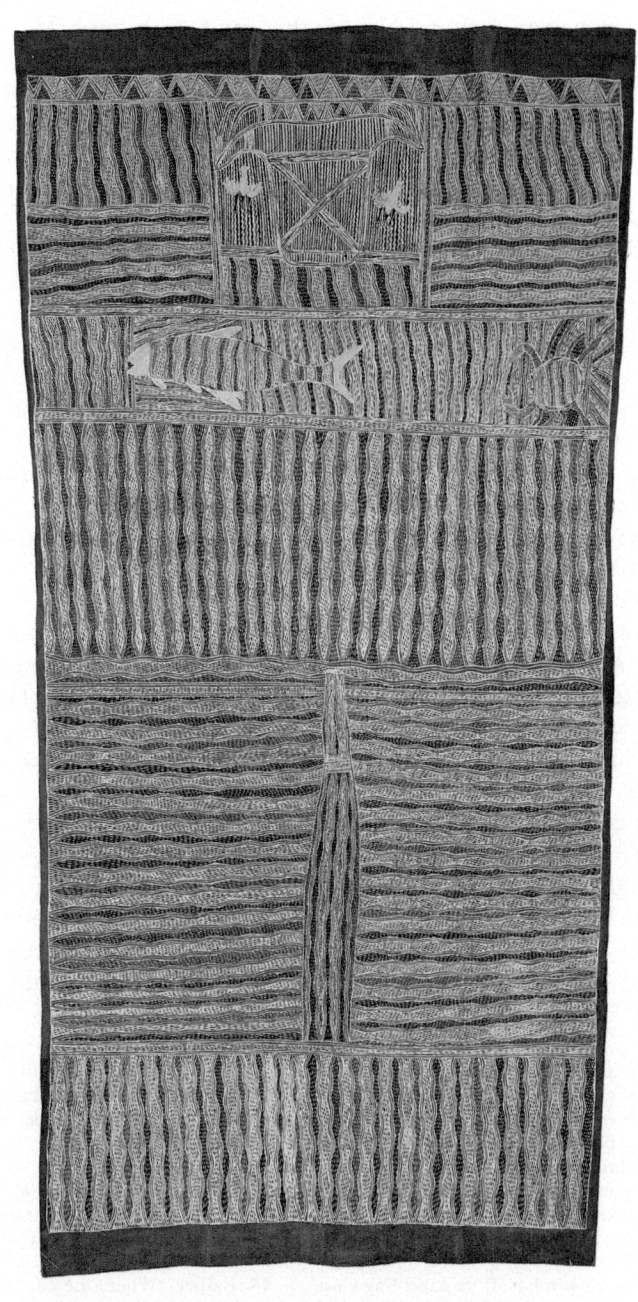

Figure 4.3 Djambawa Marawili, 'Baraltja' (1998). Courtesy of Djambawa Marawili of Buku-Larrŋgay Mulka Centre. Australian National Maritime Museum Collection purchased with the assistance of Stephen Grant of the GrantPirrie Gallery.

into deeper waters, where Nyoka the mud crab and Makani the queenfish swim.

Even in this much-simplified description, two interrelated aspects of a Yolŋu worldview are striking.[120] First, this is a cyclical vision: in the monsoon season that Marawili depicts, the clouds – themselves a place of distant, ancestral kin – shed water over the land. Fresh waters from the inland Maḏarrpa estate rush into Baraltja, mixing with brackish waters and eventually flushing into the deep saltwater, where, at the edge of the known Yolŋu world, they will be drawn up once again into the clouds. In the dry season, by contrast, Muŋurru penetrates the inland creeks and billabongs, offering a salty taste to the drinking water. Moreover, there are cycles within cycles: the daily tides, the lunar cycle of neap and spring tides – and of course the annual cycle of the trepang fishers from Makassar, whose stays coincided with the wet season.[121]

Second, this is a unified vision, where sea and land are conceptually inseparable. Here as also in other parts of Indigenous Australia, 'country' extends across sea and land – a far cry from Consul Iijima's nation-state framed articulation of 'the mutual relations of both countries'.[122] Indeed, as a number of anthropologists have noted, 'there is no Yolŋu word that translates as ocean or sea, no binary opposition [of] "sea" versus "land"'; but there are at least thirty-eight different names that Maḏarrpa clan members give to saltwater alone, referring both to clan ownership and to the water's character.[123]

Given this unified worldview, the most discombobulating element of Marawili's 'Baraltja' painting is therefore the horizontal line he draws across its centre, exactly where Burut'tji stands up from the brackish waters. This he was instructed to do by his artist father Wakuthi (c. 1921–2005), who also helped design Djambawa's 'Baraltja', in order to indicate the 'illegal border' of the low-water mark.[124] Under international law, the low-water mark delineates the boundary between the 'land' and the 'sea'. Although, under the Aboriginal Land Rights

---

[120] My description does not do justice to other aspects of the painting: for example, Burrut'tji's lightning and the travels of the Makani queenfish connect the Maḏarrpa clan with other Yirritja clans to the south, north and south-east of Blue Mud Bay: *Saltwater*, p. 45; Barber, 'Where the Clouds Stand', p. 172.

[121] Morphy and Morphy, 'Tasting the Waters', p. 76.

[122] On this point, see Peter Burdon, Georgina Drew, Matthew Stubbs, Adam Webster and Marcus Barber, 'Decolonising Indigenous Water "Rights" in Australia: Flow, Difference, and the Limits of Law', *Settler Colonial Studies* 5, 4 (2015): 334–49, here p. 336.

[123] Morphy and Morphy, 'Blue Mud Bay Case', p. 18; Barber, 'Where the Clouds Stand', p. 147.

[124] *Saltwater*, p. 34.

Delineating 167

(Northern Territory) Act (1976), Yolŋu *land* rights were deemed to extend down to this low-water line, the law said nothing about *sea* rights in the intertidal zone – that is, the water in the area above and between the low- and high-water marks. As a consequence, the waters so central to Yolŋu 'country' were regularly encroached by commercial fishers. After a particularly distressing desecration of Maḏarrpa clan land in 1996, forty-seven of the community's artists and leaders created a series of eighty bark paintings (*dhulaŋ*) with the aim, in Djambawa's words, of 'explain[ing] the country, how they became one, not only the sea but the land too'. He continued: 'That's why this paper is being written in public. It will be publicly seen by non-Aboriginal people, government and foreigners.'[125]

'This paper' was a 'Declaration', one of five taped by Yolŋu artists and transcribed at the beginning of *Saltwater: Yirrkala Bark Paintings of Sea Country*, a book published in 1999 by the Buku-Larrŋgay Mulka art centre and including reproductions of all eighty paintings. But the key media of knowledge transmission were the paintings themselves, coloured with pigments from the land and drawn onto barks from the common stringy-bark tree. The patterns (*miny'tji*) and paints 'come from the land', Marawili emphasized. The patterns were also 'etched by the smell of the sea around Walirra', noted Ḏula Ṉurruwuthun (1936–2001), referring to a body of water in Blue Mud Bay. The paintings were 'sacred art that has been etched by the sea':

This is our sacred design. Our art is for us. You are paper. We are sacred design. You make paper. Your wisdom is paper. Our intellect is sacred design, homeland and ancestral hearth of ancient origin.[126]

If this sounds like a polarizing view of the world, its intention was not. Such statements were rather born from a profound frustration that 'we show these barks and yet they still belittle our Law. They send their fishing boats to these waters without permission.'[127] Ultimately, therefore, the key audience that the bark paintings had to convince were the settler custodians of paper, namely the Australian law courts. And in a case which culminated in a high court judgement in July 2008, Yolŋu leaders used the bark paintings as evidence to support their contention

---

[125] Djambawa Marawili, 'Declaration', trans. Raymattja Marika, in *Saltwater*, pp. 14–15, here p. 15. Djambawa himself contributed seven of the eighty paintings.
[126] Ḏula Ṉurruwuthun (Munyuku clan, Yirritja moiety), 'Declaration', trans. Raymattja Marika, in *Saltwater*, pp. 9–12, here pp. 9–10. The sacred designs (*miny'tji*) are particular to each clan.
[127] Mowarra Ganambarr (c. 1917–2005, Ḏätiwuy clan, Dhuwa moiety), 'Declaration', trans. Merrkiyawuy Ganambarr, in *Saltwater*, pp. 16–18, here p. 18.

that their 'land' rights should extend also to the water above the intertidal zone – a contention which was supported in a landmark [sic] ruling.[128]

In this sense, bark paintings such as 'Baraltja' were more than 'Aboriginal art': they were also legal documents, thus continuing a history – dating at least as far back as the famous Yirrkala Bark Petitions (1963) – in which the medium was entwined with the political claim.[129] And, to use a term which has been debated by scholars for its applicability to Aboriginal representations, 'Baraltja' may also be considered a *map*, for it offered Balanda like the high court judges a representational structure to explain 'how we choose our names', how 'the water flows into clan groups', and thus the law of Yolŋu country.[130] Such propositions are analogous to those offered by the NYK map, with its country names, its lines across water and its explanatory basis in the alleged universalism of international law.

As Helen Watson (Verran) has argued, however, '[bark paintings] are maps only insofar as the landscape is itself a "text"'. In other words, the lands and waters of Blue Mud Bay are the founts of Yolŋu knowledge: how they are 'read' determines the construction of 'Baraltja' and its companion pieces. This is exactly the argument of the five declarations which preface the printed edition of the 1998 paintings: in Djambawa Marawili's words, non-Aboriginal people 'will see our intellectual

---

[128] Morphy and Morphy, 'Blue Mud Bay Case'.

[129] See www.nma.gov.au/defining-moments/resources/yirrkala-bark-petitions (last accessed 3 June 2021). It's worth pointing out that '[t]he very terms "map" and "chart" also derive from their materiality: the Latin word *carta* denotes a formal document on paper or parchment, while the term *mappa* indicates cloth': Presner, Shepard and Kawano, *HyperCities*, pp. 15–16. The practice of Yolŋu bark painting predates the colonial period. After the arrival of the Methodist mission in Yirrkala in the 1930s, clan members explained their world through the medium: *Saltwater*, p. 22. See also the collections of bark paintings from the 1940s discussed in Rebecca Conway, ed., *Djalkiri: Yolŋu Art, Collaborations and Collections* (Sydney: Sydney University Press, 2021).

[130] Djambawa Marawili, 'Declaration', pp. 14, 15; see also Ḏula Ŋurruwuthun's claim, 'This is our law and our art' ('Declaration', p. 10). On the bark paintings as maps, see Helen Watson with the Yolŋu community at Yirrkala, 'Aboriginal-Australian maps', in Turnbull, *Maps Are Territories* (exhibition 5). Peter Sutton labels Watson's framework 'highly problematic' for blurring what he considers to be two separate heuristic categories, namely icons and maps (and he also points out that there is no word for 'map' in Aboriginal languages): Sutton, 'Icons of Country: Topographic Representations in Classical Aboriginal Traditions', in David Woodward and G. Malcolm Lewis, eds., *The History of Cartography*, Vol. 2, Bk .3: *Cartography in the Traditional African, American, Arctic, Australian, and Pacific Societies* (Chicago: University of Chicago Press, 1998), pp. 353–86, here p. 364. It may also be possible to read 'Baraltja' and accompanying bark paintings as almanacs – at least in the South Asian reading suggested by Debjani Bhattacharyya, *Empire and Ecology in the Bengal Delta: The Making of Calcutta* (Cambridge: Cambridge University Press, 2018), pp. 11–19.

Delineating 169

knowledge exists in the fresh water and becomes one in the saltwater'. Such a statement would not be out of place in Michel Foucault's *Archaeology of Knowledge*: Yolŋu country is the archive which determines what can be said or what can be painted.[131] The country speaks a set of claims which counter those of the NYK map and its archival bases – especially in revealing the ontological absurdity of the low-water line.

But while I understand the explanatory value of suggesting that Yolŋu people read the landscape as text, I think it is an unhelpful metaphor.[132] It returns us to the book and the pen as the ultimate arbiters of knowledge; it thereby reinforces – if only inadvertently, given Verran's sensitivity to Indigenous epistemologies[133] – a long-held assumption that while the archive is a repository of knowledge, associated in the European scholarly tradition with the *arkheion* (the residence of a polity's magistrates or governors), the knowledge itself is to be found in the pages therein.[134] By contrast, Djambawa Marawili is adamant that 'this paper' is *not* equivalent to the knowledge which exists in the water. Rather, 'things like this book' are simply a means for 'you' – that is, Balanda, me – to learn:

About the homelands, the paintings, the floodwaters, the hunting grounds, the everlasting old dwelling places, the sovereignty, the places, the shades, the shelters. You will learn of these. Both sides, Yolŋu and Balanda knowledge. This will be done through the publishing of books, not just through bark paintings but also through print literacy.[135]

Reading these words in Switzerland, thousands of kilometres from the Maḏarrpa clan estates, I am under no illusions: I have held the Yolŋu artists' printed paper in my hands, I have seen Marawili's 'Baraltja' with my own eyes, but I have not in any way read his country archive. Nor could I make that claim, even if I had been able to fly to northern Australia as planned in 2020. For, to modify Foucault, one consequence of accepting the notion of Aboriginal country as archive is not merely that the archive determines *what can be said* but also *who can say it*. As has been noted of Torres Straits Islanders, land and sea rights are also related

---

[131] 'The archive is first the law of what can be said': Michel Foucault, *Archaeology of Knowledge*, trans. A. M. Sheridan Smith (London: Routledge Classics, 1989 [1969]), p. 145.

[132] For a wider critique, see Teresia K. Teaiwa, 'On Analogies: Rethinking the Pacific in a Global Context', *Contemporary Pacific* 18, 1 (2006): 71–87.

[133] Helen Verran (Watson), 'A Story about Doing "The Dreaming"', *Postcolonial Studies* 7, 2 (2004): 149–64.

[134] Alexandra Walsham, 'The Social History of the Archive: Record-Keeping in Early Modern Europe', *Past & Present*, Supplement 11 (2016): 9–48, here p. 14.

[135] Djambawa Marawili, 'Declaration', p. 15.

to the rights – and responsibilities – to name places and tell stories.[136] By this logic, my argument that historians must broaden our definition of 'the archive' also entails an acknowledgement of narrowed accessibility: global history cannot be synonymous with my unfettered right to access or tell everyone else's stories. If it were, then archival accessibility – or *open access, open science* or similar such buzzwords which flood Euro-American academia in the early 2020s – would be no more than discursive decoys for a neocolonial appropriation of Indigenous knowledge in line with a long tradition of such Euro-American colonialism.

And yet Djambawa Marawili also concludes, 'This talk is for wherever you are or whatever clan you are.' Unlike some stories in situ, the knowledge presented in the *Saltwater* collection is not to be hidden from outsiders. Indeed, Djambawa sees his Declaration, and his art, as 'living in the way of reconciliation'. In this spirit, I have tried in this chapter to take as my departure point certain Aboriginal epistemological strategies in my reading of colonial archival sources. For example, Minoru Hokari has written of the relationship that the Gurindji people of the Northern Territory posit between direction and morality in history, in which the 'right law/earth law' tracks from west to east, and 'the English' (represented by Captain Cook) 'came from the wrong direction and moved in the wrong direction' – thereby betraying their immorality.[137] While such an analytical framing of the past may seem alien to scholars trained in the discipline of 'history' which emerged from nineteenth-century Europe, I have argued that a basic acknowledgement of directionality *is* in fact useful for analysing the Australian colonial archive, and for understanding the historical lie of the 'empty North'.[138] Second, in pairing two graphic sources, namely the NYK map and 'Baraltja', I have tried to undermine any assumption that the former represents universal 'truths' and the latter mere local 'claims'. *Both* sources make claims about the past based on their understandings of 'country' law, and both need to be interrogated for the applicability of such claims beyond their local contexts. I do not have the skills to do so for the Yolŋu country archive (and herein lies one impetus for collaborative research projects). But within the limitations of the book-and-pen training I received in Europe and Japan, I see one of global history's contributions to be the un-settling of

---

[136] Mulrennan and Scott, '*Mare Nullius*', p. 688.
[137] Hokari, *Gurindji Journey*, pp. 113–35, especially pp. 125–9.
[138] My emphasis here is similar to Tony Ballantyne's call for 'perspectival histories' of colonialism: see, for example, Ballantyne, 'Mobility, Empire, Colonisation', *History Australia* 11, 2 (2014): 7–37, here p. 18.

colonial narratives – including the mutual reinforcement of Australian and Japanese narratives of 'emptiness' – as they have emerged from archival epistemologies to date.[139]

Finally, the world of metaphors is so littered with traps that I have no inherent wish to participate in what my Heidelberg colleagues jokingly called 'comparative metaphorology' – whereby my metaphor is better than yours.[140] But I do think that brackishness potentially offers a more convincing metaphor for analysing the claims and contradictions embodied in the NYK map than a language – which I have also used – of 'connections' or 'entanglements'. The *brackish world* better captures the ambiguous discourses of mapping, flooding, blotting, taste, purity, ecology, history and moving sites of contact which bubble through this chapter than any other metaphor I have used – and it speaks to the archival and methodological challenges raised by Djambawa Marawili's appeal for historians no less than judges to delineate the colonial boundaries between water and land.[141] Moreover, in modulating between histories of humans and the natural environment, the ship and the shore, the past and the present, *brackishness* may also offer scholars a framework for thinking about what I previously termed 'in-between' migration histories in the Pacific world. For ultimately, the careers of Hasegawa Setsutarō, or, before him, Wakamiya Yaichi, Kodama Keijirō or Fuyuki Sakazō, cannot be reduced to lessons in a book. Their lives take meaning in the brackish spaces around penned sentences – as the case of a female labourer, Hashimoto Usa, will now show.

---

[139] On 'unsettling', see Morphy and Morphy, 'Blue Mud Bay Case', p. 15; Neale and Turner, 'Other People's Country', p. 279.
[140] My thanks to Joachim Kurtz and Monica Juneja for allowing me to participate in such discussions.
[141] These challenges are not unique to Australia, of course: scholars of South Asia have used the metaphor of 'soaking' to describe the geographical fluidity between land and sea, and the colonial imposition of notions of 'property' thereon: Bhattacharyya, *Empire and Ecology*, herself drawing on Anuradha Mathur and Dilip da Cunha, *Soak: Mumbai in an Estuary* (New Delhi: Rupa Publishing, 2009).

5   The Archive and I

A Statement

Hers is an unlikely story of archival survival:

> On the 29th day of November 1897 in the presence of Torijiro Satow and Gyusaku Sugiyama –
> Usa states –
> My name is Usa Hashimoto –
> I am twenty one years of age –

As also for the Mossman Japanese, I came searching for Hashimoto Usa at the turn of the seasons in November 2013 – from autumn to winter in Europe, from spring to summer in Australia. In Canberra, I had found a reference to her statement in an article by David Sissons (1925–2006). Diverted from classics to the study of Japanese in the last year of the Second World War, Sissons had worked as a defence interpreter in war crimes trials in Morotai (Indonesia) for several months in 1945–6, before being posted to work as a translator for the British Commonwealth Force in the Allied Occupation of Japan. After his post-service university training, Sissons's primary expertise came to be in political sciences and international affairs, but he also began to study Japanese–Australian history in the mid 1960s.[1] In 1977, he published two groundbreaking essays on what – given his primary work on defence, immigration and trade policies – might at first seem to be a counter-intuitive interest in the history of Japanese prostitutes in Australia.

Sissons was an extraordinary scholar, whose work was foundational to new understandings of Japanese–Australian relations. His former

---

[1] I take these biographical details from Fukui Haruhiro, Okudaira Yasuhiro, Arthur Stockwin, Watanabe Akio and John Welfield, 'Reflections and Engagements', in Arthur Stockwin and Keiko Tamura, eds., *Bridging Australia and Japan*, Vol. 1: *The Writings of David Sissons, Historian and Political Scientist* (Acton: Australian National University Press, 2016), pp. 5–40. On Sissons's meticulousness, see Arthur Stockwin's 'Introduction', pp. 1–4.

students describe him as 'meticulous' and 'detailed', a 'modest' man, shy to the point of being unwilling to publish on a particular topic until convinced he had covered every empirical base. I could sense this myself from the day I spent among his research papers in Canberra's National Library of Australia: typewritten letters from all over the world testified to his exhaustive rigour in following up on every possible archival trail.[2] All of which makes it even more unusual that Sissons's reference to Hashimoto Usa in his first article on prostitutes contained a minor error.

Though insignificant in and of itself, the act of trying to correct Sissons's mistake took me into a much more problematic history of how women like Hashimoto had been categorized by officials in late-1890s Australia and Japan, and how, in that bureaucratic process, their voices had often come to be lost. According to Sissons, Hashimoto's testimony could be found in 'Q.S.A., Col. A/822, 97/15833'.[3] But when I later took the lead from 'Q.S.A' to fly to the Queensland State Archives in Brisbane, staff there were bemused by the 'Col. A/822' reference. If, as Sissons's citation of the document indicated, Hashimoto's statement had been recorded on Thursday Island in December 1897, then this must be a mistake, for the 'COL' series referred to documents only up to August 1896, after which it had been replaced by 'HOM'. To add a complication, the Queensland State Archives referencing system had recently been overhauled, such that even if 'Col. A/822' for 1897 *had* existed when Sissons was writing in the 1970s, it would now have a new identification number. But not to worry, the archivists reassured me: '97/15833' was a *top number* – a kind of watermark through which each document was embossed with the stamp of colonial authority.[4] So all we needed was to find the Home Office's Register of Letters (HOM), look up the 15,833rd piece of incoming correspondence which was logged in (18)97, and check what 'action' had been performed on that item. In this case, the action – recorded in tiny, cursive handwriting – was 'HOM/A15 Home Secretary's Department, General Correspondence 1897, Nos. 15006 to 16595'. So now, the archivists said, I could look up 'HOM/A15' on the Archives' online catalogue for the new identification number (ID 847553); I could then order the folder to my reading room desk – and Bob's your uncle.

---

[2] Papers of David Sissons, National Library of Australia (MS 3092, MS Acc09.106). I thank Arthur Stockwin for sharing with me his then-unpublished catalogue of the Sissons Papers in advance of my trip to Australia.
[3] David Sissons, '*Karayuki-san*: Japanese Prostitutes in Australia, 1887–1915: Part I', *Historical Studies* 17, 68 (1977): 323–41, here p. 339, fn 61.
[4] On watermarks, see Stoler, *Along the Archival Grain*, p. 8.

But Bob was not my uncle. After checking and rechecking the home secretary's incoming correspondence for this range of 1897 papers, I could find no trace of 97/15833 and thus no trace of Hashimoto Usa. Wherever Sissons had found her testimony, she was now lost in the archive.

The extent of my disappointment was irrational. I had a hunch that this young woman, whom Sissons described as a 'recently arrived prostitute' in December 1897, might have travelled on the *Yamashiro-maru* to Thursday Island, in the very far north of Queensland. This was where Japanese migrants had disembarked in large numbers throughout the 1890s, such that the *Townsville Daily Bulletin* would label the island 'an appanage of the Mikado's kingdom' in 1898;[5] and I knew that the ship had docked there in early November. Summarizing Hashimoto's evidence, Sissons explained that she had come from Nagasaki via Shanghai and Hong Kong, where a financial transaction had taken place with the proprietor of a 'lodging house'. From Hong Kong, she and other Japanese women had been escorted under the cover of midnight, without passports, to Thursday Island, and sold to a brothel-keeper called Shiosaki. He had paid her escort £100 sterling, which Hashimoto herself now had to repay to Shiosaki.

This was a story both extraordinary and all too ordinary for the time, as this chapter will show. But in the form through which I had accessed Hashimoto Usa's account, it remained at one step removed: Sissons had paraphrased her words, whereas I wanted to know what she herself had said and what language she had used (I assumed her deposition was in Japanese). That was one reason why I wanted to get hold of 97/15833 – and also to see if my hunch about the *Yamashiro-maru* was correct.

Although Hashimoto's testimony was absent, the folder I had requested on that November morning – ID 847553 – did nevertheless reveal much about the bureaucratic mindset which had produced her paperwork. Here was a debate in the Cairns Municipal Council, from September 1897, in response to calls by various aldermen to 'stamp out this *disgrace* to our civilization' – namely, 'Japanese houses of ill fame'. Here was one alderman claiming that 'when he was in the South recently he found that a number of Japanese women had *invaded* Brisbane'. And yet here was also the Cairns sub-inspector of police, in a letter to a colleague in Cooktown, begging to state 'that the whole subject has been very much exaggerated'.[6]

---

[5] See Chapter 4.
[6] Paperwork forwarded by the Inspector of Police (Cooktown), to the Commissioner of Police (Brisbane), 26 November 1897, and then on to the Under Secretary, Home Department (Brisbane), 14 December 1897. The Municipal Council debate was

The sub-inspector's letter led me to request a folder of police correspondence on 'Japanese women' from 1897, where I found a memorandum from the Queensland police commissioner, calling for all of the colony's sub-inspectors to furnish information on (i) the number of Japanese women in their respective districts, (ii) the women's marital status, and (iii) their 'general occupation'. Next in the folder was a stream of telegraphed responses: sixteen Japanese women in Cairns, four in Cooktown, one in Port Douglas, four in Townsville, three in Halifax, nine in Mackay and one in Ingham, 'all prostitutes except consuls wife at Townsville'. And here a letter from the inland settlement of Childers, detailing six 'places' and a total of fifteen Japanese females. All claimed to be married – six of that group were living with their husbands, 'one in each house', and the others were boarders while their husbands worked on Lady Elliott Island. But the reporting sergeant, referring to the alleged behaviour of Pacific Island labourers in the pejorative language of the time, believed otherwise: 'from the fact that Kanakas are Constantly resorting these houses, and although [the women] Claim their husbands sends them money, he believe that they get their living by Prostitution'.[7]

A few days later, on 8 November 2013, I requested a folder concerning Japanese immigration into Thursday Island. Here was the rawest form of frontline data collection, namely regular telegrams from the island's government resident, John Douglas (1828–1904), reporting on new arrivals: on 24 July 1897, 'Tsinan yesterday brought twenty one japanese from Hong kong males fifteen 15 females six 6'; on 4 August 1897, 'The Yamashiro Maru brought five 5 Japanese males and one 1 female for Thurs Island from Japan'; on the same day, the *Changsha*, bringing two males and two females from Hong Kong; and so on, through the southern hemisphere spring and until the end of December – the *Omi-maru*, the *Airlie*, the *Nanchang*, the *Chingdu*, the *Tainan*.[8]

This growing pile of telegrams, memoranda, letters and reports added up to what Bill Mihalopoulos has called an 'ocular regime', whereby government bureaucrats were directed to keep an eye on a particular subset of the population. As a consequence, that group became more visible to officialdom, leading to further calls for observation and

---

reported in a clipping from the *Morning Post*, September 1897; the Sub-Inspector's comments in a letter to the Cooktown Inspector, 24 November 1897: QSA, Item ID ITM847553 (top number 97/11970) (emphasis added in all cases).

[7] QSA, Item ID ITM86448, top numbers 97/2798, 97/11065, 97/11043, 97/10810. When Japan established its new consulate in Townsville in 1896, two wives of consular officials arrived on the *Yamashiro-maru*'s opening run to Australia, namely Mrs Masuda and Mrs Morikawa: *BC*, 13 November 1896.

[8] QSA, Item ID ITM861851 (top numbers 97/9491, 97/10152, 97/10153).

eventual government action.⁹ Mihalopoulos uses the ocular analogy in reference to the strategies by which Meiji bureaucrats began to classify migrating women. He draws on Ian Hacking's analysis of how the human sciences observe, record, and thereby 'create kinds of people that in a certain sense did not exist before', to show how a type of mobile Japanese woman was 'made up' in late nineteenth-century Tokyo governmental circles.¹⁰ As we shall see, this 'unsightly woman' was a new category, fit for the purposes of statistical analysis and policy intervention. Such categorizing was as equally evident in Queensland as in Japan. True, the Cairns sub-inspector's warning of a problem 'very much exaggerated' demonstrates that the new ocular regime was not uncontested; and the marriage claims of the alleged Japanese wives in Childers suggests that the targets of the regime occasionally devised strategies to thwart bureaucratic classification.¹¹ But still, what the paperwork before me evinced was the objectification of Japanese women by the archival eye.

And then I found her. The dozen or so beige papers, taller and thicker to the touch than your standard A4 sheet, and bound by a piece of string in their top-left corner, were out of place in yet another overflowing folder – sandwiched between correspondence over Japanese labourers in 1894 on the one hand, and a table of Japanese returnees, deaths and deserters from Queensland in the period 1892–8 on the other. At first, I was thrown by the forward-leaning cursive handwriting, in blue ink, and by the addressee: 'To the Honorable / The Government President / Thursday Island'. This imaginary government title suggested that the original author – the papers were marked 'Copy' – had been unsure how to address British colonial authority. And I was also thrown by the fact that the letter came from a woman called Oyaya, 'living at 29 Malabar Street Singapore'. But the top number was right – a red stamp, 'Home Secretary's Office Queensland / 13.Dec.97 / 15833' – and the third paragraph set my heart racing:

In the end of July this year your Petitioner's sister named Usa left Nagasaki Japan and proceeded to Singapore via Hong Kong on a visit to join Petitioner¹²

I read on, noting Oyaya's concern that her sister had been 'kidnapped from Hong Kong and taken to Australia', where she had been 'forced to

---

[9] Mihalopoulos, *Sex in Japan's Globalization*, p. 41.
[10] Mihalopoulos acknowledges Hacking as the inspiration for his chapter on 'Creating the Archive: The Power of the Pen', in his *Sex in Japan's Globalization*, pp. 11–12; see also Ian Hacking, 'Making Up People', *London Review of Books* 28, 16 (17 August 2006): 23–6, citation from p. 23.
[11] For other examples of such strategies, see Takai, 'Recrafting Marriage in Meiji Hawai'i'.
[12] QSA, Item ID ITM861850 (top number 97/15833).

prostitute herself against her will'. I don't really believe in 'the dead waiting to be chosen', as Alain Corbin has suggested.[13] But as I turned the final page of Oyaya's petition – signed by the mark of her finger – I noticed that it had been composed on 8 November, the same date I had rediscovered it in the archives. And, after the petition, here came Usa's own voice: 'My name is Usa Hashimoto. I am twenty one years of age.'

Or so I wanted to believe in that moment of archival euphoria. I wanted to believe that Hashimoto's first-person singular might resist the logic of Queensland's ocular regime, might be an example of an individual speaking back to the bureaucrats whose language of *civilization, invasion, ill fame* and *disgrace* had framed her archival appearance. An 'I' for an 'eye'.

But it was not that simple. For a start, the order of her names revealed a gap between the written and spoken words: the given name (Usa), followed by the family name, was evidence that the transcriber, who would turn out to be the aforementioned Thursday Island government resident John Douglas, had already edited her words to suit an English-reading audience. The 'presence' of Torajiro Satow and Gyusaku Sugiyama (that is, Satō Torajirō and Sugiyama Gensaku) would be explained at the end of Hashimoto's statement: they were her translators from Japanese to the English-language document I had in front of me (her words in Japanese were never recorded).[14] And, as I shall argue, the translators served as something like court interpreters too, intervening in subtle ways to drive, block and position Hashimoto's testimony for the listening (and questioning) John Douglas.[15]

These were the beginnings of what Carolyn Steedman has called archival 'degrees of separation': Hashimoto (Japanese, spoken) via Satō and Sugiyama (English, spoken) to Douglas (English, written), and Douglas to me.[16] But even that was an oversimplification. A few hours later, having put Hashimoto to one side and ploughed on through more correspondence about labour shortages in the Queensland sugar industry, I found the still-missing top page to the Oyaya/Usa paperwork (see Figure 5.1).

---

[13] Alain Corbin, *The Life of an Unknown: The Rediscovered World of a Clog Maker in Nineteenth-Century France*, trans. Arthur Goldhammer (New York: Columbia University Press, 2001 [1998]), p. x.

[14] Sugiyama's given name appears to have been misheard, leading to a transcription error. By a similar logic, Hashimoto's given name may have been Fusa, rather than the less common Usa. My thanks to David Ambaras for this suggestion.

[15] On the role of the court interpreter, see Chapter 3.

[16] Carolyn Steedman, 'Lord Mansfield's Voices: In the Archive, Hearing Things', in Stephanie Downes, Sally Holloway and Sarah Randles, eds., *Feeling Things: Objects and Emotions through History* (Oxford: Oxford University Press, 2018), pp. 209–25. My thanks to Frieder Missfelder for this reference.

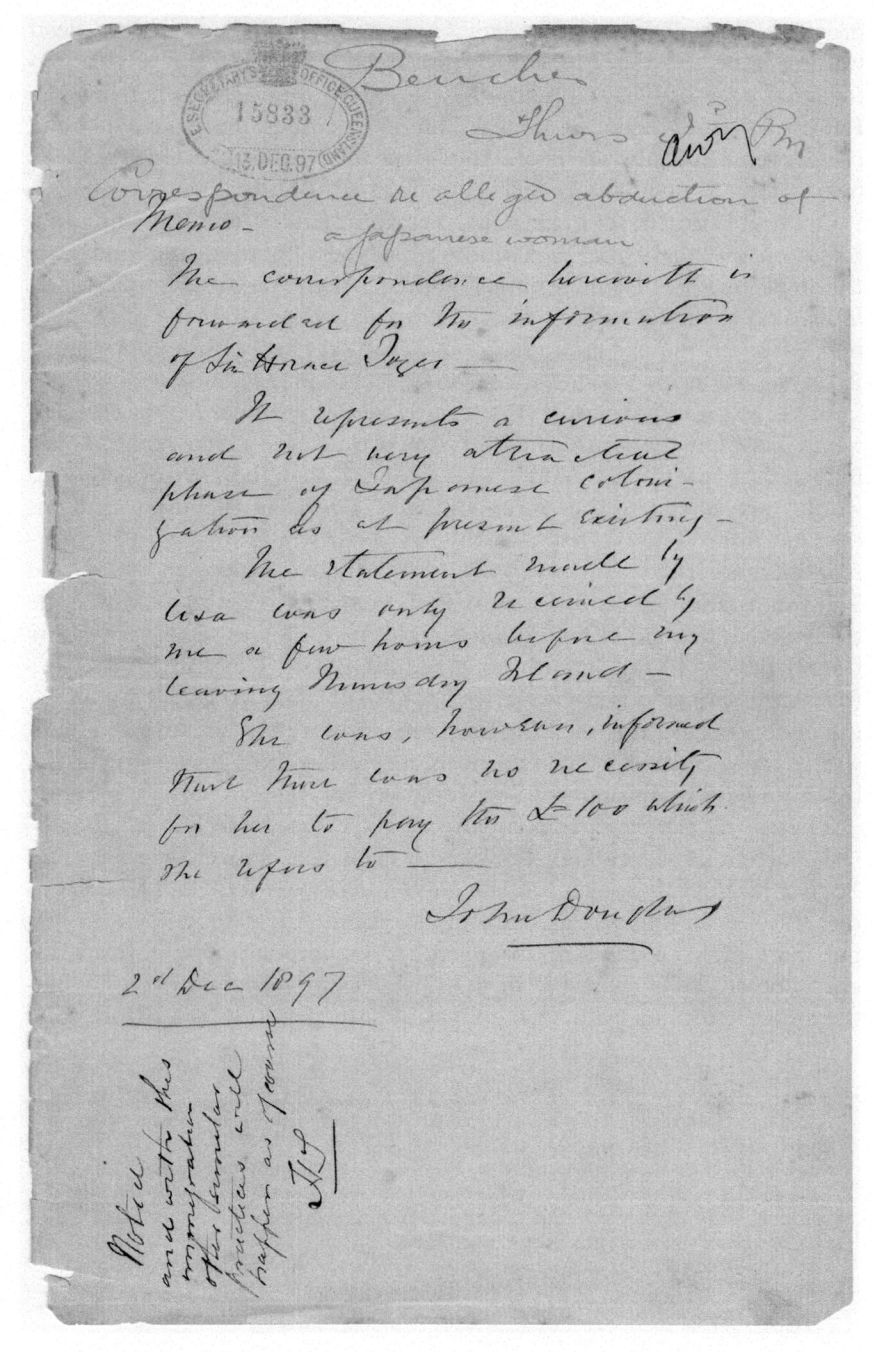

Figure 5.1 'Correspondence re alleged abduction of a Japanese woman', 1897. ITM861850. Courtesy of Queensland State Archives.

This was a 'Memo' by John Douglas, forwarding the petition and statement to home secretary Sir Horace Tozer (1844–1916) and noting that the case 'represents a curious and not very attractive phase of Japanese colonization as at present existing'. Here was yet another framing of Hashimoto Usa's words, the imposition of an interpretative filter before Sir Horace or any of the rest of us could even read her account. And, with Sir Horace's initials and perpendicular marginal comments (*'Noted and with this immigration other similar practices will happen as of course'*), and with the vermilion filing instructions and official stamp of the home secretary's office, there were at least a couple more degrees of reader separation between Douglas and me. Steedman argues that such separation renders the historian ever more 'inclined to hear voices'.[17] True, the archive may be a tonal void in terms of physical speech from the past. But, she continues, our handling of hard copies, manipulation of microfilm readers, transcriptions of texts, awareness of reading room whispers and even consciousness of travelling long distances to the archives – these actually constitute acts of training the ear to hear.

In the case of Hashimoto Usa, there were plenty of voices in the room: Satō, Sugiyama and Douglas, for a start, whose worldviews I layer into her statement in the following pages. The problem was, all these voices belonged to men. Douglas (University of Durham) and Satō (University of Michigan) – hell, Sissons (Melbourne) and me (Oxford) – typify what Virginia Woolf called the 'well-nourished, well-educated, free mind, which had never been thwarted or opposed, but had had full liberty from birth to stretch itself in whatever way it liked'. This was the male writer, the first-person singular whose 'I' was a 'straight dark bar' casting its shadow over the page:

One began to be tired of "I". [...] But – here I turned a page or two, looking for something or other – the worst of it is that in the shadow of the letter "I" all is shapeless as mist. Is that a tree? No, it is a woman. But ... she has not a bone in her body, I thought, watching Phoebe, for that was her name, coming across the beach. Then Alan got up and the shadow of Alan at once obliterated Phoebe.[18]

If, as Steedman concludes, the voices we claim to hear in the archive are ultimately those of the historian, then my channelling of them would be to impose my own straight dark bar on Hashimoto's words (or, rather, on the version of her words left by her male interlocutors). In analysing Hashimoto's statement, I could certainly try not to obliterate her; but

---

[17] Steedman, 'Lord Mansfield's Voices', p. 217.
[18] Virginia Woolf, *A Room of One's Own* (Oxford: Oxford University Press, 1992 [1929]), pp. 129–30.

then I ran the opposite risk of appearing as her one true saviour, a Rankean prince kissing life into the archived dead.[19]

Between obliteration and osculation, I was faced with the structural problem of how to write about Hashimoto's words. But as Noelani Arista has argued in her analysis of the first Hawaiian-language translations of the Gospel in the 1820s, historians should both read and *listen* to written texts which were once animated through speech. In observations pertinent also to the Thursday Island encounter between Hashimoto Usa and her Euro-Japanese interlocutors, Arista suggests that such listening will enable historians to 'attune themselves to the meaning-making systems of not just Hawaiians, but also Euro-Americans, so that we do not miss in which words and whose speech *mana* (spiritual force) inhered in a culturally diverse world of encounter – where speech *and* writing worked simultaneously to craft or dissemble power and authority'.[20]

To listen and not just to read, I attempt a two-pronged approach. At one level, I outline the basic story of a woman coming across a beach by structuring the chapter around Hashimoto's account in the order she narrated it – if, in fact, she determined that order. In terms of empirical value, her statement unshadows a very different history of Meiji Japan's engagement with the outside world, and of the routes and passages therein, to the histories I have recounted in previous chapters. Along the way, Hashimoto reveals herself to be a factually accurate witness to the phenomenon of undocumented women crossing the fluid borders between Asia and the Arafura Zone, and she disproves the thesis that such mobilities in the late nineteenth century 'may have been nearly frictionless'.[21] But although the facts of her passage are important, I am secondly interested in the archival tales historical actors tell, and the voices in which they narrate those tales. Everyone turns out to be a storyteller in the reconstruction that follows, some more flamboyantly than others.[22] Such stories both provided the data that underpinned the creation of the written archive's ocular regime, and informed its multiple textual genres – including telegraphs, letters, petitions, bureaucratic reports, purportedly first-person testimonies and newspaper clippings. But in Hashimoto's case, the provision and withholding of information equally gave her a chance to challenge the male gaze: this was her *mana*.

---

[19] On the nineteenth-century roots of the historian performing his masculinity through the archival saving of fairy princesses, see B. G. Smith, 'Gender and the Practices of Scientific History', p. 1153.

[20] Arista, *Kingdom and the Republic*, p. 103 (emphasis in original).

[21] Dotulong, '*Hyakushō* in the Arafura Zone', p. 303.

[22] For this approach, see also Natalie Zemon Davis, *Fiction in the Archives: Pardon Tales and Their Tellers in Sixteenth-Century France* (Oxford: Polity Press, 1988).

Contextualizing her history with that of other mobile Japanese women, I try to show where and how her statement performed this challenge in November 1897 – and why, in a world of increasing source digitization, her words and speech remain important today.

Doubtless there will be much to critique in the shadow which my first-person singular casts over the already gendered structures of Japanese migration archives.[23] But what follows is at least a new attempt to reply to Oyaya's 'humble petition' for 'due enquiry [to] be made into the above case'.

I Was Born at Nishiyama

My name is Usa Hashimoto –
I am twenty one years of age –
I was born at Nishiyama Nagasaki Japan –

Nishiyama is at the northeastern edge of today's Nagasaki, about two kilometres as the bird flies from Dejima, the island on which for more than two centuries European employees of the Dutch East India Company were confined. On Google Streetview from pandemic lockdown in Europe, I can read that the Nishiyama shrine is famous for its winter-flowering cherry tree, planted in January 1897 and now some seven metres tall. The shrine grounds also boast a pomelo tree, planted from a seed brought on a Qing dynasty ship from Java in 1667.[24]

In other words, the world beyond Japan was tangible to the people of mid nineteenth-century Nishiyama. If they had strolled up Tateyama, a low-lying mountain to the village's north, they could have gazed over the great vista of Nagasaki Bay, a seascape synonymous with Tokugawa Japan's connections to China, Southeast Asia and beyond to Europe (see Figure 5.2). Indeed, a party from France led by the eminent astronomer Pierre Janssen (1824–1907) had set up base on nearby Mount Konpira in December 1874 in order to observe the transit of Venus – the first such transit since 1769, when Captain Cook had been sent by the British Admiralty to Tahiti.[25] Five hundred local people had helped Janssen lug his heavy equipment up the hill; and to commemorate his

---

[23] On these structures, see Cecilia M. Tsu, 'Sex, Lies, and Agriculture: Reconstructing Japanese Immigrant Gender Relations in Rural California, 1900–1913', *Pacific Historical Review* 78, 2 (2009): 171–209.
[24] www.nagasaki-tabinet.com/guide/251 (last accessed 26 February 2021).
[25] Suzanne Débarbat and Françoise Launay, 'The 1874 Transit of Venus Observed in Japan by the French, and Associated Relics', *Journal of Astronomical History and Heritage* 9, 2 (2006): 167–71, accessible at http://articles.adsabs.harvard.edu//full/2006JAHH...9. .167D/0000167.000.html (last accessed 26 February 2021).

Figure 5.2 Nagasaki Harbour from Tateyama, after 1896. Courtesy of Nagasaki University Library Collections.

successful photographic plates, he later installed a small stone pyramid near the peak.

I wonder if Hashimoto Usa celebrated the new year of 1897 by praying at Nishiyama shrine, or whether she ascended Tateyama or Mount Konpira one last time before departing Nagasaki in June of that year. There is no way of knowing – but it nonplusses me that a perfunctory internet search reveals more about one of Nishiyama's nineteenth-century cherry trees than it will about one of its nineteenth-century residents, that it is easier to research the history of a planet crossing the sun than a woman crossing to Singapore.

Seeing My Sister at Singapore

My elder sister is keeping a lodging house in Singapore at Malabar Street –
I am one of the inmates of No 2 at the place known as Yokohama Thursday Island, a brothel kept by Shiosaki –
I departed from Nagasaki with the intention of seeing my sister at Singapore –

Like a navigator, the historian can map the locations mentioned by Hashimoto Usa in the opening sentences of her statement, and their order: Nagasaki, Singapore, the Japanese settlement of 'Yokohama' on

Thursday Island, back to Nagasaki, once again to Singapore. Her mind seems to jump without settling: having noted her place of birth, should she continue with her journey's intended destination or its unintended endpoint? The ebb and flow of her narrative may suggest emotional turmoil, caused both by her physical ordeal and also by finding herself, on this 29th day of November, suddenly 'in the presence of Torajiro Satow and Gyusaku Sugiyama' and the British official for whom they were translating. From Singapore to Thursday Island and back to Singapore may equally be a narrative consequence of the three men trying to lead the interview to the present situation and Usa resisting – to insist first on her 'intention'. Either way, the most important detail in these opening gambits is the address of her sister's lodging house in Singapore. For with her mention of 'Malabar Street', corroborated in Oyaya's own petition to the Thursday Island authorities, Usa takes us from the still air of Tateyama into the brawling, bruising heart of a magnetic Asian cityscape.

Singapore's global importance by the 1890s had been many decades in the making, its roots predating the port's founding by Sir Stamford Raffles in 1819. In the second half of the seventeenth century, increasing numbers of Chinese seafarers, including those defeated by the new Qing dynasty (1644–1912), had established themselves in the coastal waters of Southeast Asia, where they traded in commodities which both Chinese and European consumers demanded. The latter's taste for tea, for example, stimulated the need for the tin, timber, rattan and lead used in packaging. Increasing numbers of Chinese labourers migrated into the region to work in commodity production also for the Qing market – in gold- or tin-mining, in pepper-planting colonies or in the transport of rice from the Mekong Delta. But as previously prosperous trading entrepôts in Hà Tiên (present-day Vietnam) or Riau (Indonesia) declined by the late 1700s, the new Straits Settlements established by the British in Penang (1786) and Singapore expanded, thus also attracting – to the alarm of Singapore's colonial administrators in the 1830s – large numbers of Indian and especially Chinese immigrant labourers.[26]

Quickly, these labourers themselves became a commodity. As such, their transshipment in and export on from Singapore was stimulated by the growing European demand for Southeast Asian raw materials whose

---

[26] Carl A. Trocki, 'Singapore as a Nineteenth Century Migration Node', in Donna Gabaccia and Dirk Hoerder, eds., *Connecting Seas and Ocean Rims: Indian, Atlantic, and Pacific Oceans and China Seas Migrations from the 1830s to the 1930s* (Leiden: Brill, 2011), pp. 198–224, here pp. 198–207. On South Asian immigration to Singapore, see Amrith, *Crossing the Bay of Bengal*, pp. 63–100.

that the author of the November 1897 petition – Usa Hashimoto's nominal 'sister' – was a woman probably called Yaya, not Oyaya.

Shimo Sai's resting place is a beautiful site, purple bougainvilleas canopying over the cemetery's main walkway. As I take photos of her headstone, I stoop down to read the inscriptions on neighbouring plots. And here I find the grave of an unnamed woman who died on 21 April 1892. Her address is listed as Tenjin-machi in Kaminoseki town, Yamaguchi prefecture – a district I walked through every day on my way to the Municipal Archives in 2007 and 2008 (Chapter 3).[41]

On the Representations of a Man Named Konishi

This I did on the representations of a man named Konishi at the end of June 1897 –
There were ten other young women who left by a sailing ship at the same time accompanied by Konishi –
I do not know the name of the ship –
We had no passports –
It was midnight –
I intended to go to my sister at Singapore –

The women who emigrated to such entrepôts as Singapore from the last decades of the nineteenth century until the end of the Second World War are popularly known in Japan as *Karayuki* 唐行 (or, honorifically, *Karayuki-san*). The term derives from north-west Kyushu and literally means 'going to China', although in its very earliest uses, after 1868, it simply referred to women and men who sought work overseas. By the end of the nineteenth century, however, it had come to be applied only to Kyushu women who worked in the sex industry throughout the Asia-Pacific region; and, in later iterations, Karayuki-san connoted women especially from the Amakusa Islands – the birthplace of Shimo Sai – who worked in Southeast Asia.[42] According to David Sissons, a 'plaintive song' was sung about the Karayuki-san at the turn of the twentieth century:

> Carried on the drifting current,
> Her destination will be
> In the west, Siberia;

---

[41] As with several other gravestones, this one is marked as having been built by 'Futaki Tagaji' – that is, Futaki Tagajirō 二木多賀治郎, brothel owner and one of the three original landowners of the cemetery in 1891.
[42] Mihalopoulos, *Sex in Japan's Globalization*, pp. 2–3.

Or in the east, Java.
Which country will be her grave?[43]

The geography of the lyrics is unusual: from Japan, Java would be in the west. Perhaps, then, the song originates from Karayuki-san communities in North America, where 'Java' would conjure up an image of the Orient. But be that as it may, the language – as with the Hawaiian *holehole bushi* plantation songs (Chapter 3) – is of drifting bodies and currents, as if the Karayuki-san had no agency in their decision to leave Japan.

Certainly, substantial numbers of women were indeed carried on drifting currents in the late nineteenth century, against their will and with no idea of their destinations. In September 1897, for example, the *Singapore Free Press and Mercantile Advertiser* published an article, 'The Abduction of Girls from Japan', itself a reprint from the English-language *Kobe Herald* (in turn citing Kobe's Japanese-language *Yūshin nippō*). The article reported on a recently returned but unnamed eighteen-year-old girl who, after the death of her father, had moved from Shikoku to work in a fan factory in Osaka. One night, she and a friend were 'accosted' by a woman offering them work in a Yokohama teahouse. Deciding to accept, the girls were taken to Kobe for several days, and then at 2am on 12 November (1896) stowed away on board the NYK steamship *Miikemaru* in the company of four men and eleven other women. Travelling in darkness and ordered by the men to remain quiet, the women arrived ten days later in what they expected to be Yokohama but was in fact Hong Kong. There, 'quartered in a hotel', one of the girls attempted to escape but was caught; another girl was advised by a young Japanese man that it was useless for her to go to the police unless she could speak English. Another ten days later, nine of the women were shipped to Australia, while the eighteen-year-old was taken to Singapore and then on to a Japanese brothel in Batavia. Becoming ill and needing hospital treatment, her case was attended to by the Japanese consul in Singapore, who eventually arranged for her return to Kobe. The girl reportedly stated 'that there are many brothels kept by Japanese in Sumatra, all the girls being surreptitiously brought from Japan'.[44]

There survive enough such reports, both in published media and in various archives, for historians to be sure that the practice of Japanese

---

[43] Sissons, '*Karayuki-san*', p. 323, and later cited by Warren, *Ah Ku and Karayuki-san*, p. 75. The song was published in the *Japan Weekly Mail*, 30 May 1896, in turn taken from the daily *Kokumin* newspaper – but Sissons was unable to find the Japanese original.

[44] *Singapore Free Press and Mercantile Advertiser (Weekly)*, 14 September 1897. Available online through the National Library of Singapore, https://eresources.nlb.gov.sg/newspapers/ (last accessed 11 March 2021).

women being abducted and surreptitiously sent overseas was widespread at the turn of the twentieth century. Exactly how widespread is open to question: as David Ambaras has noted for a slightly later period, newspaper reports of 'abduction' constituted their own written genre, one often framed by the sensationalist agendas of reporters or editors.[45] Even a small number of factually accurate cases would be historiographically significant, however. This is because the conditions in which Japanese women and even young girls were 'recruited' to work in Southeast Asia (or, later, mainland China) have been made central to a debate about the later Japanese exploitation of so-called comfort women from imperial colonies in the 1930s and 1940s. If it could be proved (the argument goes) that there were no coercion in the period from the 1880s to the 1920s, then (by a deductive sleight of hand) it must also be true that there was no coercion of the later 'comfort women'. As many reputable scholars have pointed out, using evidence from one place and period to explain another is a deeply problematic methodology – as is the conscious misuse of later oral histories recorded by Japanese women who were, in exceptional cases, only ten years old when recruited for overseas sex labour.[46] All of which makes discussion of cases such as Hashimoto Usa's particularly fraught.

But if we follow Hashimoto's own testimony, then her departure from Japan does not appear coerced – as, indeed, Brisbane officials seem to have concluded in labelling the case as an 'alleged abduction' (see Figure 5.1). She states on two occasions that it was her 'intention' to go to Singapore. Without knowing her original Japanese phrasing, it's difficult to parse the nuances of this term. But a few key elements of her statement are consistent with those of other women who left Nagasaki to go overseas in the summer of 1897. In the archives of the Japanese Foreign Ministry in Tokyo, for example, I find first-person testimonies from five women recruited to work in Vladivostok – that is, in the 'Siberia' of the Karayuki-san song. The narrative structure of their accounts echoes that of Hashimoto's in three basic ways.[47]

First, the recruiter was a key protagonist. Rather than an unknown accoster, he was someone the women had partly come to know. In this

---

[45] Ambaras, *Japan's Imperial Underworlds*, pp. 80–8.
[46] Alexis Dudden, ed., 'Supplement to Special Issue: Academic Integrity at Stake: The Ramseyer Article – Four Letters', *Asia-Pacific Journal: Japan Focus*, 19, 5 (1 March 2021), https://apjjf.org/2021/5/ToC2.html (last accessed 11 March 2021). For an overview of the Ramseyer controversy, see Jeannie Suk Gersen, 'Seeking the True Story of the Comfort Women', *New Yorker*, 25 February 2021, www.newyorker.com/culture/annals-of-inquiry/seeking-the-true-story-of-the-comfort-women-j-mark-ramseyer (last accessed 11 March 2021).
[47] DA 3.8.8.4, vol. 3, case 7.

case, there were two such men: Maekawa Saihachi (aged 39) and Shimosaka Toyokichi (37), respectively a farmer–fisherman and a cooper. Maekawa, who in 1896 had worked as a captain transporting stowaway women to Vladivostok in a Japanese-style sailing vessel, now wanted to lead his own operation. To that end, in addition to renting a boat for 300 yen, he recruited one woman, the twenty-two-year-old Fukuhara Tsuru. Originally from Fukuoka prefecture, Fukuhara had been working in a relative's Western-style grocery shop in Nagasaki's Chinatown for all of two weeks when Maekawa, who was a frequent customer, started telling her of a 'good place' (*yokitokoro* 好き処) where she could make money. Shimosaka, for his part, appears to have groomed the other women over a number of days from occasional chance encounters: he 'met' Matsunobe Tomi (23) a few days after she had arrived, also from Fukuoka, to learn needlework from her aunt; he came to the house where Onoue Shima (25) was staying while seeking domestic service employment and posed the rhetorical question of whether this were really the kind of household from which she would eventually be able to marry; he often bought eggs at the shop where Nakamura Saku (18) was working, such that she knew his face when she bumped into him on the street one day; and, in the case of Maebara Matsu (23), he was even joined by her employer, an acquaintance, who urged her to go abroad. Thus, for Hashimoto Usa, the 'man named Konishi' may have played a similar role as had Shimosaka for these Vladivostok-bound women – as someone she felt she could trust to accompany her to Singapore.

Second, this familiar figure promised to manage the logistics. Matsunobe Tomi recalled that Shimosaka had told her he would take care of passports and everything else. Nakamuru Saku, the youngest of the Vladivostok-bound group, testified:

I said, 'If we don't have a licence [passport] to go abroad, then we can't go, right?' To which he said, 'There's no need to worry at all: I'll take care of it all'.

There may be an element of Nakamura speaking to her audience here. Her testimony, like that of the other women and the two recruiters, was taken down by a member of staff from the Japanese consulate in Wonsan, Korea, where, en route to Vladivostok, Maekawa's rented boat had landed ('having fallen into great difficulties'). Perhaps, to these particular officials, she wanted to emphasize her lack of culpability when it came to the paperwork of international travel. But still, the journey involved 'no passports' – as was also the case for Hashimoto Usa.

And third, several of the Vladivostok-bound women were also explicit in voicing their *desire* to go abroad:

I also knew that [a 'good place'] would most probably be a foreign brothel, but he recommended it to me in various ways, saying that I could make lots of money and advance in the world, so I ended up *wanting to go*. [Fukuhara Tsuru]

I thought that if I went to Vladivostok I would do service at some kind of brothel; but because [Shimosaka] said I would get lots of money and could advance in the world, I finally ended up *wanting to go*. [Nakamura Saku]

Although I thought that if I went to Vladivostok I would do service in a brothel, [Shimosaka] said I would earn lots of money, so I finally ended up *wanting to go*. [Matsunobe Tomi]

Perhaps this was the phrase Hashimoto Usa used as well, *iku ki ni naru* 行く気になる, which her Thursday Island translators then rendered as 'I intended to go'.[48]

Of course, the linguistic evidence from the Vladivostock case is not as unambiguous as it might seem. The almost identical phrasing used by the three women in their recorded dispositions raises the suspicion that they were coached by their handlers to give set responses in the event that they be apprehended. This was certainly true of some Chinese and Japanese women who ended up in Singapore;[49] and the fact that the Vladivostok-bound women denied knowing the name of the fishing port from which they were smuggled away in the cover of darkness suggests that they were trying – or had been told – to protect the ringleader Maekawa, whose home village (Fukuda) it was. That, at least, is one hypothesis to explain their rote-phrasing. An alternative is that the male consular official in Wonsan not only transcribed but also edited the women's nominal first-person voices into a series of set phrases in order to simplify his job. More perniciously, he may have done so also to imply that the problem was less groomed coercion than immoral women willing to do anything for money. Here, as often in the case of nominal first-person testimonies 'glossed by a male hand', the legibility and brevity of the account served both to simplify complex motivations on the part of the women and to encode gendered assumptions on the part of the men.[50]

But even if the evidence of 'intention' is ambiguous in the Vladivostok case, the bigger picture was that there *were* significant numbers of women willing to earn money overseas in the late nineteenth century. This may have been to 'advance in the world' (*shusse* 出世), and/or to send remittances (*sōkin* 送金) home – either to their parents and older

---

[48] Matsutome Tomi used the more humble phrase *mairu ki ni naru* 参る気になる, whose meaning is the same.
[49] Warren, *Ah Ku and Karayuki-san*, pp. 212–13.
[50] Ambaras, *Japan's Imperial Underworlds*, p. 78.

brothers, or to their village as a whole (as Matsunobe Tomi and Maebara Matsu respectively claimed in their testimonies). In this sense, the women's motivations for leaving Japan were no different from those of a male migrant such as Fuyuki Sakazō (Chapter 3), who went off to make money in Hawai'i – or from Fuyuki's cousin Hiraki Yasushirō, whom Fuyuki helped find sugar plantation work in 1897. Indeed, five years earlier, the Acting Japanese Consul in Singapore had written in English to the city's Chinese protectorate concerning four 'girls' – aged seventeen to eighteen – whom British officials had wanted investigated. Noting that they were all 'natives of Nagasaki', the consul explained their economic circumstances at home:

They informed me of their families' being in such distress that they could not even provide themselves, sometimes with daily food. They arrived in Hong Kong in the beginning of last summer for the purposes of finding some means of living there. They came on to Singapore [as] they had heard about this place being very prosperous.

Having talked to the women, he was sure that they had not 'been induced to leave or smuggled out by any one', and that they had left Japan 'entirely of their free will'. He continued:

Under these circumstances I am convinced that these girls were not brought out by others against their will, but that they really came here by their own wishes, in order to procure a better living in this place, than they could do in their native country.

The consul's language is more discreet than that of the transcribed Vladivostok women – he writes of 'a better living' where they spoke of 'lots of money' and worldly 'advance' – but the general point is the same: many of the women leaving Nagasaki in the late nineteenth century were doing so for economic reasons.[51]

Yet the pre-war archival eye in Tokyo could not acknowledge the parity of this economic push factor between male and female emigrants. The main body of pre-war diplomatic records in the Japanese Foreign Ministry archive is divided into more than twenty series (*mon*), of which the most important for the study of overseas migration in the Meiji period would seem to be Series 3 (*Commercial Relations*). The majority of files relating to the government-sponsored emigration programme to Hawai'i, for example, are to be found in various sub-series thereof, as in: 3 (*Commercial Relations*) – 8 (*The Movement of Imperial Subjects*) – 2 (*Migrants*). Yet the Vladivostok-bound women are not filed alongside

---

[51] Letter from Miki Saito to the Protector of Chinese, 28 September 1892: DA 4.2.2.27, vol. 1, section 1, sub-section 10.

Fuyuki or his migrant counterparts in 3-8-2 but rather appear in 3-8-8 (*Miscellaneous*), as if metropolitan bureaucrats did not know how to categorize single women wanting to go abroad. In fact, women only appear in the government-sponsored Hawaiian paperwork if they are listed as the wives of male emigrants – even if the status of pre-departure and post-arrival 'wife' was considerably more fluid than Japanese officials knew or wanted to believe.[52] Meanwhile, the four Nagasaki girls questioned in Singapore in 1892, whom the acting consul insisted came simply 'to procure a better living', are filed under 4 (*Judiciary and Policing*) – 2 (*Policing*) – 2 (*Policing Matters, Enforcement and Punishment*). Here, the archival eye is unambiguous: the women constituted a problem of law and order.

This apparently technical issue of filing is a classic expression of the metropolitan archive's 'ocular regime', whereby migrating single women were classified as a threat to the Meiji state – and thus in need of repatriation – in ways that single men were not.[53] The building-blocks of such a classification were the consular reports flowing into Tokyo from Southeast Asia, Australia and North America. In June 1888, for example, the honorary Japanese consul in Melbourne, Alexander Marks, wrote to Tokyo to report on information he had requested from the businessman Kanematsu Fusajirō, who had recently returned to Japan via Port Darwin.[54] Kanematsu, wrote Marks, 'says there are 15 men and 21 women [there] who are all prostitutes and the men may all live [?] on the prostitution of the women'. Calling the whole affair 'extremely unpleasant', he did 'not wish the fair name of Japan soiled by a lot of unfortunate women'.[55] Almost a decade later, in June 1897, it was the

---

[52] Takai, 'Recrafting Marriage in Meiji Hawai'i'.

[53] Barbara J. Brooks notes that due to the introduction of a diplomatic examination system in 1894, Foreign Ministry entrants 'came to strongly share common views and experiences': Brooks, *Japan's Imperial Diplomacy: Consuls, Treaty Ports, and War in China, 1895–1938* (Honolulu: University of Hawai'i Press, 2000), p. 42. For this reason, I write of a singular ocular regime. It is unclear whether the aforementioned archival categories date from the moment the paperwork was generated or from later. There was an independent archives section in the Ministry by at least 1913 (ibid., p. 20). The table of contents for some of the most voluminous folders concerning Meiji-period female emigration (e.g. DA 4.2.2.27, vol. 1, or 4.2.2.34, vol. 1) was written on paper from the Taisho period (1912–26), indicating that such categories were in place by the mid 1920s at the latest. But much else about the archivists' appraisal decisions remains unclear: see also Terry Cook, 'The Archive(s) is a Foreign Country: Historians, Archivists, and the Changing Archival Landscape', *Canadian Historical Review* 90, 3 (September 2009): 497–534.

[54] On Marks and Kanematsu, see Chapter 4.

[55] Letter from Alexander Marks to the Vice Minister of State for Foreign Affairs, Tokyo, 8 June 1888: DA 4.2.2.27, vol. 1, section 1, sub-section 2. From 1888 to 1890, Japan's Foreign Ministry received over fifteen petitions from its consuls in the Asia-Pacific

same story: Marks wrote of receiving a letter from a Japanese resident of West Australia 'complaining about the number of Japanese low characters both men and women now in that country'.[56] Many of these came from Singapore, Marks added.

In these cases, Australia-bound women who desired a better living even through the practice of sex work were framed in three ways. First, their circumstances rendered them 'unfortunate' – a language I never saw deployed by officials for Japanese males who had had to leave Japan for similar reasons of domestic impoverishment. Second, their presence undermined both the expansion of Japanese business interests overseas, as embodied by Kanematsu, and also 'hindered' those male Japanese who sought 'respectable Honest Employment' (in the words of Marks's 1897 informant).[57] Thus, thirdly, the women soiled the 'fair name of Japan'.[58] Describing them in 1888 as 'most indecently dressed and in their houses with little or no clothing on at all', Marks hoped that the presence of Japanese women would not provoke the colonies to impose immigration restrictions on *all* Japanese subjects – including on the allegedly more reputable men.

The image of working women that Marks and other Japanese consuls reported back to Tokyo in the 1880s and 1890s was an ugly one – even if, as we have seen, such reports were often exaggerated. ('These women,' the Cairns sub-inspector of police wrote in November 1897, 'although a nuisance by reason of their calling are *so orderly in their conduct* that a stranger coming to town would have to seek them before he would find

---

region calling for action to be taken against Japanese sex labourers: Mihalopoulos, *Sex in Japan's Globalization*, pp. 44–45.

[56] Letter from Alexander Marks to the Vice Minister of State for Foreign Affairs, Tokyo, 24 June 1897: DA 6.1.5.9–7, vol. 1.

[57] 'For the good name of Japan and her people who come here for trade purposes the arrival of such characters would certainly destroy the good feeling that exists at present between Japanese subjects and the people of Australia': Letter from Alexander Marks to the Vice Minister of State for Foreign Affairs, Tokyo, 12 April 1888: DA 4.2.2.27, vol. 1, section 1, sub-section 2.

[58] Sidney Xu Lu has argued that the 'shame' inflicted upon Japan's name by overseas sex labourers requires disaggregation: 'Japanese prostitutes who went to North America, Hawaii, and places in Southeast Asia under British colonial rule were seen as baring Japan's inferiority to the world's ruling powers. Japanese prostitutes in Korea, Manchuria, and other parts of China, on the other hand, were accused of sabotaging the empire by selling sex indiscriminately, especially to the subjugated and unenlightened, thus undermining Japan's hard-fought gains in prestige and status in the world community of nations.' Lu, 'The Shame of Empire: Japanese Overseas Prostitutes and Prostitution Abolition in Modern Japan, 1880s–1927', *positions* 24, 4 (2016): 830–73, here p. 852.

Given that both Usa and Yaya were unable to write, the logistics of Usa sending correspondence from Thursday Island to Singapore were considerable. Why was Usa updating her sister as opposed to the only other family relation mentioned in Yaya's petition, 'her brother in Japan' – where, Mr Ukita's translation abilities notwithstanding, *our* would surely be the more natural personal pronoun? If there had been a similar sisterly exchange of letters between Malabar Street and Nishiyama in the early months of 1897, was Konishi involved in some way as a broker working on Yaya's behalf? If so, then is it possible that the term 'sister' referred – as so often among the Karayuki-san in Singapore – not to a biological relationship but to the hierarchical relationship between a keeper and her prospective employee?[65] And that Usa intended, through Konishi's representations, to work in a lodging house at Malabar Street?

And thus: is it possible that Yaya's appeal to the British authorities in Queensland via Singapore was motivated less by sisterhood than by a recruitment process gone wrong, an asset kidnapped by competitors?

Transferred without Landing

On reflection, I don't much like the tone of my questions. My voice has bled into that of Hashimoto Usa's investigators on Thursday Island. Which is unfortunate because, regardless of her pre-departure plans or the exact nature of her relationship to Yaya in Singapore, the next part of her statement, beginning with her and ten other women leaving Nagasaki on a sailing ship, reveals a system in which her intentions counted for nothing. Indeed, we need not define Hashimoto by her passage nevertheless to accept that her period of transit, from Nagasaki through Hong Kong to her eventual arrival on Thursday Island, was a formative moment in her story.[66]

> *The ship took us to Shanghai, and there we were transferred without landing to a Steamer for Hong Kong where we arrived on the 13th of July –*
> *We were all put up at a lodging house kept by a Japanese called Yoishi Otaka –*
> *I was then told that it would be impossible for me to go to my sister in Singapore as no woman who has not a passport from the Japanese authorities is allowed to land at Singapore –*

---

[65] See Warren, *Ah Ku and Karayuki-san*, pp. 230–1.
[66] On transit encompassing more than simply the ship passage, see Chapter 2.

Transferred without Landing 199

The visit to my sister at Singapore was my inducement to leave Japan –
My disappointment was so great that I did not know what to do –

In these sentences, Hashimoto offers a series of realizations which must have washed over her like waves of seasickness during her weeks in transit: that Konishi was not the man she had imagined him to be; that a new regime of passports initiated by the Meiji state constrained her movements in ways that sisterly correspondence between Malabar Street and Nishiyama had surely not explained (assuming such correspondence existed);[67] and, most importantly, that she had become a sellable commodity in a transnational infrastructure which, by 1897, had been years in the making.

The key nodes in this infrastructure were all referenced in Hashimoto's account, namely the port cities of Nagasaki (described by Consul Alexander Marks in 1888 as the 'hunting ground' for 'unprincipled traffickers'), Shanghai, Hong Kong and Singapore (the last two constituting 'great sinks of iniquity').[68] Two weeks prior to Hashimoto's departure, for example, a group of two Japanese men and eight women – the latter aged between seventeen and thirty-six – had boarded a German steamer in Nagasaki bound for Shanghai, where they arrived four days later. Without landing, they had attempted to transfer to another steamship bound for Hong Kong but were detected and taken to the Japanese consulate. Along the way, the two male ringleaders escaped, but the women were promptly returned to Nagasaki. Consular officials recorded their addresses, which included both Nagasaki city and also the Shimabara peninsula, another south-western Kyushu region which was particularly associated in the post-war Japanese popular imagination with the Karayuki-san. Two of the eight women, it turned out, were sisters who had already been repatriated from Shanghai the previous October; another, the thirty-six-year-old Ishimoto Tayo, had been working in Hong Kong for nine years but had returned home temporarily to visit her sick mother.[69] (Again, these histories force us to query Marks's language of 'hunting', with its implication that all women departing Nagasaki were captured against their will.)

This and numerous other cases reveal that the infrastructure of female trafficking was connected partly to the steamship economy – as also in

---

[67] On the early-Meiji passport regime, see Yamamoto, 'Japan's Passport System'.
[68] Letters from Alexander Marks to the Vice Minister of State for Foreign Affairs, Tokyo, 8 June 1888 and 10 August 1888: DA 4.2.2.27, vol. 1, section 1, sub-section 2.
[69] DA 3.8.8.4, vol. 3, section 4. The women left Nagasaki on the evening of 12 June 1897 and were repatriated exactly a week later.

the aforementioned 1896 case of the eighteen-year-old girl and her friend who stowed away on the NYK-owned *Miike-maru* with the expectation that they would disembark in Yokohama, not Hong Kong. More specifically, the trafficking networks were associated with Kyushu's most important export item in the late nineteenth century, coal. As part of an ongoing policy to expand its foreign trade, the Meiji government opened nine 'special ports of export' in 1889, including four in Kyushu – Kuchinotsu, Karatsu, Moji and Misumi – which specialized in coal.[70] But this also had unintended consequences, as noted by the Japanese consul in Hong Kong in 1890: 'The increase in the flow of foreign ships entering and leaving recently opened special export ports such as Kuchinotsu and Karatsu for the purposes of exporting coal, has also increased the opportunity [for women] to slip secretly abroad.'[71]

Coal could of course be carried on steamships, but the most important mode of transport was sailing ships. The 715-ton *Sumanoura-maru*, with which the *Yamashiro-maru* collided in October 1884, was one such vessel: bound for Nagasaki carrying only ballast and forty boxes of dynamite (presumably for Mitsubishi-owned mines), its main function was to transport coal from Kyushu back to Yokohama.[72] Similarly, sailing ships traversing the East China Sea were central to Meiji Japan meeting the exponential increase in demand for Japanese coal in late nineteenth-century Shanghai (see Chapter 6). We must assume that Konishi had arranged for Hashimoto and her ten female companions to travel on one such ship in late June 1897 before transferring 'without landing onto a steamer for Hong Kong'.

Between them, Hashimoto Usa and her questioners are curiously reticent about this hybrid sail–steam passage from Nagasaki to Hong Kong. Where elsewhere in her statement there are hints of Usa being interrupted, here there are none. And if she chose not to go into the details, that may be because the realities of being a stowaway were too traumatic to dwell upon. Several decades later, retired captain Katō Hisakatsu, who had begun his career on an 850-ton coal-carrying ship sailing from Yokohama to Karatsu and later worked all around maritime Asia, recalled the 'ingenuity' (*kōmyōsa* 巧妙さ) with which ringleaders such as Konishi concealed their human cargo 'in places unfit to accommodate humans'. Katō also noted how easily things could go wrong:

---

[70] Phipps, *Empires on the Waterfront*, pp. 25, 43–8. As Phipps points out, Kuchinotsu (in the Shimabara peninsula) had been the key port for the export of coal from the Miike mines since 1877 (ibid., pp. 47, 101).
[71] Quoted in Mihalopoulos, *Sex in Japan's Globalization*, p. 22.
[72] Mitsubishi gōshi kaisha, *Mitsubishi shashi*, vol. 12, p. 337.

[The women] might be crowded into the ship's water tank when the engineer, not knowing they were there, would fill the tank mid-passage and they would be submerged alive, ending up as swollen blue corpses. Or there would be women poisoned by coal gas [carbon monoxide], who would die writhing and screaming and vomiting blood. Or there would be ghost-like women, hair dishevelled and nothing more than bones, starving for food and parched for water, who would eat lumps of coal until they breathed their last. Or there was once a male procurer who was surrounded as the women became ravenous. They gnawed on him as a rat nibbles rice-cakes – women who hated his cold-heartedness and tortured him to death, eating at him while baring their bloody teeth, gouging his eyes out and ripping off his nose.[73]

In this passage, there is a sense that Katō offers graphic details with a little too much relish. 'Such horrific stories to make your hair stand on end,' he continues, slipping almost into a genre of sailor's yarns: 'No matter how many I write, I would not run out of them.'

But lest Katō be thought to be exaggerating, the international press had reported in 1890 on the NYK-owned steam coal-hauler *Fushikimaru*, which left Nagasaki on 21 March. After a few days, a 'bad smell' was noticed in the engineers' mess room, at first attributed to dead rats. But following arrival in Hong Kong on 26 March, the stench was traced to the cofferdam, a compartment some three feet high and two feet wide (91 cm by 61 cm), stretching across the width of the ship above one of the water tanks. Having removed coal from the main hold to get to the compartment's sliding door, the crew discovered the naked corpses of seven women and a man, all 'in a more or less advanced state of decomposition', and four other naked women alive but in a 'shocking condition'. The survivors described having been lured to Hong Kong by the deceased man, a cooking-oil salesman, who had gone house-to-house selling promises of a better life in Hong Kong. The women had made it on board dressed as coal 'coolies', but after entering the cofferdam their exit had been blocked by coal loaded into the hold. To secure relief from the intense heat of the compartment's iron plates, the survivors reported having lain across the bodies of the dead.[74]

That Hashimoto Usa and her ten female companions did not meet such a fate does not detract from the terror that they presumably felt in the depths of the ship, cooped up in the stultifying darkness of the coal

---

[73] Katō Hisakatsu 加藤久勝, *Kanpan ni tachite* 甲板に立ちて [From the deck] (Kobe: Kaibundō shoten, 1926), p. 134.

[74] 'Fate of Smuggled Passengers', *SMH*, 5 May 1890. Available online through the National Library of Australia, http://nla.gov.au/nla (last accessed 18 March 2021). See also Mihalopoulos, *Sex in Japan's Globalization*, p. 47, and Sissons, '*Karayuki-san*', p. 340. The case is covered in DA 3.8.8.4, vol. 1.

bunkers with the air – at least from Shanghai to Hong Kong – pounding to the engine's rhythm. If a summer typhoon were to come, with waves 'running mountains high', the hold's coal might shift and even combust – as happened with the *Cheang Hye Teng* (1,436 tons), steaming with a cargo of coal from Moji to Hong Kong in August 1897; the ship eventually sank with the loss of thirty-six lives.[75] On top of all this, depending on which of the ship's male crew knew that there were stowaways on board – and there were always some bribed members of the traffickers' networks – the women also faced the prospect of rape day and night in the pitch black of the bunkers.[76] For foreign crew members in particular, according to Katō, the women were 'an offering to be pinned down while they sated their lust'.

This was an 'unimaginable world'.[77]

Otaka the Keeper of the Lodging House

Konishi the man who brought me from Japan went back to Japan –
Perhaps he had received a considerable sum of money from Otaka –
I found myself alone in a strange country without a friend to help me –
While I was in such distressed and terrified condition Otaka the keeper of the lodging house told me that Thursday Island in Australia was a very good place to make money, and that I could freely land there without passports –
He strongly advised me to go to Thursday Island –
I followed his advice thinking that in doing so I might find an opportunity to get afterwards to my sister at Singapore –

Although Hashimoto Usa does not name any of the women with whom she travelled or was sequestered, nor indeed her sister by name, she is explicit about four men: Konishi and Matsubara, who accompanied her from Nagasaki to Hong Kong and from Hong Kong to Thursday Island respectively; her brothel keeper on Thursday Island, Shiosaki; and, in Hong Kong, 'a Japanese called Yoishi Otaka' – from whom, she suspects, Konishi 'had received a considerable sum of money'.

---

[75] 'Loss of the "Cheang Hye Teng": A Terrible Tale of the Sea', *Singapore Free Press and Mercantile Advertiser (Weekly)*, 14 September 1897. Available online through the National Library of Singapore, https://eresources.nlb.gov.sg/newspapers/ (last accessed 18 March 2021).

[76] For detailed foreign crew testimonies from 1888 and 1894 respectively, see Warren, *Ah Ku and Karayuki-san*, p. 207 (originally in DA 4.2.2.34, vol. 1), and Mihalopoulos, *Sex in Japan's Globalization*, pp. 22–3 (originally DA 3.8.8.4, vol. 1).

[77] Katō, *Kanpan ni tachite*, pp. 134–5 (*bettenchi* 別天地).

These men were the 'procurers' (*zegen* 女衒), or, to use a term I saw more often in the particular sources I used, the 'ringleaders' (*shubōsha* 首謀者). Hundreds of them are named in the Japanese Foreign Ministry's archives – sometimes by consular officials and sometimes by concerned Japanese visitors or residents.[78] Back in April 1889, Alexander Marks received a letter from a Hokkaido government official who, on his way to Melbourne, had passed through Port Darwin (whence the businessman Kanematsu had reported the previous year). The official detailed a conversation he had had with two Japanese ship carpenters living there, who testified:

That another Japanese named Takada Tokujiro of Osaka came to that town with five young women all of whom belong to Nagasaki but had been residing in Hon Kong [sic] just previous to their removal to Port Darwin, and that he gave one of them to a Malaya hair dresser for £50, and two to a Chinese at £40 each, keeping one for his concubine and the other under his employment as a public woman.

The two carpenters, the letter continued, had tried to take Takada to a local court but were unable to do so before he had 'run away' to Singapore 'owing to their inferiority in the English speaking capacity'.[79]

Nagasaki – Hong Kong – Australia – Singapore: once again, the key nodes of the traffickers' network appear in the course of a routine account. As in Hashimoto's case, Hong Kong was often not the women's final destination but rather a place of 'transfer' (*iten* 移転), as the Japanese consul noted in 1890, whence women were shipped to 'ports in Australia or to Sandakan in British-controlled Borneo'.[80] Similarly, one of the leading Japanese residents on Thursday Island, Sasaki Shigetoshi, confirmed in an 1892 petition to Tokyo that the fifteen sex labourers there had been bought by their brothel owners through five different procurers in Hong Kong. He named two: from Chikuzen, Nishiyama Yoshizō; and, from Nagasaki, Ōtaka Yūichi – that is, the same man named by Hashimoto Usa:

These men put up a 'Hotel' sign and seem to be in the lodging-house business, but this is just a surface painting and behind the scenes the main business is

---

[78] On pimps and traffickers as 'the first important male Japanese imperialists in Asia', see Mark Driscoll, *Absolute Erotic, Absolute Grotesque: The Living, Dead, and Undead in Japan's Imperialism, 1895–1945* (Durham, NC: Duke University Press, 2010), pp. 57–80, here p. 69.

[79] Letter from H. Satow to Alexander Marks, Melbourne, 12 April 1889: DA 3.8.4.8. Mihalopoulos also mentions this case: *Sex in Japan's Globalization*, p. 29.

[80] Report to the Japanese Foreign Ministry from the Japanese Consul in Hong Kong, 20 February 1890: DA 4.2.2.27, vol. 1, section 3. For context, see Elizabeth Sinn, 'Women at Work: Chinese Brothel Keepers in Nineteenth-Century Hong Kong', *Journal of Women's History* 19, 3 (2007): 87–111.

actually to be found in the trading of unsightly women (*shūgyōfujo*). From what I hear of how they trade in prostitutes, they direct subordinating underlings who, with various devious tricks, abduct women of the right age from Kyushu or any other convenient place.[81]

Five years prior to Hashimoto's arrival on Thursday Island, Sasaki was foreshadowing the infrastructures of her passage: the steamship routes; the Ōtaka 'lodging house' in Hong Kong; the transnational networks of the recruiters; and the rhetorical tricks possibly used by Ōtaka to 'strongly advise' women like Hashimoto (her words). As Sasaki's account in the Tokyo archives and a stream of telegrams in the Brisbane archives make clear, Hashimoto Usa was not the first such woman caught up in this infrastructure. Nor would she be the last: four days before she arrived in Hong Kong in July 1897, the Japanese consul there reported eight Japanese brothels and sixty-six Japanese prostitutes in the colony – but maybe as many as fifteen or twenty additional 'mistresses' (to Westerners) or trafficked women.[82] The arrival of Hashimoto's group from Shanghai would merely have added to this total, had it been detected.

Thus, regardless of her intentions, Hashimoto Usa's fate had quite probably been set in motion even before she left Nishiyama: by Ōtaka, a man pretending to run a hotel in Hong Kong, with a view to her eventual sale in Australia. And yet, as we shall see, she would speak of 'boldly' going to Thursday Island, as if this were her decision as much as his. Perhaps naively, I hear her voice in the adverb, suggesting as it does a kind of empowerment, her subjective framing of a situation which she must have known was beyond her control.[83] I also hear her voice in her adjectives, 'distressed' and 'terrified'. Here, however, I suspect that she

---

[81] Petition sent by Sasaki Shigetoshi and forty-one others to the Foreign Ministry, Tokyo, via Alexander Marks, 15 September 1892: DA 4.2.2.27, vol. 1, section 2. Sasaki had a personal interest in these matters, as he had previously been signatory to a letter complaining about a certain Okeyo 'keeping a Disorderly house, Bawdey [sic] House, Brothel or house of ill fame at the back of Sasaki's Laundry near the road to the Burial Ground Thursday Island': Letter from twenty-two Japanese residents of Thursday Island to John Douglas, 23 October 1891: QSA, Item ID ITM847411 (top number 91/14105).

[82] Japanese Consul in Hong Kong to Foreign Minister Komura Jutarō, 9 July 1897: DA 4.2.2.99, section 13. On 24 July 1897, Douglas telegrammed Brisbane to advise, 'it will be necessary in controlling Japanese Immigration to supervise departures from Hongkong almost all the females come from Hongkong and not from Japanese ports': QSA, Item ID ITM861851 (top number 97/9451).

[83] On 'whispers of the women's subjectivity that prevent [historians] from completely transforming them into subaltern objects of discrimination', see Kirsten L. Ziomek, *Lost Histories: Recovering the Lives of Japan's Colonial Peoples* (Cambridge, MA: Harvard University Asia Center, 2019), p. 46.

speaks for a plural experience, on behalf of the other women who also found themselves alone in a strange country – but whom Hashimoto will protect by not naming.[84]

I Boldly Decided to Go

> *So I boldly decided to go to Thursday Island, and was accompanied there by Matsubara from Otaka's lodging house –*
> *We arrived at Thursday Island on the 11th day of September –*
> *There were other women with Matsubara whom he brought to sell along with me –*

After all that, Hashimoto Usa did not travel to Australia on the *Yamashiro-maru*. In a folder in the Japanese Foreign Ministry archives in Tokyo, I find a note stating that the *Nanchang*, a China Steam Navigation company steamship, departed Hong Kong on 27 August 1897 and landed at Thursday Island on 11 September. There it discharged, presumably among other passengers, two Japanese men and five Japanese women.[85] Even here, then, Hashimoto tries to protect her female compatriots by talking vaguely of 'other women' rather than giving her questioners a precise number.

The Japanese note is filed in a nine-volume folder, 'Concerning restrictions to the passage of Japanese migrants in Australia' – which gives a good sense of how Hashimoto's journey was framed by concerned Japanese bureaucrats. A few pieces of paperwork later, the Japanese consul in Townsville sent his Tokyo colleagues a brief clipping from a Brisbane newspaper reporting on a question the home secretary, Sir Horace Tozer, had been asked in the Legislative Assembly on 21 September. (The member questioning Sir Horace, the consul added in a hasty postscript, was a Labour Party politician known for his radical Japanese-exclusion views.) Sir Horace had replied that 'he had a record of every Japanese who had arrived since the recent discussion in the House on the question of Japanese immigration'.[86] This wasn't strictly true; but it was nevertheless the case that Hashimoto Usa's journey

---

[84] My reading of Hashimoto here is influenced by Julie Otsuka's nameless, first-person plural narrative voice in her novel, *The Buddha in the Attic* (New York: Anchor Books, 2011).

[85] DA 3.8.2.33, vol. 2. The details of the journey are confirmed by 'Late Shipping', *Evening News* (Sydney), 20 September 1897: available through https://trove.nla.gov.au (last accessed 20 April 2021). The *Nanchang* was a Glasgow-built steamer of 1,715 gross tons.

[86] DA 3.8.2.33, vol. 2. This paperwork is also reprinted in the *NGB* (1897), pp. 616–17 (item 419).

coincided with a frenzy of record-making in both Tokyo and Brisbane, thus producing her as an archival subject in a way that might not have occurred had she departed Nagasaki a year or two earlier.

From Tokyo, this documentary drive was initiated in March 1897 by deputy foreign minister Komura Jutarō (1855–1911), who directed Japanese consuls to report biannually on 'the total number of unsightly women' in their jurisdiction. (One outcome of this directive was the Hong Kong consul's aforementioned figures on prostitutes and brothels in July 1897.) As Mihalopoulos has argued, this attempt to render the women visible stemmed from the assumption that the opacity of their lives was synonymous with their alleged unruliness.[87] By this logic, archivally to know was practically to control; and with such control, which included both stemming the numbers leaving Japan and deporting alleged delinquents back to Japan, the reputational damage to respectable overseas actors such as businessmen would be reduced. The performance of control was particularly urgent by 1897, given that New South Wales was in the process of passing an immigration act that would potentially constrain future Japanese business interests, and Queensland seemed likely to follow suit (see Chapter 4).

Meanwhile, in Brisbane the intensification of data collection was initiated by Sir Horace, who requested from his officials information on the impact of Japan's 1896 Emigrants' Protection Law – by which all Japanese emigrants were to be issued with passports – 'upon the arrival of Japanese laborers and artisans'.[88] (One outcome of this request was the police reports from Cairns, Cooktown, Childers and so on, cited at the beginning of this chapter.) By September 1897, a few days after he had been questioned in the Legislative Assembly, Sir Horace had his numbers: 116 Japanese women in the colony as a whole, all of whom, with one exception (the consul's wife in Townsville), 'gain their living by prostitution'. Fully 34 of these women were to be found on Thursday Island, an increase from the 15 mentioned by petitioner Sasaki Shigetoshi five years earlier. Moreover, the regular telegrams that John Douglas sent to Brisbane from mid 1897 onwards – including noting the arrival of the *Nanchang* on 11 September – were also an archival manifestation of Sir Horace's eye for record-keeping.[89]

Thus, Hashimoto Usa happened to arrive on Thursday Island in a period of heightened bureaucratic production. Her interview was the outcome of two different archival agendas, in Tokyo and Brisbane respectively, aligning for a fleeting moment. Channelling his instructions

---

[87] Mihalopoulos, *Sex in Japan's Globalization*, p. 58.
[88] QSA, Item ID ITM861851 (top numbers 97/9354 and 97/11085).
[89] QSA, Item ID ITM861851 (top number 97/11771).

from Sir Horace, it was John Douglas, I fancy, who asked her the question about passports, and who took particular interest in her reporting of Ōtaka's advice that she *could freely land [in Thursday Island] without passports*. Echoing both the Japanese government's view and the language of Sasaki's anti-prostitution activism, it was John Douglas who declared, in an interview he gave to the Brisbane *Telegraph* two weeks after questioning Hashimoto, that women 'smuggled out [from Japan] and brought on from Hongkong' were 'contraband'. 'The evil,' he continued, 'is an increasing one, and ought to be checked'.[90] But over the years, Douglas had also displayed a more nuanced understanding of these Japanese women than many of his counterparts in Tokyo – as when he claimed that two women he had been asked to deport in 1891 were 'undoubtedly prostitutes of a respectable and orderly type'.[91] Did he perhaps therefore have Hashimoto Usa freshly in mind when he noted, in his *Telegraph* interview, that although such 'Japanese ladies [...] are not a desirable addition to our population', they nevertheless 'behave very properly'?

We cannot know. But the fact that Hashimoto Usa's statement was taken down is a testament not just to the production of knowledge generated by bureaucrats working in mutually complementary ways across transimperial space – that is, Tokyo, Wonsan, Singapore, Hong Kong, Thursday Island and Brisbane. It was also a testament to Douglas. Though he had been ordered to collect quantitative data, he also generated something qualitative in his archival paperwork. Hashimoto's statement was a small victory for stories over statistics.

A Brothel at No 2 Yokohama Thursday Island

Matsubara is not himself the keeper of a brothel –
Matsubara made arrangement with Shiosaki the keeper of a brothel at
No 2 Yokohama – Thursday Island –
I have entered into agreement with Shiosaki to pay him the sum of one
hundred pounds sterling out of my earnings –
I think Matsubara has received from Shiosaki my large sum of money
for passage lodging commission and other expenses alleged to be
incurred on my behalf –

---

[90] 'Hon. John Douglas – An Interesting Interview. Japanese Problems. New Guinea Questions', *Telegraph* (Brisbane), 13 December 1897. Available through https://trove.nla.gov.au (last accessed 20 April 2021). By coincidence, Douglas's interview appeared on the day that his Hashimoto-related paperwork was processed by officials in Brisbane.

[91] Letter from John Douglas to the Queensland Chief Secretary, 17 November 1891: QSA, Item ID ITM847411 (top number 91/14105).

> *Unfortunately I fell into such a miserable state, but the act is voluntary and not against my will, and as Shiosaki has paid the amount demanded by Matsubara with my consent I am now under obligation to pay him £100 –*

In the wealth of detail provided by Hashimoto Usa to her interrogators, one question was so obvious as to go unasked: why Thursday Island? A young migrant's intention to go to Singapore or Hong Kong, either for a visit or for work, makes sense to a twenty-first-century reader given the economic magnetism of both metropolises well beyond her time. But why did *Otaka the keeper of the lodging house* tell Hashimoto that a tiny island off the northernmost tip of Queensland was *a very good place to make money*? (By which, of course, he meant a good place for him to make money by trading her.)

An encyclopaedic two-volume book, *A History of Overseas Japanese Development*, published between 1936 and 1938 and digitized by Japan's National Diet Library, offers one answer to that question. The author, Irie Toraji, explained that the island was – and remained, when he was writing – a key centre for shell diving (see Figure 5.3). (Pearl shells were used for the global production of buttons and wristwatch faces.) In 1897, wrote Irie, there were more than 1,500 people involved in the shell-diving industry on Thursday Island, of whom approximately 900 were Japanese. By June 1898, there were 32 Japanese-owned diving boats on the island (out of 221), each boat able to harvest eight tons of pearl shells a year. Given that a ton of pearl shells was worth approximately £90 sterling (compare to the £100 Shiosaki seems to have paid for Hashimoto), this meant an annual turnover per boat of £720 and, after the deduction of expenses, a boat-owner's profits of more than £200 a year. In other words, pearl shelling could be hugely lucrative for the small number of Japanese who might become independent boat owners; and, he implied, the industry provided an excellent income to any skilled diver or seaman who contracted his services either to Japanese or non-Japanese boats.[92]

Irie did not footnote his sources, but it's obvious that he closely consulted the monthly reports compiled by the Colonization Society of

---

[92] Irie Toraji 入江寅次, *Hōjin kaigai hattenshi* 邦人海外発展史 [A history of overseas Japanese development] (Tokyo: Ida shoten, 1942 [1936, 1938]), vol. 1, pp. 399–400. Available through the National Diet Library of Japan, https://dl.ndl.go.jp/info:ndljp/pid/1461457 (last accessed 16 April 2021). Irie's figures should be treated with caution, as the number of pearling boats could fluctuate by season; boats from neighbouring islands may also have found their way into his numbers. On the use of the pearl shells, see Julia Martínez and Adrian Vickers, *The Pearl Frontier: Indonesian Labor and Indigenous Encounters in Australia's Northern Trading Network* (Honolulu: University of Hawai'i Press, 2015), p. 10.

Figure 5.3 View of Thursday Island, 1899 (detail). Courtesy of the National Library of Australia.

Japan, a key think tank and pressure group established in March 1893 by a group of prominent Tokyo-based politicians, journalists, intellectuals and business leaders. Irie's calculations on profits, for example, were taken from a report written by a Thursday Island resident in the Colonization Society's March 1894 issue; and at regular intervals over the following years, the journal carried other contributions from Thursday Island visitors and settlers.[93] In January 1896, member Sugiyama Gensaku published a detailed account recalling his two-week journey from Hong Kong to Thursday Island via the Philippines and Port Darwin. Like many of the journal's authors, Sugiyama devoted much attention to the island's geography, climate and natural resources (or lack thereof: in describing the dearth of fresh water, he was unwittingly echoing Thursday Island's Indigenous name, Waiben, or 'place of no water'). 'The [pearl] shelling industry is the island's very life', he wrote, going on to detail how the value of annual exports to imports in 1894 was £111,942 to £41,885, and therefore all of the island's labourers and capitalists were in a position to send remittances back to their home country. At the end of his report, Sugiyama listed the price of everyday items on the island, followed by the wages one could make even in the economy's secondary sectors – as a cook or carpenter, for example. The cost of living is substantial, he acknowledged, but wages are also high: 'It's normal for a labourer to make £30 a year – and, by economising, it's easy to save 200 yen a year.'[94] This was a fortune, when set against the wages of day labourers in rural Hiroshima, Yamaguchi, Kumamoto or Nagasaki prefectures (see Chapter 2).

In publishing such accounts, not only from Australia but from all over the Pacific world, Sugiyama and his peers in the Colonization Society were both recording the lives of overseas Japanese and also providing information which they hoped would stimulate further emigration. This was the empirical data, as it were, which sustained their vision of an expansionist imperial Japan. Such expansionary zeal had partly to do

---

[93] The article on which Irie based his summaries about pearl-boat tonnage and profits was by Matsuoka Yoshikazu 松岡好一, in *Shokumin kyōkai hōkoku* 殖民協會報告 11 (21 March 1894), reprinted in Shokumin Kyōkai 殖民協會, *Shokumin Kyōkai hōkoku* 殖民協會報告 [Colonization Society journal] (Tokyo: Fuji shuppan, 1986), vol. 3, pp. 227–35, here pp. 231–4.

[94] Sugiyama Gensaku 杉山源作, 'Nansei kikō oyobi Sāsudē-tō' 南征紀行及サースデー島 [Diary of a journey to the south and to Thursday Island], *Shokumin Kyōkai hōkoku* 33 (28 January 1896), reprinted in Shokumin Kyōkai, vol. 7, pp. 11–26, here p. 20 (water), p. 21 (trade balance) and pp. 25–6 (wages). Sugiyama was working on an exchange rate of £1 = ¥10 (see fn 106). Newspaper clippings preserved by staff in the Foreign Ministry of Japan from 1897 note that 'the cost [of living] is double what it is in other places not far off': 'Rambling Notes', probably in *Beaver Stout*, 25 September 1897, in DA 3.8.2.33.

with the particular moment of the mid 1890s: the victory over Qing China in the Sino-Japanese War (1894–5), the phasing out of the unequal treaty system, and even the international zeitgeist that surrounded the term 'expansion'.[95] But it was also part of a longer-term trend by which both intellectuals in Tokyo and well-educated elites in the overseas communities imagined Japan's place in the Asia-Pacific world. This was an imagination which posited Japanese 'frontiers' not just in the sites where the Meiji state would establish formal colonies – Taiwan, southern Sakhalin, Korea, later Micronesia and Manchuria – but also in Australia, Hawai'i, and particularly in the Americas. By the late 1930s, this vision had coalesced around the term 'overseas development' (*kaigai hatten* 海外発展). Thus, Irie's two-volume tome was itself constitutive of Japan's expansionist knowledge production, just as the efforts of men such as Sugiyama Gensaku had been in the mid-Meiji years.[96]

But this vision did not go uncontested on the ground. Japanese settlers in the Americas and in the European colonies of the Pacific confronted the realities of white settler racism and associated immigration restrictions. Equally significantly, though less studied by subsequent historians, they faced internal opposition from some of their own compatriots in the diaspora communities.[97] These were men and women who had very different imaginations of 'Japan' from the Tokyo elites and whose voices consequently didn't make it into the pages of the society's reports, nor – for the most part – into public debates over the value of overseas migration to the Meiji state in the mid 1890s. But they were present in Thursday Island, as the aforementioned Sasaki Shigetoshi noted in his 1892 petition to Tokyo. Sasaki had opened his densely handwritten, fourteen-page petition by noting that there were fifteen 'unsightly' Japanese women on the island – five years before Hashimoto's arrival – and that they all came from Kyushu, especially from Nagasaki. They worked in four establishments which their proprietors (whom Sasaki named) had built in woods apart from the island's main settlement. 'Just like the licensed quarters in our own country,' he wrote, the four businesses give the appearance of being normal shops, but they sell not a thing and, just like Tokyo's Yoshiwara district, offer rooms out for rent in

---

[95] Martin Dusinberre, 'J. R. Seeley and Japan's Pacific Expansion', *Historical Journal* 64, 1 (2021): 70–97.
[96] Azuma, *In Search of Our Frontiers* (for the discussion of Irie, see pp. 222–4).
[97] For one example of constant tensions between metropole elites and grassroot settlers, see Jun Uchida, *Brokers of Empire: Japanese Settler Colonialism in Korea, 1876–1945* (Cambridge, MA: Harvard University Asia Center, 2011).

1897 newspaper interview, he mentioned 'gentlemen among [the Japanese] who have proved intellectually quite our equals'.[103]

Sugiyama and Satō were officially present in their capacity as translators of Hashimoto Usa's account. But the fact that two men were called upon, when Satō clearly had the ability to translate alone, suggests that their role went beyond linguistic mediation. Before them was a woman who, in their minds, was an anathema to Japanese 'national power abroad' – who undermined the very principles of the Thursday Island Japanese Club (as whose president Satō had previously served), namely 'that the members become law-abiding, respectful to their superiors (the Europeans) and [...] live in peace and amity among themselves'.[104] The pair's antipathy to what Hashimoto represented explains their interest in the logistics of her journey rather than in her experience of it. Not once, it seems, is she invited to elaborate on her 'distressed and terrified condition'. The name of the ship, however, the question of passports, the exact sum of money: *these* are important questions. Indeed, the debt in which Hashimoto Usa found herself may well have been of interest to Satō and Sugiyama less because of their concern to help her – which Douglas eventually did – than because an overseas migrant who could not pay their passage home, and who was therefore dependent on the beneficent intervention of the colonial powers in the Pacific, constituted a problem which served only to exacerbate the alleged gap between the Japanese and 'their superiors (the Europeans)'.[105]

And then there is the strange structure of this sentence: 'Unfortunately I fell into such a miserable state, but the act is voluntary and not against my will'. Again, I read this as a kind of rhetorical sparring, reminiscent of that between Sasaki and the 'unsightly women' in his petition. Having been encouraged to itemize her debt, using an oddly legalistic turn of phrase (the 'large sum of money for passage lodging commission and other expenses *alleged to be incurred on my behalf*'), Hashimoto Usa offers an emotional response: she fell into 'such a miserable state' (or perhaps

---

https://trove.nla.gov.au (last accessed 19 April 2021). I am grateful to Giorgio Scherrer for this reference.

[103] 'Hon. John Douglas', *Telegraph* (Brisbane), 13 December 1897.

[104] 'Torres Straits', *Queenslander* (Brisbane), 14 July 1894 (available through https://trove.nla.gov.au), itself citing the *Torres Strait Pilot*. In 1891, the twenty-two signatories of a letter to John Douglas had described themselves as 'being a well conducted law abiding and orderly portion of the Community of Thursday Island': see fn 81.

[105] From the very beginning of the Meiji passport system, officials had worried that emigrants who fell into debt and could not pay their passage home would damage the reputation of Japan: Yamamoto, 'Japan's Passport System', p. 1009.

'miserable' here means 'deplorable'.) Immediately, the trained lawyer seems to step in once again, proffering and perhaps even inserting a phrase which protects his civilized nation from any scurrilous claim that there may have been structural factors leading to Hashimoto's all-too-common story: *the act is voluntary and not against my will.*

That the voices of the Japanese 'translators' are present in Hashimoto Usa's first-person singular is to my mind incontestable. Their agenda was to try and emphasize her personal responsibility in representing 'a curious and not very attractive phase of Japanese colonization' – in the words of Douglas's cover memo (see Figure 5.1) – which contrasted to their society's more civilized imagination of colonization. And yet, though Hashimoto's recorded turn of phrase may well reflect the translators' interventions in her statement, it is also possible that she *did* take responsibility for her 'voluntary' departure from Nagasaki. In other words, as with the ambiguities raised by Hashimoto's mention of Konishi's 'representations', it need not be contradictory for a historian to emphasize her 'free will' *and* the fact that she was duped *and* the fact that she had words put into her mouth by her translators. But no analytical term adequately captures these layerings of intention, complicity and exploitation in Hashimoto Usa's nominal voice – 'nominal' because the posturing and positioning evident in the construction of her narrative was not hers alone.

Hashimoto's language of 'earnings' is also striking. For someone who planned simply to visit her sister in Singapore, Hashimoto adapted quickly – or, again, the written statement suggests she did – to new economic realities. Economists would doubtless talk of her 'purchasing power', although the word *power* jars in light of her circumstances. Still, depending on the number of sexual encounters she was expected to have each day, then Hashimoto might have made as much as 400 yen (£40) a month on Thursday Island, following Sissons's calculations.[106] The settling of her £100 debt to Shiosaki would have been a significant burden, as she makes clear, but it was not unimaginable. And, in the meantime, if she did not share the worldview of the women cited by Sasaki, she might still have been able to afford herself the odd purchase or treat, even if at overpriced Japanese shops (another way of exploiting poor labourers): a haircut for 0.75 yen, a silk handkerchief for anything upwards of 1.5 yen – or, at 4 yen, a bottle of brandy to drown her sorrows.[107]

---

[106] The figure is from Sissons, '*Karayuki-san*', p. 323, citing the *Japan Mail* from 30 May 1896.
[107] Sugiyama, 'Nansei kikō', pp. 24–5.

Her Finger Mark

I am aware that my interruptions of Hashimoto Usa's story have been no less frequent than those of her inquisitors. So here, in full, is what she is recorded as saying:

> *My name is Usa Hashimoto –*
> *I am twenty one years of age –*
> *I was born at Nishiyama Nagasaki Japan –*
> *My elder sister is keeping a lodging house in Singapore at Malabar Street –*
> *I am one of the inmates of No 2 at the place known as Yokohama Thursday Island, a brothel kept by Shiosaki –*
> *I departed from Nagasaki with the intention of seeing my sister at Singapore –*
> *This I did on the representations of a man named Konishi at the end of June 1897 –*
> *There were ten other young women who left by a sailing ship at the same time accompanied by Konishi –*
> *I do not know the name of the ship –*
> *We had no passports –*
> *It was midnight –*
> *I intended to go to my sister at Singapore –*
> *The ship took us to Shanghai, and there we were transferred without landing to a Steamer for Hong Kong where we arrived on the 13th of July –*
> *We were all put up at a lodging house kept by a Japanese called Yoishi Otaka –*
> *I was then told that it would be impossible for me to go to my sister in Singapore as no woman who has not a passport from the Japanese authorities is allowed to land at Singapore –*
> *The visit to my sister at Singapore was my inducement to leave Japan –*
> *My disappointment was so great that I did not know what to do –*
> *Konishi the man who brought me from Japan went back to Japan –*
> *Perhaps he had received a considerable sum of money from Otaka –*
> *I found myself alone in a strange country without a friend to help me –*
> *While I was in such distressed and terrified condition Otaka the keeper of the lodging house told me that Thursday Island in Australia was a very good place to make money, and that I could freely land there without passports –*
> *He strongly advised me to go to Thursday Island –*
> *I followed his advice thinking that in doing so I might find an opportunity to get afterwards to my sister at Singapore –*

Her Finger Mark 217

So I boldly decided to go to Thursday Island, and was accompanied there by Matsubara from Otaka's lodging house –
We arrived at Thursday Island on the 11th day of September –
There were other women with Matsubara whom he brought to sell along with me –
Matsubara is not himself the keeper of a brothel –
Matsubara made arrangement with Shiosaki the keeper of a brothel at No 2 Yokohama – Thursday Island –
I have entered into agreement with Shiosaki to pay him the sum of one hundred pounds sterling out of my earnings –
I think Matsubara has received from Shiosaki my large sum of money for passage lodging commission and other expenses alleged to be incurred on my behalf –
Unfortunately I fell into such a miserable state, but the act is voluntary and not against my will, and as Shiosaki has paid the amount demanded by Matsubara with my consent I am now under obligation to pay him £100 –
Unless my sister will pay the amount, or I can pay it out of my earnings I am not free to go to my sister –
I declare that the above statements are correct –
Usa Hashimoto
0
Her finger mark –

* * *

There is a final point to be made about marks in the archives. It concerns correspondence I have already briefly mentioned, from the coincidentally named Alexander Marks (Honorary Consul of Japan in Victoria) to Komura Jutarō (Vice-Minister of Foreign Affairs in Tokyo) on 24 June 1897 – just days before Hashimoto departed Nagasaki.[108] Marks enclosed a letter from S. Sakurai, a Japanese labourer living in Coolgardie, Western Australia, in which Sakurai complained that (male) 'Japanese find it very hard to get Honest Employment on account of my Countrywomen who carry on an Immoral business'. He lamented the 'Great Shame that those who wishes [sic] to get respectable Honest Employment should be hindered by those of Ill fame & Classed all alike'. That Sakurai penned his letter in English constituted a performance of his own respectability.

---

[108] See fn 56 above: Letter from Alexander Marks to the Vice Minister of State for Foreign Affairs, Tokyo, 24 June 1897: DA 6.1.5.9–7, vol. 1.

Marks contextualized Sakurai's letter by noting that for some time he'd had 'quite a number of personal complaints' from Japanese residing in Western Australia. Noting that the colony was outside his formal consular jurisdiction, he nevertheless suggested he take a trip there to lobby government members not to impose immigration restrictions on 'respectable' Japanese.[109] Moreover, 'I might possibly be able in a quiet way to get rid of some of the worst characters by deporting them at their own expense, and feel sure the Western Australian authorities will assist me.' But Komura declined the honorary consul's offer to take up the problem: 'In reply I have to say that I deem it almost impossible practically to keep such persons of low character under efficient control, owing to the tendency of [their] constantly changing their places of abode'.

These three letters encapsulate the 'ocular regime' by which young Japanese women migrating overseas in the late nineteenth century were framed. In short: male residents or businessmen on the ground conveyed their concerns about 'immoral' work to Japanese consuls; the consular network forwarded such concerns to Tokyo, adding comments about the reputational damage to Japan; and Tokyo bureaucrats filed the paperwork under 'miscellaneous' migration problems, or under discussion of anti-Japanese legislation, or under policing matters – before requesting more information to fill their files. The overseas actors were of a type: they could have been called Sakurai or Marks; Sasaki, Satō, Sugiyama or Douglas. But between them, and in dialogue with Tokyo, they also strove to produce a type of mobile and thereby uncivilized Japanese woman. That is, to write and to file was also to construct an ontological space in which women were 'unsightly', such that the very act of them moving rather than staying at home was deemed transgressive – unlike the mobilities practised by their male counterparts.[110] In all this, Komura's admission was unusual because it acknowledged the difficulties that Tokyo faced in keeping mobile women 'under efficient control', either practically or discursively.

Indeed, Komura's point about the difficulty of identifying the women's 'places of abode' may be read as a metaphor for the archives. The first-person testimonies of women such as those bound for Vladivostok or

---

[109] In June 1897 the premiers of the Australian colonies and of other British dominions gathered in London to discuss immigration legislation with Joseph Chamberlain (secretary of state for the colonies): Jeremy Martens, 'A Transnational History of Immigration Restriction: Natal and New South Wales, 1896–97', *Journal of Imperial and Commonwealth History* 34, 3 (2006): 323–44, here pp. 336–8.

[110] On sources constructing space, see Ambaras, *Japan's Imperial Underworlds*, pp. 25–6. On the association of masculinity with movement and femininity with stasis in a South Asian migrant setting, see Khatun, *Australianama*, p. 81.

those who ended up in Thursday Island occasionally survive; their places in the archives are unstable, however, because their lives crossed the epistemological boundaries by which bureaucrats tried to order the world – including the Tokyo archival boundaries between Series 3 (*Commercial Relations*) and Series 4 (*Judiciary and Policing*).[111] In this sense, there is an unintended historical logic to Hashimoto's paperwork in Brisbane having been filed out of place: for the women in my story, the archive admits no fixed abode.

Despite all this, however, it was ultimately possible for me to find Hashimoto, and to draw a line connecting the histories represented by her finger mark to those of countless other migrating Japanese women in the mid 1890s. But without physical archival visits, this would have been impossible. In the 2010s, hundreds of thousands of pages from the pre-war Diplomatic Archives of Japan's Ministry of Foreign Affairs were painstakingly photographed and uploaded to the Japan Center for Asian Historical Records (JACAR), creating an invaluable online resource for scholars of Japan's place in the world. But of the aforementioned Series 3 (*Commercial Relations*), both sub-series 8 (*The Movement of Imperial Subjects*) and 9 (*The Movement of Foreigners*) are undigitized and absent from JACAR, as is the whole of Series 4 (*Judiciary and Policing*).[112] No official explanation is given for this absence, but several experts told me that there is bureaucratic concern about the illegitimate use of 'personal data' (*kojin jōhō*) – a problem which affects much other demographic historical research in Japan (see Chapter 2).

Laudable and legally necessary though these concerns are, their consequence is to exacerbate the problem of archival abode. Admittedly, this is not a new phenomenon. Scholars of the period 1868–1941 who use the Foreign Ministry-published 222-volume *Records of Japanese Diplomacy* (*Nihon gaikō bunsho*) often fail to discuss the winnowing process by which the edited volumes took shape.[113] The note which recorded the *Nanchang*'s arrival on Thursday Island, for example, is excluded from reprints of documents 'Concerning Restrictions to the Passage of Japanese Migrants in Australia', as is a letter from Satō Torajirō in which

---

[111] My thinking here is influenced by David Ambaras's analysis of bodies taking on 'the material and symbolic functions of borders': Ambaras, *Japan's Imperial Underworlds*, p. 111.

[112] The same is true of emigration-related documents from the pre-war Showa-period collections (e.g. Series K and J): for full details, see the downloadable spreadsheets (Japanese only) available from JACAR (www.jacar.go.jp/english/about/documentstable/index.html) (last accessed 23 June 2022).

[113] The NGB were published in three batches, in 1936, 1963 and 1987: http://www.mofa.go.jp/mofaj/annai/honsho/shiryo/bunsho/index.html (last accessed 22 April 2021).

he discusses anti-Japanese newspaper coverage with regard to pearl-shelling boat ownership on Thursday Island. But this silencing has taken on a new dimension with the exclusion of exactly those series of documents from the digitized JACAR by which a historian might access different voices from those of the consul or the (male) labourer seeking respectable Honest Employment.[114] If digitization funnels historians towards the citation of easily accessible sources over those found in expensive archival visits, then the already faint marks left by Meiji Japan's Hashimoto Usas will be overlooked to an even greater extent than to date; and the politics of digital migration will have inadvertently assisted Alexander Marks in his quiet quest 'to get rid of some of the worst characters by deporting them' – not from Western Australia, but from the online archive.[115]

Voicing

'The very use of the figure of woman as the point of reference for a historiographic investigation,' Betty Joseph has written, 'can transform the premises and blind spots of the dominant history that has marginalized women as actors and agents on the one hand, and the domains of social production and reproduction on the other.'[116] In this chapter, I have tried to make Hashimoto Usa's narrative the premise for a different history of Japanese global migrations from those I sketched in previous chapters on Hawai'i: one that focuses not only on women but also on the kinds of mobilities which occurred in the shadows of state oversight rather than with its official support.[117] In so doing, I have also tried to reveal some of the processes by which she and other migrating women were produced and reproduced in the archives of Japan, Singapore and Australia. Such processes are rendered visible if historians consciously read along the so-called archival 'grain', thereby grasping the epistemic

---

[114] The Sakurai–Marks correspondence is filed under DA 6 (*Personnel Affairs*) – 1 (*Government Organizations and Posts*) – 5 (*Appointment and Dismissal, Rewards and Punishments*), and is therefore available from JACAR (www.jacar.go.jp) (reference code B16080178700, images 0246–0252).

[115] Although not explicitly addressed, the main body of sources by which David Ambaras traces female abduction narratives into the 1920s and 1930s are also undigitized, e.g. the DA K series: see Ambaras, *Japan's Imperial Underworlds*, pp. 115–61.

[116] Betty Joseph, *Reading the East India Company 1720–1840: Colonial Currencies of Gender* (Chicago: University of Chicago Press, 2003), p. 2.

[117] On centring global histories to include female narratives, see Amy Stanley, 'Maidservants' Tales: Narrating Domestic and Global History in Eurasia, 1600–1900', *American Historical Review* 121, 2 (2016): 437–60.

habits and practices by which the physical authors of documents such as Hashimoto's statement – the Sugiyamas, Satōs or Douglases of the world – made 'the rubrics of rule correspond to a changing imperial world'.[118] But the 'grain' was also constructed in the spaces *between* archives. Analysing some of the dynamics of this transimperial epistemological space in the late nineteenth century helps historians better understand both the sources and the silences through which we might reconstruct mobile women such as Hashimoto Usa.

But although I would love to think that Hashimoto's statement *does* highlight blind spots in the dominant history of so-called respectable Japanese emigration, that her statement constitutes the individual voice of the 'someone' through which a historian can chip away at the archival facades of The Past, I fear it does not.[119] Her voice is never alone. Into her first-person singular are stacked multiple other individual histories, a few of which I have discussed: those of her translators, of her British colonial interrogator, of other Japanese women ferried across the Asian maritime world in the late 1890s and of their male transcribers. I myself am also inseparable from this collective sharing and threatened obliteration of Hashimoto Usa's words. For in my repeated language of 'finding' her statement in Brisbane, I have unwittingly adopted the mode of an 1890s consular or port official, searching for a stowaway amidst the archive's paper bunkers. Thus, it turns out that the preservation of 'difference between our words and theirs' is easier said than done.[120] Historians need not go so far as to claim that 'what we find in the archives is ourselves';[121] but at least acknowledging first-person voicings in our interactions with the sources might be a useful initial step towards identifying more clearly what 'we' are seeing when – despite the ocular regimes in Japan, Australia and in between – we claim to make out the historical shape of an individual woman.[122]

★ ★ ★

I don't know what happened to Hashimoto Usa after 29 November 1897. Douglas's memo suggests that she was repatriated without her having to

---

[118] Stoler, *Along the Archival Grain*, p. 4.
[119] Trouillot, *Silencing the Past*, p. 142: 'History did not need to be mine in order to engage me. It just needed to relate to someone, anyone. It could not just be The Past. It had to be someone's past.'
[120] Ginzburg, 'Our Words, and Theirs', p. 109.
[121] Bradley, 'Seductions of the Archive', p. 119.
[122] In all of this, I am aware that some languages – especially pre-colonial languages – do not have a first-person pronoun: see Ben Tran, 'I Speak in the Third Person: Women and Language in Colonial Vietnam', *positions* 21, 3 (2013): 579–605.

pay the £100 to Shiosaki, but there are insufficient details to trace the route of her return. And anyway, did she go back to her brother in Nagasaki or her 'sister' in Singapore?[123] If she ended up living into old age, I wonder if this encounter in a Thursday Island government office remained the formative life event that my reconstruction has made it out to be – or whether, as one of the less unpleasant moments in the tumultuous post-departure months of 1897, it quickly slipped her memory. Not for her the troving of paper across a lifetime so as to shape a personal archive in the quiet of retirement.[124]

By contrast to Hashimoto, the other protagonists in her story have left numerous other genres of historical marks. In October 1898, the *Torres Straits Pilot* published the names of all the Japanese residents of Thursday Island who had financially contributed to the construction of a new hospital.[125] 'Dr Gensaku Sugiyama' is listed as having donated one pound, one shilling (£1/1): this is the first and last mention I will find of his having been a doctor. Although the entries are mainly those of individual men, several couples are also listed, including Tsuruma and Oyaye (£1/1). This, I suddenly realize, may be the name of a brothel owner and his wife or business partner. And so it is intriguing to read that the same amount was also donated by a certain 'Shiosaki and Oume': this must have been Hashimoto's employer at No 2 Yokohama, with Oume – that is, Ume – her probable manager. Meanwhile, the single largest donation belonged to 'Mrs Torajiro Satow' (£2/2), who would die shortly after. In the aftermath of her death, and also in response to Queensland's subsequent anti-immigration laws, her husband would leave Thursday Island in 1901 and return to Japan. There, he authored several books and became a member of the House of Representatives – before, in 1910, moving to the newly annexed Korea, where he strove for the 'assimilation' of Koreans into the empire. Satō Torajirō would die in 1928 of wounds sustained in an attack where a would-be assassin mistook him for a more senior Japanese colonial official.[126]

As for John Douglas, he would remain until his death in 1904 the British government resident of Thursday Island, relentlessly penning letters, dictating telegrams, perhaps even enquiring into the lives of women distressed and in a strange land. On 8 November 1898, exactly

---

[123] It may be that another scholar was trying to answer that question when they accidentally left her paperwork in the wrong Queensland State Archive folder, adjacent to a list of Japanese returnees in the period 1892–8.
[124] Joan Wallace Scott, 'Archival Angst', *History of the Present* 11, 1 (2021): 107–18.
[125] *Torres Straits Pilot*, 14 October 1898, clipped and preserved in DA 3.8.2.33.
[126] Kira, 'Yokohama jānarisuto retsuden'; see also Uchida, *Brokers of Empire*, pp. 166–7.

Voicing 223

a year after Oyaya's petition had started off the process which culminated in Hashimoto Usa's statement, Douglas cabled the Under Secretary of the Home Office in Brisbane: 'Four male Japanese and one female by Yamashiro Maru all with passports'.[127]

What, I wonder, was this woman's story?

---

[127] QSA, Item ID ITM861851 (top number 98/13812).

6 The Burned Archive

A Diary

On a sunny spring morning in 1900, the industrialist Yasukawa Keiichirō (1849–1934) left his company headquarters in Wakamatsu, northern Kyushu, for a business trip east:

[Meiji 33] March 27. Fine. Departure. At half-past eight, I departed on a small tug and then headed up to Osaka on the *Yamashiro-maru*.

The next day, the weather again fine, Yasukawa records that he arrived in Osaka, via the port of Kobe, in the late morning. Spending the afternoon with one of his key associates, the two men discussed the division of profits from their recent sale of the Tagawa coal mines, in northern Kyushu, to the Mitsui Mining Company.[1]

I happen to find this reference to the *Yamashiro-maru* in the first of four published but as yet undigitized volumes of Yasukawa's private diary. (When I say, 'happen to find', what I mean is: a kind colleague who has studied the diaries told me he seemed to remember a mention of the ship sometime around 1900.) Yasukawa kept twenty notebooks of his daily activities; thirteen have survived, dating from October 1898 to his death in November 1934. They offer a ringside view of Japan's early twentieth-century transformations by a man who, from the chaos of Kyushu's anti-Meiji uprisings in the early 1870s, established a coal-selling business in 1877 and went on to become a key figure in what

---

[1] Yasukawa Keiichirō 安川敬一郎, *Yasukawa Keiichirō nikki: Daiikkan* 安川敬一郎日記：第一巻 [Yasukawa Keiichirō's diary: Volume 1] (Kitakyushu: Kitakyūshū shiritsu shizenshi/rekishi hakubutsukan, 2007), p. 140. I am very grateful to Nakamura Naofumi for introducing me to Yasukawa's diary in 2012. On the sale of the Tagawa mines to Mitsui, for 1.65 million yen, see Nakamura Naofumi 中村尚史, *Chihō kara no sangyō kakumei: Nihon ni okeru kigyō bokkō no gendōryoku* 地方からの産業革命：日本における企業勃興の原動力 [The industrial revolution from the regions: The driving force behind the rise of business in Japan] (Nagoya: Nagoya daigaku shuppankai, 2010), p. 214.

has been called Japan's 'industrial revolution from the regions'.[2] In later years, Yasukawa founded many other companies, in fields ranging from cotton spinning to electricity; he was also elected a member of the House of Representatives in 1914 and joined the House of Peers in 1924. The period at the turn of 1900, therefore, was a crucial one in the expansion of Yasukawa's business activities from the regional to the national stage. As Hibino Toshinobu's close reading of the diary has shown, Yasukawa spent approximately a third of each year in Osaka or Tokyo between 1899 and 1902, and the opening of the San'yō Railway between Kobe and Shimonoseki in 1901 would further facilitate the expansion of his networks in central and eastern Japan – this in an age when face-to-face meetings still lay at the heart of the business relationship.[3]

Such a reading of Yasukawa's diary implicitly looks forward: it posits his overnight journey on the *Yamashiro-maru* as a fin-de-siècle moment in the gradual usurpation of the ship by the train. But it would be equally possible to read the 27 March entry with a backward glance. If Yasukawa had made the same journey, say, 100 years earlier, he would not have arrived in Osaka until a week or even three after departing Wakamatsu, as his ship negotiated the weather and waters of the Inland Sea. That it took him only twenty-four hours to do so in 1900 was therefore due to a technological innovation whose uptake in many ways epitomized the global transformations of the nineteenth century: the invention of the rotating steam engine, patented by James Watt in 1784, and its subsequent application to riverboats, lake ferries, coastal freight ships and oceanic vessels across the world.[4] By the time of the *Yamashiro-maru*'s launch in 1884, the advent of steamships, along with the introduction of the telegraph, had already begun to transform the economies of some of the Inland Sea ports through which Yasukawa passed on the morning of 27 March. For example, the *Yamashiro-maru* did not stop in Fuyuki Sakazō's home town of Murotsu, in eastern Yamaguchi prefecture (see Chapter 3). For centuries, ships had anchored here, or just across the straits in Kaminoseki, to restock ahead of the next day's sailing and, if

---

[2] Nakamura, *Chihō kara no sangyō kakumei*. On Yasukawa's background see pp. 202–6: one of his brothers was executed as a rebel in the Fukuoka uprising (1871); another died fighting on the government side in the Saga rebellion (1874).
[3] Hibino Toshinobu 日比野利信, 'Nisshin/Nichiro senkanki ni okeru Yasukawa Keiichirō' 日清・日露戦間期における安川敬一郎, in Arima Manabu 有馬学, ed., *Kindai Nihon no kigyōka to seiji: Yasukawa Keiichirō to sono jidai* 近代日本の企業家と政治：安川敬一郎とその時代 [Politics and the entrepreneur in modern Japan: Yasukawa Keiichirō and his age] (Tokyo: Yoshikawa kōbunkan, 2009), pp. 12–39, here p. 16.
[4] On the early and transformative application of steam engines to riverboats, see Walter Johnson, *River of Dark Dreams: Slavery and Empire in the Cotton Kingdom* (Cambridge, MA: Harvard University Press, 2013), pp. 73–96.

necessary, await appropriate winds and tides. Local expertise was priceless to ships and their crews. In late March (as Murotsu fishermen could have told Yasukawa), a change in cloud patterns presages a warm southerly wind, the *maji*, which in its wake brings rain; more often than not, a west wind then follows the rain, one favourable for those sailing towards Osaka.[5] Yet the *Yamashiro-maru*'s crew did not need this old knowledge any more than they needed new provisions. Whether the weather was fine or not, the ship would steam on – or so we might imagine.[6]

This image of the steamship cutting serenely through the seas finds apt expression in another of the three (known) surviving photographs of the *Yamashiro-maru*, published in the fifty-year celebration history of the NYK company.[7] The black vessel crosses from left to right across open water (see Figure 6.1). Smoke unfurls at an almost perfect ninety-degree angle from its only funnel, while the two masts stand high both fore and aft. The *Yamashiro-maru* would seem, in this framing, to be apart from space and time: the ship could be anywhere, the moment anytime in the late nineteenth century. Yet readers familiar with one of the most famous literary depictions of steamships in that period would have known such images to be an illusion. In Jules Verne's *Le Tour du Monde en Quatre-Vingts Jours* (1872), Phileas Fogg's passage to India is punctuated by his ship's regular need to call at port, with each stop counted on the clock – four hours in Suez, every second precious, before onward to Aden – and calculated against his apparently foolhardy bet.[8] Thus, the steamship could never be nowhere. The steam which compressed its engine's cylinder(s) was generated by the burning of coal beneath one or more water boilers. The coal, in turn, must be loaded into the ship's holds at ports sufficiently large for the job, be they in Suez or in Aden – or in Wakamatsu, where Yasukawa's eponymous coal-selling business had been based since 1886. In this sense, as Allan Sekula once noted, 'steam tethered ships more firmly to the land, by a line that stretched back to the bowels of the earth'.[9]

---

[5] I picked up this knowledge from local fishermen during a period of fieldwork in Kaminoseki in May 2004.
[6] For one example of steam not overcoming nature, see Amrith, *Crossing the Bay of Bengal*, pp. 112–14.
[7] Nippon Yusen Kaisha, *Golden Jubilee History of Nippon Yusen Kaisha* (Tokyo: Nippon Yusen Kaisha, 1935), p. 9. For my discussion of another of these photographs, see Chapter 1.
[8] Jules Verne, *Around the World in Eighty Days*, trans. George Makepeace Towle (Boston: James R. Osgood, 1873 [1872]), pp. 34–40. Available through https://archive.org.
[9] Sekula, *Fish Story*, p. 106. The *Yamashiro-maru* had a compound engine with two cylinders, both 54 inches in length: the high-pressure cylinder was 42 inches in diameter, the low-pressure, 78 inches: 'The Yamashiro Maru', *PCA*, 21 July 1885.

A Diary 227

Figure 6.1 The *Yamashiro-maru* (1884–1910). Courtesy of the NYK Maritime Museum.

The black smoke filtering back across the *Yamashiro-maru*'s photograph was one atmospheric trace of this tethering line. Its presence in the photo serves as a reminder that in resource terms, the steamship could never simply 'steam on'. Nor, contrary to my earlier assertion, were tides or the weather completely irrelevant to the determination of steam-powered routes.[10] Rather, the steamship's passage was 'terraqueous' – that is, part of a history which encompassed the transmutation of earth, water and air (as early modern European scholars understood the term).[11] The ship's course at sea was bound to the ground. Thus, the photograph's smoky trail raises the question: if the penned past ultimately leads historians to the paper archive, then from what archival place can we read terraqueous traces?

We might begin to answer this question by siting the relevant 'bowels of the earth' – in this case, by identifying where the *Yamashiro-maru*'s

---

[10] Peter A. Shulman, *Coal and Empire: The Birth of Energy Security in Industrial America* (Baltimore, MD: Johns Hopkins University Press, 2015), points out that 'steamships still relied a great deal on winds and currents', especially in terms of crossing the Pacific (p. 83).

[11] Alison Bashford, 'Terraqueous Histories', *Historical Journal* 60, 2 (2017): 253–72, here p. 260.

coal came from at any particular moment in time. On the morning of 27 March 1900, assuming that the only reason the ship had stopped in the coal transit hub of Wakamatsu was to refuel, its likely origin was one of the mines in Chikuhō, a north-eastern Kyushu coalfield equivalent in land area to today's New York City.[12] The coal with which the *Yamashiro-maru* supplied the imperial navy during the Sino-Japanese War of 1894–5 likewise came from this field and probably also from mines in Nagasaki prefecture. At the beginning of the *Yamashiro-maru*'s career, by contrast, the picture is more precise. Thanks to a combination of the loquaciousness of the ship's chief engineer, Mr Crookson, and the curiosity of the *Daily Pacific Commercial Advertiser*'s representative on the Honolulu docks, we know the following:

> The speed of the vessel is 14¼ knots, with sixty-five revolutions of the propeller per minute. The consumption of coal is about forty-eight tons a day of the soft kind called "Karatsu," which is mined about the centre of Japan. To supply the consumption, the vessel can carry 350 tons of coal in her bunkers, and a further supply of 320 tons for long voyages of about sixteen days.[13]

And so Karatsu, in the western Kyushu prefecture of Saga (not at all 'about the centre of Japan'), is one place we might begin to source the tethering line.

As such, this chapter's first archival port of call would ideally be the earth itself, in the form of any surviving material traces of the nearly 400 pitheads which in the late nineteenth century were dotted around the Matsuura river and its tributaries, some ten to twenty kilometres south of the coastal castle town of Karatsu.[14] The pitheads, or even better the endpoint of the underground shafts, would be my archival ground zero – signified, to borrow from David Sepkoski, by the notation, $archive_0$.[15] But unfortunately the world was a far from ideal place to conduct archival research in March 2020, when I had scheduled to visit Karatsu. Moreover, even if I had been able to hire a car and drive to any of the nineteen villages where the late nineteenth-century pitheads were clustered, it is extremely unlikely I would have got anywhere near a

---

[12] For an overview of Chikuhō, see Phipps, *Empires on the Waterfront*, pp. 116–27; the size of New York is according to the 2010 United States Census.

[13] 'The Yamashiro Maru', *PCA*, 21 July 1885.

[14] Tōjō Nobumasa 東定宣昌, 'Meiji zenki, Hizen Matsuuragawa no sekitan yusō' 明治前期、肥前松浦川の石炭輸送 [The transportation of coal from the Matsuura river in Hizen, in the early Meiji period], *Enerugii-shi kenkyū* 17 (2002): 31–46, here pp. 32–3.

[15] David Sepkoski, 'The Earth as Archive: Contingency, Narrative, and the History of Life', in Lorraine Daston, ed., *Science in the Archives: Pasts, Presents, Futures* (Chicago: University of Chicago Press, 2017), pp. 53–83.

shaft (if any still survive); and, in any case, I am not trained to read the earth.

Thus, the empirical base for the journeys this chapter reconstructs is a series of archival reconfigurations, in which we follow historical actors as they visited ground zero (or worked therein) and tried to transcribe the 'original' archive into meaningful words or images. I call their resulting paperwork, $archive_1$ – although unlike the scholars to whose work Sepkoski applies this term, the key initial transcriber of the Karatsu earth was no geologist or paleontologist but rather a German doctor working for the Dutch East India Company in Nagasaki in the mid 1820s. (Perhaps appropriately, his book had the subtitle, *Archiv zur Beschreibung von Japan und dessen Neben- und Schutzländern Jezo mit den südlichen Kurilen, Sachalin, Korea und den Liukiu-Inseln.*) The doctor's account, in turn, was taken up by the US commodore Matthew Perry and abstracted into a new geopolitical imagination of the mid nineteenth-century Pacific world: that is, $archive_2$. And so on.

These indications of distance from archival ground zero in Karatsu run the danger of becoming parodic ends in themselves – $archive_4$? $archive_6$? – rather than, as intended, a heuristic means to identify the transcriptions necessary to render the soil a historical source. But my primary interest in this chapter lies not in archival notation per se but rather in rebraiding the tethering line between the earth and the engine. I do this by following the migration of a piece of coal from seam to ship. Taking my lead from William Cronon's argument that an environmental history must root itself 'in the depths of the earth', I start in Karatsu and follow the line(s) out – from mine to river to market to port to lighter to bunker and finally, burned up and exhausted, to a puff of smoke.[16] But as I have recreated this human history of a fossil fuel's journey, my story has coalesced with a second migration, namely of the archive from its 'original' material form to verbal and visual forms which, due to their digitization, have been accessible to me even during a global pandemic. Comprising a selection of diary entries, newspaper articles, technical reports, memoirs, paintings, handwritten scrolls and much more, this digital constellation of $archives_1$ and $archives_2$ is, by necessity, my own invention.[17] But its principle is the same as a place-based archive: it offers an abstract

---

[16] William Cronon, 'Kennecott Journey: The Paths out of Town', in William Cronon, George Miles and Jay Gitlin, eds., *Under an Open Sky: Rethinking America's Western Past* (New York: Norton, 1992), pp. 28–51, here p. 48.

[17] '[W]e invent an archive every time we have a question to answer; and then someone reinvents the archive in the service of a new question': Benjamin Zachariah, 'Travellers in Archives, or the Possibilities of a Post-Post-Archival Historiography', *Práticas da História* 3 (2016): 11–27, here p. 27.

equivalence between its constituent elements – just as the telegraphs and police reports and transcribed testimonies and politicians' letters in the Queensland State Archives are, at the most basic level, afforded equivalent value simply by dint of their accessibility in the same physical location.[18]

One outcome of this invented, migrated archive is an argument concerning the social history of extraction.[19] Beneath the transpacific journeys of the plantation labourers or the brothel workers I traced in earlier chapters toiled men and women whose bodies made possible new lives overseas and yet who are generally overlooked in migration histories. The artifice of my personalized 'Karatsu archive' draws equal attention to these labour histories and the ways they shaped shipboard passages – just as Utagawa Kunisada's woodblock print, detailing dozens of imaginary blue-uniformed labourers inside the human body, brought to the fore the work necessary for a healthy dietary life in the 1850s (Figure 3.1). More generally, my assembled archive reminds us of the extractive contexts which lay behind other histories I have hitherto described in passing or in detail, from the Whitby collier repurposed as Captain Cook's *Endeavour*, to the dynamite-carrying *Sumanoura-maru* with which the *Yamashiro-maru* collided in October 1884, to the holds in which terrified young women were made to hide during transportation to Southeast Asia in the late nineteenth century. This chapter's focus on subterranean histories in Kyushu offers a labour history counterpoint to the simplicity of Yasukawa Keiichirō's diary entry on 27 March 1900; but the chapter could equally well have been placed at the beginning of the book, thus framing my analyses of transoceanic migrations in the 1880s and 1890s.

Indeed, my second contribution in these pages is to suggest a revised framing for Japan's geopolitical engagement with the Asia-Pacific world across the second half of the nineteenth century as a whole. The work of Catherine L. Phipps has highlighted the value of narrating the Sino-Japanese War from the perspective of the recoaling port of Moji (just along the northern Kyushu coast from Wakamatsu), so as to demonstrate some of the energy infrastructures that lay behind Japan's late nineteenth-century military ascendance in East Asia.[20] Similarly, my Karatsu archive projects a revised reading of the epochal encounter between Tokugawa

---

[18] Concerning photographs, Sekula observes that 'archives establish a relation of *abstract visual equivalence* between pictures': Allan Sekula, 'Reading an Archive: Photography between Labour and Capital', in Liz Wells, ed., *The Photography Reader* (London: Routledge, 2019), pp. 443–52, here p. 445 (emphasis in the original).

[19] Cf. Gabrielle Hecht's innovative labour history of uranium mining: Hecht, *Being Nuclear: Africans and the Global Uranium Trade* (Cambridge, MA: MIT Press, 2012).

[20] Phipps, *Empires on the Waterfront*, pp. 189–216.

Japan and the US squadron led by Commodore Perry in 1853–4 – an encounter in which the significance of the 'geo-' has been understudied relative to the '-political'. Here too, I argue, historians should focus their attention less on Perry's famous 'black ships' than on the oft-ignored black smoke: its origins are the real 'matter of history'.[21]

The narrative seam of the mid nineteenth-century US–Japanese encounter which burrows through the chapter may appear counter-intuitive, given that Perry arrived in Japan three decades before the *Yamashiro-maru* was even launched. But it is important because the logistical realities which drove US policymakers towards Japan in the early 1850s were fundamentally the same as those which affected the quotidian calculations of NYK ships carrying migrant labourers to Hawai'i at the turn of the 1890s. That is, assuming that the *Advertiser* correspondent noted down Mr Crookson's technical descriptions accurately in 1885, then at a constant speed of 14¼ knots, the *Yamashiro-maru*'s 'long voyage' from Yokohama to Honolulu (3,410 nautical miles, with one knot equal to one nautical mile per hour) would have taken just under ten days and consumed about 480 tons of coal. From Honolulu port records, we know that it actually took two weeks, with Captain Mahlmann remembering 'not having pressed the engines in order to save coal'.[22] Either way, with a maximum coal bunker capacity of 670 tons, the *Yamashiro-maru* would have needed to recoal in Hawai'i in order to return to Japan. This basic fact of steamship life thus underlined the calculations which US naval strategists made from the mid nineteenth century onwards about the geopolitical importance of the recoaling facilities at Pearl Harbor – calculations which, alongside archipelago politics and sugar planter interests, were a key factor in the eventual US annexation of the Hawaiian islands in 1898.[23] The *Advertiser*'s profile of the *Yamashiro-maru* was thus one point in a longer energy history whose trajectory arced, like the lines that US strategists drew across Pacific maps, from the mid to the late nineteenth century.

Tethering lines and cartographic lines notwithstanding, what follows is no linear analysis, at least in chronological terms. It would be practically impossible – at least with my training – to scale in any meaningful way a history whose temporal units range from millions of years to half-past

---

[21] LeCain, *Matter of History*.
[22] On the nautical mile distance from Yokohama to Honolulu, https://developer.searoutes .com/docs (last accessed 21 June 2021); Mahlmann, *Reminiscences*, p. 184. It's possible that Mahlmann also utilized the *Yamashiro-maru*'s square-rigged sails during the journey, further to reduce coal consumption while maintaining speed.
[23] William M. Morgan, *Pacific Gibraltar: US–Japanese Rivalry over the Annexation of Hawai'i, 1885–1898* (Annapolis, MD: Annapolis Naval Institute Press, 2011).

eight on a March morning, and thus impossible to do justice to the basic profundity of archive$_0$ over all subsequent transfigurations. And yet, as Dipesh Chakrabarty observed in a groundbreaking essay on how historians might respond to the crisis of climate change, a greater awareness of humans as geological agents, whose initial scrabbling for coal in places like Karatsu eventually culminated in planetary-transforming releases of carbon dioxide into the atmosphere, requires new narrative forms. Chakrabarty urges us to 'cross-hatch' different modes of historical analysis (in his case, between 'the immiscible chronologies of capital and [human] species history'), without spelling out what such a cross-hatching might look like in practice.[24] In this chapter, my small nod towards such narrative challenges comes in the form of textual divisions between generic 'port' and 'passage' sections. The 'port' sections moor the analysis at a particular time or place, while the 'passage' sections indicate history – coal, people, ships – on the move.[25] Thus, for the reader as also for the steamship passenger, the journeys are interrupted, the geographies of fuel consumption unstable. For the labourers on and in the ground, however, the infrastructures of passage were all too constant.

Port: 'At Wukumoto We Visited…'

In 1762, in one of the perennial reshuffles of domain management which characterized the Tokugawa shogunate's rule, the feudal lord of Okazaki was ordered to move to Karatsu, many days' travel to the west. Unfamiliar with his domain's socio-economic profile, he commissioned the painter Kizaki Moritaka (1711–92), who had accompanied him from central Honshu, to document local industries. Kizaki's first work, 'Scroll about the Whale Incident', was completed in 1773. Over the next decade, he continued to paint and gather information, culminating in the magnificent eight-scroll 'Illustrations of Products from Hizen Province' (1784). This depicted not only whaling but also nineteen other types of livelihoods, including horse breeding, pottery production, deer and wild boar hunting, falconry, cormorant fishing, coastal fishing, papermaking, textile bleaching, blacksmithery, incense production – and, as I shall shortly discuss, coal mining.[26]

---

[24] Dipesh Chakrabarty, 'The Climate of History: Four Theses', *Critical Inquiry* 35, 2 (2009): 197–222, citation from p. 220.
[25] On the need to bring 'passage' back into spatial imaginations of the world, see Carter, *Dark Writing*, pp. 16–48.
[26] Kizaki Moritaka 木崎盛標, 'Hizen-shū sanbutsu zukō' 肥前州産物図考 [Illustrations of products from Hizen Province] (1784), digitized by the National Archives of Japan Digital Archive, www.digital.archives.go.jp (last accessed 23 June 2021). Kizaki was

At around the same time as Kizaki was completing his scroll, a new coal mine opened in Fukumo, in the southern part of Hizen Province. Though some thirty-five kilometres distant from Karatsu, in geological terms Fukumo was located at the southern end of what a 1913 map called the 'Karatsu Coal Field', in today's municipality of Ōmachi (see Map 4, p. 240).[27] And here, doubtless to the surprise of the mine's labourers, a couple of European visitors appeared in 1826. In his diary entry for 18 February, a day after his thirtieth birthday, one visitor mangled the mine's name as he noted, 'Bei Wukumoto besuchten wir eine Steinkohlengrube'.[28]

The diarist was Philipp Franz Balthasar von Siebold (1796–1866), a German physician and botanist who had been working at the Dutch East India Company outpost of Dejima, in Nagasaki, since 1823. At the beginning of 1826 he joined the company's delegation on its mission to the shogunal capital in Edo, and as part of this trip he and a companion took a detour to the coal mine in 'Wukumoto'. Siebold was not the first German doctor to write about Japanese coal production. The Dejima-based Engelbert Kaempfer (1651–1716) had noted coal mines in central Kyushu on his way to Edo in 1691 and again on his return the following year, when he commented that the people around the post station of Koyanose 'were very dirty, perhaps because of the hard coal'.[29] In 1826, Siebold would also pass by 'coal-burning mountains' (*Kohlenbrenner Gebirge*) near Koyanose – in the region later known as Chikuhō. But it was his account of Fukumo that was to have a lasting geopolitical impact:

The coal was brought to the surface through a shaft, which gently slopes downward in 120 deep steps. It was foliated coal (Houille feuilletée), alternating in thin layers with clay shale. Up to about sixty steps down, because our Japanese guides did not permit us to descend any further, the thickness of the

also known by the given name Yūken 攸軒. For the scroll's composition, see Mori Hiroko 森弘子 and Miyazaki Katsunori 宮崎克則, *Kujiratori no shakaishi: Shiiboruto ya Edo no gakushatachi ga mita Nihon hogei* 鯨取りの社会史：シーボルトや江戸の学者たちが見た日本捕鯨 [A social history of whale catching: Japanese whaling as seen by Siebold and Edo scholars] (Tokyo: Karansha, 2016), pp. 100–7.

[27] 'Coal Resources of the World. Japan. Map No. 17, Plate IV. Karatsu and Sasebo Coal Fields. After Y. Otsuki' (Toronto: Morang, 1913), available through the David Rumsey Map Collection, www.davidrumsey.com/luna/servlet/detail/RUMSEY~8~1~205124~3002 286:Karatsu-and-Sasebo,-Japan–Coal-Res (last accessed 23 June 2021).

[28] It is unclear when the Fukumo 福母 (also 布久母) mine opened, but one suggestion is sometime in the 1770s or 1780s: Ōmachi-chō 大町町, *Ōmachi-chōshi* 大町町史 [A history of Ōmachi town] (Ōmachi: Ōmachi chōshi hensanshitsu, 1987), p. 332 (and p. 333 for Siebold's visit).

[29] Kaempfer, *Kaempfer's Japan*, pp. 297, 400.

coal strata was inconsiderable and a matter of only a few inches. But deeper down the strata are apparently several feet in size – something one could also gather from the extracted coal pieces.[30]

Siebold then described what he considered to be an elementary system for extracting ground water, before concluding: 'Because the coal is of strongly bituminous composition, it is usually burned as coke, which happens both at the actual pit and in free-standing ovens.'

In this passage, Siebold's language reveals the extent to which late eighteenth-century 'geognostic' (Earth-knowing) mineralogy framed his vision of the natural world. One of the leading geognosts of the day, Abraham Gottlob Werner (1749–1817), professor of mining and mineralogy at the Bergakademie Freiberg in Saxony, had emphasized in his *Kurze Klassifikation und Beschreibung der verschiedenen Gebirgsarten* (1787) the need for a precise 'description' of different rock strata.[31] Consequently, when Siebold wrote of 'thin layers' (*dünne Schichten*) of 'foliated coal' (*Blätterkohlen, Houille feuilletée*) alternating with 'clay shale' (*Schieferton*), he was employing a stratigraphic vocabulary whereby – to cite Georges Cuvier's 'Preliminary Discourse' to his 1812 *Recherches sur les ossemens fossiles de quadrupedes* – 'nature everywhere maintains the same language'.[32] Siebold's 'reading' of the earth was thus an act of archival transcription, in which he began to abstract the particular characteristics of the Fukumo mine into a universal geological terminology. Future scholars – or commodores, or consuls – would themselves not need to read the archive$_0$ of the earth because they now had Siebold's *Nippon: Archiv zur Beschreibung von Japan* (1832).

---

[30] Philipp Franz von Siebold, *Nippon: Archiv zur Beschreibung von Japan und dessen Neben- und Schutzländern Jezo mit den südlichen Kurilen, Sachalin, Korea und den Liukiu-Inseln*, Alexander Freiherr von Siebold and Heinrich Freiherr von Siebold, eds., 2nd edn (Würzburg: KUK Hofbuchhandlung von Leo Woerl, 1897 [1832]), vol. 1, p. 88. Digitized by the Internet Archive, https://archive.org/details/b29352411_0001 (last accessed 8 January 2020). Siebold's journey to Edo was in the company of Heinrich Bürger (see 'Port: No Further than Sixty Steps Down', later in this chapter), the Dutch East India Company's chief factor (Opperhoofd) in Dejima, Johan Willem de Sturler (1777–1855), and fifty-seven Japanese men: Arlette Kouwenhoven and Matthi Forrer, *Siebold and Japan: His Life and Work* (Leiden: Hotei Publishing, 2000), p. 33.

[31] Rudwick, *Earth's Deep History*, pp. 82–5. For the influence of Werner on Siebold, see Togo Tsukahara, 'An Unpublished Manuscript *Geologica Japonica* by Von Siebold: Geology, Mineralogy, and Copper in the Context of Dutch Colonial Science and the Introduction of Western Geo-sciences to Japan', *East Asian Science, Technology, and Medicine* 40 (2014): 45–80, here pp. 56–8. According to Tsukahara, Siebold had a copy of Werner's *Letztes Mineral-System: Aus dessen Nachlasse auf oberbergamtliche Anordnung herausgegeben und mit Erläuterungen versehen* (1817) with him in Japan.

[32] Cited in Sepkoski, 'Earth as Archive', p. 61.

And indeed, two decades later, this brief diary entry would be pored over by powerful actors in the corridors of Washington, DC – a fuel, as it were, for a new imagination of the Pacific world.[33]

Passage: 'The Great Mineral Agent of Civilization'

The lithograph entitled 'Landing of Commodore Perry, Officers & Men of the Squadron', by the Dresden-born Wilhelm Heine (also known as William, 1827–85), has become one of the most famous visualizations of US–Japanese engagement in the mid nineteenth century. Commemorating Perry's second visit to Japan in February–March 1854, it offers a shoreside view of the commodore's ceremonial landing in the then-village of Yokohama on 8 March. From behind two lines of immaculately attired troops, their white trousers pristine and their bayonets standing to attention, a crowd of Japanese onlookers strains to catch a glimpse of the navy-uniformed central group, headed by Perry, as it marches in formation up the beach to awaiting shogunal officials. Just to the rear of Perry and his officers, three African-American men serve as the commodore's personal guards. In the distance, the US squadron is anchored in calm waters, the steam-powered *Susquehanna*, *Mississippi*, and *Powhatan* identifiable by their funnels. Heine's image records detailed choreographies of power in the beach encounter, from the minstrel diplomacy of racial hierarchies performed by the Americans to the theatre of gift exchange between the two sides.[34] Indeed, in another famous lithograph from March 1854, often wrongly attributed to Heine, US engineers explain the workings of a quarter-size steam locomotive to enchanted samurai, while up to three miles of telegraph wire stretch along the shore into the distance.[35]

This model train and the telegraph were just a few of the presents which Perry lavished upon his Tokugawa counterparts in order to showcase US technology and systems of knowledge – a collection which Heine himself later described as 'one of the most valuable gifts ever brought and

---

[33] China's place in the world was similarly reconceptualized through mineral resources in the late nineteenth century: Shellen Xiao Wu, *Empires of Coal: Fueling China's Entry into the Modern World Order, 1860–1920* (Stanford, CA: Stanford University Press, 2015).

[34] On the performance of blackface minstrel shows by Perry's crew in Japan, see Brian Rouleau, *With Sails Whitening Every Sea: Mariners and the Making of an American Maritime Empire* (Ithaca, NY: Cornell University Press, 2014), pp. 46–55.

[35] The lithograph is thought to be by W. T. Peters, a New York artist, and based on a now-lost daguerreotype by the Perry mission's photographer, Eliphalet Brown, Jr: see John W. Dower, 'Black Ships & Samurai: Commodore Perry and the Opening of Japan (1853–54)', MIT Visualizing Cultures, https://visualizingcultures.mit.edu/black_ships_and_samurai/index.html (last accessed 2 July 2021).

presented by one nation to another'.³⁶ But Perry's gift-giving equally had a strategic purpose: in offering objects of great financial and intellectual value to Japanese officials, he was attempting both to impress upon them American 'advancement' and also to force them into a position of reciprocal diplomacy. As Courtney Fullilove has argued, this was 'an exercise of power', in which 'largess became a weapon rather than homage'.³⁷ But although the asymmetries of gift-giving in 1854 were undoubtedly important, the problem with such analyses is that they follow the Heine framing of encounter, thus foregrounding the significance of the shore and relegating the ships and the sea to mere background details. In fact, the challenges raised by the transoceanic passage from the United States to Japan were central to the Perry expedition's goals – and, in pursuing those goals, the commodore was exposed to a very different exercise of power from that represented in the mission's visual records.

On his initial arrival in Edo Bay, in July 1853, Perry had carried a letter from President Millard Fillmore for the emperor of Japan that framed the geopolitical ambition of the expedition according, first, to the US's recent expansion to Oregon and California (and the latter's production of 'about sixty millions of dollars in gold every year'), and, second, to the fact that '[o]ur steamships can go from California to Japan in eighteen days'. Fillmore was 'desirous' of mutual trade, and he also sought protection for American whalers who had become shipwrecked in Japan. (The significance of the whaling industry was alluded to in one of Perry's gifts for the Japanese empress, namely perfume produced from ambergris.)³⁸ But the expedition's key goal – or so it has been argued – came in the paragraph which followed the president's request for 'kindness' to be shown to the whalers:

Commodore Perry is also directed by me to represent to your imperial majesty that we understand there is a great abundance of coal and provisions in the Empire of Japan. Our steamships, in crossing the great ocean, burn a great deal of coal, and it is not convenient to bring it all the way from America. We wish that

---

[36] Wilhelm Heine, *With Perry to Japan: A Memoir*, trans. Frederick Trautmann (Honolulu: University of Hawai'i Press, 1990 [1856]), pp. 126–7, cited in Courtney Fullilove, 'Gift and Gunboat: Meanings of Exchange in the Perry Expedition', *Diplomatic History* 42, 1 (2018): 90–108, here p. 96.

[37] Fullilove, 'Gift and Gunboat', pp. 97, 98.

[38] Ian Jared Miller, 'Writing *Japan at Nature's Edge*: The Promises and Perils of Environmental History', in Ian Jared Miller, Julia Adeney Thomas and Brett L. Walker, eds., *Japan at Nature's Edge: The Environmental Context of a Global Power* (Honolulu: University of Hawai'i Press, 2013), pp. 1–17, here p. 15fn.

our steamships and other vessels should be allowed to stop in Japan and supply themselves with coal, provisions, and water.[39]

Crossing the great ocean was indeed inconvenient: so much so that Perry himself did not traverse the Pacific to reach Japan. Drawn by the much cheaper coal which could be purchased on the US East Coast, his mission instead crossed the Atlantic and then the Indian Oceans, sending its coal supplies in advance. Even then, the coal alone cost more than US $600,000 dollars, while its acquisition – in Madeira, Singapore or Shanghai, for example – threw up all kinds of logistical challenges.[40]

Thus, in terms of fuel access, the goal of Perry's expedition may be considered as much to 'open' the Pacific to the conveniences of transoceanic passage as to 'open' Japan (itself a deeply problematic notion).[41] This was a perspective ignored for many years in popular portrayals of Perry's arrival – partly because those portrayals tended to overlook the logistics of his lengthy passage to Japan.[42] But when Perry himself later came to dictate the *Narrative* of his expedition, he emphasized – with italics – the importance of US access to Japanese fuel. In the very first paragraph of chapter I, he claimed that California's statehood had rendered America, not China, the new 'Middle Kingdom': 'If the shortest route between Eastern Asia and Western Europe be (in this age of steam) across our continent, then was it obvious enough that our continent must, in some degree at least, become a highway for the world'. The discovery of California gold, he continued, had given

---

[39] Cited in Matthew Calbraith Perry, *Narrative of the Expedition of an American Squadron to the China Seas and Japan, Performed in the Years 1852, 1853, and 1854, under the Command of Commodore M. C. Perry, United States Navy, by Order of the Government of the United States. Compiled from the Original Notes and Journals of Commodore Perry and His Officers, at His Request, and under His Supervision, by Francis L. Hawks*, D. D., L. L. D., Washington, DC, vol. 1, pp. 256–7. Digitized by ETH-Zürich, https://doi.org/10.3931/e-rara-14667 (last accessed 2 July 2021). For the argument that Perry's principal interest was coal, and that he 'chose instead to make the public face of his efforts a remonstrance against the mistreatment of shipwrecked American sailors and whaling crews who increasingly washed up on Japanese shores', see Shulman, *Coal and Empire*, p. 80.

[40] On the expedition's costs, and on its logistical challenges, see Shulman, *Coal and Empire*, pp. 37 and 79–91 respectively. A ton of coal procured on the west coast of North America in 1850 cost up to ten times more than one on the Atlantic seaboard (p. 35).

[41] For the argument that Japan's 'opening' lay primarily in new Japanese geographic imaginations of the Pacific Ocean, rather than in older notions of an awakening from slumber, see Endō, 'Cultural Geography of the Opening of Japan'. Cf. Perry, *Narrative*, vol. 1, p. 62: 'The Pacific ocean is destined to be the theatre of immense commercial undertakings.'

[42] Sheila Hones and Yasuo Endo, 'History, Distance and Text: Narratives of the 1853–1854 Perry Expedition to Japan', *Journal of Historical Geography* 32 (2006): 563–78, here p. 566.

'additional interest to the obvious reflections suggested by our geographical position':

> Direct trade from our western coast with Asia became, therefore, a familiar thought; the agency of steam was, of course, involved, and fuel for its production was indispensable. Hence arose inquiries for that great mineral agent of civilization, *coal*.[43]

'Hence arose inquiries' is an oddly distant formulation, similar to President Fillmore's 'understanding' of Japan's 'great abundance of coal'. But the introductory chapter to Perry's *Narrative* reveals the sources of this knowledge: the Americans had read Kaempfer's description of coal from 1691–2; and they were familiar with Siebold's account of his visit to Fukumo:

> Dr. Siebold also speaks of coal as being in common use throughout the country; and on visiting one of the mines he saw enough to convince him that it was skillfully worked. For domestic purposes they convert the coal into coke. Viewed in the light of commercial intercourse between the two hemispheres, this coal is worth more than all the metallic deposits we have enumerated.[44]

(Which were, to be clear: silver, copper, mercury, lead, tin and iron.)

That Siebold influenced Perry's reading of Japan is well known. While the commodore rejected the doctor's entreaties to be allowed to join the expedition, he did purchase Siebold's *Archiv* for US$503 (out of a total budget of US$30,000 for the expedition's library of maps and books). Perry also used maps which Siebold had sent to Wilhelm Heine, one of two German-speaking members of the expedition with whom the doctor was in correspondence in 1852–3: here, the artist was a mediator of knowledge with more than just his paintbrush.[45] But Siebold's relatively short description of the southern Karatsu coalfield seems to have taken on an oversized significance for the Americans, becoming central to a vision of 'commercial intercourse between the two hemispheres'.

Even though Siebold himself would critique Perry's alleged ignorance of Japanese coal in 1854, the Fukumo pithead remained a lodestar for US imaginations of transpacific passages. In August 1856, on his way to Japan under orders to conclude a comprehensive trade treaty, the new consul Townsend Harris (1804–78) recorded a diary entry which

---

[43] Perry, *Narrative*, vol. 1, p. 75 (emphasis in original).
[44] Perry, *Narrative*, vol. 1, p. 60.
[45] On this correspondence, see Herbert Plutschow, *Philipp Franz von Siebold and the Opening of Japan: A Re-Evaluation* (Leiden: Brill, 2007), pp. 53–60. On the expedition's budget, see pp. 50–1.

revealed his onboard reading as his ship steamed away from Hong Kong (having coaled there two days earlier):

> Von Siebold says that coal exists in the Island of Kyushu. At Koyanosi [sic] he saw a coal fire. At Wukumoto [sic] he visited a coal mine. Although he was not permitted to descend the shaft for more than sixty steps, he saw enough to convince him that the shaft was well and judiciously worked. He was told the lower *strata* were several feet in thickness, and the size of the blocks he saw drawn up confirmed the statement. The coal is bituminous, and is converted into *coke* for use by the Japanese.[46]

Port: No Further than Sixty Steps Down

What Harris paraphrased as a 'block' and Siebold had called 'extracted coal pieces' (*gewonnene Kohlen*) was, in the very distant past, perhaps a fern or a palm tree. Between 56 and 23 million years in the past, to be precise – that is, in the Eocene and Oligocene epochs, when the landmass today called 'Japan' was still attached to the continental coastline of Eurasia. This was a younger coal than that mined in the *Yamashiro-maru*'s birthplace in north-east England: it had a more complex chemical composition than those seams, as around Newcastle upon Tyne, which had been formed in the eponymous Carboniferous period (c. 360–300 million years ago), due partly to the relative coolness of the Oligocene, when the Antarctic ice cap was beginning to form.[47] On the aforementioned 1913 map of the Karatsu Coal Field, these deposits would be coloured in two blocks of orange: one in the area encompassing Fukumo, and the other, stretching north, along the western side of the Matsuura river (see Map 4). The river's eastern bank was coloured in pink, to represent granite – a rock predating the region's coal by up to 90 million years. (Such maps were also archival transcriptions: the earth was abstracted into a visual form which could offer other interested parties an ersatz reading of the underground.)[48]

---

[46] Townsend Harris, *The Complete Journal of Townsend Harris: First American Consul General and Minister to Japan* (New York: Japan Society, 1930), pp. 188–9 (13 August 1856). Available through the Internet Archive (https://archive.org) (last accessed 3 July 2021) (emphasis in original).

[47] Teresa Moreno, Simon Wallis, Tomoko Kojima and Wes Gibbons, *The Geology of Japan* (London: Geological Society, 2016), p. 450; Larry Thomas, *Coal Geology* (Chichester: Wiley, 2013 [2nd edn]), pp. 46–7.

[48] Geological Survey of Japan (地質調査総合センター), GeomapNavi for Karatsu, https://gbank.gsj.jp/geonavi/geonavi.php#12,33.28920,130.10084 (last accessed 5 July 2021). See also Sepkoski, 'Earth as Archive', pp. 61–3.

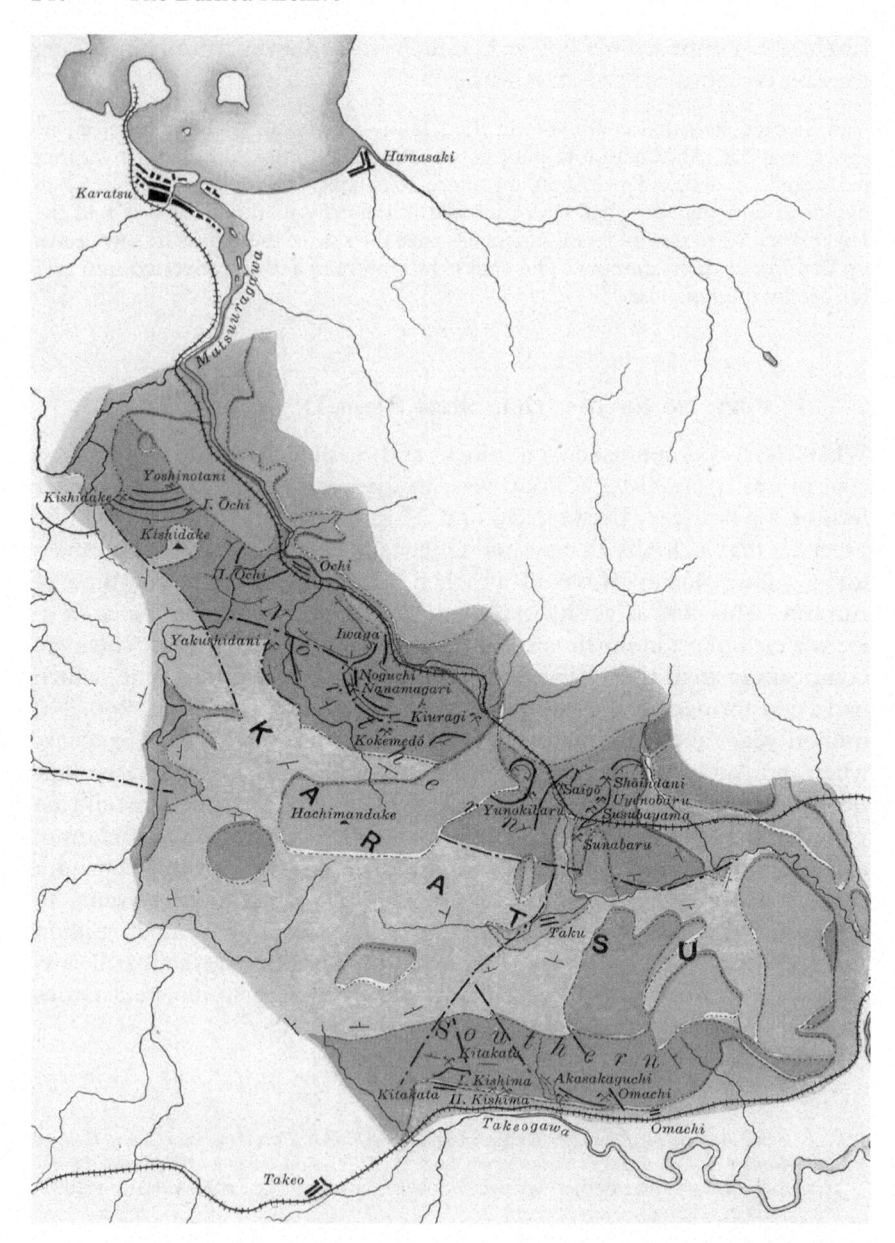

Map 4 Karatsu and Sasebo Coal Fields (1913), detail, with Karatsu to the north and Fukumo (Ōmachi) in the south. Courtesy of David Rumsey Map Collection, David Rumsey Map Center, Stanford Libraries.

In the years after the fern or palm tree died, it came to be covered by layer upon layer of marine and non-marine sediments (mainly non-marine, in the Karatsu case). The pressure of this weight generated heat; gradually, the peat – 'a melange of spores, seed coats, wood, bark, leaves, and roots which looks like chewing tobacco and burns about as well', in John McPhee's memorable description – began to cook.[49] The extent of this cooking, and the amount of hydrogen, oxygen, nitrogen, sulphur and most importantly carbon that escaped or remained trapped within, would determine the coal's classification. Any fossil with more than 50 per cent of carboniferous material counted as a 'coal'. But the famous seams of Pennsylvania, southern Wales, or indeed Amakusa – whence so many women departed on coal ships for Southeast Asia – had a carbon content of between 86 per cent and 98 per cent. This qualified them to be described as *anthracite*, indicating a hard, iridescent fuel which had a high calorific value.[50] This was important because if coal A had a higher calorific value than coal B, a ship would need to carry less of A than B in order to travel the same distance – thus leaving more space in the cargo holds to carry freight, for which a ship owner could charge money. As we shall see, calorific value was not the only determination of a coal's appropriateness for a steamship, but it was important.

In 1826, Siebold did not have steamship fuel in mind when he entered the mine at Fukumo. But he knew enough to identify the coal there as 'of strongly bituminous composition' – that is, as having a lower calorific value than anthracite. Indeed, his later criticism of Perry's great expectations centred on his belief (mistaken, as it would turn out) that Japan's coal was overwhelmingly lignite – that is, 'brown', with an even lower carbon content than bituminous coal.[51] Once again, the Karatsu field took on an oversized significance in Siebold's imagination of 'Japanese' coal.

And there we might leave the story. Except that the most interesting phrase from Siebold's 1826 diary entry, in my view, is the almost par-

---

[49] John A. McPhee, *Annals of the Former World* (New York: Farrar, Straus and Giroux, 2006), pp. 246–7.
[50] On calorific value, see Steven Gray, *Steam Power and Sea Power: Coal, The Royal Navy, and the British Empire, c. 1870–1914* (London: Palgrave Macmillan, 2018), pp. 263–4; on carbon content, 'How Is Coal Formed – A Process Spanning Eras', www.planete-energies.com/en/medias/close/how-coal-formed-process-spanning-eras (last accessed 5 July 2021). A calorie indicates how much heat an engine would need to raise one gram of water by one degree Celsius.
[51] Siebold brought back two samples of Japanese coal, both 'brown' and 'black', from his travels: Tsukahara, 'Unpublished Manuscript', p. 79.

enthical subclause, 'Up to about sixty steps down, *because our Japanese guides did not permit us to descend any further* [...]'. This is because it would be possible to characterize the presence and analyses of Siebold and his assistant, pharmacist Heinrich Bürger (1806–58), in mid-1820s Japan in terms of the gradual 'dissemination of modern Western science and medicine' to non-European arenas.[52] Other than the two men's trip to Fukumo, however, much of Siebold's pidgin knowledge about Japanese coal mining was gleaned from his medical students at his school in Nagasaki, thereby pointing to the mediation of local expertise in the production of knowledge about Japan.[53] Similarly, in Fukumo, Siebold and Bürger's descent was restricted by the mediation of 'Japanese guides' to only sixty steps, thereby limiting his direct observational analysis to the upper-level foliated coal. Perhaps the guides were concerned about their visitors' safety. But it seems equally likely that they were protecting their pit from prying outside eyes: denying, as it were, access to the earth's deep archive.

Whether Perry remembered this detail in his reading of Siebold's *Archiv* is unknown. But it may be no coincidence that one of his least satisfactory interactions with the Japanese in 1853–4 came about because of a local reluctance to share coal knowledge. In Shimoda, he writes, the Japanese authorities supplied the US steamers with some 'native coal' – 'brought from their mines, at considerable trouble and expense, in hampers made of rice-straw'. Yet Perry was dismayed to discover that this was only a low-grade surface coal (obtained from fewer than sixty steps down, he might have surmised). 'On being tried on board the steamers,' he continued, 'the engineers reported that it was of a quality so inferior that they were unable to keep up steam with it.' This then prompted the observation:

Whether the shrewd Japanese supplied an inferior quality to deceive their visitors, or whether from ignorance of the article and want of mining skill they innocently brought that which was inferior, cannot be certainly decided; but as good coal certainly exists in Japan, and as the natives not only use it, but, according to Von Siebold, know very well how to mine it, the probabilities are that they purposely furnished the poorest samples. [...] We are inclined to think, after a careful examination of the particulars of the interviews and conferences with them on all topics, that on no one subject did they misrepresent more unscrupulously than on that of coal.[54]

---

[52] For a partial critique of this view, see Tsukahara, 'Unpublished Manuscript', citation from p. 54.

[53] Tsukahara, 'Unpublished Manuscript', p. 59. See also Harald Fischer-Tiné, *Pidgin-Knowledge: Wissen und Kolonialismus* (Zurich: Diaphanes, 2013).

[54] Perry, *Narrative*, vol. 1, pp. 481–2, 483–4.

If coal was the 'great mineral agent of civilization', then for all the pomp of Perry's landing ceremonies and performance of US gift-giving, considerable agency lay in Japanese hands in 1853–4 – including the agency of alleged misrepresentation. A similar dynamic had been at play when Siebold was permitted to descend no further than sixty steps in Fukumo. Thus, coal was a leveller in the encounter of Japan and the outside world, its power political as much as calorific.

Passage: From Mine to Market

Siebold's past participle was a grammatical occlusion, of course: behind the 'extracted coal pieces' were men and women engaged in the heavy labour of extraction.

Their passage to the mine had begun long before 1826, in the economic and environmental transformations of the first Tokugawa century. Deforestation, caused partly by the construction boom in the new metropolis of Edo, and partly by an archipelago-wide population growth (necessitating ever more forest clearance for rice paddies and firewood for cooking), was one factor which led local people to burn surface coal deposits where they naturally occurred – as near the village of Koyanose, visited by Kaempfer in 1692.[55] After that area of north-central Kyushu had been devastated by a famine in 1732–3, killing 70,000 people (a fifth of the population), short-term economic hardship also pushed desperate farmers into the nascent coal-mining industry. For years afterwards, as if to recall their need to earn extra money in the agricultural off-season, mining was stigmatised as the 'famine industry'.[56]

Meanwhile, as mainland capitalists expanded their fishing interests north into the islands of Ezo and the world of the Indigenous Ainu peoples, greater amounts of salt were needed in order to preserve springtime catches of herring for transportation back south. From the eighteenth century onwards, central Kyushu coal was shipped both to Kyushu's northern coast and to the western Inland Sea's inshore salt fields, where it was burned to purify brine. Compared to saltwater cauldrons heated by pine boughs and needles, coal's hotter fires produced a cloudier, irregular crystal, one which was adequate for food preservation or for the manufacture of condiments but less good for table

---

[55] Conrad Totman, *Early Modern Japan* (Berkeley: University of California Press, 1993), pp. 225–9.
[56] Arne Kalland and Jon Pederson, 'Famine and Population in Fukuoka Domain during the Tokugawa Period', *Journal of Japanese Studies* 10, 1 (1984): 31–72, here pp. 44–5; Phipps, *Empires on the Waterfront*, p. 119.

244   The Burned Archive

Figure 6.2 Detail from Kizaki Moritaka, 'Illustrations of Products from Hizen Province' ('Hizen-shū sanbutsu zukō' 肥前州産物図考), 1784. Courtesy of the National Archives of Japan.

salt.[57] Even so, until the mid 1880s half of all the coal mined for domestic purposes in Karatsu and in the Chikuhō fields around Koyanose was burned for the manufacture of salt.[58]

These, then, were some of the socio-economic contexts which animated the lives of the near-naked coal miners portrayed in the third scroll of Kizaki Moritaka's 1784 'Illustrations of Products from Hizen Province' (see Figure 6.2). As if reflecting the process by which local villagers initially cleared flora and detritus from the Karatsu hills before extracting surface deposits of coal,[59] the scroll first depicts two men hacking directly at the mountainside. Reading right to left, we then encounter another pair of labourers entering an opening in the mountain, one carrying an unprotected flame to illuminate the way, while the next group works adjacent to a human-made entrance, replete with

[57] Shunsaku Nishikawa, 'The Economy of Chōshū on the Eve of Industrialization', *Economic Studies Quarterly* 38, 4 (1987): 323–37, here p. 330; Arne Kalland, *Fishing Villages in Tokugawa Japan* (Richmond: Curzon Press, 1995), pp. 76, 92–3; Totman, *Early Modern Japan*, p. 272.
[58] Richard J. Samuels, *The Business of the Japanese State: Energy Markets in Comparative and Historical Perspective* (Ithaca, NY: Cornell University Press, 1987), p. 73.
[59] W. Donald Burton, *Coal-Mining Women in Japan: Heavy Burdens* (London: Routledge, 2014), p. 28.

supporting overhead beams.[60] The latter was much closer to what Siebold and Bürger would have seen four decades later, namely a horizontal entrance to the pithead, from which steps followed the seam down into the hillside. On the other side of the world, in eighteenth-century Northumberland and County Durham, this was known as walk-in drift mining.[61] Thus, drawn in the same year as James Watt patented his new steam engine, the Hizen scroll's depiction of Japanese mining is yet another reminder that proto-industrialization was occurring in parts of Japan even as industrialization took off in Britain, and that Japan's subsequent late nineteenth-century industrialization cannot be explained simply as the inscription of Euro-American expertise onto a blank Japanese slate.

Indeed, in the years immediately after the Meiji revolution, when the new Navy Ministry surveyed its domestic fuel supplies, there were 376 such pitheads recorded in the Karatsu region, clustered around nineteen villages.[62] This points to an extraordinary expansion of coal mining in mid nineteenth-century Karatsu in particular and Kyushu more generally, justifying American and European imaginations of a Japanese 'abundance'. But by this time, as miners were forced to dig deeper into the mountainside, many of the pithead entrances were less sculpted than those depicted in the 1784 Hizen scrolls. Instead, narrow shafts known as *tanuki-bori* 狸掘り (badger holes) followed the seam downwards into the earth. Usually working in teams of two, the male *sakiyama* 先山 (hewer, literally 'pit fronter') crouched on his haunches or lay sideways, chipping away at the coal with a pickaxe or mattock. Brute hacking – as in the Hizen scrolls – would produce nothing but shards and powder, so the *sakiyama* sought out cracks in the seam, wedged his pick in, and loosened the cracks until whole lumps of coal gave way. These he pushed and kicked behind him to the *atoyama* 後山 (assistant, 'pit backer'), often a woman, who raked and scraped the pieces into a wicker basket and then, once she'd manoeuvred herself into more space, into two deeper baskets to yoke over her back. Such a load-bearing practice was adapted from the farm fields, whence labourers carried vegetables, tools and rice back to the village balanced over their shoulders. The coal baskets could load up to 80 *kin* 斤 (48 kg) in front and 100 *kin* (60 kg)

---

[60] The scroll, Hizen-shū sanbutsu zukō 肥前州産物図考, is digitized by the National Archives of Japan Digital Archive, www.digital.archives.go.jp/. On the visual similarities between the Hizen scrolls and Hirase Tessai's 平瀬徹斎 'Nippon sankai meibutsu zue' 日本山海名物図絵 (1754), see Mori and Miyazaki, *Kujiratori no shakaishi*, pp. 102–7.
[61] Visitors to County Durham's Beamish – The Living Museum of the North (www.beamish.org.uk) can enter the Mahogany Drift Mine, first opened in 1855.
[62] Tōjō, 'Meiji zenki, Hizen Matsuuragawa', p. 32. The ministry was established in 1872.

behind; even if both were only half-filled, an assistant might lug more than 50 kilograms back through the tunnels, either to a haulier or all the way to the pithead.[63]

Kizaki Moritaka did not offer visual depictions of such details: perhaps, like Siebold, he was not permitted to descend very deep into the Karatsu shafts, and thus was prevented from witnessing the brutal working conditions underground. (This may be another reason why the 'Japanese guides' restricted Siebold's access.) Nearly two centuries later, however, a retired coal miner from Tagawa – the mines owned by the diarist Yasukawa, until he sold them to Mitsui in 1900 – began to paint scenes from his working life and thereby bequeath the world an extraordinary archive of the subterranean.[64] Born in Fukuoka in 1892, Yamamoto Sakubei first joined his older brother in the Chikuhō mines of north-central Kyushu when he was seven or eight years old and still at elementary school. He became a full-time miner in 1906, the same year Mitsui Tagawa identified its ideal unit of labour recruitment as 'three people comprised of a couple with a 12- or 13-year-old child, all working, and an elder to cook'. (For context: there were officially 17,570 men, 8,316 women and 115 children working as hewers or assistants in the Chikuhō mines in 1906.)[65]

Many of the nearly 600 watercolour and ink paintings that Yamamoto composed between his retirement in 1955 and his death in 1984 look back to the turn of the twentieth century. They may therefore be taken as the best surviving record of what working life was like for the men and women in whose calloused fingertips the passage of coal from Karatsu to the *Yamashiro-maru* began. In 'Mining Coal in a Lying Position', for example (see Figure 6.3), Yamamoto depicts a hewer/assistant team working on a seam thinner than 1.5 metres (which the team could approach from a standing position) or even 0.45 metres (which might allow them to squat). The painting's power is to offer a full sensory vision of the labour. The underground heat is suggested through the bare torsos of both the male hewer and the female assistant – the former's tattoos alluding to the fact that many Meiji-era miners were convicts or social outcasts, or were stigmatized as such. The exaggerated gradations of colour extending outwards from the hanging lamps – yellow to cream to grey to black – connote the intense darkness of the couple's daily

---

[63] For details of these working conditions, see Burton, *Coal-Mining Women*, pp. 29–33.
[64] The Yamamoto Collection became Japan's first entry in UNESCO's 'Memory of the World' programme in 2011: www.y-sakubei.com/english/mow/index.html (last accessed 6 July 2021).
[65] Tagawa Mitsui citation from Burton, *Coal-Mining Women*, p. 17. For the figures from Chikuhō, ibid., p. 15: compare to 3,153 men, 1,561 women and 144 children working as hewers or assistants in the Karatsu mines in 1906.

Figure 6.3 Yamamoto Sakubei, 'Mining Coal in a Lying Position' (*Nebori* 寝掘り), December 1964. © Yamamoto Family. Courtesy of The Tagawa City Coal Mining Historical Museum Collection.

world. Though both labourers wear bandana-like cloths to protect their heads from sharp rocks above, they eschew facecloths attached to the ears: many miners, Yamamoto writes in his customary comments on another painting, hated such coverings because they muffled the warning sounds of collapsing roofs. But the ears could play tricks, too. Yamamoto recalls hearing a raccoon dog in the summer of 1899 making noises as if it were driving or dragging a pickaxe – a terrifying illusion for a seven-year-old boy. Thus, to the right of the diagrammatic inset in 'Mining Coal in a Lying Position', he records the lyrics to a mining song. The words reveal the calculations the hewer was making as he inched forward, but also the comfort of hearing fellow human voices in this domain of raccoons, rockfalls and the spirits of colleagues killed in accidents:

> *Noborya horinasanna me ni ishi ga iru.*
> *Orosha horinasanna mizu ga tsuku.*
> *Gotton!*

> Don't mine coal of an ascending coalface, or your eyes will catch coal dust.
> Don't mine coal of a descending coalface, or the coal will get soaked with water.
> *Gotton!* [chant]

So: from pickaxe to basket, the coal must now be hauled to the pithead entrance – a job that in both the Chikuhō and Karatsu regions accounted for another 4 per cent or so of the total underground labour force in the early twentieth century.[66] There, it must be sifted, sorted, picked and packed (another job often for women), and then carried down to the depots, which in Karatsu were built adjacent to the Matsuura river. In his 1784 scroll, Kizaki depicted the journey from pithead to depot in human-drawn, open-topped carts. This remained the case a century later, as Tōjō Nobumasa's meticulous research has shown: of twenty-five Karatsu pitheads surveyed in 1883, for example, only two used horses to transport the coal. For the other twenty-three, the need for human labour made this the most expensive leg of the journey to market.[67]

From riverside depot downstream to the wholesale merchants based in the shadow of the former domain castle in Karatsu town, the coal now entered the penultimate stage of its migration to the steamship bunker. And it was the relative ease of this riverine transportation which prompted Meiji naval officials to establish a supply infrastructure in the central Karatsu field in the 1870s.[68] One key cluster of depots was to be found near where the Matsuura river forks at today's Ōchi town – that is, north of the Fukumo mine visited by Siebold in 1826 (see Map 4). There were almost 200 pitheads in the vicinity of the Navy Ministry's branch office here (established in 1879), and the distance from the furthest depot to Karatsu was only fifteen kilometres – a two-day round trip at most, and one that an unusually enterprising boatman called Kōshichi made some 113 times in 1880.[69] Again, this was a supply line which had hardly changed since Kizaki's 1784 depiction of single-manned coal barges carrying between 2,000 and 4,000 *kin* (between approximately 1.2 and 2.4 tons, depending on the water level). But despite relatively small barges, the Matsuura river itself gave Karatsu coal a significant advantage over Chikuhō coal in the 1870s and 1880s. This is because the complex flow of the Onga river in Chikuhō – despite its barges carrying up to 10,000 *kin* (approximately 6 tons) – rendered the fastest journey from pithead depots to Wakamatsu market five or six days, increasing to two weeks in bad conditions. In other words, even though Chikuhō coal was known to have a higher calorific value than that of Karatsu, the ease of the

---

[66] Burton, *Coal-Mining Women*, p. 15 (the figures are for 1906).
[67] Tōjō, 'Meiji zenki, Hizen Matsuuragawa', pp. 41, 38.
[68] On direct mine management, see Tōjō Nobumasa 東定宣昌, 'Karatsu kaigun tankō no settei to sono kei'ei' 唐津海軍炭坑の設定とその経営 [The establishment and management of navy coal collieries in Karatsu], *Keizaigaku kenkyū* 59, 3–4 (1993): 81–109.
[69] Tōjō, 'Meiji zenki, Hizen Matsuuragawa', pp. 36–7.

latter's riverine transportation network – served with a peak of 1,780 coal barges at the time of the Sino-Japanese War – made the Karatsu region of central strategic importance to Meiji Japan well into the third decade after the revolution.[70] Only the opening of the first railway line connecting the Chikuhō mines to Wakamatsu in August 1891 eroded the hitherto superior infrastructure offered by the Matsuura river, making Onga boatmen such as the artist Yamamoto's father unemployed in the process.[71]

And so the coal has arrived in Karatsu town by river, as it will do until the opening of the first Karatsu railway in 1899.[72] There, the highest quality fuel will be sold by the wholesalers – for an unusually low price of 23 yen per 10,000 *kin* in December 1884, just as the post-crash repairs to the *Yamashiro-maru* are completed.[73] Yet the likely coal-carrying functionality of the *Sumanoura-maru*, the ship with which the *Yamashiro-maru* had collided two months previously, is a reminder that the coal's final passage, onwards from Karatsu, would have been impossible without the countless sail-powered ships which transported it to ports big enough to handle steamships. In Japan, those were ports such as Yokohama, Kobe, Nagasaki – and, at least if the ships anchored in deeper waters offshore, Wakamatsu.[74]

---

[70] Tōjō, 'Meiji zenki, Hizen Matsuuragawa', pp. 37, 43. For the navy's survey of forty-nine river bargemen whom it directly contracted in 1881, ibid., pp. 34–5: some 71 per cent of the Matsuura river's coal barges were between 4,500 and 5,500 *kin* in 1881.

[71] On the bargemen's response to the Chikuhō railways, see Yamamoto's painting, 'Sendō to okajōki' 舟頭と陸蒸気 [The bargeman and the steam train] (April 1965), in which the boatman glowers at the coal freight train and complains, 'Oh shit! That damned steam train came here to finally rob me of my job'. On Yasukawa's shares in the Chikuhō Railway Company in the 1890s, see Nakamura, *Chihō kara no sangyō kakumei*, p. 212. In terms of the share of Japan's total coal production, Chikuhō coal rose from 27.7 per cent in 1890 to 54.4 per cent in 1900, even as total production trebled from 2.6 million tons to 7.5 million tons in this period, suggesting the transformative effect of rail transportation on Chikuhō production (p. 197).

[72] Tōjō Nobumasa 東定宣昌, 'Karatsu tanden no yusō taikei no kindaika: Karatsu Kōgyō Tetsudō Gaisha no seiritsu to sekitan yusō' 唐津炭田の輸送体系の近代化：唐津興業鉄道会社の成立と石炭輸送 [The modernization of the transportation system in Karatsu Coalfield: The founding of the Karatsu Kōgyō Railway Company and coal transportation], *Hikaku Shakai Bunka* 1 (1995): 49–60. The railways carried 29 per cent of the 906,000 tons produced in Karatsu by 1902, and 62 per cent of the 1.03 million tons produced there in 1906 (p. 58).

[73] *AS*, 10 December 1884. By contrast, in times of unusually high prices, 10,000 *kin* of Karatsu coal could sell for 41 yen: *AS*, 22 August 1882.

[74] In an 1881 survey ordered by the Ministry of Agriculture and Commerce, Wakamatsu was not considered as one of the forty ports suitable for foreign steamship anchorage: Kokaze, *Teikokushugika no Nihon kaiun*, pp. 203–4. That Wakamatsu was a port of call for ships such as the *Yamashiro-maru* by 1900 was due in no small part to the modernization efforts led by entrepreneurs such as Yasukawa, who served on the municipal council from 1898 onwards: Hibino, 'Nisshin/Nichiro senkanki ni okeru Yasukawa Keiichirō', pp. 30–3.

Port: Alternative Geographies of Japan's 'Opening'

As a small tug conveyed Yasukawa Keiichirō from Wakamatsu to the *Yamashiro-maru* on the morning of 27 March 1900, he may or may not have known that the ship had just arrived from Shanghai.[75] In fact, after its final return to Japan from Melbourne in January 1899, the *Yamashiro-maru* ran the NYK's Yokohama–Shanghai line once or twice a month until mid 1900 – a route which sometimes also extended from Yokohama to Vladivostok. The ship carried passengers and freight across the East China Sea, including (to Shanghai) Japanese green tea for transshipment to North America, and (from Shanghai) groups of Chinese students who were going to study in Japan.[76] But the embarkation of one of Japan's leading coal industrialists, on a ship steaming the Shanghai line and in a port synonymous with coal transportation: this serves as an opportunity for us briefly to consider how coal from Karatsu and Chikuhō was central not just to the fuelling of Japanese ships across the Pacific but, more generally, to a transformation of shipping infrastructures in late nineteenth-century East Asia.

When Commodore Perry first navigated his four-vessel squadron into Edo Bay in July 1853, it is not known exactly which coal his two steamships were burning.[77] All that's clear, according to one of the iconic Japanese woodblock prints of his arrival, is that the ships belched vast amounts of black smoke (see Figure 1.4). But on second thoughts, perhaps the billowing clouds merely represented, like so many other aspects of the print (the figurehead, the paddlewheel, the stern, the monkey-like sailors on the rigging), artistic licence: that is, one of several exaggerations to emphasize the foreignness of the 'black ships' (*kurofune* 黒船) to Japanese eyes. In fact, a key consideration for naval officials across the Euro-American world in the mid nineteenth century was the ability to source coal which offered as *little* smoky discharge as possible,

---

[75] 'Shanghai Shipping Intelligence', *North China Herald*, 28 March 1900 (the *Yamashiro-maru* reportedly departed Shanghai on 24 March). I am grateful to Rudolph Ng for his research assistance on this aspect of the *Yamashiro-maru*'s history.

[76] For example, 'Commercial Intelligence', *North China Herald*, 9 October 1899, reporting that 440,906 pounds (lb) of green tea carried by the *Yamashiro-maru* had been cleared for ports in Canada and the United States, and 9,315 lb for London; and the Chinese-language *Shenbao* 申報 newspaper (Shanghai), 17 November 1899, for brief mention of a group of thirty-five Chinese students bound for Tokyo. See also Robert Hellyer, *Green with Milk and Sugar: When Japan Filled America's Tea Cups* (New York: Columbia University Press, 2021); Paula Harrell, *Sowing the Seeds of Change: Chinese Students, Japanese Teachers, 1895–1905* (Stanford, CA: Stanford University Press, 1992).

[77] On the 1854 mission, the *Mississippi* consumed 2,336 lb of coal per hour, compared to the *Susquehanna* (3,310 lb) and the *Powhatan* (3,248 lb): Dower, 'Black Ships & Samurai'.

thus to increase – should it be necessary – the element of surprise in any maritime engagement.

Again, anthracite was in theory the panacea to this problem, for in addition to its high calorific value, it was a relatively smokeless coal. At the same time, however, anthracite was also very hard. This made it difficult to ignite, meaning that once shovelled into an already-lit furnace, it could have an initial cooling effect, followed by a surge in heat once it did ignite – thereby creating an uneven temperature in the fire and thus in the production of steam. Equally, a very hard fuel was less likely to adhere to the furnace's sides, increasing the likelihood of an imbalanced fire when the ship rolled in high seas (the same problem of potential imbalance was true in the coal bunkers).[78] Softer, bituminous coals – '[the *Yamashiro-maru's*] consumption of coal is about forty-eight tons a day of the *soft* kind called "Karatsu"' – ignited faster and dislodged less easily than anthracite. They produced more smoke, however, and, due to their lower calorific value, demanded higher consumption and thus more frequent recoaling. Bituminous coals also had a greater tendency to self-combust – as indeed occurred during the *Yamashiro-maru's* first crossing to Hawai'i, causing what Captain Mahlmann recalled to be a small fire in one of the ship's coal bunkers.[79]

But as naval engineers on both sides of the Atlantic experimented with different classifications in the 1840s and 1850s, the British Admiralty discovered that the coal extracted from the South Wales Field, especially the central area served by the port of Cardiff, was the ideal steamship fuel. With an average carbon content of 92.5 per cent, the calorific value of 'Best Welsh' was competitive with anthracite – meaning that, per unit of energy, it required less onboard bunker space than bituminous coals. It was also a smokeless coal and produced less ash than softer coals, reducing the labour required of the ship's firemen (about whom more later).[80] In short, no other coal held a flame to Best Welsh.

With Royal Navy warships designed for the consumption of Best Welsh by the late nineteenth century, this particular coal became the standard fuel for the maintenance of British interests around the world. From the east coast of Latin America to East Asia, Welsh coal was to be found in every port of strategic significance for Britain – even when there were 'local' coal industries.[81] In Shanghai, for example, more than half of

---

[78] Shulman, *Coal and Empire*, p. 46; Brian Lavery, *SS Great Britain, 1843–1937 Onwards: Enthusiasts' Manual* (Yeovil: Haynes Publishing, 2012), p. 99.
[79] Mahlmann, *Reminiscences*, p. 184.   [80] Gray, *Steam Power and Sea Power*, p. 70.
[81] Trevor Boyns and Steven Gray, 'Welsh Coal and the Informal Empire in South America, 1850–1913', *Atlantic Studies* 13, 1 (2016): 53–77; on the relative failure of British attempts to develop coal mining in mid-century Labuan (Borneo), see Robert Bickers,

the coal was imported from Britain in the mid 1860s. Together with coal from Newcastle (New South Wales), British imperial coal thus accounted for around 90 per cent of the port's coal imports. (Mahlmann was employed on a coal barque from Newcastle to Shanghai in 1868.)[82] This predominance of Best Welsh, despite the vast distances in question, was partly explained by economic factors. British imports from India and Burma back to the metropole tended to be bulk commodities (including cotton, jute, rice and teak), whereas British exports to the Asian colonies were higher-value but less bulky manufactured products. The resulting extra capacity in Asia-bound shipping therefore facilitated the export of coal from Wales and contributed to relatively low coal freight costs from Britain to Shanghai or Hong Kong – costs which declined even further after the opening of the Suez Canal in 1869.[83]

From Perry's difficulties in securing a supply of coal in Singapore and Shanghai to the ways in which French colonial officials in Indochina were cognisant of their dependence on what one scholar has called the 'British carbon system', the time was ripe for the emergence of a major new coal supplier in East Asia.[84] This was another reason why President Fillmore's letter expressed such interest in Japanese 'abundance': Japanese coal had the potential to disrupt the British coal monopoly in the crucial port of Shanghai and thus 'open' the Pacific to US steamships – and China to US cotton exports.[85] For their part, British planners were also interested in developing new sources of coal in East Asia so as

---

'The *Challenger*: Hugh Hamilton Lindsay and the Rise of British Asia, 1832–1865', *Transactions of the RHS* (2012): 141–69, here pp. 157–65.

[82] Kokaze Hidemasa 小風秀雅, '19 seiki ni okeru kōtsū kakumei no shinten to Nihontan no yakuwari' 19世紀における交通革命の進展と日本炭の役割 [The development of the nineteenth-century transportation revolution and the role of Japanese coal], in Nagasaki-shi 長崎市, ed., *Takashima tankō chōsa hōkokusho* 高島炭鉱調査報告書 (Nagasaki: Nagasaki-shi, 2014), pp. 2-6–2-27, here p. 2-20. On Mahlmann, see Chapter 1.

[83] Yrjö Kaukiainen, 'Coal and Canvas: Aspects of the Competition between Steam and Sail, c. 1870–1914', *International Journal of Maritime History* 4 (1992): 175–91, here p. 181. The bulk cost of transporting Welsh coal to Asia declined by between a third and a quarter over the decade 1873–83: Kokaze, *Teikokushugika no Nihon kaiun*, p. 41. See also On Barak, 'Outsourcing: Energy and Empire in the Age of Coal, 1820–1911', *International Journal of Middle East Studies* 47, 3 (2015): 425–45.

[84] Shulman, *Coal and Empire*, p. 85; James R. Fichter, 'Imperial Interdependence on Indochina's Maritime Periphery: France and Coal in Ceylon, Singapore, and Hong Kong, 1859–1895', in James R. Fichter, ed., *British and French Colonialism in Africa, Asia and the Middle East: Connected Empires across the Eighteenth to the Twentieth Centuries* (London: Palgrave Macmillan, 2019), pp. 151–79.

[85] One context for Perry's expedition was the United States having lost out to Britain in trying to establish new coal supplies in Labuan: Shulman, *Coal and Empire*, pp. 70–9.

to reduce fuel costs in the Royal Navy's budget.[86] In 1866, British consular officials in Nagasaki singled out the nearby coalfields of Takashima, Karatsu, Hirado and Hizen (Saga) as sites ripe for vertical mining technology, and, in the same year, Japanese coal was first exported to Shanghai.

Like historians surveying an archive's potential, geologists and entrepreneurs rushed to analyse Japan's fossil past so as to position themselves favourably in exploiting its fuel future. The British businessman Thomas Blake Glover (1838–1911), based in Nagasaki since 1859, focused his efforts on Takashima island, some fourteen kilometres offshore from the city, where the coal was of a higher quality but also more expensive than that mined in Karatsu.[87] The *Journal of the Tokyo Geographical Society* discussed Karatsu in the context of Japan's 'underground resources' in 1881, while in the same year the British consulate in Nagasaki offered a carbon, sulphur and ash comparison of Takashima and Karatsu coals.[88] In November 1883, two months before the *Yamashiro-maru*'s launch, the *Asahi shinbun* reported on tests carried out by the KUK company, comparing Karatsu coal to that from Horonai (Hokkaido): for eight hours of steaming in identical conditions, 7 tons of Karatsu coal were consumed compared to 6.25 tons of Horonai. The latter produced less ash, too, and weaker smoke than Takashima or Karatsu coals, thus – in the newspaper's optimistic reading – rendering Horonai coal 'no different from high grade British coal'.[89] But, of course, Hokkaido was much further away from East Asian ports hitherto monopolized by Welsh fuel than the coalfields of northern and western Kyushu.

Thus, in exactly the years when steamship tonnage in East Asia began to grow exponentially due to the US-based Pacific Mail Steamship Company commencing its transpacific line (1867), to the concomitant connection of the east and west coasts by transcontinental railway (1869), and especially due to the opening of the Suez Canal, Japanese coal became available to meet the new demand. And not just any coal, but fuel of sufficient calorific value and yet softness to be, if not in the league of Best Welsh, then at least more than adequate for steamship

---

[86] Fichter, 'Imperial Interdependence', p. 167. On Prussia's attempts to exploit Chinese coal reserves from the 1860s onwards, see Wu, *Empires of Coal*, pp. 33–65.
[87] John McMaster, 'The Takashima Mine: British Capital and Japanese Industrialization', *Business History Review* 37, 3 (1963): 217–39.
[88] Sano Tsuneki 佐野常樹, 'Chika tōgen no gaikyō' 地下當源ノ概況 [Overview of underground resources], *Tōkyō chigaku kyōkai hōkoku* 10, 3 (1881), reprinted in *Tōkyō chigaku kyōkai hōkoku* 東京地学協会報告 (Tokyo: Tōkyō chigaku kyōkai, 1990), vol. 4, pp. 279–88.
[89] *AS*, 1 November 1883.

consumption. Because of Kyushu's relative proximity to Shanghai, and the resulting low transportation costs, the proportion of Japanese coal – particularly from Takashima (shipped via Nagasaki), then later from the Miike mines in central Kyushu (shipped via Kuchinotsu) – relative to all coal sold on the Shanghai market increased from 40 per cent to 78 per cent between 1873 and 1881, and it was a similar story in Hong Kong, too. By the early 1900s, Japanese coal also supplied between one-third and one-half of the total coal sold in Singapore. As an absolute figure, 450,790 tons of Japanese coal were exported to Shanghai as the *Yamashiro-maru* ran the Yokohama–Shanghai line in 1900 – the majority from Chikuhō and shipped via Moji.[90]

In turn, this transformation of Japan's resource relationship to East Asia forces historians to reconsider the geographies of the archipelago's late nineteenth-century engagement with the outside world. Standard narratives of Japan's 'opening' draw a line from Perry's conclusion of the Treaty of Kanagawa in 1854, to the arrival of Townsend Harris two years later and the signing of comprehensive if 'unequal' commercial treaties between Japan and the Western powers after 1858, to the subsequent key role of the five international ports defined in those agreements as hubs for Japan's foreign connections – that is, the so-called treaty ports of Yokohama, Nagasaki, Kobe, Niigata and (in Hokkaido) Hakodate. And yet, as Phipps has argued, 'a framework that relies on the treaty ports alone misses the much more complex system of maritime relations that developed in East Asia during this pivotal era'. For in fact, when the abolition of the unequal treaties came into effect in 1899, the Japanese metropole – excluding the newly acquired Taiwan and the Pescadores – was equipped with an additional twenty-one 'special' ports whose denizens were engaged in overseas trade. Ninety per cent of the trade through these trading ports was handled by Japanese merchants – men such as Yasukawa – by the 1890s, compared to the 80 per cent of trade handled by non-Japanese in Yokohama.[91] In other words, shifting our focus away from the five well-known treaty ports brings a range of new actors into view in the history of Japan's overseas relations, and it brings to the fore

---

[90] On Shanghai and Hong Kong, see Kokaze, '19 seiki ni okeru kōtsū kakumei', pp. 2-22 and 2-24 respectively (p. 2-21 for 1900 tonnage). On Singapore, Fichter, 'Imperial Interdependence', p. 166. The value of Japanese coal sold in the Straits Settlements increased from US$1.6 million in 1894 to US$5.3 million in 1913, making it the most valuable Japanese export commodity there: Shimizu, 'Karayuki-san', p. 127. On Kuchinotsu and Moji, see Phipps, *Empires on the Waterfront*, pp. 101, 146.

[91] Phipps, *Empires on the Waterfront* (citation from p. 4). In addition to the twenty-one 'special' ports, Taketoyo (near Nagoya) also opened in 1899. On the handling of international trade, see p. 248.

sites of international trade that otherwise make at best marginal appearances in the mainstream narratives of Meiji Japan.

For example, four of the nine nationwide 'special export ports' (*tokubetsu yushutsukō* 特別輸出港) designated by the Ministry of Finance in 1889 were located in Kyushu. All four – the aforementioned Kuchinotsu, plus Karatsu, Misumi and Moji – were authorized to handle the export of coal, one of the Meiji government's five key export products.[92] Such designations built on the previous export histories of all nine ports: in Karatsu's case, coal had been directly shipped by a private entrepreneur to Shanghai since 1882, despite the Navy Ministry having requisitioned key Karatsu pitheads for state use in the 1870s.[93] But with the new 'special export port' status, the coal trade could remain largely in Japanese hands, thereby generating profits for Japanese businesses and additional customs revenue for the state. Moreover, the proximity of these ports to the coal mining regions of Karatsu, Chikuhō and Miike simplified the logistics of international export – especially to the key markets of Shanghai, Hong Kong or Singapore. (As noted in Chapter 5, the opening of Kuchinotsu and Karatsu had the unexpected consequence, according to the Japanese consul in Hong Kong in 1890, of facilitating the opportunities for young women 'to slip secretly abroad'.)

Thus, in the case of Karatsu, its designation as a special port in 1889 was effectively an opportunity to expand into East Asia the riverine transportation networks first depicted in the Hizen scrolls of 1784 – such that we may think rather of a basic historical *continuity* across the supposedly epochal events of the 1850s. That is, in terms of international relations, and from the archival perspective of Edo/Tokyo, Perry's arrival might seem to be *the* pivotal event of the mid nineteenth century, his ships' smoke casting a pall over subsequent decades. Meanwhile, from the perspective of Yokohama, itself transformed from fishing village to international port, the late nineteenth-century story might seem to be one of still nascent Japanese trading networks (e.g. with Australia) and newly emerging industries (e.g. transpacific shipping). But from the starting point of a coal seam in Karatsu, the line connecting 1784 to 1889 might be considered entirely natural if somewhat unexpected, uncoiling as it did from an already established local industry and merely extending – with the aid of central government finance and

---

[92] Phipps, *Empires on the Waterfront*, p. 46. One other special export port handled coal exports, namely Otaru, in Hokkaido. The other products were rice, sulphur, wheat and wheat flour (p. 62). In 1896, Karatsu, Kuchinotsu and Misumi were redesignated as 'world trade ports' (*kaikōgai bōekikō* 開港外貿易港), giving merchants greater freedom to engage in international exports *and* imports (pp. 51–2).

[93] Phipps, *Empires on the Waterfront*, pp. 99–100.

management – the infrastructure of coal transportation from the Matsuura river to an East Asian arena.

Idling in the domestic coaling hub of Wakamatsu on the morning of 27 March 1900, fresh from a run to Shanghai and refuelled for the final journey to Yokohama with coal from Kyushu, the *Yamashiro-maru* epitomized these alternative geographical frameworks by which historians might understand Meiji Japan. Honolulu, Sydney, Singapore or Shanghai were indisputably central to the story I have told in this book, their roles documented in the paperwork of Japan's Foreign Ministry and other institutions. But so too were the subterranean spaces of the Karatsu and other Kyushu mines, an archive which reveals the extent to which the need for coal indeed tethered ship-shaped histories to the bowels of the earth.

Passage: Stevedores and Bronze Buddhas

Anthropomorphizing the ship with an unfortunate want of care, I have ascribed to it a human emotion – *fresh*! – which erases the labour histories rigged to its refuelling. The coal did not magically spirit itself from port to ship bunker, wisping through the air like the ghosts of the dead miners who haunt Yamamoto Sakubei's underground paintings. Rather, it was carried: on the backs of men, women and children.

In the digital archives of the Smithsonian Institute, there survives a photograph from 1904 which depicts this heavy labour in the port of Nagasaki.[94] Close enough in both time and place that we may assume a similar process occurred when the *Yamashiro-maru* docked in Wakamatsu in March 1900 (or, indeed, anywhere else during its career in Japan), the photograph profiles the starboard side of the Pacific Mail Steamship Company's *Siberia*, launched in 1901. This was a huge ship by comparison to the *Yamashiro-maru* – at 572 feet, almost twice as long, and more than six times as big in terms of gross tonnage (18,000 tons). The image's waterline perspective thus dramatizes an already large vessel's draft, while four of the *Siberia*'s lifeboats hang over the

---

[94] 'Coaling the Pacific Mail S. S. "Siberia" at the fortified naval station of Nagasaki, Japan', Underwood & Underwood, 1904 or earlier, The Henry and Nancy Rosin Collection of Early Photography of Japan, Freer Gallery of Art and Arthur M. Sackler Gallery Archives (Smithsonian Institution: Washington, DC), https://sova.si.edu/record/FSA.A1999.35?s=216&n=12&t=D&q=Japan&i=217, call number FSA A1999.35.609 (last accessed 16 July 2021). The photograph also survives in the Library of Congress, www.loc.gov/resource/cph.3c34388/ (last accessed 16 July 2021). My thanks to David Fedman (@dfedman) for posting a link to this image on Twitter, 7 February 2021.

scene like mini versions of the Zeppelins being contemporaneously trialled in Germany.[95]

From the pointed bow of the wooden lighter on which the camera must have been balanced, the viewer's eye is directed towards three other lighters drawn up perpendicular to the *Siberia* – that is, long narrow boats which were capable of carrying up to sixty tons of coal from the pier to the offshore steamship.[96] We are thus cast into the middle of a multistep process. The lighters have already been loaded by onshore stevedores (*okanakashi* 陸仲仕) working at the pier, the coal there sometimes blended according to a particular steamship's needs. Now, standing thigh-deep in the lighters, a dozen or so offshore stevedores (*okinakashi* 沖仲仕) stoop down to shovel and hoe the coal into bamboo baskets. These are relayed to the bottom of a ladder-like structure which angles at approximately sixty degrees up the ship's metal hull. Like the coal, our eyes are drawn upwards: on each of the ladder's shelflike steps stand one or two labourers, who pass the baskets to their colleagues above in what the photograph implies to be a metronomic rhythm. I can count labourers at nine different levels of the ladder, which is attached to the ship's bulwarks by rope. Hanging over those bulwarks from the *Siberia*'s promenade deck, passengers look down at the industrious scene below.

In the photograph's foreground, three such ladders have been tied to the *Siberia*. Just below the bulwark, the ladders are connected by two horizontal cross-shelves, onto each of which are crowded another half-dozen labourers who are busy tipping the coal into the bunkers and stacking the empty baskets. This is because the *Siberia* was equipped with sideloading coal bunkers on its main deck. But on ships like the *Yamashiro-maru*, the coal would have been carried over the bulwarks, across the main deck and then lowered down into the coal bunker(s) two decks below – where another group of stevedores levelled the fuel to make it safe in high seas and accessible to the ship's passers.

Although one or two of the labourers in the 1904 photograph glance towards the camera and seem aware of its presence (and why not? Such a device would not ordinarily have made an appearance on a lighter), for the most part this is a normal work scene. The male labourers wear straw

---

[95] The draft refers to the measurement from keel to waterline, which would therefore increase as the ship was loaded. On the *Siberia*'s dimensions and architecture in this and the following paragraphs, 'Cabin Plan of the Pacific Mail Steamship Co's New Twin Screw Steamships, Transpacific Service, "Korea" & "Siberia"' (c. 1906), John Haskell Kemble Collection, Huntingdon Digital Library, call number priJHK 00187, https://hdl.huntington.org/digital/collection/p9539coll1/id/22028/ (last accessed 16 July 2021).

[96] I take some additional details in this paragraph from Phipps, *Empires on the Waterfront*, p. 174.

258 The Burned Archive

Figure 6.4 'Loading Women', date and photographer unknown. Courtesy of Nagasaki University Library Collections.

hats or *hachimaki* headbands to keep the sweat and dirt from their eyes. Perhaps between a third and half of the workforce are female, their distinctive bleached cotton head towels, tied in the *anesan-kaburi* style, offering some protection against the dust – but also shadowing their faces from view. By contrast, another photograph, preserved in Nagasaki University Library, shows a contemporaneous group of stevedore women in a pose, the ground around them littered with large lumps of coal (see Figure 6.4).[97] In truth the women seem no older than teenagers, their hands resting on each other's shoulders, one girl offering another an affectionate clasp from behind. These were the kinds of workers rendered faceless and voiceless in the Honolulu *Advertiser*'s observation that 'the [*Yamashiro-maru*] can carry 350 tons of coal in her bunkers, and a further supply of 320 tons for long voyages of about sixteen days'. In fact, if the ship had carried a full load – say, for a crossing to Hawai'i – then it would have taken a group of fifty stevedores, hauling at a load of between

[97] 'Loading Women', photographer and date unknown, Nagasaki University Library Collection, 'Japanese Old Photographs in Bakumatsu-Meiji Period', http://oldphoto.lb.nagasaki-u.ac.jp/top/en_top.php, catalogue number 7081 (last accessed 15 July 2021).

twenty-five and thirty-five tons an hour, approximately eleven hours to render the ship capable of carrying 670 tons in its bunkers.[98]

But the carrying is not complete. As the ship prepares to depart, a team of passers (also known as trimmers) must manoeuvre the coal by wheelbarrow from bunker to furnace – a job that could be dangerous in high seas and, due to the necessity of bringing fuel from the ship's more distant bunkers, increasingly difficult the longer the journey lasted. Only now can the engine be fired – and that is where the firemen took centre stage.

'The importance of skilful firemen cannot be too much insisted upon,' British civil engineer Robert Murray wrote in his grippingly entitled *Rudimentary Treatise on Marine Engines and Steam Vessels; Together With Practical Remarks on the Screw and Propelling Power as Used in the Royal and Merchant Navy* (3rd edn, 1858). He continued: 'It is a great mistake to suppose, as too many captains and owners of steam vessels do, that any able-bodied man who can throw coals on a fire is fit for a stoker'. This was because 'ignorance of the despised art of stoking' could lead to as much as one quarter of a ship's fuel being discarded during a journey. The skilled and conscientious fireman in fact had to consider the weight of coal upon each square foot of grate surface per hour; the frequency of when to stoke and when to open the furnace door to check (for to open the doors and let in cold air was to hinder the steady generation of steam); the state of the fire from its colour; the even spread of coal upon the grate; the need to break up 'very bituminous coal [...] owing to the tendency of such coal to cake upon the bars, and thus prevent the passage of air through them'; and the importance of cleaning the fires after each watch, including clearing ashes and collecting cinders to be re-burned.[99] In short, many of the calorific and smoke-related benefits offered by a ton of Best Welsh over, say, a ton of Karatsu coal would go to waste if the firemen did their job badly.

In the previous chapter, I introduced the seaman Katō Hisakatsu, who began his career in February 1897 as a deckhand on the 850-ton *Koto'omaru*, sailing from Yokohama to Karatsu to pick up coal, and who in retirement penned several books about his experiences at sea. In one

---

[98] For this loading calculation, see Phipps, *Empires on the Waterfront*, p. 172.
[99] Robert Murray, C. E., *Rudimentary Treatise on Marine Engines and Steam Vessels; Together with Practical Remarks on the Screw and Propelling Power as Used in the Royal and Merchant Navy*, 3rd edn (London: John Weale, 1858), pp. 49–53 (quotations on pp. 50 and 51 respectively). Digitized by HathiTrust Digital Library, www.hathitrust.org (last accessed 18 July 2021). See also Alston Kennerley, 'Stoking the Boilers: Firemen and Trimmers in British Merchant Ships, 1850–1950', *International Journal of Maritime History* 20, 1 (2008): 191–220.

collection of reminiscences, he described the work of the firemen and passers:

All day and night, their bodies discoloured by soot and sweat and oil until they resemble bronze Buddhas, they run to-and-fro like squirrels in the coal holds. In the eyes of the ladies and gentlemen strolling with easy-sounding footsteps on the upper deck, these are the men – 'Golly, the crew!' – barely regarded as humans. They work in a world of darkness never visited by the sun, a place where the mouldy black air drifts constantly and thickly, where both clouds of fine coal powder and tepid airs or hot winds begin to blow in all directions after grazing your body, where with the sound of a dripping tap you sweat black ink and feel as if lukewarm water is washing over your skin; they work in the depths of a fiery hell. And their work, continuing to carry coal with the loyalty of an army of ants – the coal that drives the power, the power that drives the ship – this job is truly the most invaluable on the whole ship.[100]

As with his graphic descriptions of women stowed away on ships from Japan to Southeast Asia, there is more than a hint of late-night yarn in Katō's characterization of 'bronze Buddhas' (*kanabutsu-sama* 金佛さま). The everyday, all-day realm of the firemen was very much of the here and now, not the enlightened afterlife – although, as Frances Steel has observed, there was also a 'startling rate' of suicides among steamship firemen, attributed by contemporaries to 'a kind of heat insanity'.[101]

Like the 'ghost workers' who power today's internet, who at some level have made it possible for me to read Robert Murray's *Rudimentary Treatise* online, the firemen and the passers described by Katō were 'the unseen workers of the steam age'.[102] I cannot see or name the person who digitized Murray. But I do know the names of the *Yamashiro-maru*'s firemen and passers in August 1898, when the ship deposited 100 sugar labourers at Port Douglas. They are only single-line entries in a Burns, Philp & Co crew list (itself also anonymously digitized) – but perhaps they go some way towards counterbalancing the weight this chapter has ascribed to Yasukawa Keiichirō's one-line diary entry:

T. Akushi	38 (age)	Fireman
S. Katayama	20	Fireman
S. Naito	24	Fireman

[100] Katō Hisakatsu 加藤久勝, *Madorosu yawa* マドロス夜話 [A sailor's night tales] (Tokyo: Shōkōdō shobō, 1931), p. 20. For details on the *Koto'o-maru*, see pp. 23–7.
[101] Frances Steel, *Oceania under Steam: Sea Transport and the Cultures of Colonialism, c. 1870–1914* (Manchester: Manchester University Press, 2011), p. 83.
[102] Steel, *Oceania under Steam*, p. 77; Mary L. Gray and Siddharth Suri, *Ghost Work: How to Stop Silicon Valley from Building a New Global Underclass* (Boston, MA: Houghton Mifflin Harcourt, 2019); cf. also Hecht on the 'invisibility' of uranium labourers: Hecht, *Being Nuclear*, pp. 183–212.

K. Fujino	24	Fireman
T. Aoki	32	Fireman
H. Ifuji	29	Fireman
S. Takisa	26	Fireman
S. Kashiwabara	26	Fireman
N. Utsu	22	Fireman
T. Tamaki	21	Fireman
T. Ishii	25	Fireman
K. Koyoshi	20	Fireman
M. Hisakata	23	Coal Passer
Y. Nakao	25	Coal Passer
T. Honda	21	Coal Passer
H. Nabeoka	25	Coal Passer
K. Yoshida	27	Coal Passer
H. Matsuo	21	Coal Passer
B. Takahashi	31	Coal Passer
K. Zaima	21	Coal Passer
D. Nematsu	19	Coal Passer
J. Kawagoi	21	Coal Passer Apprentice[103]

Mining

In John Oliver's words, coal is 'basically cocaine for Thomas the Tank Engine'.[104] It's a funny and appropriate analogy, speaking as it does to some of the histories of labour exploitation, consumer addiction, international commerce and supply logistics which I have touched upon in this chapter. Historians' figures of speech, by contrast, are far more earnest. From our apparently extraordinary repertoire of practical skills, we *map*, we *sketch*, we *navigate* (all of which I have done over the course of this book) – and we also *mine*. The Italian archives, wrote Carlo Ginzburg and Carlo Poni in the late 1970s, are 'precious deposits of primary materials, in large part never mined'.[105] 'Students of the colonial experience "mine" the *content* of government commissions and reports,' Ann Laura Stoler has observed, conscious of the extractive metaphor,

---

[103] Burns, Philp & Co, 'A List of the Crew and Passengers arrived in the Steamship *Yamashiro Maru* [...] from the Port of Japan via Brisbane to Sydney, New South Wales, 19 8 1898 (Inward)', digitized by www.ancestry.com (last accessed 24 October 2013). I have been unable confidently to decipher the first letter of the surname, 'Zaima'.

[104] 'Coal: Last Week Tonight with John Oliver (HBO)', 19 June 2017, www.youtube.com/watch?v=aw6RsUhw1Q8 (last accessed 17 July 2021).

[105] Carlo Ginzburg and Carlo Poni, 'The Name and the Game: Unequal Exchange and the Historiographic Marketplace', in Edward Muir and Guido Ruggiero, eds., *Microhistory and the Lost Peoples of Europe*, trans. Eren Branch (Baltimore, MD: Johns Hopkins University Press, 1991 [1979]), pp. 1–10, here p. 2.

'but rarely attend to their peculiar *form* or *context*'.[106] By contrast, Allan Sekula warns that '[a]rchives are not like coal mines: meaning is not extracted from nature, but from culture'.[107]

In tracing the journey of a piece of coal to its burned-up conclusion, this chapter has experimented with turning figures of speech literal, such that the coal mine exists not *like* the archive but *as* the archive. What is the value, intellectual if not calorific, of such an experiment?

The first point is that my focus on the particular pitheads of the Karatsu coalfield highlights the contingency even of deep histories of the earth. This is exactly the argument that natural scientists advanced in the eighteenth century as they began to apply the language of archives to the study of fossils.[108] 'Contingency' might feel like an awkward term to describe change across tens of millions of years – at least for scholars whose training in the discipline of history habituates them to think in units of decades or at most a couple of centuries. The contingencies I have discussed in this book, for example, concern themselves with why economic contraction in a particular decade may have led young men to board a Hawai'i-bound steamship a few years later, or how a young woman was diverted from travelling to Singapore by dint of being 'kidnapped' in Hong Kong. That said, it does matter to the human histories I reconstructed in this chapter that the formation of fossil fuels in today's Kyushu, contingent as it partly was on the climatic conditions of the Oligocene Epoch, led to a carbon composition in Karatsu coal which was more than adequate for the onboard requirements of steamship engines. It matters that the stratigraphic profile of Karatsu was such that, as the demand for coal grew in Japan in the second half of the nineteenth century, it could be extracted without vertical mining technologies. And it matters that Karatsu coal in particular – as opposed to that in Chikuhō – was located serendipitously close to navigable waterways, such that the fuel could be quickly transported to market. In short, if the earth is this chapter's archive, then its exact geographical location and stratigraphic composition, or its *context* and *form*, fundamentally shape the history it can tell – in Karatsu no less than in the archival collections I have discussed in Honolulu or Brisbane. The matter of coal, to paraphrase Timothy J. LeCain, has played an essential role in the human

---

[106] Ann Laura Stoler, 'Colonial Archives and the Arts of Governance', *Archival Science* 2 (1–2) (2002): 87–109, here p. 90 (emphasis in the original).

[107] Sekula, 'Reading an Archive', p. 445. Historians using digital methodologies also text mine: for a reflective consideration, see Christian Henriot, 'Rethinking Historical Research in the Age of NLP', *Elites, Networks and Power in Modern China* blog, https://enepchina.hypotheses.org/3275, 21 May 2020 (last accessed 23 July 2021).

[108] Sepkoski, 'Earth as Archive', pp. 57–60.

history this chapter has covered – and coal's deep history offers new material contexts to the analyses of Japanese overseas migration that scholars have undertaken to date.[109]

The contingent question of where and what kind of coal was to be found in nineteenth-century East Asia also invites historians to reconsider one of the most contentious historiographical debates of the early twenty-first century, namely why 'Europe' industrialized at an exponentially greater intensity after 1800 than 'China'. One reason, Kenneth Pomeranz advanced in *The Great Divergence* (2000), concerned the ways in which British coal consumption reduced demographic and resource pressure on the land. This, in turn, could be explained by the relative proximity of northern coalfields to British centres of industrialization. By contrast, in Qing China, major coal deposits in the north and north-west were sufficiently distant from the proto-industrializing Lower Yangzi region for technological advancements analogous to those in British industries to remain unsupported by steam engines. Thus, in terms of coal consumption, 'Europe's advantage rested as much on geographic accident as on overall levels of technical skill'.[110]

The evidence in this chapter suggests that 'geography' is somewhat of a misnomer when talking about Karatsu – at least if defined in terms of nation-state units. On the one hand, the location of the Karatsu coalfield, and especially its riverine access, facilitated regional industrial development prior to the arrival of Commodore Perry, in particular the development of the salt industry in northern Kyushu and the western Inland Sea. That this did not lead to accelerated economic growth comparable to that of nineteenth-century north-western Europe thus suggests that other 'divergence' factors were more important than geographical accident, including the sufficiency of wood as a source of fuel (thanks to Tokugawa afforestation policies). On the other hand, Pomeranz's postulation of a relationship between coal mine location and economic growth is more convincing when we consider the extent to which Japanese coal – especially Kyushu coal – was exported to Shanghai, Hong Kong and Singapore in the late nineteenth century. Here, however, it is more useful to think about East Asian rather than Japanese economic growth per se. In other words, be it for Karatsu coal's contribution to regional economic growth *within* Japan prior to 1850 or for its contribution to regional industrialization *beyond* Japan after 1850, the story of coal mining

---

[109] LeCain, *Matter of History*, p. 11.
[110] Kenneth Pomeranz, *The Great Divergence: China, Europe, and the Making of the Modern World Economy* (Princeton, NJ: Princeton University Press, 2000), pp. 59–68, citation from p. 62.

I have sketched in this chapter is not one that necessarily aligns with the polity of 'Japan' across the nineteenth century.[111]

My second observation departs from Siebold, the man whose writings were directly or indirectly referenced so often in the Euro-American imagination of Japanese coal 'abundance'. Following David Sepkoski's notation, I have assumed that what Siebold described was the 'original' archive of the earth – that is, archive$_0$. In fact, however, his access to that archive was restricted by his 'guides' (or minders): what he saw was already shaped by human hands, both in terms of the samples brought up from below sixty steps, and in terms of the mine shaft, which literally tunnelled his vision of the stratigraphic record. In this sense, and to return to Sekula, the coal mine *is* like the archive, because the fossil documentation therein is not unmediated – just as the materials a historian calls up from an archive's stacks are never an 'unprocessed historical record'.[112] This is important because it calls into question Sekula's unwritten assumption – at least in the previous citation – that the coal mines are 'nature' while the archive is 'culture'. Rather, as William Cronon argues from his study of the copper mines in Kennecott (Alaska), '[t]he special task of environmental historians is to tell stories that carry us back and forth across the boundary between people and nature to reveal just how culturally constructed that boundary is – and how dependent upon natural systems it remains'.[113] There *was* a natural coal system at some point in Karatsu's history, as formed in the millions of years between the Oligocene and the Holocene. But whether it is useful for historians to apply a language of 'archive' to this natural record is a different question. Given the extent to which I have argued in this book that archives are (human) constructions, it would seem that Karatsu may only usefully be considered an archive *after* curious farmers started clearing, burrowing, digging and extracting from its hillsides. Perhaps, therefore, there is no such thing as an archive$_0$, and historians

---

[111] For understanding the applicability of the 'Great Divergence' to Japanese economic history, see Penelope Francks, *Japan and the Great Divergence: A Short Guide* (London: Palgrave Macmillan, 2016). For using 'Japan' to think through some of the Great Divergence debates, see Julia Adeney Thomas, 'Reclaiming Ground: Japan's Great Convergence', *Japanese Studies* 34, 3 (2014): 253–63.
[112] *Pace* Hayden White: 'I take "chronicle" and "story" to refer to "primitive elements" in the *historical account*, but both represent processes of selection and arrangement of data from the *unprocessed historical record* in the interest of rendering that record more comprehensible to an *audience* of a particular kind.' See Hayden White, *Metahistory: The Historical Imagination in Nineteenth-Century Europe* (Baltimore, MD: Johns Hopkins University Press, 1973), p. 5.
[113] Cronon, 'Kennecott Journey', p. 33.

need a different vocabulary by which to conceptualize the earth's prehuman record.

My final point is axiomatic but bears repeating. Along with the railways and the telegraph, steamships were one mechanism by which the world was commonly imagined to be shrinking in the late nineteenth century, with time and space allegedly 'annihilated' by ever faster transits.[114] (Remember: 'Our steamships can go from California to Japan in eighteen days.') But if steam engines were one catalyst of this transformation, then any study of the 'great mineral agent of civilization' which fuelled the engines requires historians, conversely, to *expand* our temporal units of analysis – from days to millions of years. How to 'cross-hatch' these multiple imaginations of time, or of agency, raises a separate problem of narrative structure. My slowing down of the coal's journey from bowels to bunkers has been one attempt to indicate non-linear temporalities in this story, even as I have tried to rebraid what Sekula so persuasively calls the steamship's tethering line back to the earth.

As with some of the other interventions I have tried to make in *Mooring the Global Archive*, these points can be loosely tethered to Kodama Keijirō's gravestone. Marking Kodama's arrival in 'Hawaii Nei' in June 1885 and his death in Meiji XXIX (1896), the inscription posited four temporal regimes I have already discussed: Japanese imperial time, Gregorian time, international time and of course Kodama's own lifetime. But there was a fifth regime inherent in the numerals '1885' and '1896' – not Gregorian time per se but *Christian* time. Indeed, *Anno Domini* referred to more than God's human incarnation. For many believers well into the nineteenth century, Christian time was synonymous with *world* time (*Anno Mundi*): in particular, with James Ussher's (1581–1656) theory that the Creation had occurred 'upon the entrance of the night preceding the twenty-third day of October' in the year 4004 BCE.[115] In 1885, however, Ussher's claim was cut from the margins of the Revised Version of the King James Bible. In the same year, the International Geological Congress met in Bologna to debate the proposition that the epoch of the 'entirely recent' be termed the Holocene, thereby continuing the revolution in understandings of planetary time which disciplines

---

[114] Yrjö Kaukiainen, 'Shrinking the World'; Wolfgang Schivelbusch, 'Railroad Space and Railroad Time', *New German Critique* 14 (1978): 31–40. For an important recent critique of 'annihilation' as an analytical language for understanding social histories of space, see Alexis D. Litvine, 'The Annihilation of Space: A Bad (Historical) Concept', *Historical Journal* 65 (2022): 871–900.

[115] McPhee, *Annals of the Former World*, p. 70.

such as geology and paleontology had already started.[116] Seen in this light, the notation '1885' on Kodama's gravestone is a subtle invitation for historians to consider his life, and global migrations more generally, in terms of expanded temporalities: to acknowledge that histories of geographical breadth must also entail material depth.[117]

---

[116] Rudwick, *Earth's Deep History*, p. 17; Simon L. Lewis and Mark A. Maslin, 'Defining the Anthropocene', *Nature* 519 (2015): 171–80, here pp. 172–3.

[117] In this sense, my approach in this chapter has encapsulated the so-called volumetric turn in history: Franck Billé, 'Volumetric Sovereignty: Introduction', *Society & Space* (2019), accessible at www.societyandspace.org/forums/volumetric-sovereignty (last accessed 30 June 2022).

Epilogue

Mooring the Global Archive has highlighted what kinds of histories can be heard when divergent archival contexts and epistemologies are brought into conversation with one other. Through archival dialogue, for example, we can better understand both the complex factors which drove young Japanese women to travel to Southeast Asia and Australia in the late nineteenth century, and the agendas of the state and non-state actors who attempted to frame those women's voices. We can better picture the often nameless and faceless labourers who powered the coal revolution in East Asia or the sugar revolution in Hawai'i. We have a better sense of why those Japanese who worked overseas did so, and the ways they conceived of the world – in song, in deed, and in their posthumous inscriptions.

These empirical insights in turn offer new historiographical interventions. Most prosaically, although no less important for that, I hope that it will no longer be viable to publish surveys of modern Japan with little more than a passing mention of overseas migration. The histories of Kodama Keijirō, Wakamiya Yaichi, Fuyuki Sakazō, Hasegawa Setsutarō, Hashimoto Usa and even the Matsuura river boatman Kōshichi speak to a different historiographical imagination of Meiji Japan's 'world' than a traditional focus on high diplomacy, trade or elite cultural entanglements. Their mobilities across different bodies of water delineated a set of spaces in and between the archives that offer scholars new ways of thinking about issues of gender, labour, social exclusion, Indigenous rights and resource extraction. For example, I have suggested some ways in which historians might study the economics and politics of settler colonialism far away from the actual site of Indigenous-settler encounters, thereby broadening our designation of 'colonial' archives to include not just the Diplomatic Archives in Tokyo but also haphazardly preserved records in rural Japan. I have pointed out how historians trained in epistemologies derived from nineteenth-century Europe, including in the discipline of history itself, could productively reimagine the 'global' through learning Indigenous epistemologies and languages.

Indeed, my reading of archival materiality along and against the grain of digitization complements a recent call for 'slow' archival engagement as a way of foregrounding Indigenous understandings of time and space.[1] The identification of new interfaces between 'global' and 'Indigenous' historiographies is, in my view, one of the most exciting trends in contemporary scholarship – as is the possibility for new research questions in global history to emerge from Indigenous Studies methodologies.

While my empirical mooring has limited me to discussing the history primarily of Japanese people on the move, I hope that the arguments in this book can also be adapted to other arenas and other historiographical debates. In particular, I would like to think that this experiment in offering the reader what Marc Bloch called 'the sight of an investigation, with its successes and reverses', begins to shift the burden of investigative proof away from an avoidance of self-reflection towards a greater acknowledgement of authorial metadata in the writing of history.[2] It has long been an article of faith – certainly during my own training in Britain and still in many history departments in the Germanic world – that, in the words of Keith Thomas, '[i]t never helps historians to say too much about their working methods'. Offering an analogy pregnant with meaning from his own illustrious scholarship, Thomas continues: 'For just as the conjuror's magic disappears if the audience knows how the trick is done, so the credibility of scholars can be sharply diminished if readers learn everything about how exactly their books came to be written.'[3] This acceptance that there should be, on the one hand, members of a guilded elite who know each other's tricks and then, on the other, passive consumers of history, reinforces a long-standing epistemological divide – one paralleled in colonial settings – between knowledge producers and knowledge recipients.[4] Partly to encourage more transparent conversations between practitioners of history from diverse knowledge backgrounds, *Mooring the Global Archive* proposes

---

[1] Kimberly Christen and Jane Anderson, 'Toward Slow Archives', *Archival Science* 19 (2019): 87–116. On how digitization must avoid exacerbating traumas arising from the colonial archive, see Temi Odumosu, 'The Crying Child: On Colonial Archives, Digitization, and Ethics of Care in the Cultural Commons', *Current Anthropology* 61, Supplement 22 (October 2020): 289–302.

[2] On Bloch, see the Preface.

[3] Keith Thomas, 'Working Methods', *London Review of Books* 32, 11 (10 June 2010), available to subscribers on www.lrb.co.uk (last accessed 17 June 2021). Marina Rustow evokes a similar metaphor of performer(s) and audience when she argues (contrary to Thomas) for breaking down the 'fourth wall' between the two: Rustow, *The Lost Archive: Traces of a Caliphate in a Cairo Synagogue* (Princeton, NJ: Princeton University Press, 2020), p. 12.

[4] For one critique of colonial knowledge produced as if to deny positionality, see Chang, *World and All the Things upon It*, especially pp. 103–55.

Epilogue   269

the opposite to the conjuror's tricks: the book's gauntlet is for scholars groping their way towards a better understanding of the 'global' in history to prove that *not* discussing their archival methodologies is intellectually defensible. I would prefer for our default mode to be one in which the absence of authorial metadata diminishes scholarly credibility; or, formulated less negatively, for the acknowledged situatedness of our knowledge production to enrich the potency – even the objectiveness – of our historical analysis.[5] If the investigation is to be in sight, then so should be the sites of investigation.

Throughout *Mooring the Global Archive*, the ship has served as a model for such siting. For a couple of years between 2016 and 2018, as I settled into a new job in Zurich and tried, for the umpteenth time, to work out what this book was actually about, I would pop into the Johann Jacobs Museum and visit the model of the *Yamashiro-maru* for some form of inspiration. But this was also an archival trap of sorts. As I slowly came to realise, the model ship no less than the museum bound me to a set of European epistemologies encompassing the practice of history in particular and the production of scientific knowledge more generally.[6] And the miniature on display drew me all too easily into a set of European literary associations: on the relationship between ships and thought, ships and books, or – closer to home – ships and fools.[7]

Perhaps that particular vessel has sailed its course. Some fifteen years after I first had the idea to write about the *Yamashiro-maru*, it may be time to scrap the metaphor of the ship-shaped archive. For as I finish this project, I find I am gravitating towards a different set of metaphors: a language of *waves*, and how they might speak to the physical materiality and violence of colonial encounters in history;[8] and a language of *shoals*. Indeed, in words which are applicable to what I see as the opportunities

---

[5] '[I]t is precisely in the politics and epistemology of *partial* perspectives that the possibility of sustained, rational, objective inquiry rests': Haraway, 'Situated Knowledges', p. 584 (emphasis added).

[6] On the historian's insistence that theoretical models must be contingent, and float 'like a ship on the waters of a particular time', see Fernand Braudel, 'Unity and Diversity in the Human Sciences', in *On History*, trans. Sarah Matthews (Chicago: University of Chicago Press, 1980 [1960]), pp. 55–63, here p. 60. On models and practices of natural science in eighteenth-century Britain, see Simon Schaffer, 'Fish and Ships: Models in the Age of Reason', in Soraya De Chadarevian and Nick Hopwood, eds., *Models: The Third Dimension of Science* (Stanford, CA: Stanford University Press, 2004), pp. 71–105.

[7] E.g. Wintroub, *Voyage of Thought*. Cf. also 'Books are the anchors / Left by the ships that rot away': Clive James, *The River in the Sky* (London: Picador, 2018), p. 3; Michel Foucault, *Madness and Civilization: A History of Insanity in the Age of Reason*, trans. Jonathan Murphy and Jean Khalfa (London: Routledge, 2006 [1961]), pp. 5–10.

[8] Sujit Sivasundaram, *Waves across the South: A New History of Revolution and Empire* (London: William Collins, 2020).

presented by global history, Tiffany Lethabo King has noted that 'as an in-between, ecotonal, unexpected, and shifting space, the shoal requires new footing, different chords of embodied rhythms, and new conceptual tools to navigate its terrain'.[9] I am interested in the brackishness arising from such unexpected archival spaces, in knowledge stirred and unsettled. In a discipline still belatedly coming to terms with its colonial sites and sights, perhaps these processes of un-settling are what historians should aim for in our analyses of the global and the archival.

[9] Tiffany Lethabo King, *The Black Shoals: Offshore Formations of Black and Native Studies* (Durham, NC: Duke University Press, 2019), p. 4.

Bibliography

Abbreviations

AS	*Asahi shinbun* 朝日新聞 newspaper; accessed digitally through Kikuzo II Visual (https://database.asahi.com/help/jpn/about.html) (subscription)
BC	*Brisbane Courier* newspaper; accessed through National Library of Australia Trove (https://trove.nla.gov.au)
DA	Gaikō shiryōkan 外交資料館 [Diplomatic Archives of the Ministry of Foreign Affairs, Japan] (Tokyo)
HG	*Hawaiian Gazette* newspaper; accessed first in microfilm and then through https://chroniclingamerica.loc.gov.
HN	*Hiogo News* newspaper (Kobe); accessed in paper form
HSA	Hawai'i State Archives (Honolulu)
HSPA	Hawaiian Sugar Planters' Association Plantation Archives, Hamilton Library, University of Hawai'i-Mānoa (Honolulu)
JACAR	Japan Center for Asian Historical Records (www.jacar.co.jp)
MYM	Murotsu yakuba monjo 室津役場文書 [Murotsu village archives], Kaminoseki town
NGB	*Nihon gaikō bunsho* 日本外交文書 [Records of Japanese diplomacy], multiple volumes, 1867–1941 (www.mofa.go.jp/mofaj/annai/honsho/shiryo/archives/mokuji.html)
PCA	*Daily Pacific Commercial Advertiser*; accessed first in microfilm and then through https://chroniclingamerica.loc.gov.
PM	*Planters' Monthly* (Honolulu) (https://evols.library.manoa.hawaii.edu/handle/10524/1687)
QPD	Hansard: Queensland Parliamentary Debates (www.parliament.qld.gov.au/work-of-assembly/hansard)
QSA	Queensland State Archives (Brisbane)
SMH	*Sydney Morning Herald*; accessed through National Library of Australia Trove (https://trove.nla.gov.au)
YS	*Yomiuri shinbun* 読売新聞 newspaper; accessed digitally through Yomiuri Database Service (https://database.yomiuri.co.jp/) (subscription)

Archives, Museums and Libraries

Australian National Maritime Museum, Sydney
Australian Sugar Heritage Centre, Mourilyan, Queensland
Beamish, The Living Museum of the North, County Durham
Bernice Pauahi Bishop Museum, Honolulu
Brunel's SS Great Britain museums, Bristol
Caird Library and Archive, National Maritime Museum, Greenwich, London
Cairns Historical Society Research Centre, Queensland
Diplomatic Archives of the Ministry of Foreign Affairs of Japan (Gaikō shiryōkan 外交資料館), Tokyo
Hamilton Library, University of Hawai'i-Mānoa, Honolulu
Hawai'i State Archives, Honolulu
Hiroshima Prefectural Library (Hiroshima kenritsu toshokan 広島県立図書館), Hiroshima
Internationales Maritimes Museum Hamburg
Japanese Cultural Center of Hawai'i, Honolulu
Japanese Overseas Migration Museum (Kaigai ijū shiryōkan 海外移住資料館), Yokohama
Johann Jacobs Museum, Zurich
Kaiwomaru Park 海王丸パーク, Toyama prefecture
Kaminoseki Town Office Board of Education (Kaminoseki-chō yakuba kyōiku iinkai 上関町役場教育委員会)
Kobe City Archives (Kōbe-shi bunshokan 神戸市文書館), Kobe
Kumamoto Prefectural Library (Kumamoto kenritsu toshokan 熊本県立図書館), Kumamoto
Legal Affairs Bureau, Ministry of Justice (Japan), Yanai branch (Hōmukyoku Yanai shutchōsho 法務局柳井出張所), Yamaguchi prefecture
Mitsubishi Archives (Mitsubishi shiryōkan 三菱史料館), Tokyo
Mitsui Archives (Mitsui bunko 三井文庫), Tokyo
Mossman Library, Queensland
Museum am Rothenbaum – Kulturen und Künste der Welt (MARKK), previously the Museum für Völkerkunde Hamburg
Museum of Japanese Emigration to Hawai'i (Nihon Hawai imin shiryōkan 日本ハワイ移民資料館), Suō-Ōshima, Yamaguchi prefecture
National Archives of Australia, Brisbane branch
National Archives of Japan (Kokuritsu kōbunshokan 国立公文書館), Tokyo
National Diet Library (Kokuritsu kokkai toshokan 国立国会図書館), Tokyo
National Library of Australia, Canberra
National Library of Singapore
National Museum of Singapore
New Bedford Whaling Museum, Massachusetts
Newcastle City Library (UK)

Noel Butlin Archives Centre, Australian National University, Canberra
NYK Maritime Museum (Nippon Yūsen rekishi hakubutsukan 日本郵船歴史博物館), Yokohama
Queensland State Archives, Brisbane
Research Institute for Economics and Business Administration, Kobe University
Shōtōen museum 松濤園, Kure city, Hiroshima prefecture
State Library of Queensland, Brisbane
Tyne & Wear Archives, Discovery Museum, Newcastle (UK)
Villa of the Minister to the Kingdom of Hawai'i (Hawai ōkoku kōshi bettei ハワイ王国公使別邸), Ikaho town, Gunma prefecture
Yokohama Archives of History (Yokohama kaikō shiryōkan 横浜開港資料館), Yokohama

Databases and Online Resources

Ancestry (www.ancestry.com) (subscription)
Australian Institute of Aboriginal and Torres Strait Islander Studies database (https://collection.aiatsis.gov.au/austlang/about)
British Newspaper Archive, Part I database (www.britishnewspaperarchive.co.uk/) (subscription)
Chronicling America: Historic American Newspapers (https://chroniclingamerica.loc.gov)
'Colonial Frontier Massacres in Australia, 1788–1930' database (https://c21ch.newcastle.edu.au/colonialmassacres/)
Greatorex, John. *Yolngu Matha Dictionary* (2014): (https://yolngudictionary.cdu.edu.au)
Hoji Shinbun Digital Collection: Japanese Diaspora Initiative, Hoover Institution, Stanford University (https://hojishinbun.hoover.org)
Internet Archive (https://archive.org)
Japan Center for Asian Historical Records (www.jacar.archives.go.jp)
National Library of Australia, TROVE (https://trove.nla.gov.au)
NewspaperSG (https://eresources.nlb.gov.sg/newspapers/)
Papakilo Database (www.papakilodatabase.com)
Papers Past (https://paperspast.natlib.govt.nz)
Yamamoto Collection (www.y-sakubei.com/english/mow/index.html)

Historical Periodicals and Newspapers

Please refer to individual footnotes to see whether these newspapers were accessed online or in paper/microfilm form.

Age (Melbourne)
Argus (Melbourne)
Asahi shinbun (朝日新聞)
Auckland Star
Australian Town and Country Journal

Brisbane Courier
Capricornian (Rockhampton)
Daily Bulletin (Honolulu)
Daily Pacific Commercial Advertiser (Honolulu)
Daily Telegraph (Sydney)
Evening News (Sydney)
Evening Post (New York)
Guardian
Hawaiian Gazette
Hiogo News (Kobe)
Honolulu Republican
Honolulu Star
Japan Punch (Yokohama)
Japan Weekly Mail (Yokohama)
Ka Nupepa Kuokoa (Honolulu)
Maitland Weekly Mercury (NSW)
Mercury (Hobart)
Morning Bulletin (Rockhampton, QLD)
Morning Post
Newcastle Daily Journal (UK)
New York Herald
Nippu jiji 日布時事 (Honolulu)
North China Herald (Shanghai)
Northern Territory Times and Gazette
North Queensland Register (Townsville)
Overland Monthly
Pall Mall Gazette
Paradise of the Pacific (Honolulu)
Planters' Monthly (Honolulu)
Queenslander (Brisbane)
Shenbao 申報 (Shanghai)
Shokumin kyōkai hōkoku 殖民協會報告
Singapore Free Press and Mercantile Advertiser (Weekly)
South Australian Register
Sydney Morning Herald
Telegraph (Brisbane)
Tōkyō chigaku kyōkai hōkoku 東京地学協会報告
Townsville Daily Bulletin
Worker (Brisbane)
Yomiuri shinbun 読売新聞

Published Primary Sources

53rd Congress, House of Representatives: Appendix II: Foreign Relations of the United States 1894, Affairs in Hawaii (Washington, DC: United States Government Printing Office, 1895).

Bird, Isabella Lucy. *Unbeaten Tracks in Japan: An Account of Travels in the Interior including Visits to the Aborigines of Yezo and the Shrine of Nikkô and Isé*, Vol. 1 (London: John Murray, 1880).
Braisted, William Reynolds, trans. *Meiroku Zasshi: Journal of the Japanese Enlightenment* (Tokyo: University of Tokyo Press, 1976).
The Chronicle & Directory for China, Japan, Corea, Indo-China, Straits Settlements, Malay States, Siam, Netherlands India, Borneo, The Philippines, &c. for the year 1898 (Hong Kong: Daily Press, 1898). Available through Google Books.
Ethnic Studies Oral History Project. *A Social History of Kona*, Vol. 1 (Honolulu: Ethnic Studies Program, University of Hawaii, Manoa, 1981). Available through the University of Hawai'i Scholar Space: https://hdl.handle.net/10125/29788.
Fujii Shūgorō 藤井秀五郎. *Shin Hawai* 新布哇 [New Hawai'i] (Tokyo: Taiheikan, 1900). Digitized by the National Diet Library, Japan: https://dl.ndl.go.jp/info:ndljp/pid/767370.
Fujita Toshirō 藤田敏郎. *Kaigai zaikin shihanseiki no kaiko* 海外在勤四半世紀の回顧 [Reminiscences of a quarter-century of overseas postings] (Tokyo: Kyōbunkan, 1931).
Fukuzawa Yukichi 福沢諭吉. *Sekai kuni zukushi: Taiyōshū kan no 5, 6* 世界国盡大洋洲巻之五六 [All the countries of the world: The Pacific, Vols 5, 6] (n.p., 1871 [1869]). Digitized by the National Diet Library, Japan: http://dl.ndl.go.jp/info:ndljp/pid/993094.
Hansard: *Queensland Parliamentary Debates* (1893–7).
Harris, Townsend. *The Complete Journal of Townsend Harris: First American Consul General and Minister to Japan* (New York: Japan Society, 1930). Available through the Internet Archive: https://archive.org.
Hiroshima Kenritsu Monjokan 広島県立文書館. *Hiroshima-ken ijūshi: Shiryō-hen* 広島県移住史：資料編 [A migration history of Hiroshima prefecture: Sources] (Hiroshima: Hiroshima-ken, 1991).
Irie Toraji 入江寅次. *Hōjin kaigai hattenshi* 邦人海外発展史 [A history of overseas Japanese development] (Tokyo: Ida shoten, 1942 [1936, 1938]), Vol. 1. Available through the National Diet Library, Japan: https://dl.ndl.go.jp/info:ndljp/pid/1461457.
Japan Directory for the Year 1884 (Yokohama: Japan Gazette, 1884).
Japanese Association of Singapore. *Shingapōru Nihonjin bochi: Shashin to kiroku* シンガポール日本人墓地：写真と記録 [The Singapore Japanese cemetery: Photographs and records] (Singapore: Japanese Association of Singapore, 1993).
Kaempfer, Engelbert. *Kaempfer's Japan: Tokugawa Culture Observed*, trans. and ed. Beatrice M. Bodart-Bailey (Honolulu: University of Hawai'i Press, 1999).
Kansenkyoku dai-sanji nenpō 管船局第三次年報 [Third annual report of the marine bureau] (1884). Available through www.jacar.go.jp (reference code A07062251700).
Katō Hisakatsu 加藤久勝. *Kanpan ni tachite* 甲板に立ちて [From the deck] (Kobe: Kaibundō shoten, 1926).
— *Madorosu yawa* マドロス夜話 [A sailor's night tales] (Tokyo: Shōkōdō shobō, 1931).

Kume, Kunitake. *The Iwakura Embassy 1871–73: A True Account of the Ambassador Extraordinary & Plenipotentiary's Journey of Observation Through the United States of America and Europe*, Vol. 5, trans. Graham Healey and Chushichi Tsuzuki (Richmond: Curzon Press, 2002).

Locke, John. *Two Treatises of Government*, ed. Peter Laslett (Cambridge: Cambridge University Press, 1988).

Mahlmann, John James. *Reminiscences of an Ancient Mariner* (Yokohama: Japan Gazette Printing and Publishing, 1918). Available through the Internet Archive: https://archive.org.

Masuda Takashi 益田孝 and Nagai Minoru 長井実. *Jijo Masuda Takashi-ō den* 自叙益田孝翁伝 [Autobiography of Masuda Takashi, Esq.] (Kanagawa: private publication, 1939).

Mitsubishi gōshi kaisha 三菱合資会社. *Mitsubishi shashi* 三菱社誌 [Mitsubishi company history], Vol. 12 (Tokyo: Mitsubishi, 1980).

Mori Arinori 森有禮. 'Kaika dai-ichiwa' 開化第一話 [First essay on enlightenment], *Meiroku zasshi dai-sangō* (n.d.): unpaginated.

Murray, D. A., Rev. *Inductive English Lessons; Japanese Text*, 3rd edn (Osaka: Osaka kokubunsha, 1892); https://collections.museumsvictoria.com.au/items/1556835.

Murray, Robert, C. E. *Rudimentary Treatise on Marine Engines and Steam Vessels; Together with Practical Remarks on the Screw and Propelling Power as Used in the Royal and Merchant Navy*, 3rd edn. (London: John Weale, 1858). Digitized by HathiTrust Digital Library, www.hathitrust.org.

Narrative of Five Youth from the Sandwich Islands: Published by Order of the Agents Appointed to Establish a School for Heathen Youth (New York: J. Seymour, 1816), p. 30. Downloadable from the HathiTrust Digital Library, www.hathitrust.org.

Nihon gaikō bunsho 日本外交文書 [Records of Japanese diplomacy], multiple volumes (1867–1941). Available online, www.mofa.go.jp/mofaj/annai/honsho/shiryo/archives/mokuji.html.

Nihon Kei'eishi Kenkyūjo 日本経営史研究所, ed. *Nippon Yūsen Hyakunenshi: Shiryō* 日本郵船百年史：資料 [The NYK centennial: Documents] (Tokyo: Nippon yūsen, 1988).

Nippon Yusen Kaisha. *Golden Jubilee History of Nippon Yusen Kaisha* (Tokyo: Nippon Yusen Kaisha, 1935).

Ōtsuka Takematsu 大塚武松, ed. *Kengai shisetsu nikki sanshū* 遣外使節日記纂輯 [The diary collections of overseas embassies] (Tokyo: Nihon shiseki kyōkai, 1928).

Perry, Matthew Calbraith. *Narrative of the Expedition of an American Squadron to the China Seas and Japan, Performed in the Years 1852, 1853, and 1854, under the Command of Commodore M. C. Perry, United States Navy, by Order of the Government of the United States*. Compiled from the original notes and journals of Commodore Perry and his Officers, at his request, and under his supervision, by Francis L. Hawks, D. D., L. L. D., Washington, DC, Vol. 1, pp. 256–7. Digitized by ETH-Zürich: https://doi.org/10.3931/e-rara-14667.

Shibusawa Eiichi Denki Shiryō Kankōkai 渋沢栄一：伝記資料刊行会. *Shibusawa Eiichi: Denki shiryō daihakkan* 渋沢栄一伝記資料第8巻 [Shibusawa Eiichi: Biographical sources, Vol. 8] (Tokyo: Ryūmonsha, 1956).

Siebold, Philipp Franz von. *Nippon: Archiv zur Beschreibung von Japan und dessen Neben- und Schutzländern Jezo mit den südlichen Kurilen, Sachalin, Korea und den Liukiu-Inseln*, ed. Alexander Freiherr von Siebold and Heinrich Freiherr von Siebold, 2nd edn (Würzburg: KUK Hofbuchhandlung von Leo Woerl, 1897 [1832]), Vol. 1, p. 88. Digitized by the Internet Archive: https://archive.org/details/b29352411_0001.

Verne, Jules. *Around the World in Eighty Days*, trans. George Makepeace Towle (Boston: James R. Osgood, 1873 [1872]). Available through the Internet Archive: https://archive.org.

Yanagita Kunio 柳田国男. *Kokyō shichijū nen* 故郷七十年 [Seventy years of home] (Kobe: Kobe shinbun sōgō shuppan sentā, 2010 [1957]).

Yasukawa Keiichirō 安川敬一郎. *Yasukawa Keiichirō nikki: Daiikkan* 安川敬一郎日記: 第一巻 [Keiichirō Yasukawa's diary: Vol. 1] (Kitakyushu: Kitakyūshū shiritsu shizenshi/rekishi hakubutsukan, 2007).

Secondary Sources

Adler, Jacob. *Claus Spreckels: The Sugar King in Hawaii* (Honolulu: University of Hawai'i Press, 1966).

Affeldt, Stefanie. 'A Paroxysm of Whiteness: "White" Labour, "White" Nation and "White" Sugar in Australia', in Wulf D. Hund, Jeremy Krikler and David Roediger, eds., *Wages of Whiteness and Racist Symbolic Capital* (Berlin: Lit Verlag, 2011), pp. 99–130.

Alexanderson, Kris. *Subversive Seas: Anticolonial Networks across the Twentieth-Century Dutch Empire* (Cambridge: Cambridge University Press, 2019).

Amano Masatoshi 天野雅敏. 'Senzen ni okeru Nihon shōsha no Gōshū shin-shutsu ni tsuite: Kanematsu Shōten to Mitsui Bussan no jirei o chūshin ni shite' 戦前における日本商社の豪州進出について：兼松商店と三井物産の事例を中心にして [Concerning the pre-war advance of Japanese trading firms into Australia: With a focus on the examples of Kanematsu Shōten and Mitsui Bussan], in Andō Sei'ichi 安藤精一, Takashima Masaaki 高嶋雅明, and Amano Masatoshi 天野雅敏, eds., *Kinsei kindai no rekishi to shakai* 近世近代の歴史と社会 [The history and society of the early modern and modern] (Tokyo: Seibundō shuppan, 2009), pp. 260–89.

Ambaras, David R. *Japan's Imperial Underworlds: Intimate Encounters at the Borders of Empire* (Cambridge: Cambridge University Press, 2018).

Amrith, Sunil S. *Crossing the Bay of Bengal: The Furies of Nature and the Fortunes of Migrants* (Cambridge, MA: Harvard University Press, 2013).

Anderson, Christopher and Norman Mitchell. 'Kubara: A Kuku-Yalanji View of the Chinese in North Queensland', *Aboriginal History* 5, 1/2 (1981): 20–37.

Anderson, Clare. *Subaltern Lives: Biographies of Colonialism in the Indian Ocean World, 1790–1920* (Cambridge: Cambridge University Press, 2012).

Araragi Shinzō 蘭信三, ed. *Nihon teikoku o meguru jinkō idō no kokusai shakaigaku* 日本帝国をめぐる人口移動の国際社会学 [An international sociology of population movement in the Japanese empire] (Tokyo: Fuji shuppan, 2008).

Archer, Seth. *Sharks upon the Land: Colonialism, Indigenous Health, and Culture in Hawai'i, 1778–1855* (Cambridge: Cambridge University Press, 2018).

Arista, Noelani. *The Kingdom and the Republic: Sovereign Hawai'i and the Early United States* (Philadelphia: University of Pennsylvania Press, 2019).

Armitage, David. 'John Locke, Carolina, and the *Two Treatises of Government*', *Political Theory* 32, 5 (2004): 602–27.

Ashley, Scott. 'How Navigators Think: The Death of Captain Cook Revisited', *Past & Present* 194, 1 (2007): 107–37.

Ashmore, Paul. 'Slowing Down Mobilities: Passengering on an Inter-war Ocean Liner', *Mobilities* 8, 4 (2013): 595–611.

Azuma, Eiichiro. *In Search of Our Frontier: Japanese America and Settler Colonialism in the Construction of Japan's Borderless Empire* (Berkeley: University of California Press, 2019).

Ballantyne, Tony. 'Mobility, Empire, Colonisation', *History Australia* 11, 2 (2014): 7–37.

Barak, On. 'Outsourcing: Energy and Empire in the Age of Coal, 1820–1911', *International Journal of Middle East Studies* 47, 3 (2015): 425–45.

Barber, Marcus. 'Where the Clouds Stand: Australian Aboriginal Relationships to Water, Place, and the Marine Environment in Blue Mud Bay, Northern Territory', unpublished PhD dissertation, Australian National University (2005).

Bartky, Ian R. *One Time Fits All: The Campaigns for Global Uniformity* (Stanford, CA: Stanford University Press, 2007).

Basalla, George. 'The Spread of Western Science', *Science* 156, 3775 (5 May 1967): 611–22.

Bashford, Alison. 'Terraqueous Histories', *Historical Journal* 60, 2 (2017): 253–72.

Bastos, Cristiana. 'Portuguese in the Cane: The Racialization of Labour in Hawaiian Plantations', in Sofia Aboim, Paulo Granjo and Alice Ramos, eds., *Changing Societies: Legacies and Challenges*, Vol. 1: *Ambiguous Inclusions: Inside Out, Outside In* (Lisbon: Imprensa de Ciências Sociais, 2018), pp. 65–96.

Bayly, C. A. *The Birth of the Modern World, 1780–1914: Global Connections and Comparisons* (Oxford: Blackwell, 2004).

Belich, James, John Darwin and Chris Wickham. 'Introduction: The Prospect of Global History', in James Belich, John Darwin, Margret Frenz and Chris Wickham, eds., *The Prospect of Global History* (Oxford: Oxford University Press, 2016), pp. 1–22.

Bell, Daniel A. 'This Is What Happens When Historians Overuse the Idea of the Network', *New Republic*, 26 October 2013.

Benton, Lauren. *A Search for Sovereignty: Law and Geography in European Empires, 1400–1900* (Cambridge: Cambridge University Press, 2010).

Bernault, Florence. 'Suitcases and the Poetics of Oddities: Writing History from Disorderly Archives', *History in Africa* 42 (2015): 269–77.

Besomi, Daniele. 'Crises as a Disease of the Body Politick: A Metaphor in the History of Nineteenth-Century Economics', *Journal of the History of Economic Thought* 33, 1 (2011): 67–118.

Bhattacharyya, Debjani. *Empire and Ecology in the Bengal Delta: The Making of Calcutta* (Cambridge: Cambridge University Press, 2018).

Bickers, Robert. 'The *Challenger*: Hugh Hamilton Lindsay and the Rise of British Asia, 1832–1865', *Transactions of the RHS* (2012): 141–69.
Billé, Franck. 'Volumetric Sovereignty: Introduction', *Society & Space* (2019). www.societyandspace.org/forums/volumetric-sovereignty
Bloch, Marc. *The Historian's Craft*, trans. Peter Putnam (Manchester: Manchester University Press, 2015 [1949]).
Bojanowska, Edyta M. *A World of Empires: The Russian Voyage of the Frigate Pallada* (Cambridge, MA: Harvard University Press, 2018).
Botsman, Daniel V. 'Freedom without Slavery?: "Coolies", Prostitutes and Outcastes in Meiji Japan's "Emancipation Moment"', *American Historical Review* 116, 5 (2011): 1323–47.
Bottoms, Timothy. *Conspiracy of Silence: Queensland's Frontier Killing Times* (Sydney: Allen & Unwin, 2013).
Boyns, Trevor and Steven Gray. 'Welsh Coal and the Informal Empire in South America, 1850–1913', *Atlantic Studies* 13, 1 (2016): 53–77.
Bradley, Harriet. 'The Seductions of the Archive: Voices Lost and Found', *History of the Human Sciences* 12, 2 (1999): 107–22.
Braudel, Fernand. *The Mediterranean and the Mediterranean World in the Age of Philip II*, trans. Sian Reynolds (London: Harper & Row, 1972 [1966]).
'Unity and Diversity in the Human Sciences', in *On History*, trans. Sarah Matthews (Chicago: University of Chicago Press, 1980), pp. 55–63.
Brooks, Barbara J. *Japan's Imperial Diplomacy: Consuls, Treaty Ports, and War in China, 1895–1938* (Honolulu: University of Hawai'i Press, 2000).
Brown, Laurence. '"A Most Irregular Traffic": The Oceanic Passages of the Melanesian Labor Trade', in Emma Christopher, Cassandra Pybus and Marcus Rediker, eds., *Many Middle Passages: Forced Migration and the Making of the Modern World* (Berkeley: University of California Press, 2007), pp. 184–203.
Brügger, Niels. *The Archived Web: Doing History in the Digital Age* (Cambridge, MA: MIT Press, 2018).
Buku-Ḻarrngay Mulka Centre. *Saltwater: Yirrkala Bark Paintings of Sea Country: Recognising Indigenous Sea Rights* (Neutral Bay, NSW: Jennifer Isaacs Publishing, 2003 [1999]).
Burdon, Peter, Georgina Drew, Matthew Stubbs, Adam Webster and Marcus Barber. 'Decolonising Indigenous Water "Rights" in Australia: Flow, Difference, and the Limits of Law', *Settler Colonial Studies* 5, 4 (2015): 334–49.
Burton, W. Donald. *Coal-Mining Women in Japan: Heavy Burdens* (London: Routledge, 2014).
Caldeira, Leah. 'Visualizing Hoʻoulu Lāhui', in Healoha Johnston, ed., *Hoʻoulu Hawaiʻi: The King Kalākaua Era* (Honolulu: Honolulu Museum of Art, 2018), pp. 11–35.
Carter, Paul. *Dark Writing: Geography, Performance, Design* (Honolulu: University of Hawai'i Press, 2009).
Catton, Eleanor. *The Luminaries* (London: Granta Books, 2013).
Chakrabarty, Dipesh. 'The Climate of History: Four Theses', *Critical Inquiry* 35, 2 (2009): 197–222.

Provincializing Europe: Postcolonial Thought and Historical Difference, 2nd edn (Princeton, NJ: Princeton University Press, 2008 [2000]).

Chan, Shelly. *Diaspora's Homeland: Modern China in the Age of Global Migration* (Durham, NC: Duke University Press, 2018).

Chang, David A. 'Borderlands in a World at Sea: Concow Indians, Native Hawaiians, and South Chinese in Indigenous, Global, and National Spaces', *Journal of American History* 98, 2 (2011): 384–403.

The World and All the Things upon It: Native Hawaiian Geographies of Exploration (Minneapolis: University of Minnesota Press, 2016).

Chapman, David. 'Geographies of Self and Other: Mapping Japan through the *koseki*', *Asia-Pacific Journal*, 9, 29 (18 July 2011), https://apjjf.org/2011/9/29/David-Chapman/3565/article.html.

Chilton, Lisa and Yukari Takai. 'East Coast, West Coast: Using Government Files to Study Immigration History', *Histoire sociale / Social History* 48, 96 (May 2015): 7–23.

Christen, Kimberly and Jane Anderson. 'Toward Slow Archives', *Archival Science* 19 (2019): 87–116.

Christian, David. *Maps of Time: An Introduction to Big History* (Berkeley: University of California Press, 2004).

Christopher, Emma. 'An Illegitimate Offspring: South Sea Islanders, Queensland Sugar, and the Heirs of the British Atlantic Slave Complex', *History Workshop Journal* 90 (2020): 233–52.

Christy, Alan S. *A Discipline on Foot: Inventing Japanese Native Ethnography, 1910–1945* (Lanham, MD: Rowman & Littlefield, 2012).

Clark, Marshall and Sally K. May, eds. *Macassan History and Heritage: Journeys, Encounters and Influences* (Canberra: Australian National University E-Press, 2013).

Cobbing, Andrew. *The Satsuma Students in Britain: Japan's Early Search for the 'Essence of the West'* (Abingdon: Routledge, 2000).

Cobble, Dorothy Sue. 'The Promise and Peril of the New Global Labor History', *International Labor and Working-Class History* 82 (2012): 99–107.

Cohen, Daniel J., Michael Frisch, Patrick Gallagher, Steven Mintz, Kirsten Sword, Amy Murrell Taylor, William G. Thomas III and William J. Turkel. 'Interchange: The Promise of Digital History', *Journal of American History* 95, 2 (2008): 452–91.

Conrad, Joseph. *The Mirror of the Sea*, 10th edn (Edinburgh: Methuen, 1906).

Conrad, Sebastian. 'Enlightenment in Global History: A Historiographical Critique', *American Historical Review* 117, 4 (October 2012): 999–1027.

What Is Global History? (Princeton, NJ: Princeton University Press, 2016).

Conte-Helm, Marie. *Japan and the North East of England: From 1862 to the Present Day* (London: Athlone Press, 1989).

Conway, Rebecca, ed. *Djalkiri: Yolŋu Art, Collaborations and Collections* (Sydney: Sydney University Press, 2021).

Cook, Terry. 'The Archive(s) is a Foreign Country: Historians, Archivists, and the Changing Archival Landscape', *Canadian Historical Review* 90, 3 (September 2009): 497–534.

Cooper, Frederick. *Colonialism in Question: Theory, Knowledge, History* (Berkeley: University of California Press, 2005).
Corbin, Alain. *The Life of an Unknown: The Rediscovered World of a Clog Maker in Nineteenth-Century France*, trans. Arthur Goldhammer (New York: Columbia University Press, 2001 [1998]).
Cothran, Boyd and Adrian Shubert. 'Maritime History, Microhistory, and the Global Nineteenth Century: The *Edwin Fox*', *Global Nineteenth-Century Studies* 1, 1 (2022): 73–80.
Cronon, William. 'Kennecott Journey: The Paths out of Town,' in William Cronon, George Miles and Jay Gitlin, eds., *Under an Open Sky: Rethinking America's Western Past* (New York: Norton, 1992), pp. 28–51.
Crossley, Pamela Kyle. *What Is Global History?* (Cambridge: Polity Press, 2008).
Crymble, Adam. *Technology and the Historian: Transformations in the Digital Age* (Champaign: University of Illinois Press, 2021).
Cushman, Gregory T. *Guano and the Opening of the Pacific World: A Global Ecological History* (Cambridge: Cambridge University Press, 2013).
Daley, Ben and Peter Griggs. 'Mining the Reefs and Cays: Coral, Guano and Rock Phosphate Extraction in the Great Barrier Reef, Australia, 1844–1940', *Environment and History* 12 (2006): 395–433.
Davis, Natalie Zemon. *Fiction in the Archives: Pardon Tales and Their Tellers in Sixteenth-Century France* (Oxford: Polity Press, 1988).
Débarbat, Suzanne and Françoise Launay. 'The 1874 Transit of Venus Observed in Japan by the French, and Associated Relics', *Journal of Astronomical History and Heritage* 9, 2 (2006): 167–71, http://articles.adsabs.harvard.edu//full/2006JAHH...9..167D/0000167.000.html.
Demos, John. *The Unredeemed Captive: A Family Story from Early America* (London: Papermac, 1996).
Dening, Greg. *The Death of William Gooch: A History's Anthropology* (Honolulu: University of Hawai'i Press, 1995).
  Mr Bligh's Bad Language: Passion, Power and Theatre on the Bounty (Cambridge: Cambridge University Press, 1992).
Derrida, Jacques. 'Archive Fever: A Freudian Impression', *Diacritics* 25, 2 (1995): 9–63.
de Vries, Jan. 'The Industrial Revolution and the Industrious Revolution', *Journal of Economic History* 54 (1994): 249–70.
  The Industrious Revolution: Consumer Behaviour and the Household Economy, 1650 to the Present (Cambridge: Cambridge University Press, 2008).
Doan, Natalia. 'The 1860 Japanese Embassy and the Antebellum African American Press', *Historical Journal* 62, 4 (2019): 997–1020.
Doi Yatarō 土井彌太郎. *Yamaguchi-ken Ōshima-gun Hawai iminshi* 山口県大島郡ハワイ移民史 [A history of emigration to Hawai'i from Ōshima county, Yamaguchi prefecture] (Tokyo: Matsuno Shoten, 1980).
Dotulong, Manimporok. 'Hyakushō in the Arafura Zone: Ecologizing the Nineteenth-Century "Opening of Japan"', *Past & Present* 257, 1 (November 2022): 280–317.
Drayton, Richard and David Motadel. 'Discussion: The Futures of Global History', *Journal of Global History* 13, 1 (2018): 1–21.

Dresner, Jonathan. 'Instructions to Emigrant Workers, 1885–1894: "Return in Triumph" or "Wander on the Verge of Starvation"', in Nobuko Adachi, ed., *Japanese Diasporas: Unsung Pasts, Conflicting Presents and Uncertain Futures* (Abingdon: Routledge, 2006), pp. 52–68.

Driscoll, Mark. *Absolute Erotic, Absolute Grotesque: The Living, Dead, and Undead in Japan's Imperialism, 1895–1945* (Durham, NC: Duke University Press, 2010).

Dudden, Alexis, ed. 'Supplement to Special Issue: Academic Integrity at Stake: The Ramseyer Article – Four Letters', *Asia-Pacific Journal: Japan Focus*, 19, 5 (1 March 2021), https://apjjf.org/2021/5/ToC2.html.

Dusinberre, Martin. *Hard Times in the Hometown: A History of Community Survival in Modern Japan* (Honolulu: University of Hawai'i Press, 2012).

'J. R. Seeley and Japan's Pacific Expansion', *Historical Journal* 64, 1 (2021): 70–97.

'Of World History and Great Men: A Japanese Village and Its Worlds', in Tosh Minohara, Tze-ki Hon and Evan Dawley, eds., *The Decade of the Great War: Japan and the Wider World in the 1910s* (Leiden: Brill, 2014), pp. 372–93.

'Unread Relics of a Transnational "Hometown" in Rural Western Japan', *Japan Forum* 20, 3 (2008): 305–35.

'Writing the On-board: Meiji Japan in Transit and Transition', *Journal of Global History* 11, 2 (2016): 271–94.

Dusinberre, Martin and Mariko Iijima. 'Transplantation: Sugar and Imperial Practice in Japan's Pacific', *Historische Anthropologie* 27, 3 (2019): 325–35.

Dusinberre, Martin and Roland Wenzlhuemer. 'Being in Transit: Ships and Global Incompatibilities', *Journal of Global History* 11, 2 (2016): 155–62.

Edgerton, David. *The Shock of the Old: Technology and Global History since 1900* (Oxford: Oxford University Press, 2007).

Edmond, Rod. *Leprosy and Empire: A Medical and Cultural History* (Cambridge: Cambridge University Press, 2006).

Endō, Yasuo. 'The Cultural Geography of the Opening of Japan: The Arrival of Perry's Squadron and the Transformation of Japanese Understanding of the Pacific Ocean during the Edo Period', *Acta Asiatica* 93 (2007): 21–40.

Entman, Robert M. 'Framing: Toward Clarification of a Fractured Paradigm', *Journal of Communication* 43, 4 (1993): 51–8.

Ernst, Wolfgang. 'History or Resonance? Techno-Sonic Tempor(e)alities', *Journal of Visual Culture* 14, 1 (2015): 99–110.

Espeland, Wendy Nelson and Mitchell L. Stevens. 'Commensuration as a Social Process', *Annual Review of Sociology* 24 (1998): 313–43.

Farge, Arlette. *The Allure of the Archives*, trans. Thomas Scott-Railton (New Haven, CT: Yale University Press, 2013).

Fichter, James R. 'Imperial Interdependence on Indochina's Maritime Periphery: France and Coal in Ceylon, Singapore, and Hong Kong, 1859–1895', in James R. Fichter, ed., *British and French Colonialism in Africa, Asia and the Middle East: Connected Empires across the Eighteenth to the Twentieth Centuries* (London: Palgrave Macmillan, 2019), pp. 151–79.

Fickers, Andreas. 'Towards a New Digital Historicism? Doing History in the Age of Abundance', *VIEW Journal of European Television History and Culture* 1, 1 (2012): 19–26, http://doi.org/10.18146/2213-0969.2012.jethc004.
Fischer, John Ryan. *Cattle Colonialism: An Environmental History of the Conquest of California and Hawai'i* (Chapel Hill: University of North Carolina Press, 2015).
Fischer-Tiné, Harald. *Pidgin-Knowledge: Wissen und Kolonialismus* (Zurich: Diaphanes, 2013).
Fogel, Joshua. *Articulating the Sinosphere: Sino-Japanese Relations in Space and Time* (Cambridge, MA: Harvard University Press, 2009).
Maiden Voyage: The Senzaimaru and the Creation of Modern Sino-Japanese Relations (Berkeley: University of California Press, 2014).
Forbes, David. *Encounters with Paradise: Views of Hawaii and Its People, 1778–1941* (Honolulu: University of Hawai'i Press, 1992).
Foucault, Michel. *Archaeology of Knowledge*, trans. A. M. Sheridan Smith (London: Routledge Classics, 1989 [1969]).
Madness and Civilization: A History of Insanity in the Age of Reason, trans. Jonathan Murphy and Jean Khalfa (London: Routledge, 2006 [1961]).
Francks, Penelope. *Japan and the Great Divergence: A Short Guide* (London: Palgrave Macmillan, 2016).
Frawley, Jodi. 'Containing Queensland Prickly Pear: Buffer Zones, Closer Settlement, Whiteness', *Journal of Australian Studies* 38, 2 (2014): 139–56.
Friedrich, Markus. *The Birth of the Archive: A History of Knowledge*, trans. John Noël Dillon (Ann Arbor: University of Michigan Press, 2018 [2013]).
Fujikane, Candace and Jonathan Y. Okamura, eds. *Asian Settler Colonialism: From Local Governance to the Habits of Everyday Life in Hawai'i* (Honolulu: University of Hawai'i Press, 2008).
Fukui Haruhiro, Okudaira Yasuhiro, Arthur Stockwin, Watanabe Akio and John Welfield. 'Reflections and Engagements', in Arthur Stockwin and Keiko Tamura, eds., *Bridging Australia and Japan*, Vol. 1: *The Writings of David Sissons, Historian and Political Scientist* (Acton, ACT: Australian National University Press, 2016), pp. 5–40.
Fullilove, Courtney. 'Gift and Gunboat: Meanings of Exchange in the Perry Expedition', *Diplomatic History* 42, 1 (2018): 90–108.
Gänger, Stefanie. 'Circulation: Reflections on Circularity, Entity, and Liquidity in the Language of Global History', *Journal of Global History* 12, 3 (2017): 303–18.
Ganter, Regina. 'Remembering Muslim Histories of Australia', *La Trobe Journal* 89 (2012): 48–62.
'Turning the Map Upside Down', *History Compass* 4, 1 (2006): 26–35.
Garon, Sheldon. *Molding Japanese Minds: The State in Everyday Life* (Princeton, NJ: Princeton University Press, 1997).
Ghobrial, John-Paul A. 'Introduction: Seeing the World like a Microhistorian', *Past & Present* 242, Supplement 14 (2019): 1–22.
'Moving Stories and What They Tell Us: Early Modern Mobility Between Microhistory and Global History', *Past & Present* 242, Supplement 14 (2019): 243–80.

Gibbs, Fred and Trevor Owens. 'The Hermeneutics of Data and Historical Writing', in Jack Dougherty and Kristen Nawrotzki, eds., *Writing History in the Digital Age* (Ann Arbor: University of Michigan Press, 2013), pp. 159–70.

Gillis, John R. *Islands of the Mind: How the Human Imagination Created the Atlantic World* (New York: Palgrave Macmillan, 2004).

Ginzburg, Carlo. 'Our Words, and Theirs: A Reflection on the Historian's Craft, Today,' in Susanna Fellman and Marjatta Rahikainen, eds., *Historical Knowledge: In Quest of Theory, Method, and Evidence* (Newcastle: Cambridge Scholars Publishing, 2012), 97–119.

Ginzburg, Carlo and Carlo Poni. 'The Name and the Game: Unequal Exchange and the Historiographic Marketplace', in Edward Muir and Guido Ruggiero, eds., *Microhistory and the Lost Peoples of Europe*, trans. Eren Branch (Baltimore, MD: Johns Hopkins University Press, 1991), pp. 1–10.

Godsen, Chris and Yvonne Marshall. 'The Cultural Biography of Objects', *World Archaeology* 31, 2 (1999): 169–78.

Goebel, Michael. 'Ghostly Helpmate: Digitization and Global History', *Geschichte und Gesellschaft* 47 (2021): 35–57.

Gordon, Andrew. *A Modern History of Japan: From Tokugawa Times to the Present*, 3rd edn (Oxford: Oxford University Press, 2014).

Gray, Steven. *Steam Power and Sea Power: Coal, The Royal Navy, and the British Empire, c. 1870–1914* (London: Palgrave Macmillan, 2018).

Griggs, Peter D. *Global Industry, Local Innovation: The History of Cane Sugar Production in Australia, 1820–1995* (Bern: Peter Lang, 2011).

Guterl, Matthew Pratt. 'After Slavery: Asian Labor, the American South, and the Age of Emancipation', *Journal of World History* 14, 2 (2003): 209–41.

Hacking, Ian. 'Making Up People', *London Review of Books* 28, 16 (17 August 2006): 23–6.

Hall, Ivan Parker. *Mori Arinori* (Cambridge, MA: Harvard University Press, 1973).

Hammond, Joyce D. 'Hawaiian Flag Quilts: Multivalent Symbols of a Hawaiian Quilt Tradition', *Hawaiian Journal of History* 27 (1993): 1–26.

Haneda Masashi 羽田正. *Atarashii sekaishi e: Chikyū shimin no tame no kōsō* 新しい世界史へ：地球市民のための構想 [Towards a new world history: Making citizens of the earth] (Tokyo: Iwanami shoten, 2014).

Hanlon, David L. *Upon a Stone Altar: A History of the Island of Pohnpei to 1890* (Honolulu: University of Hawai'i Press, 1988).

Haraway, Donna. 'Situated Knowledges: The Science Question in Feminism and the Privilege of Partial Perspective', *Feminist Studies* 14, 3 (1988): 575–99.

Harms, Robert. *The Diligent: A Voyage through the Worlds of the Slave Trade* (New York: Basic Books, 2000).

Harrell, Paula. *Sowing the Seeds of Change: Chinese Students, Japanese Teachers, 1895–1905* (Stanford, CA: Stanford University Press, 1992).

Hart, Douglas. 'Sociability and "Separate Spheres" on the North Atlantic: The Interior Architecture of British Atlantic Liners, 1840–1930', *Journal of Social History* 44, 1 (2010): 189–212.

Hatsukaichi-chō 廿日市町, ed. *Hatsukaichi chōshi* 廿日市町史 [Hatsukaichi town history] (Hiroshima: Hatsukaichi-chō, 1988).

Hayami, Akira. *Japan's Industrious Revolution: Economic and Social Transformations in the Early Modern Period* (London: Springer, 2015).

Heald, Henrietta. *William Armstrong: Magician of the North* (Newcastle upon Tyne: Northumbria Press, 2010).

Hecht, Gabrielle. *Being Nuclear: Africans and the Global Uranium Trade* (Cambridge, MA: MIT Press, 2012).

Heere, Cees. *Empire Ascendant: The British World, Race, and the Rise of Japan, 1894–1914* (Oxford: Oxford University Press, 2019).

Heerten, Lasse. 'Mooring Mobilities, Fixing Flows: Towards a Global Urban History of Port Cities in the Age of Steam', *Journal of Historical Sociology* 34 (2021): 350–74.

Heinsen, Johan. *Mutiny in the Danish Atlantic World: Convicts, Sailors and a Dissonant Empire* (London: Bloomsbury, 2017).

Hellyer, Robert. *Green with Milk and Sugar: When Japan Filled America's Tea Cups* (New York: Columbia University Press, 2021).

  'The West, the East, and the Insular Middle: Trading Systems, Demand, and Labour in the Integration of the Pacific, 1750–1875', *Journal of Global History* 8, 3 (2013): 391–413.

Henriot, Christian. 'Rethinking Historical Research in the Age of NLP', *Elites, Networks and Power in Modern China* blog, https://enepchina.hypotheses.org/3275, 21 May 2020.

Herman, R. D. K. 'Out of Sight, Out of Mind, Out of Power: Leprosy, Race and Colonization in Hawai'i,', *Journal of Historical Geography* 27, 3 (2001): 319–37.

Hibino Toshinobu 日比野利信. 'Nisshin/Nichiro senkanki ni okeru Yasukawa Keiichirō' 日清・日露戦間期における安川敬一郎, in Arima Manabu 有馬学, ed., *Kindai Nihon no kigyōka to seiji: Yasukawa Keiichirō to sono jidai* 近代日本の企業家と政治：安川敬一郎とその時代 [Politics and the entrepreneur in modern Japan: Yasukawa Keiichirō and his age] (Tokyo: Yoshikawa kōbunkan, 2009), pp. 12–39.

Hirai Kensuke 平井健介. *Satō no Teikoku: Nihon Shokuminchi to Ajia Shijō* 砂糖の帝国：日本植民地とアジア市場 [Official translation: Empire of Sugar: External Forces of Change in the Economy of the Japanese Colonies] (Tokyo: Tōkyō daigaku shuppankai, 2017).

Hoerder, Dirk. 'Migrations and Belongings', in Emily S. Rosenberg, ed., *A World Connecting, 1870–1945* (Cambridge, MA: Harvard University Press, 2012), pp. 435–589.

Hokari, Minoru. *Gurindji Journey: A Japanese Historian in the Outback* (Sydney: University of New South Wales Press, 2011 [2004]).

Hones, Sheila and Yasuo Endo. 'History, Distance and Text: Narratives of the 1853–1854 Perry Expedition to Japan', *Journal of Historical Geography* 32 (2006): 563–78.

Horne, Gerald. *The White Pacific: US Imperialism and Black Slavery in the South Seas after the Civil War* (Honolulu: University of Hawai'i Press, 2007).

Hosaka Hirooki 保坂裕興. 'Ākaibuzu to rekishigaku' アーカイブズと歴史学 [Archives and the discipline of history], in Ōtsu Tōru 大津透, Sakurai Eiji

桜井英治, Fujii Jōji 藤井讓治 et al., eds., *Iwanami kōza: Nihon rekishi* 岩波講座：日本歴史, Vol. 21 (Tokyo: Iwanami shoten, 2015), pp. 181–207.

Howell, David L. 'Proto-Industrial Origins of Japanese Capitalism', *Journal of Asian Studies* 51, 2 (1992): 269–86.

Hu-DeHart, Evelyn. 'La Trata Amarilla: The "Yellow Trade" and the Middle Passage, 1847–1884', in Emma Christopher, Cassandra Pybus and Marcus Rediker, eds., *Many Middle Passages: Forced Migration and the Making of the Modern World* (Berkeley: University of California Press, 2007), pp. 166–83.

Hyslop, Jonathan. 'The Politics of Disembarkation: Empire, Shipping and Labor in the Port of Durban, 1897–1947', *International Labor and Working Class History* 93 (2018): 176–200.

Ichioka, Yuji. *The Issei: The World of the First Generation Japanese Immigrants, 1885–1924* (New York: Free Press, 1988).

Iijima, Mariko. 'Japanese Diasporas and Coffee Production', in David Ludden, ed., *The Oxford Research Encyclopedia of Asian History* (2019), https://oxfordre.com/asianhistory/.

Iijima, Shuji. 'Australian Aboriginal Studies in Japan, 1892–2006', *Japanese Review of Cultural Anthropology* 7 (2006): 51–70.

Indelicato, Maria Elena. 'Beyond Whiteness: Violence and Belonging in the Borderlands of North Queensland', *Postcolonial Studies* 23, 1 (2020): 99–115.

Irwin Yukiko アーウィン・ユキコ. *Furankurin no kajitsu* フランクリンの果実 [The Offspring of Franklin] (Tokyo: Bungei Shunjū, 1988).

Ishihara Shun 石原俊. *'Guntō' no rekishishakaigaku: Ogasawara shotō, Iōtō, Nihon, Amerika, soshite Taiheiyō sekai* 「群島」の歴史社会学：小笠原諸島・硫黄島、日本・アメリカ、そして太平洋世界 [A historical-sociology of 'islands': The Ogasawaras, Iwojima, Japan, America and the Pacific World] (Tokyo: Kōbundō, 2013).

Ishikawa Tomonori 石川友紀. 'Hiroshima wangan Jigozenson keiyaku imin no shakai chirigakuteki kōsatsu' 広島湾岸地御前村契約移民の社会地理学的考察 [A social and geographic study of contract emigration from Jigozen village, Hiroshima bay], *Jinbun chiri*, 19 (1967): 75–91.

Jackson, S. E. 'The Water Is Not Empty: Cross-Cultural Issues in Conceptualising Sea Space', *Australian Geographer* 26, 1 (1995): 87–96.

Jacob, Christian. *Qu'est-ce qu'un lieu de savoir?* (Marseille: Open Edition Press, 2014), http://books.openedition.org/oep/423.

James, Clive. *The River in the Sky* (London: Picador, 2018).

Johnson, Walter. *River of Dark Dreams: Slavery and Empire in the Cotton Kingdom* (Cambridge, MA: Harvard University Press, 2013).

Joseph, Betty. *Reading the East India Company 1720–1840: Colonial Currencies of Gender* (Chicago: University of Chicago Press, 2003).

Kaeppler, Adrienne. 'Eduard Arning: Hawai'is ethnografischer Fotograf/ Ethnographic Photographer of Hawai'i', in Wulf Köpke and Bernd Schmelz, eds., *Blick ins Paradies / A Glimpse into Paradise* (Hamburg: Museum für Völkerkunde Hamburg, 2014), pp. 86–103.

Kalland, Arne. *Fishing Villages in Tokugawa Japan* (Richmond: Curzon Press, 1995).

Kalland, Arne and Jon Pederson. 'Famine and Population in Fukuoka Domain during the Tokugawa Period', *Journal of Japanese Studies* 10, 1 (1984): 31–72.
Kamehiro, Stacy L. *The Arts of Kingship: Hawaiian Art and National Culture of the Kalākaua Era* (Honolulu: University of Hawai'i Press, 2009).
Kaminoseki Chōshi Hensan Iinkai 上関町史編纂委員会. *Kaminoseki chōshi* 上関町史 [Kaminoseki town history] (Kaminoseki: Kaminoseki-chō, 1988).
Katelaar, Eric. 'Tacit Narratives: The Meanings of Archives', *Archival Science* 1 (2001): 131–41.
Kaukiainen, Yrjö. 'Coal and Canvas: Aspects of the Competition between Steam and Sail, c. 1870–1914', *International Journal of Maritime History* 4 (1992): 175–91.
  'Shrinking the World: Improvements in the Speed of Information Transmission, c. 1820–1870', *European Review of Economic History* 5, 1 (2001): 1–28.
Kennerley, Alston. 'Stoking the Boilers: Firemen and Trimmers in British Merchant Ships, 1850–1950', *International Journal of Maritime History* 20, 1 (2008): 191–220.
Kerr, John. *Northern Outpost* (Mossman: Mossman Central Mill Co, 1979).
Khatun, Samia. *Australianama: The South Asian Odyssey in Australia* (London: C. Hurst, 2018).
Kimura Kenji 木村健二. 'Senzenki Nihon ni okeru kaigai imin: Yamaguchi-ken no jirei o chūshin ni' 戦前期日本における海外移民：山口県の事例を中心に [Overseas emigration in prewar Japan: The case of Yamaguchi prefecture], in Komai Hiroshi 駒井洋, Chin Tenji 陳天璽 and Kobayashi Tomoko 小林知子, eds., *Higashi Ajia no diasupora* 東アジアのディアスポラ [East Asian diasporas] (Tokyo: Akashi shoten, 2011), pp. 126–51.
  Zaichō Nihonjin no shakaishi 在朝日本人の社会史 [A social history of the Japanese in Korea] (Tokyo: Miraisha, 1989).
Kimura, Yukiko. *The Issei: Japanese Immigrants in Hawaii* (Honolulu: University of Hawai'i Press, 1992).
King, Tiffany Lethabo. *The Black Shoals: Offshore Formations of Black and Native Studies* (Durham, NC: Duke University Press, 2019).
Kinski, Michael. 'Admonitions Regarding Food Consumption,' *Japonica Humboldtiana* 7 (2003): 123–78.
Kira Yoshie 吉良芳恵. 'Yokohama jānarisuto retsuden: Satō Torajirō, sono sūki na isshō' 横浜ジャーナリスト列伝：佐藤虎次郎、その数奇な一生 [Biographies of Yokohama journalists: The chequered life of Satō Torajirō], *Yokohama kaikō shiryōkan kanpō* 37 (29 April 1992): 6–7.
Kodama Masaaki 児玉正昭. 'Shoki imingaisha no imin boshū to sono jittai' 初期移民会社の移民募集とその実態 [The conditions and recruitment strategies of the first emigration companies], *Hiroshima kenshi kenkyū* 3 (1978): 20–44.
Kokaze Hidemasa 小風秀雅. '19 seiki ni okeru kōtsū kakumei no shinten to Nihontan no yakuwari' 19世紀における交通革命の進展と日本炭の役割 [The development of the nineteenth-century transportation revolution and the role of Japanese coal], in Nagasaki-shi 長崎市, ed., *Takashima tankō*

chōsa hōkokusho 高島炭鉱調査報告書 (Nagasaki: Nagasaki-shi, 2014), pp. 2-6 – 2-27.

Teikokushugika no Nihon kaiun: Kokusai kyōsō to taigai jiritsu 帝国主義下の日本海運：国際競争と対外自立 [Japanese maritime transportation under imperialism: International competition and independence in external affairs] (Tokyo: Yamakawa shuppansha, 1995).

Kōno Shinji 河野信治, *Nihon tōgyō hattatsu-shi: Jinbutsu-hen* 日本糖業発達史：人物篇 [A developmental history of the sugar industry in Japan: People] (Kobe: Nihon tōgyō hattatsu-shi hensanjo, 1934).

Köpke, Wulf and Bernd Schmelz, eds. *Blick ins Paradies / A Glimpse into Paradise* (Hamburg: Museum für Völkerkunde Hamburg, 2014).

Kopytoff, Igor. 'The Cultural Biography of Things: Commoditization as Process', in Arjun Appadurai, ed., *The Social Life of Things: Commodities in Cultural Perspective* (Cambridge: Cambridge University Press, 1986), pp. 64–91.

Korhonen, Pekka. 'Leaving Asia? The Meaning of *Datsu-A* and Japan's Modern History', *Asia-Pacific Journal* 12, 9 (3 March 2014), https://apjjf.org/2014/11/50/Pekka-Korhonen/4083/article.html.

Kosasa, Eiko. 'Ideological Images: US Nationalism in Japanese Settler Photographs', in Candace Fujikane and Jonathan Y. Okamura, eds., *Asian Settler Colonialism: From Local Governance to the Habits of Everyday Life in Hawai'i* (University of Hawai'i Press, 2008), pp. 209–32.

Koselleck, Reinhart. 'The Temporalisation of Concepts', *Finnish Yearbook of Political Thought* 1, 1 (1997): 16–24.

Kouwenhoven, Arlette and Matthi Forrer. *Siebold and Japan: His Life and Work* (Leiden: Hotei Publishing, 2000).

Kōyama Toshio 鴻山俊雄. 'Gaijin bochi ni nemuru hitobito' 外人墓地に眠る人々 (中) [Those who sleep in the foreigners' cemetery], *Nikka geppō 16* (1968).

Kreitman, Paul. *Japan's Ocean Borderlands: Nature and Sovereignty* (Cambridge: Cambridge University Press, 2023).

Kuhn, Philip A. *Chinese among Others: Emigration in Modern Times* (Lanham, MD: Rowman & Littlefield, 2008).

Kuriyama, Shigehisa. 'The Historical Origins of Katakori', *Japan Review* 9 (1997): 127–49.

  'The Travel of Anxieties: Rethinking Western Medicine in Edo Japan', public lecture at the Heidelberg Center for Transcultural Studies, 22 January 2015.

Kuwata Etsu 桑田悦. 'Nisshin sensō ni okeru yusō, hokyū' 日清戦争における輸送・補給 [Transportation and supply in the Sino-Japanese War], in *Kindai Nihon sensō* 近代日本戦争 [Japan's modern wars] (Tokyo: Dōdai keizai konwakai, 1995), pp. 251–68.

Lake, Marilyn and Henry Reynolds. *Drawing the Global Colour Line: White Men's Countries and the International Challenge of Racial Equality* (Cambridge: Cambridge University Press, 2008).

Lavery, Brian. *SS Great Britain, 1843–1937 Onwards: Enthusiasts' Manual* (Yeovil: Haynes Publishing, 2012).

LeCain, Timothy J. *The Matter of History: How Things Create the Past* (Cambridge: Cambridge University Press, 2017).

Levine, Philippa. 'The Mobile Camera: Bodies, Anthropologists, and the Victorian Optic', *Nineteenth-Century Contexts* 37, 5 (2015): 473–90.
  Prostitution, Race and Politics: Policing Venereal Disease in the British Empire (New York: Routledge, 2003).
Lewis, Simon L. and Mark A. Maslin. 'Defining the Anthropocene', *Nature* 519 (2015): 171–80.
Litvine, Alexis D. 'The Annihilation of Space: A Bad (Historical) Concept', *Historical Journal* 65 (2022): 871–900.
Livingstone, David N. *Putting Science in Its Place: Geographies of Scientific Knowledge* (Chicago: University of Chicago Press, 2003).
Lu, Sidney Xu. 'Colonizing Hokkaido and the Origin of Japanese Trans-Pacific Expansion, 1869–1894', *Japanese Studies* 36, 2 (2016): 251–74.
  The Making of Japanese Settler Colonialism: Malthusianism and Trans-Pacific Migration, 1868–1961 (Cambridge: Cambridge University Press, 2019).
  'The Shame of Empire: Japanese Overseas Prostitutes and Prostitution Abolition in Modern Japan, 1880s-1927', *positions* 24, 4 (2016): 830–73.
Macknight, C. Campbell. 'The View from Marege': Australian Knowledge of Makassar and the Impact of the Trepang Industry across Two Centuries', *Aboriginal History* 35 (2011): 121–43.
  The Voyage to Marege': Macassan Trepangers in Northern Australia (Melbourne: Melbourne University Press, 2017 [1976]).
MacLennan, Carol A. *Sovereign Sugar: Industry and Environment in Hawai'i* (Honolulu: University of Hawai'i Press, 2014).
Manjapra, Kris. *Colonialism in Global Perspective* (Cambridge: Cambridge University Press, 2020).
  'Transnational Approaches to Global History: A View from the Study of German–Indian Entanglement', *German History* 32, 2 (2014): 274–93.
Marcon, Federico. *The Knowledge of Nature and the Nature of Knowledge in Early Modern Japan* (Chicago: University of Chicago Press, 2015).
Martens, Jeremy. 'A Transnational History of Immigration Restriction: Natal and New South Wales, 1896–97', *Journal of Imperial and Commonwealth History* 34, 3 (2006): 323–44.
Martínez, Julia and Adrian Vickers. *The Pearl Frontier: Indonesian Labor and Indigenous Encounters in Australia's Northern Trading Network* (Honolulu: University of Hawai'i Press, 2015).
Marumoto, Masaji. '"First Year" Immigrants to Hawaii & Eugene van Reed,' in Hilary Conroy, ed., *East Across the Pacific: Historical and Sociological Studies of Japanese Immigration and Assimilation* (Santa Barbara, CA: American Bibliographical Center–Clio Press, 1972), pp. 5–39.
Mathur, Anuradha and Dilip da Cunha. *Soak: Mumbai in an Estuary* (New Delhi: Rupa Publishing, 2009).
Matsuda, Hiroko. *Liminality of the Japanese Empire: Border Crossings from Okinawa to Colonial Taiwan* (Honolulu: University of Hawai'i Press, 2019).
Matsuda, Matt. *Pacific Worlds: A History of Seas, Peoples, and Cultures* (Cambridge: Cambridge University Press, 2012).
Mawani, Renisa. *Across Oceans of Law: The* Komagata Maru *and Jurisdiction in the Time of Empire* (Durham, NC: Duke University Press, 2018).

'The Politics of Empire: Minor History on a Global Scale', in Rita Dhamoon, Davina Bhandar, Renisa Mawani and Satwinder Kaur Bains, eds., *Unmooring the Komagata Maru: Charting Colonial Trajectories* (Vancouver: University of British Colombia Press, 2019), pp. 280–9.

Mawson, Stephanie. 'The Deep Past of Pre-Colonial Australia', *Historical Journal* 64, 5 (2021): 1477–99.

McCormack, Noah. '*Buraku* Migration in the Meiji Era: Other Ways to Become "Japanese"', *East Asian History* 23 (2002): 87–108.

McFadzean, Moya. 'Setsutaro Hasegawa, Japanese Migrant, 1897–circa 1952', in *Museums Victoria Collections* (2009), https://collections.museumsvictoria.com.au/articles/2935.

McIntosh, Ian S. 'Unbirri's Pre-Macassan Legacy, or How the Yolngu Became Black', in Clark and May, *Macassan History and Heritage*, pp. 95–105.

McKeown, Adam M. *Melancholy Order: Asian Migration and the Globalization of Borders* (New York: Columbia University Press, 2008).

McMaster, John. 'The Takashima Mine: British Capital and Japanese Industrialization', *Business History Review* 37, 3 (1963): 217–39.

McNeill, J. R. and Peter Engelke. *The Great Acceleration: An Environmental History of the Anthropocene since 1945* (Cambridge, MA: Harvard University Press, 2016).

McPhee, John A. *Annals of the Former World* (New York: Farrar, Straus and Giroux, 2006).

Mervart, David. 'The Republic of Letters Comes to Nagasaki: Record of a Translator's Struggle', *Transcultural Studies* 2 (2015): 8–37.

Metzler, Mark and Gregory Smits. 'Introduction: The Autonomy of Market Activity and the Emergence of Keizai Thought', in Bettina Gramlich-Oka and Gregory Smits, eds., *Economic Thought in Early Modern Japan* (Leiden: Brill, 2010): 1–19.

Mihalopoulos, Bill. *Sex in Japan's Globalization, 1870–1930: Prostitutes, Emigration and Nation-Building* (London: Pickering & Chatto, 2011).

Miller, Ian Jared. 'Writing *Japan at Nature's Edge*: The Promises and Perils of Environmental History', in Ian Jared Miller, Julia Adeney Thomas and Brett L. Walker, eds., *Japan at Nature's Edge: The Environmental Context of a Global Power* (Honolulu: University of Hawai'i Press, 2013), pp. 1–17.

Miller, Nicholas B. 'Trading Sovereignty and Labour: The Consular Network of Nineteenth-Century Hawai'i', *International History Review* 42, 2 (2020): 260–77.

Milligan, Ian. *History in the Age of Abundance? How the Web is Transforming Historical Research* (Montreal: McGill–Queen's University Press, 2019).

Mintz, Sidney W. *Sweetness and Power: The Place of Sugar in Modern History* (New York: Viking, 1985).

Mishra, Pankaj. *From the Ruins of Empire: The Revolt Against the West and the Remaking of Asia* (London: Penguin, 2013).

Miyoshi, Masao. *As We Saw Them: The First Japanese Embassy to the United States (1860)* (Berkeley: University of California Press, 1979).

Mizushima Tsukasa 水島司. *Gurōbaru hisutorī nyūmon* グローバル・ヒストリー入門 [An introduction to global history] (Tokyo: Yamakawa shuppansha, 2010).

Moreno, Teresa, Simon Wallis, Tomoko Kojima and Wes Gibbons. *The Geology of Japan* (London: Geological Society, 2016).
Morgan, William M. *Pacific Gibraltar: US–Japanese Rivalry over the Annexation of Hawai'i, 1885–1898* (Annapolis, MD: Annapolis Naval Institute Press, 2011).
Mori Hiroko 森弘子 and Miyazaki Katsunori 宮崎克則. *Kujiratori no shakaishi: Shiiboruto ya Edo no gakushatachi ga mita Nihon hogei* 鯨取りの社会史：シーボルトや江戸の学者たちが見た日本捕鯨 [A social history of whale catching: Japanese whaling as seen by Siebold and Edo scholars] (Tokyo: Karansha, 2016).
Moriyama, Alan Takeo. *Imingaisha: Japanese Emigration Companies and Hawaii 1894–1908* (Honolulu: University of Hawai'i Press, 1985).
Morphy, Frances and Howard Morphy. 'The Blue Mud Bay Case: Refractions through Saltwater Country', *Dialogue* 28 (2009): 15–25.
Morphy, Howard and Frances Morphy. 'Tasting the Waters: Discriminating Identities in the Waters of Blue Mud Bay', *Journal of Material Culture* 11, 1–2 (2006): 67–85.
Moulton, Kimberly. 'Djambawa Marawili AM: Change Agent', to accompany Marawili's collaboration, *where the water moves, where it rests*, with the Kluge-Ruhe Aboriginal Art Collection, University of Virginia, 1 August 2015 – 24 January 2016, https://kluge-ruhe.org/collaboration/djambawa-marawili/.
Mulrennan, Monica E. and Colin H. Scott. '*Mare Nullius*: Indigenous Rights in Saltwater Environments', *Development and Change* 31 (2000): 681–708.
Nagata, Yuriko. 'Japanese Internment in Australia during World War II', unpublished PhD thesis, University of Adelaide (1993).
Nakamura Naofumi 中村尚史. *Chihō kara no sangyō kakumei: Nihon ni okeru kigyō bokkō no gendōryoku* 地方からの産業革命：日本における企業勃興の原動力 [The industrial revolution from the regions: The driving force behind the rise of business in Japan] (Nagoya: Nagoya daigaku shuppankai, 2010).
Neale, Timothy and Stephen Turner. 'Other People's Country: Law, Water, Entitlement', *Settler Colonial Studies* 5, 4 (2015): 277–81.
Nicholson, Bob. 'The Digital Turn: Exploring the Methodological Possibilities of Digital Newspaper Archives', *Media History* 19, 1 (2013): 59–73.
Nippon Yūsen Kaisha 日本郵船会社. *Yōjō no interia II* 洋上のインテリアII/ *The Interiors of Passenger Ships II* (Yokohama: Nippon yūsen rekishi hakubutsukan, 2011).
Nishikawa, Shunsaku. 'The Economy of Chōshū on the Eve of Industrialization', *Economic Studies Quarterly* 38, 4 (1987): 323–37.
Nishizawa Yasuhiko 西澤泰彦. 'Meiji jidai ni kensetsu sareta Nihon no dorai dokku ni kansuru kenkyū' 明治時代に建設された日本のドライドックに関する研究 [Official translation: A Study on the Dry Docks Built Up in the Meiji Period in Japan], *Dobokushi kenkyū* 19 (1995).
Noble, Safiya Umoja. *Algorithms of Oppression: How Search Engines Reinforce Racism* (New York: New York University Press, 2018).
Nogelmeier, Puakea. *Mai Pa'a I Ka Leo: Historical Voice in Hawaiian Primary Materials: Looking Forward and Listening Back* (Honolulu: Bishop Museum Press, 2010).

Odo, Franklin. *Voices from the Canefields: Folksongs from Japanese Immigrant Workers in Hawai'i* (New York: Oxford University Press, 2013).
Odo Franklin 王堂フランクリン and Sinoto Kazuko 篠遠和子. *Zusetsu Hawai Nihonjinshi, 1885–1924* 図説ハワイ日本人史 1885–1924 [A pictorial history of the Japanese in Hawai'i, 1885–1924] (Honolulu: Bishop Museum, 1985).
Odumosu, Temi. 'The Crying Child: On Colonial Archives, Digitization, and Ethics of Care in the Cultural Commons', *Current Anthropology* 61, Supplement 22 (October 2020): 289–302.
Ogle, Vanessa. *The Global Transformation of Time, 1870–1950* (Cambridge, MA: Harvard University Press, 2015).
Ōmachi-chō 大町町. *Ōmachi-chōshi* 大町町史 [A history of Ōmachi town] (Ōmachi: Ōmachi chōshi hensanshitsu, 1987).
Ondaatje, Michael. *The Cat's Table* (London: Jonathan Cape, 2011).
Osorio, Jonathan Kay Kamakawiwo'ole. *Dismembering Lāhui: A History of the Hawaiian Nation to 1887* (Honolulu: University of Hawai'i Press, 2002).
Osterhammel, Jürgen. 'Arnold Toynbee and the Problems of Today', 2017 Toynbee Prize Lecture, *Bulletin of the GHI Washington* 60 (2017): 69–87.
  The Transformation of the World: A Global History of the Nineteenth Century, trans. Patrick Camiller (Princeton, NJ: Princeton University Press, 2014 [2009]).
Otsuka, Julie. *The Buddha in the Attic* (New York: Anchor Books, 2011).
Park, Joohyun Jade. 'Missing Link Found, 1880: The Rhetoric of Colonial Progress in Isabella Bird's *Unbeaten Tracks in Japan*', *Victorian Literature and Culture* 43 (2015): 371–88.
Pearn, John. *Outback Medicine: Some Vignettes of Pioneering Medicine* (Brisbane: Amphion Press, 1994).
Phipps, Catherine L. *Empires on the Waterfront: Japan's Ports and Power, 1858–1899* (Cambridge, MA: Harvard University Asia Center, 2015).
Pietsch, Tamson. 'A British Sea: Making Sense of Global Space in the Late Nineteenth Century', *Journal of Global History* 5, 3 (2010): 423–46.
Plutschow, Herbert. *Philipp Franz von Siebold and the Opening of Japan: A Re-Evaluation* (Leiden: Brill, 2007).
Pomeranz, Kenneth. *The Great Divergence: China, Europe, and the Making of the Modern World Economy* (Princeton, NJ: Princeton University Press, 2000).
Ponsonby-Fane, Richard. *The Nomenclature of the N. Y. K. Fleet* (Tokyo: Nippon yusen kaisha, 1931).
Pratt, Edward E. *Japan's Protoindustrial Elite: The Economic Foundations of the Gōnō* (Cambridge, MA: Harvard University Asia Center, 1999).
Presner, Todd, David Shepard and Yoh Kawano. *HyperCities: Thick Mapping in the Digital Humanities* (Cambridge, MA: Harvard University Press, 2014).
Putnam, Lara. 'The Transnational and the Text-Searchable: Digitized Sources and the Shadows They Cast', *American Historical Review* 121, 2 (2016): 377–402.
Putney, Clifford. *Missionaries in Hawai'i: The Lives of Peter and Fanny Gulick, 1797–1883* (Amherst: University of Massachusetts Press, 2010).
Pwee, Timothy. '"The German Medicine Deity": Singapore's Early Pharmacies', *biblioasia* 14, 3 (Oct–Dec 2018): 46–9, https://biblioasia.nlb.gov.sg/past-issues/pdf/BiblioAsia%20Oct-Dec%202018.pdf.

Raj, Kapil. 'Beyond Postcolonialism ... and Postpositivism: Circulation and the Global History of Science', *Isis* 103 (2013): 337–47.

Ravina, Mark. 'Locally Ancient and Globally Modern', in Robert Hellyer and Harald Fuess, eds., *The Meiji Restoration: Japan as a Global Nation* (Cambridge: Cambridge University Press, 2020), pp. 212–31.

To Stand with the Nations of the World: Japan's Meiji Restoration in World History (New York: Oxford University Press, 2017).

Rediker, Marcus. *The Amistad Rebellion: An Atlantic Odyssey of Slavery and Freedom* (London: Verso, 2013).

The Slave Ship: A Human History (London: John Murray, 2007).

Ricci, Ronit. *Islam Translated: Literature, Conversion, and the Arabic Cosmopolis of South and Southeast Asia* (Chicago: University of Chicago Press, 2011).

Richards, Thomas. *The Imperial Archive: Knowledge and the Fantasy of Empire* (London: Verso, 1993).

Rouleau, Brian. *With Sails Whitening Every Sea: Mariners and the Making of an American Maritime Empire* (Ithaca, NY: Cornell University Press, 2014).

Rudwick, Martin J. S. *Earth's Deep History: How It Was Discovered and Why It Matters* (Chicago: University of Chicago Press, 2014).

Rüger, Jan. *The Great Naval Game: Britain and Germany in the Age of Empire* (Cambridge: Cambridge University Press, 2007).

Ruoff, Kenneth J. *Imperial Japan at Its Zenith: The Wartime Celebration of the Empire's 2,600th Anniversary* (Ithaca, NY: Cornell University Press, 2010).

Rustow, Marina. *The Lost Archive: Traces of a Caliphate in a Cairo Synagogue* (Princeton, NJ: Princeton University Press, 2020).

Sachsenmaier, Dominic. *Global Entanglements of a Man Who Never Traveled: A Seventeenth-Century Chinese Christian and His Conflicted Worlds* (New York: Columbia University Press, 2018).

Saito, Osamu. 'An Industrious Revolution in an East Asian Market Economy? Tokugawa Japan and Implications for the Great Divergence', *Australian Economic History Review* 50, 3 (2010): 240–61.

'Population and the Peasant Family Economy in Proto-industrial Japan', *Journal of Family History* 8 (1983): 30–54.

Samuels, Richard J. *The Business of the Japanese State: Energy Markets in Comparative and Historical Perspective* (Ithaca, NY: Cornell University Press, 1987).

Sand, Jordan. 'Gentleman's Agreement 1908: Fragments for a Pacific History', *Representations* 107 (2009): 91–127.

Saranillio, Dean Itsuji. 'Haunani-Kay Trask and Settler Colonial and Relational Critique: Alternatives to Binary Analyses of Power', *Verge: Studies in Global Asias* 4, 2 (2018): 36–44.

Satia, Priya. *Time's Monster: How History Makes History* (Cambridge, MA: Belknap Press, 2020).

Satow, Ernst. *A Diplomat in Japan: The Inner History of the Critical Years in the Evolution of Japan When the Ports Were Opened and the Monarchy Restored* (San Diego: Stone Bridge Press, 2006 [1921]).

Saunders, David. 'Charles Mitchell, Tyneside and Russia's First Ironclads', *Northern History* 48, 1 (2011): 75–95.

Schaffer, Simon. 'Fish and Ships: Models in the Age of Reason', in Soraya De Chadarevian and Nick Hopwood, eds., *Models: The Third Dimension of Science* (Stanford, CA: Stanford University Press, 2004), pp. 71–105.

Schaffer, Simon, Lissa Roberts, Kapil Raj and James Delbourgo, eds. *The Brokered World: Go-Betweens and Global Intelligence, 1770–1820* (Sagamore Beach, MA: Science History Publications, 2009).

Schivelbusch, Wolfgang. 'Railroad Space and Railroad Time', *New German Critique* 14 (1978): 31–40.

Scott, Joan Wallace. 'Archival Angst', *History of the Present* 11, 1 (2021): 107–18.

Sekiguchi Kaori 関口かをり and Takeda Haruhito 武田晴人. 'Yūbinkisen Mitsubishi Kaisha to Kyōdō Un'yu Kaisha no "kyōsō" jittai ni tsuite' 郵便汽船三菱会社と共同運輸会社の「競争」実態について [On the 'competitive' state between the companies Yūbinkisen Mitsubishi Kaisha and Kyōdō Un'yu Kaisha], *Mitsubishi shiryōkan ronshū* 11 (2010): 13–48.

Sekula, Allan. *Fish Story* (Düsseldorf: Richter Verlag, 1995).

 'Reading an Archive: Photography between Labour and Capital', in Liz Wells, ed., *The Photography Reader* (London: Routledge, 2019), pp. 443–52.

Sepkoski, David. 'The Earth as Archive: Contingency, Narrative, and the History of Life', in Lorraine Daston, ed., *Science in the Archives: Pasts, Presents, Futures* (Chicago: University of Chicago Press, 2017).

Shepherd, Hannah. 'Fukuoka's Meiji Migrants and the Making of an Imperial Region', *Japan Forum* 30, 4 (2018): 474–97.

Shepherd, Verene A. *Maharani's Misery: Narratives of a Passage from India to the Caribbean* (Kingston: University of the West Indies Press, 2002).

Shibamura Keijirō 芝村敬次郎. *Yamaguchi-ken Kaminoseki Yoshida-ke shiryō to Yoshida-shi* 山口県上関吉田家資料と吉田氏 [The Yoshidas and the Yoshida household of Kaminoseki, Yamaguchi prefecture] (Hiroshima: Shimo-Kamagari-chō, 2000).

Shimazu, Naoko. *Japanese Society at War: Death, Memory, and the Russo-Japanese War* (Cambridge: Cambridge University Press, 2009).

 Japan, Race and Equality: The Racial Equality Proposal of 1919 (London: Routledge, 1998).

Shimizu, Hiroshi. 'Karayuki-san and the Japanese Economic Advance into British Malaya, 1870–1920', *Asian Studies Review* 20, 3 (1997): 107–32.

Shiode Hiroyuki 塩出浩之. *Ekkyōsha no seijishi: Ajia Taiheiyō ni okeru Nihonjin no imin to shokumin* 越境者の政治史：アジア太平洋における日本人の移民と植民 [A political history of border-crossers: Japanese emigrants and colonists in the Asia-Pacific] (Nagoya: Nagoya daigaku shuppankai, 2015).

Shulman, Peter A. *Coal and Empire: The Birth of Energy Security in Industrial America* (Baltimore, MD: Johns Hopkins University Press, 2015).

Siegert, Bernhard. 'Ficticious [sic] Identities: On the Interrogatorios and *registros de pasajeros a Indias* in the Archivo General de Indias (Seville) (16th century)', in Wolfram Nitsch, Matei Chihaia and Alejandra Torres, eds., *Ficciones de los medios en la periferia: Técnicas de comunicación en la ficción hispanoamericana moderna* (Cologne: Universitäts- und Stadtbibliothek Köln, 2008), pp. 19–30.

Sinn, Elizabeth. 'Women at Work: Chinese Brothel Keepers in Nineteenth-Century Hong Kong', *Journal of Women's History* 19, 3 (2007): 87–111.
Sissons, David. 'Japan and the Australian Wool Industry, 1868–1936', in Arthur Stockwin and Keiko Tamura, eds., *Bridging Australia and Japan*, Vol. 1: *The Writings of David Sissons, Historian and Political Scientist* (Acton, ACT: Australian National University Press, 2016 [1978]), pp. 311–18.
  '*Karayuki-san*: Japanese Prostitutes in Australia, 1887–1915: Part I', *Historical Studies* 17, 68 (1977): 323–41.
Sivasundaram, Sujit. *Islanded: Britain, Sri Lanka, and the Bounds of an Indian Ocean Colony* (Chicago: University of Chicago Press, 2013).
  Waves across the South: A New History of Revolution and Empire (London: William Collins, 2020).
Skwiot, Christine. 'Migration and the Politics of Sovereignty, Settlement, and Belonging in Hawai'i', in Donna Gabaccía and Dirk Hoerder, eds., *Connecting Seas and Ocean Rims: Indian, Atlantic, and Pacific Oceans and China Seas Migrations from the 1830s to the 1930s* (Leiden: Brill, 2011), pp. 440–63.
Smith, Bonnie G. 'Gender and the Practices of Scientific History: The Seminar and Archival Research in the Nineteenth Century', *American Historical Review* 100, 4 (1995): 1150–76.
Smith, Henry D., II. 'Hokusai and the Blue Revolution in Edo Prints', in John T. Carpenter, ed., *Hokusai and His Age: Ukiyo-e Painting, Printmaking, and Book Illustration in Late Edo Japan* (Amsterdam: Hotei Publishing, 2005), pp. 234–69.
Smith, Linda Tuhiwai. *Decolonizing Methodologies: Research and Indigenous Peoples*, 3rd edn (London: Zed Books, 2021 [1999]).
Smith, Thomas C. 'Farm Family By-Employments in Preindustrial Japan', *Journal of Economic History* 29, 4 (1969): 687–715.
  Native Sources of Japanese Industrialization, 1750–1920 (Berkeley, CA: University of California Press, 1988).
  'Peasant Time and Factory Time in Japan', *Past & Present* 111 (1986): 165–97.
Smits, Gregory. *Seismic Japan: The Long History and Continuing Legacy of the Ansei Edo Earthquake* (Honolulu: University of Hawai'i Press, 2013).
Sonoda Hidehiro 園田英弘. *Seiyōka no kōzō: Kurofune, bushi, kokka* 西洋化の構造:黒船・武士・国家 [Constructions of Westernization: Black ships, samurai, state] (Kyoto: Shibunkaku shuppan, 1993).
Spiekermann, Uwe. 'Das gekaufte Königreich: Claus Spreckels, die Hawaiian Commercial Company [sic] und die Grenzen wirtschaftlicher Einflussnahme im Königtum Hawaii, 1875 bis 1898', in Harmut Berghoff, Cornelia Rauh and Thomas Welskopp, eds., *Tatort Unternehmen: Zur Geschichte der Wirtschaftskriminalität im 20. und 21. Jahrhundert* (Berlin: de Gruyter, 2016), pp. 47–67.
Stalker, Nancy. 'Suicide, Boycotts and Embracing Tagore: The Japanese Popular Response to the 1924 US Immigration Exclusion Law', *Japanese Studies* 26, 2 (2006): 153–70.
Stanley, Amy. 'Maidservants' Tales: Narrating Domestic and Global History in Eurasia, 1600–1900', *American Historical Review* 121, 2 (2016): 437–60.

Stranger in the Shogun's City: A Woman's Life in Nineteenth-Century Japan (London: Chatto & Windus, 2020).
Steedman, Carolyn. *Dust* (Manchester: Manchester University Press, 2001).
  'Lord Mansfield's Voices: In the Archive, Hearing Things', in Stephanie Downes, Sally Holloway and Sarah Randles, eds., *Feeling Things: Objects and Emotions through History* (Oxford: Oxford University Press, 2018), pp. 209–25.
Steel, Frances. *Oceania under Steam: Sea Transport and the Cultures of Colonialism, c. 1870–1914* (Manchester: Manchester University Press, 2011).
Steele, William M. *Alternative Narratives in Modern Japanese History* (London: Routledge, 2003).
Stoler, Ann Laura. *Along the Archival Grain: Epistemic Anxieties and Colonial Common Sense* (Princeton, NJ: Princeton University Press, 2009).
  'Colonial Archives and the Arts of Governance', *Archival Science* 2 (1–2) (2002): 87–109.
Sugihara, Kaoru and R. Bin Wong. 'Industrious Revolutions in Early Modern World History', in Jerry H. Bentley, Sanjay Subrahmanyam and Merry E. Wiesner-Hanks, eds., *The Cambridge World History*, Vol. 6: *The Construction of a Global World, 1400–1800 CE* (Cambridge: Cambridge University Press, 2015), pp. 282–310.
Suk Gersen, Jeannie. 'Seeking the True Story of the Comfort Women', *New Yorker*, 25 February 2021. www.newyorker.com/culture/annals-of-inquiry/seeking-the-true-story-of-the-comfort-women-j-mark-ramseyer
Sutton, Peter. 'Icons of Country: Topographic Representations in Classical Aboriginal Traditions', in David Woodward and G. Malcolm Lewis, eds., *The History of Cartography*, Vol. 2, Bk. 3: *Cartography in the Traditional African, American, Arctic, Australian, and Pacific Societies* (Chicago: University of Chicago Press, 1998), pp. 353–86.
Swale, Alastair. *The Political Thought of Mori Arinori: A Study in Meiji Conservatism* (Richmond: Japan Library, 2000).
Taitō Kyūjūnen Tsūshi Hensan Iinkai 台糖90年通史編纂委員会. *Taitō kyūjūnen tsūshi* 台糖90年通史 [A ninety-year history of Taitō] (Tokyo: Taitō kabushiki kaisha, 1990).
Takai, Yukari. 'Recrafting Marriage in Meiji Hawai'i, 1885–1913', *Gender & History* 31, 3 (2019): 646–64.
Takaki, Ronald. *Pau Hana: Plantation Life and Labor in Hawaii* (Honolulu: University of Hawai'i Press, 1983).
Tanaka, Stefan. 'History without Chronology', *Public Culture* 28, 1 (2016): 161–86.
Teaiwa, Teresia K. 'On Analogies: Rethinking the Pacific in a Global Context', *Contemporary Pacific* 18, 1 (2006): 71–87.
Thigpen, Jennifer. *Island Queens and Mission Wives: How Gender and Empire Remade Hawai'i's Pacific World* (Chapel Hill: University of North Carolina Press, 2014).
Thomas, Julia Adeney. 'Reclaiming Ground: Japan's Great Convergence', *Japanese Studies* 34, 3 (2014): 253–63.

Thomas, Keith. 'Diary: Working Methods', *London Review of Books* 32, 11 (10 June 2010).
Thomas, Larry. *Coal Geology*, 2nd edn (Chichester: Wiley, 2013).
Thomas, Nicholas. *Discoveries: The Voyages of Captain Cook* (London: Penguin Books, 2018).
Thomas, Paul. 'Interpreting the Macassans: Language Exchange in Historical Encounters', in Marshall Clark and Sally K. May, eds., *Macassan History and Heritage: Journeys, Encounters and Influences* (Canberra: Australian National University E-Press, 2013), pp. 69–93.
Thompson, E. P. 'Time, Work-Discipline and Industrial Capitalism', *Past & Present* 38 (1967): 56–94.
Tōjō Nobumasa 東定宣昌. 'Karatsu kaigun tankō no settei to sono kei'ei' 唐津海軍炭坑の設定とその経営 [The establishment and management of navy coal collieries in Karatsu], *Keizaigaku kenkyū* 59, 3–4 (1993): 81–109.
'Karatsu tanden no yusō taikei no kindaika: Karatsu Kōgyō Tetsudō Gaisha no seiritsu to sekitan yusō' 唐津炭田の輸送体系の近代化：唐津興業鉄道会社の成立と石炭輸送 [The modernisation of the transportation system in Karatsu Coalfield: The founding of the Karatsu Kōgyō Railway Company and coal transportation], *Hikaku shakai bunka* 1 (1995): 49–60.
'Meiji zenki, Hizen Matsuuragawa no sekitan yusō' 明治前期、肥前松浦川の石炭輸送 [The transportation of coal from the Matsuura river in Hizen, in the early Meiji period], *Enerugii-shi kenkyū* 17 (2002): 31–46.
Torget, Andrew J. and Jon Christensen. 'Building New Windows into Digitized Newspapers', *Journal of Digital Humanities* 1, 3 (2012), http://journalofdigitalhumanities.org.
Totman, Conrad. *Early Modern Japan* (Berkeley: University of California Press, 1993).
Toyosawa, Nobuko. *Imaginative Mapping: Landscape and Japanese Identity in the Tokugawa and Meiji Eras* (Cambridge, MA: Harvard University Asia Center, 2019).
Tran, Ben. 'I Speak in the Third Person: Women and Language in Colonial Vietnam', *positions* 21, 3 (2013): 579–605.
Trask, Haunani-Kay. *From a Native Daughter: Colonialism and Sovereignty in Hawaii* (Honolulu: University of Hawai'i Press, 1999 [1993]).
'Settlers of Color and "Immigrant" Hegemony: "Locals" in Hawai'i', *Amerasia Journal* 26, 2 (2000): 1–24.
Trocki, Carl A. 'Singapore as a Nineteenth Century Migration Node', in Donna Gabaccía and Dirk Hoerder, eds., *Connecting Seas and Ocean Rims: Indian, Atlantic, and Pacific Oceans and China Seas Migrations from the 1830s to the 1930s* (Leiden: Brill, 2011), pp. 198–224.
Trouillot, Michel-Rolph. *Silencing the Past: Power and the Production of History* (Boston: Beacon Press, 2015 [1995]).
Tsu, Cecilia M. 'Sex, Lies, and Agriculture: Reconstructing Japanese Immigrant Gender Relations in Rural California, 1900–1913', *Pacific Historical Review* 78, 2 (2009): 171–209.
Tsubota-Nakanishi, Miki. 'The Absence of Plantations in the Taiwanese Sugar Industry', *Historische Anthropologie* 27, 3 (2019): 385–409.

Tsukahara, Togo. 'An Unpublished Manuscript *Geologica Japonica* by Von Siebold: Geology, Mineralogy, and Copper in the Context of Dutch Colonial Science and the Introduction of Western Geo-sciences to Japan', *East Asian Science, Technology, and Medicine* 40 (2014): 45–80.

Tsurumi, E. Patricia. *Factory Girls: Women in the Thread Mills of Meiji Japan* (Princeton, NJ: Princeton University Press, 1990).

Tubiana, Jérôme and Clotilde Warin. 'Diary: Migrant Flows', *London Review of Books* 41, 6 (21 March 2019): 42–3.

Turnbull, David with Helen Watson. *Maps Are Territories: Science Is an Atlas: A Portfolio of Exhibits* (Chicago: University of Chicago Press, 1993), http://territories.indigenousknowledge.org/index.html.

Uchida, Jun. *Brokers of Empire: Japanese Settler Colonialism in Korea, 1876–1945* (Cambridge, MA: Harvard University Asia Center, 2011).

van Goethem, Ellen. *Nagaoka: The Forgotten Capital* (Leiden: Brill, 2008).

van Sant, John. *Pacific Pioneers: Japanese Journeys to America and Hawaii, 1850–1880* (Champaign: University of Illinois Press, 2000).

Verran (Watson), Helen. 'A Story about Doing "The Dreaming"', *Postcolonial Studies* 7, 2 (2004): 149–64.

Wakayama-ken 和歌山県. *Wakayama-ken iminshi* 和歌山県移民史 [A history of Wakayama prefecture migration] (Wakayama: Wakayama-ken, 1957).

Walker, Alan and R. David Zorc. 'Austronesian Loanwords in Yolngu-Matha of Northeast Arnhem Land', *Aboriginal History* 5 (1981): 109–34.

Walker, David. *Anxious Nation: Australia and the Rise of Asia, 1850–1939* (St. Lucia: University of Queensland Press, 1999).

Walsham, Alexandra. 'The Social History of the Archive: Record-Keeping in Early Modern Europe', *Past & Present* 230, Supplement 11 (2016): 9–48.

Warren, James Francis. *Ah Ku and Karayuki-san: Prostitution in Singapore, 1870–1940* (New York: Oxford University Press, 2003).

Watt, Lori. *When Empire Comes Home: Repatriation and Reintegration in Postwar Japan* (Cambridge, MA: Harvard University Asia Center, 2009).

White, Hayden. *Metahistory: The Historical Imagination in Nineteenth-Century Europe* (Baltimore, MD: Johns Hopkins University Press, 1973).

Whitehead, Judith. 'John Locke, Accumulation by Dispossession and the Governance of Colonial India', *Journal of Contemporary Asia* 42, 1 (2012): 1–21.

Wigen, Kären. *The Making of a Japanese Periphery, 1750–1920* (Berkeley: University of California Press, 1995).

A Malleable Map: Geographies of Restoration in Central Japan, 1600–1912 (Berkeley: University of California Press, 2010).

Willis Burden, Pam. *Raindrops and Sugar Crops: Tales from South of the Daintree* (Port Douglas, QLD: Douglas Shire Historical Society, 2010).

Wintroub, Michael. *The Voyage of Thought: Navigating Knowledge across the Sixteenth-Century World* (Cambridge: Cambridge University Press, 2017).

Wolfe, Patrick. 'Settler Colonialism and the Elimination of the Native', *Journal of Genocide Research* 8, 4 (2006): 387–409.

Wood, Denis with Jon Fels and John Krygier. *Rethinking the Power of Maps* (New York: Guilford Press, 2010).

Woolf, Virginia. *A Room of One's Own* (Oxford: Oxford University Press, 1992 [1929]).
Wray, William D. *Mitsubishi and the N. Y. K., 1870–1914* (Cambridge, MA: Harvard University Asia Center, 1984).
Wu, Shellen Xiao. *Empires of Coal: Fueling China's Entry into the Modern World Order, 1860–1920* (Stanford, CA: Stanford University Press, 2015).
Wyllie, Arthur. *The Confederate States Navy* (n.p.: private publication, 2007).
Yamada Michio 山田迪生. *Fune ni miru Nihonjin iminshi: Kasato-maru kara kurūzu kyakusen e* 船にみる日本人移民史：笠戸丸からクルーズ客船へ [Japanese emigration history as seen through ships: From the *Kasato-maru* to passenger cruise liners] (Tokyo: Chūkō shinsho, 1998).
Yamamoto, Takahiro. 'Japan's Passport System and the Opening of Borders, 1866–1878', *Historical Journal* 60, 4 (2017): 997–1021.
Yamashita, Samuel Hideo. *Master Sorai's Responsals: An Annotated Translation of Sorai Sensei Tomonsho* (Honolulu: University of Hawai'i Press, 1994).
Yonemoto, Marcia. 'Maps and Metaphors of Japan's "Small Eastern Sea" in Tokugawa Japan (1603–1868)', *Geographical Review* 89, 2 (1999): 169–87.
Yun, Lisa. *The Coolie Speaks: Chinese Indentured Laborers and African Slaves of Cuba* (Philadelphia, PA: Temple University Press, 2008).
Zachariah, Benjamin. 'Travellers in Archives, or the Possibilities of a Post-Post-Archival Historiography', *Práticas da História* 3 (2016): 11–27.
Zimmerman, Andrew. 'Africa in Imperial and Transnational History: Multi-Sited Historiography and the Necessity of Theory', *Journal of African History* 54, 3 (2013): 331–40.
Ziomek, Kirsten L. *Lost Histories: Recovering the Lives of Japan's Colonial Peoples* (Cambridge, MA: Harvard University Asia Center, 2019).

Index

Page numbers in italics refer to primary-source quotations.

Aboriginal history, *See* settler colonialism, *See* Queensland, *See* Yolŋu people
anti-Japanese discrimination, 123, 126, 140–4, 150–1, 211
archives
   as 'country', 128, 168–71
   as earth, 234, 264
   as ontologies, 169
   brackishness, 5, 171, 269–70
   carbon footprint, 15, 20, 35
   Chronicling America (Library of Congress), 19–20, 45
   contingency, xxi, 262
   digitization, xxii, 14–22, 30, 70, 74, 122, 128, 136, 208, 219–20, 260, 268
   Diplomatic Archives of MOFA (Japan), 19, 46–7, 62, 99, 105, 153–5, 190, 193–6, 203–7, 217–20, 256, 267
   Hawai'i State Archives, 26–31, 51, 85–90, 109
   Hawai'i State Library, 26–31, 39
   Internet Archive, 19
   Kaminoseki Municipal Archives, 103–6, 118–21, 188
   National Library of Australia, 156, 173
   National Maritime Museum (Sydney), 127, 160
   ocular regime, 175, 180, 194, 218, 221
   ontologies, 4, 20, 176, 218
   positionality, 3, 22, 35, 36, 153–60, *See* authorial metadata
   Queensland State Archives, 158, 159, 173–9, 230
   silences, 5, 30, 36, 85, 89, 118, 155, 221
   traps, xxii, 269, *See* Chapter 1
   Tyne and Wear Archives, 11, 14
Arista, Noelani, 112, 180
Armstrong company (later Armstrong-Mitchell), 7, 11, 76

Arning, Eduard (1855–1936), 58–61, 64, 72, 73, 76
Australia, 16, 189, *See* Queensland, *See* Yolŋu people, *See* settler colonialism
   'Kanaka' (Pacific Island) labour, 155, 157, 175, *See* Pacific Ocean
   as dominion of Britain, 144–7
   Federation (1901), 127, 146, 160
   New South Wales, 140, 142, 146, 206, *See* Newcastle
   Port Darwin, 194, *203*, 210
   trade with Japan, 138–40, 195, 255
authorial metadata, xxi, 35, 268–9

Bayly, C. A., 3, 13
beaches, 167, 179, 180, 235
Bird, Isabella (1831–1904), 72
Bloch, Marc, xxi–xxii, 268
Braudel, Fernand, 158
Brazil, xx, 78, 150
Burns, Philp & Co., 124–7, 137, 139, 156, 159, 260, *See* Nippon Yūsen Kaisha (NYK)
Byrnes, Thomas J. (1860–1898), 136, 140, 151

Canada, xx, 124, 250
cartography, 36, 38, 127, 131–5, 161–2, 168
catch-up, discourses of, 11, 15, 29
Chakrabarty, Dipesh, 13, 232
China, xx, *28*, 183, 195
   'coolie' labour, 54, 111, 183–5
   China, discourses of, 71–2, 86
   Chinese medicine, 93
   market for Pacific commodities, 17, 139, 162, 183
   overseas diaspora, 34, 149, 155, 157, 159, 250

300

Index

Qing Empire, 6–8, 181, 183, 237, 263, *See* Sino-Japanese war (1894–5)
Sinosphere, 133–5
transpacific migration, 71, 111, 123, *146*, 148
circulation, 36, 90, 92–103, 115, 118, 189
City of Peking, 47, 55, 65
City of Tokio, 47, 52–3, 59–61, 65–7, 70, 74–6, 105, 108
coal
  Britain, 14, 251–3, 263
  Chikuhō mines, 100, 228, 233, 254, 255, *See* Yamamoto, Sakubei
  Japanese export to Asia, 200, 253–6, 263
  Karatsu mines, 228, 233–5, 238–41, 244–6, 248–9, 253
  modes of transportation, 200, 243, 248–9
  Nagasaki mines, 200, 228, 253–4
  onboard bunkers, 202, 231, 251, 257
  Shanghai market, 16, 17, 237, 251, 254, 255
  smoke, 226, 231, 250–1, 255, 259
  US consumption, 236–9
Cook, James (1728–79), 18, 57, 73, 129, 170, 181, 230
cotton, 49, 59, 103, 139, 225, 252, 258
Covid-19 pandemic, 129, 228, 229
Cuvier, Georges (1769–1832), 23, 234

digitization, *See* archives
Douglas, John (1828–1904), 143, 175, 177–9, 206–7, 213–15
Dutch East India Company, 162, 181, 229, 233–5, 242

Edo, *See* Tokyo
England, 7, 112, 239, *See* Great Britain

fertilizer, 92, 115, 138
fossil fuels, 2, 37, 229, 241, 253, 262, *See* coal
Fujita, Toshirō (1862–1937), 44, 184
Fukuzawa, Yukichi (1835–1901), 71, 73, 134
Fuyuki, Sakazō, 42, 89–90, 171, 193
  Hāna plantation, 113–18
  Kapa'a, 31, 32, 85
  Murotsu village, 88, 99–101, 104–6, 109–11, 119, 225

Ganter, Regina, 160, 162
Gibson, Walter M. (1822–88), 28, 39, 45, 66–9, 70, 76
gold rushes, 16, 147, 148, 236
Great Britain, 6, 8, 102, 128, 139, 245, 268
  Anglo-Japanese Treaty of Commerce and Navigation (1894), 126, 144, 151

empire, 124, 140, 144–7, 183–5, *See* coal
Great Britain, SS, 23–4, 25
Great Eastern, SS, 24, 25

Hamburg, 13, 16, 65, 102
Harris, Townsend (1804–78), 238–9, 254
Hasegawa, Setsutarō (1871–1952), 122–3, 126, 144, 171
Hashimoto, Usa
  as filed, 172–4, 176–9, 205
  as narrator, 36, 180, 183, 190, 200, 202, 204, 214–15, 220
  in Nagasaki, *176*, 181–2, 215, 222
  sister in Singapore, 176, 184–7, 197–8
Hawai'i, *See* Irwin, Robert W., *See* migration, from Japan
'Iolani Palace, 26–31, 88
'paradise', 18, 110
annexation, 110, *117*, 231, *See* settler colonialism
Kaua'i, 31, 57, 105
missionaries, 68, 72, 88, 111–13
monarchy, 30, 86, 88–9, 112, 115, 117, *See* Kalākaua, David (1836–91)
Native Hawaiian depopulation, 57, 74–6
Native Hawaiian dispossession, 31, 113, 115–18
Native Hawaiian voices, 36, 73–6, 88–9
pre-contact, 2, 57, 73
Royal Hawaiian Band, 18, 88
Hayami, Akira, 106–9
Heine, Wilhelm (1827–85), 235–8
Hiroshima prefecture, *See* Japan
Hokari, Minoru, 128, 170
Hong Kong, 124, 174, *175*–6, 189, 198–202, 202–4, *207*, 239, 252, 254–5

Iijima, Kametarō, 153–6, 159, 166
imperialism, *See* Great Britain, *See* Japan, *See* settler colonialism
India, 13, *28*, *71*, 124, *139*, 226, 252
Indigenous knowledge, 84, 161–71, 226, 241–3, 267
industrious, discourses of, *28*, 29, 36, 60, 90, 105–9, 111–13, 118, 213
Inoue, Kaoru (1836–1915), 32, 47
Inoue Katsunosuke, 53, 70
interpretation, *See* translation
Irwin, Robert W. (1844–1925), 42–4, 46–7, 66–9, 85–7, 89, 90, 101, 106
  KUK employee, 17, 26, 83
  Takechi, Iki, 42, 83

Index

Irwin, Robert W. (1844–1925) (cont.)
   Yamashiro-maru (1885), 18, 28, *39*, 55, 64, 70–3

Japan, *See* Tokugawa shogunate,
   See migration, *See* labour
   Asiatic, discourses of, 26–9, 67, 158
   Colonization Society of Japan, 208–11, 213
   consuls, 32, 47, 53, 61, 154, 175, 189, 191–3, 199–200, 203, 205–7, 255, *See* Fujita, Toshirō; Iijima, Kametarō; Marks, Alexander
   Emperor Meiji (r. 1868–1912), 23, 33, 39, 66–73, 136
   Hiroshima prefecture, 48–50, 61–2, 87, 91, 98, *101*, 150, 210, *See* Wakamiya, Yaichi
   Hokkaido (Ezo), 122, 130, 203, 243, 253, 254
   imperialism, xx, 34, 70, 124, 133–6, 155, 190, 215, *See* settler colonialism
   industrialization, 86–8, 120, 245, 263
   Inland Sea, 48–9, 52, 62, 63, 87, 96–100, 103, 225, 243, 263
   Iwakura Mission (1871–3), 102
   Kumamoto prefecture, 50, 62, 67, 69–70, 77–9, 150, 187, 210, *See* Kodama, Keijirō
   nation, discourses of, *62*, 63–5, 211–13
   overpopulation, 100, *101*, 150
   Ritsuryō state, 130–1, 133
   Wakayama, 24, 64, 213
   Yamaguchi prefecture, 47, 48, 87–8, 100, *101*, 106, 108, 210, 225, *See* Fuyuki, Sakazō

Kaempfer, Engelbert (1651–1716), 233, 238, 243
Kaibara Ekiken (1630–1714), 95
Kalākaua, David (1836–91), 17–18, 30, 39, 58, 59, 68, 72, 75–6, 86, 117
Karatsu, *See* coal
Karayuki-san, *See* migration, from Japan
Katō, Hisakatsu, 200, 259
Kobe, xix, 15, 18, 23, 113, 224, 254, *See* Yokohama–Kobe line
Kodama, Keijirō (d. 1896), 105, 138, 171, 265
   gravestone, 1, 32–5, 46, 265
   in transit, 50–2
   Orisaki village, 50, 77–9, 150
   Spreckelsville plantation, 40, 68
Komura, Jutarō (1855–1911), 206, 217–19
Korea, xx, 124, 130, 191, 195, 207, 211, 222
Kuku Yalanji people, *See* Queensland
Kumamoto prefecture, *See* Japan, *See* Kodama, Keijirō
Kuriyama, Shigehisa, 93, 107

Kyōdō Un'yu Kaisha (KUK), 9, 17, 23, *27*, 44, 47, 80–4, 91, 130, 253
Kyoto, 130, 131

labour, within Japan, 60, 230, *See* migration, within Japan
   by-employments, 49, 87–8, 98–100, 102
   dock workers, 256–9
   industrious revolution, 106–9
   mine workers, 244–7
   transport workers, 248–9
Latin America, xx, 23, 251
LeCain, Timothy J., 37, 262
leprosy, 58
Locke, John (1632–1704), 112

Mahlmann, John J. (1838–1930), 15–22, 26, 148, 231, 251, 252
Manchuria, xx, 139, 195, 211
Marks, Alexander (1838–1919), 126, 145, 155, 194–5, 199, 203, 217–20
Meiji revolution (1868), xx, 3, 6, 8, 33, 49, 99, 130, 245
microhistory, 36, 261
migration, from Japan, xx, 2, 32, 210, 262, *See* remittances, *See* City of Tokio
   canefield songs, 90, 91
   farmer migrants, 47–50, 70, 99–101, 114
   female migrants, 38, 63, 64, 126, 174–5, 188–202, 211–13, 230, 267
   Gannenmono (1868), 74
   Japan-Hawai'i sponsored programme (1885–94), xiii, 2, 17, 26–30, 40, 46–56, 61, 70, 86, 91, 101
   private companies, 115, 150
   recruitment, 47, 67, 101, 114–18, 190–3, 201, 202–5
migration, within Japan, xix, 100, 191, *See* labour, within Japan
Mihalopoulos, Bill, 175, 196, 206
Mitsubishi company, 9, 23, 26, 80–4, 91, 200, *See Sumanoura-maru*
Mitsui Bussan company, 47, 50
Mitsui Mining Company, 224, 246
modernity, 3, 13–14, *See* 'progress', discourses of
Moji, 200, 202, 230, 254, 255
Mori, Arinori (1847–89), 8–14, 23, 32

Nagakubo Sekisui (1717–1801), 131, *132*
Nagasaki, 7–8, 133, 181–2, 190–3, 200–1, *203*, 210, 229, 233, 242, 256–8, *See* coal, *See* Dutch East India Company
Nagasaki–Shanghai line, 124, 199, *See* Yokohama–Shanghai line

Index

New York, 23, 25
Newcastle (New South Wales), 16, 252
Newcastle upon Tyne, 6–14, 26, 130, 239
Nippon Yūsen Kaisha (NYK), 23, 36, 91, 122, 123–7, 131, 189, 200, 201, 226, 250

Omi-maru, 11, 23, 64, 130, 175
Osaka, 48, 55, 96–8, 113, 189, *203*, 224

Pacific Mail Steamship Company, 47, 253, 256
Pacific Ocean, 235
  'blackbirding', 16, 54, 148, *See* Australia
  'coolie' trade, 54, 148
  'great eastern sea', 2, 131
  ecological transformation, 139
  Melanesia, 54, 59, 157
  Micronesia, xx, 16, 124, 211
paintings, *See* Yamamoto, Sakubei, *See* Yolŋu people, *See* Strong, Joseph Dwight, *See* Heine, Wilhelm, *See* Utagawa, Kunisada
passports, 122, 151, *188*, 191, 197, 199, 206–7, 214, *223*
Perry, Matthew (1794–1858), 24, 38, 229, 231, 235–9, 250
Philippines, xx, 139, 210
Phipps, Catherine L., 230, 254
photography, 6, 56, 58–60, 72, 73, 256–9
Prendergast, Eleanor Kekoaohiwaikalani Wright (1865–1902), 88–90, 115, 117
prints, *See* Utagawa, Kunisada, *See* Heine, Wilhelm
progress, discourses of, *10*, 13–14, *28*, 29, *32*, *45*, *61*, 71, 73, *135*, *137*

Queensland
  'empty North', 147, 149, 152, 158–60, 170
  Cairns, 137, 156, 174–5, 206
  immigration debates, 142–4, 146, 158–9, 174, 205
  Kuku Yalanji people (Mossman), 129, 147–8, 155
  Mossman, 129, 147–58
  Port Douglas, 127, 129, 149, 152–3, 156, 160, 175, 260
  Rockhampton, 135, 144–6, 152, 159
  Thursday Island, 129, 147, 151, *159*, 173–7, 197–8, 203–4, 206–15, 219, 222
  Townsville, 153, 154, 156, 159, 175, 205, 206

racism, *See* anti-Japanese discrimination
railways, 225, 235, 249, 265
remittances, 32, 104–6, 108, 109, 119, 120, 192, 210

Russia, 8, 142, *See* Vladivostok
Russo-Japanese War (1904–5), 3, 63

Sasaki, Shigetoshi, 203–4, 206–7, 211–13, 215, *See* Queensland
Satō, Torajirō (1864–1928), 177, 183, 213–15, 219, 222, *See* Queensland
Sekula, Allan, 226, 262, 264, 265
settler colonialism, xx, 3, 112, 267, 270
  in Australia, 128, 139, 147–9, 159–71
  in Hawaiʻi, 30–1, 36, 74, 109, 115–18, 119–20
Shanghai, 7, 198–9, 204, *See* coal
shipbuilding, 8, *9*, 11, 23
Siebold, Philipp Franz von (1796–1866), 229, 233–5, 238–9, 241–3, 246, 264
silk, 100, 103, 138
  as fashion, 3, *50*, 212, 215
Singapore, 44, 189, *193*, 195, 199, 203, 207, 237, 252, 254, 263
  as entrepot, 183–4, 188
  entertainment district, 176, 184–7
Sino-Japanese War (1894–5), xix–xx, 115, 126, 133–6, 211, 228, 230, 249
Sissons, David, 172–3, 179, 188, 215
smallpox, 17, *26*, *28*, 51, 52, 57
Smith, Thomas C., 86–8, 90, 103, 107, 118
songs, 88–9, 90, 91–2, 102–3, 115, 117, 120, 188–9, 247
Southeast Asia, 124, 131, 163, 181, 188, 230, 252
Spreckels, Claus (1828–1908), 68, 112, 117, *See* sugar plantations, Hawaiʻi
Steedman, Carolyn, 177–9
Stoler, Ann Laura, 4, 20, 261
Strong, Joseph Dwight (1853–99), 39–43, 45, 51, 53, 57–8, 65–8, 71–4, 76
subaltern histories, 18, 37, 204
Suez Canal, 124, 184, 226, 252, 253
sugar industry, Queensland, 148–9, *152*, 177
sugar plantations, Hawaiʻi, *17*, 29, 149
  accommodation, 52, 55
  bango system, 51, 109
  canefield songs, 90–2, 102–3, 115, 189
  Kauaʻi plantations, 51, 116, 119
  labour disputes, 52, 68–9, 108
  luna (overseers), 51, 53, 70, 102, 108
  Maui plantations, 52–3, 66–8, 103, 108, 109, *114*, 114, 117
  planter politics, *28*, 46, 68, 76, 112, 117
  Spreckelsville, *39*, 40, 66–70, 83, 112, 116, 153
  wages, 50, 105
Sugiyama, Gensaku, 177, 210–11, 213, 222, *See* Queensland

Index

Sumanoura-maru, 80–4, 200, 230, 249, *See* Mitsubishi company
Switzerland, 16, 76, 169

Taiwan, xx, 124, 211, 254
Taiwan Sugar Company, 40–3, 47, 70, 73, 155
Takechi, Tadamichi (1870–1962), 43, 73, *See* Irwin, Robert W.
tea, 53, 97, 108, 183, 250
teahouses, 96, 98, 189
telegraph, *10*, 99, 151, 159, 175, 180, 204, 225, 235, 265
Thursday Island, *See* Queensland
Thurston, Lorrin A. (1858–1931), 85, 89, 101
time
  Biblical time, 23, 265
  geological time, 37, 231, 234, 239–41, 262, 264, 265
  imperial time, 33, 265
  plantation time, 55, 69, 106–9
  standardization, 13, 33, 133
  steamship time, 24, 55, 81, 226, 231, 265
Tokugawa shogunate, 2, 6–8, 10, 48, 96–100, 131, 181, 232–9, 243–5, 263
'opening' of Japan, 24, 237, 250–6
Tokyo, xix, 9, 40, 61–2, 80, 82, 150, 210–11, 213, 225, 255
  Edo, 95, 233, 243
Tozer, Sir Horace (1844–1916), 179, 205–7
transit, 43–4, 46, 50–2, 54–6, 61–5, 188–202
translation, 82–5, 109, 177, 214–15
Trask, Haunani-Kay, 89, 115–16
Trouillot, Michel-Rolph, 5, 83, 85, 90

United States, xx, 6, 8, 24–5, 78, 102, 110, 111–12, *117*, 119, 126, 231, 236–9, 250
  Civil War, 47, 81
  Fillmore, Millard (1800–74), 236, 238, 252
University College London, 8, 32
Utagawa, Kunisada (1786–1864), 93–4, 98, 107, 108, 119, 230

Vladivostok, 190–4, 196, 197, 250

Wakamiya, Yaichi, 171

in transit, 49–52, 55
Jigozen village, 48–50, 61–2, 96, 98, 150
return, 91, 105
Watt, James (1736–1819), 225, 245
whaling, 232, 236
Woolf, Virginia (1882–1941), 179
World War, First, 120, 123, 142
World War, Second, xx, 123, 172

Yamaguchi prefecture, *See* Japan, *See* Fuyuki, Sakazō
Yamamoto, Sakubei (1892–1984), 77, 246–7, 256
Yamashiro-maru
  captains, 15–22, 82, 84, 136, 138, 231, *See* Mahlmann, John J.
  cargo, 138, 143
  coal bunkers, *228*, 251, 257
  conversion for war service, 29, 133, 135, 228
  crash (1884), 80–4, 200, 230, 249
  crew, 80–4, 226, 228, *260*
  engine, 11, 226, *228*
  first-class accommodation, xix, 54, 136
  launch, 6–14, 25
  model, 76, 269
  name, 25, 129–31
  scrapping, 23
  steerage accommodation, *28*, 54–5, 63, 64, 123
Yanagita, Kunio (1875–1962), xix–xx, 17, 91
Yasukawa, Keiichirō (1849–1934), 224–6, 246, 250, 254
Yokohama, 28, 50, 51, 62, 200, 231, 235, 249, 254, 255, 259
Yokohama–Kobe line, xix, 17, 80–1, 91, 189
Yokohama–Melbourne line, xx, 36, 122–7, 250
Yokohama–Shanghai line, 250, 254, 256, *See* Nagasaki–Shanghai line
Yolŋu people (Australia), 36, 161–71
  Saltwater Visions exhibition, 128, 160
  Yolŋu-Makassar connections, 162–3, 166

C4. ethnogenesis
Dr Sarina Nasar @ Bristol.ac.uk